The MEDIEVAL MEDEA

The legends of Jason and Medea have inspired writers of many kinds. In this new analysis of the legends, Prof. Morse shows how disparate and sometimes contradictory stories were combined in the creation of this first secular princely quest, which became a benchmark of western chronology and took its place as part of the legends of Troy – a story of adventure, politics, and of dangerous, order-threatening women. Prof. Morse demonstrates how the innovations of Euripides and Apollonius were imitated throughout Antiquity for other female characters: the multiple examples of murderous mothers appear to give independent evidence of the lethal disruptions of which women in the grasp of irrational passion were believed capable. For a variety of authors – Dante, Chaucer, Boccaccio, Gower, Christine de Pizan and others – the problem of a hero who betrays his oath, exemplified by Jason, and a heroine who murders and escapes – Medea – offered insoluble and tragic subjects. The legends thus contribute not only to ideas of history, but also to ideas of the power and ruthlessness of women.

Dr RUTH MORSE is Professeur des Universités at Université Paris VII.

The
MEDIEVAL MEDEA

Ruth Morse

D. S. BREWER

First published 1996
D. S. Brewer, Cambridge

ISBN 0 85991 459 3

D S. Brewer is an imprint of Boydell & Brewer Ltd
PO Box 9, Woodbridge, Suffolk IP12 3DF, UK
and of Boydell & Brewer Inc.
PO Box 41026, Rochester, NY 14604–4126, USA

British Library Cataloguing in Publication Data
Morse, Ruth
    The medieval Medea
    1. Euripides. Medea   2. Greek drama –
    History and criticism
    I. Title
    882'.01
    ISBN 0859914593

Library of Congress Cataloging-in-Publication Data
Morse, Ruth.
    The medieval Medea / Ruth Morse.
        p.   cm.
    Includes bibliographical references and index.
    ISBN 0–85991–459–3
    1. Literature, Medieval – History and criticism. 2. Medea
(Greek mythology) in literature. I. Title.
PN687.M42M67   1996
809'.93351–dc20   96–17091

This publication is printed on acid-free paper

Printed in Great Britain by Boydell & Brewer Ltd

CONTENTS

PLATES

ABBREVIATIONS

BEC	*Bulletin de l'Ecole des Chartes*
BNf. f.fr.	Bibliothèque Nationale Française fonds français
Caxton	*The History of Jason,* trans. William Caxton, ed. John Munro, EETS e.s. 111 (London, Kegan Paul, 1913)
EETS e.s.	Early English Text Society extra series
EETS o.s.	Early English Text Society old series
Lefèvre	Raoul Lefèvre, *L'Histoire de Jason,* ed. Gert Pinkernell (Frankfurt, Athenäum Verlag, 1971)
MAe	*Medium Aevum*
MLR	*The Modern Language Review*
PMLA	Publications of the Modern Language Society of America
Woledge	*Bibliographie des Romans et nouvelles en prose française antérieurs à 1500,* ed. Brian Woledge (Geneva, Droz, 1954) and supplément (Geneva, Droz, 1975)

for the usual suspects

Finding is the first Act
The second, loss,
Third, Expedition for
The 'Golden Fleece'
Fourth, no Discovery –
Fifth, no Crew –
Finally, no Golden Fleece –
Jason – sham – too.

Emily Dickinson

Quis iter Jasonis, labores Herculis, Alexandri gloriam,
Caesaris victorias nosset, si scriptorum beneficia defuissent?

Itinerarium peregrinorum et gesta regis Ricardi

PREFACE AND ACKNOWLEDGEMENTS

In my childhood copy of myths and legends of Ancient Greece retold, Jason appeared as the hero who led the Argonauts to the adventure of the Golden Fleece; in my office now hangs a seventeenth-century star map illustrating the adventures which gave the constellations their names: the stars appear against a background in which the Argo is just escaping the Clashing Rocks by the nautical equivalent of a whisker. In the etching the rocks are merely rocks, not the essentially female Symplegades of Greek myth. If I remember correctly, Medea appeared in the children's version of the story like one of those ogre's daughters whose hand in marriage is part of the hero's reward. There is no sign of her presence in my etching. Hypsipyle of Lemnos, where according to some versions the Argonauts stopped for a time, was a later discovery for me, and appeared to belong to another story altogether, as did Theseus, or the wars against Thebes and Troy. But to remember 'the story' is already to accept – if not to impose – a kind of coherence which recognizes that stories develop and harden into what then seems an inevitable shape. This rationalizing impulse deserves study, because of what it does to the non-systematic presentation of a number of formerly discrete legends. Unusually among legends, this one has an oath-breaking hero who is defeated not by a monster – or at least not by a beast – but by his wife, a heroine who (as sister, in-law, mother, and step-mother) murders where she can and gets away scot-free. So far from being the ogre's innocent daughter, Medea appears as the ogre herself, one who tears apart, who dismembers, who disrupts. And yet, as one more victim of one more seducer and betrayer, her subjectivity could be turned to use by poets whose speeches of hurt and anger immortalize her as a sufferer with a claim upon our sympathy. The speech Ovid gave her, translated by Arthur Golding, passed, perhaps, through John Heywood's *Brazen Age* to reappear metamorphosed by Shakespeare into Prospero's farewell to his magic. Corneille, Cherubini and Charpentier, Milhaud and Vincent d'Indy brought her to the stage, or summoned her in music. The legends ramify, not just into other legends.

About the legends there is a coherent story to be told, but it is a story of incoherences and incompatabilities, of invention and its limits, of the ways that writers could believe and play with belief. One might begin by considering point of view. Historians made rational calculations to incorporate *Jason's* voyage into historical time. To rationalize a powerful and threatening Medea out of existence, they silenced her: that is, made her the object of fear, or contingent within another story. This story of rewriting, too, belongs to other stories. Part of the larger story belongs to the inheritance of classical antiquity; another to the modes and styles of historical representation; yet a third to a story about essentialist and contradictory patterns of drawing, and drawing upon, ideas about women (which themselves developed in association with characters like Medea); a fourth to the growth of what has traditionally been categorized as medieval romance. The search for origins which, in the Middle Ages and Renaissance, was a claim to the prestige which accrued to precedence, yielded in later scholarship to a modern myth that the reconstitution of the primitive would reveal the truth, not only of *the* story, but the truth about essential human experience. In the twentieth century, Jason's voyage could be an allegory of male conquest of the Great Mother, and another fantasy of mankind's fall from grace. Medea as an aspect of the Great Mother is only one more of the fantasies to which these stories have been recruited, an embodiment of another kind. In retelling some of them, I assume throughout a distinction between *myth* (gods, goddesses, aetiological explanations for natural phenomena) and *legend* (the actions of men and women who may have been in contact with gods and goddesses, but whose interactions took place in a human past); Jason and Medea belong to the moment when myth (because Jason is favoured by Hera and Medea is the granddaughter of the sun) becomes legendary time. Incorporation and embodiment: the absorption of a foreign bride, the regaining of a kingdom, the control of progeny and kin – these themes are constant.

Or, if one makes *Medea* the centre of study, there is a tragic story to be told of love and betrayal. Driven from her husband's side by her husband himself, Medea becomes one of the most active of Love's Martyrs. Stories which focus on her are often generically distant from the histories of Jason, and suggest a certain timelessness in her predicament (if not her reaction to it). If women are asserted as universals, universally powerless, then Medea contradicts that assertion. 'Woman' as an irrational force capable of terrible revenge becomes one of the topics at issue. The importance of Ovid in 'hardening' the implicit contradictions cannot be overstated, yet nor can the possibility of adversarial reading.

Thus, although the shape of this book is largely chronological (because it seemed the way to organize the material which would run least risk of repetition of the main points of the argument) chronology is abandoned at several strategic points, and not all of one author's works are considered together. A long first section surveys the origins and beginnings of the legends through Euripides and Hellenistic epic to Seneca; I am much indebted to the work of classicists such as Ben Edwin Perry, whose Sather Classical Lectures were one of the inspirations which started me along what then seemed a primrose path. His phrase for malleable (and much-moulded) fictions told in the style of history, 'plasmatic narrative', identifies both a kind of content and a range of stylistic overlap. Without the subsequent enquiries of anthropologically-informed French research, associated with names such as Françoise Desbordes, Marcel Detienne, Nicole Loraux, and, above all, Jean-Pierre Vernant and Pierre Vidal-Naquet, I would have seen the steps less clearly. The first departure from chronology comes in the chapter devoted to Ovid and Ovidianism.

For the middle of the book, which looks at the high medieval period, mainly in western Europe, I have been much influenced by historiographical, as well as literary, research. The imitation of antiquity is always a matter of creative misinterpretation, and each period is characterized by its own varieties. It is also a chapter of accidents, since the blunder of a Burgundian aristocrat in choosing Jason as the Patron of his chivalric order eventuated in a large-scale defence of the hero that was much read in the waning of the Middle Ages. There are patterns to the medieval interpretations of Jason (as part of the history of Troy) and Medea (both as heroine and as threat). Chapters Two and Four are oriented more toward the former, Three and Five to the latter. But it is part of my contention that 'history' and 'romance' are often terminological conveniences of interpretation that established themselves in the early modern period and that occlude as much as they illuminate. The multiplication of 'Medeas' (which assume *a* Medea) influenced depictions of 'Woman' which went well beyond genre categories to create an essentialist definition by which women were judged. This is part of the justification for transferring some of the discussions from their natural chronological place to later ones in order to discuss particular works and their influences together. There is an unavoidable hazard in the analysis of Essentialism: many depictions of Medea appeal to, while they construct, ideas of 'Woman' which can all too easily collapse into one ahistorical prejudice. I have attempted to remain alert to the seductions of the abandoned. One other decision, about classical names, may require explanation: since I shall throughout be emphasizing certain cultural differences in the representations of legendary figures, I have sometimes named them inconsistently (e.g. Odysseus for a Greek author but Ulysses for a Roman). This is deliberate.

I am grateful to the editors of *The Modern Language Review* and *Common Knowledge* for permission to re-employ material on Raoul Lefèvre and on medieval historiography which was first published in those journals. Other specific debts are, I hope, acknowledged in the footnotes and bibliography. But I began to collect, and to ponder upon, this material just over twenty years ago, and there must be influences upon me that I have internalized so far as to have forgotten who is responsible. Certainly Derek Brewer's will be felt. I am grateful to him for energetic support and gentle encouragement from the archaic period before this research ever began, but, if I am altogether fair in apportioning blame, the indefatigable persuasions of Barry Windeatt were what, in the end, proved irresistible. The ground had been prepared by James Laidlaw, who first encouraged my taste for fifteenth-century France, and who has been instrumental in the study of one of the book's heroines, Christine de Pizan. Richard Marienstras simply took it for granted that Medea was a subject worth pursuing. Professors A. J. Boyle and Peter Rickard saved me from my own ignorance of Latin and French, respectively. To my readers, my usual readers, rounded up in the dedication, I owe the debt I can best discharge by crossing out their choicest formulations in my turn, but let me, in the meantime, record once more my gratitude to Stefan Collini, Helen Cooper, and Barry Windeatt for once more insisting I meet their objections. They might wish me to stress the limits of my will, and that for those errors that remain I alone am responsible.

For permission to reproduce photographs of illustrations of manuscripts in their possession, I am grateful to the Bibliothèque de l'Arsenal for illustrations from Lefèvre's autograph of the *Histoire de Jason*, MS 5067 (Plates 3 and 5) and to the Bibliothèque Nationale for plates from BNf. MS f.fr. no. 331 (Plates 1, 2, and 6) and 12570 (Plate 4). The photographs of the Angers Apocalypse were prepared by the Cambridge University Audiovisual unit, and I am grateful to them as well as to the City of Angers for permission to reproduce Plate 7. To the staff of the University Library, Cambridge, who have given me aid and sustenance for a quarter of a century, I am constantly thankful.

INTRODUCTION

When, opening Euripides' great tragedy, Medea's nurse rails against the chain of events which has brought her and her charge to the verge of banishment from Corinth, it is not of a human being she speaks, but a tree, a pine on the heights of Mount Pelion. It is as if she traces circumstances back in the hardest argument of necessity, and fatality, which she can think of: had that tree, that tree among many others, not formed the keel of the Argo. . . . One is reminded of the missing nail which brought defeat in battle through the horseshoe which did not hold, which brought down the horse, which threw the rider carrying the message – until the lost nail explains the overthrow of a kingdom. Such trails of causality are part of children's songs, as alternative worlds traced from contingent decisions are part of literature of many kinds. So, too, the use of a metonym (a pine for the past) evokes what may not be exposed without scandal, because the public rehearsal of that chain of cause and effect, with its terrible events, would change the case to be argued. The nurse's metonym appeals to chance as necessity and avoids human agency; it appeals to the natural world as part of a conspiracy. Tragic inevitability has, however, a hold upon our imaginations which transcends that of history, or palimpsestic fictions based on history, because of its double unfolding. It insists that the deeds narrated or dramatized mean more than themselves. Especially in the theatre's compression, tragic irony represents the point of view of agents who did not know, as we know, what was to come, who believed, against our foreknowledge, in an ostensible range of possible choices and deeds, from which we anticipate the only possible conclusion. Tragic action happens within historical action, to a small group of agents, while history always reports only a part of what happened to a much larger group; even within a tragedy, what is reported is not all. Yet it is impossible to separate and define some pure kind of tragic mode against a mode which is purely historical, impossible, too, to distinguish allegory from symbol, or isolate (within the range of figurative expression) metaphors of human possibility. If history is cyclical because generations of men and women behave similarly under the goad of repeated stimuli and circumstances, its 'lessons' include claims about gender, motive, and action, class (or status) and place of origin. The cycles may then be tragic beyond the claims of individual lives because of the patterns they reveal more than the events they depict. That is, Hypsipyle's failure to evade the fate of power-

1

less women may have significance about the world and women in it beyond her own importance.

The dangers in tracing the accumulation of stories which became 'the legends of Jason and Medea' are easier to describe than to avoid. An aetiology may presuppose a march toward completeness, when, in effect, the bringing together of disparate stories was rather a drive toward coherence, an avoidable tidying-up exercise which brought with it more problems than it solved. Even with material as disparate and as ramifying as these legends, one risks both a whig history of legend and a unit idea of its content.[1] There is no 'essential' Jason or Medea to be realized, and it is for that reason that this book provides only the sketchiest of synoptic retellings.[2] Such synopses exist, of course, and are useful, but one has to be alert to how inevitable they make a retrospective history of accretion look. Even to speak of 'a' history is already, perhaps, to beg the question of the variety of possible – and actual – accidents of transmission. To speak of transmission, too, is to assume something, some thing, transmitted. Since one of the questions to which this book will return is that of the authority

---

[1] In my insistence upon 'Medeas' readers will recognize my own allusion to George Steiner, *Antigones* (Oxford, Clarendon Press, 1984). By contrast to Antigones, of course, Medeas explore revenge rather than right and power rather than guilt; if there is no Medea-complex, there is a complex of Medeas. The standard summaries are to be found in *Paulys Real-Encyclopädia der Classischen Altertumswissenschaft* (Stuttgart, 1914–), ed. G. Wilson, rev. W. Kroll; and W. H. Roscher, *Ausfürliches Lexikon der Griechischen und Römischen Mythologie* (Leipzig, 1890–7). Most studies emphasize the unifying features of 'a' Medea. Léon Mallinger, *Médée: étude de littérature comparée* (Louvain, 1897; Paris, A. Fontemoing, 1898) is still a rich source, as is R. W. Hash, *The Jason Theme in Greek and Roman Literature* (Vanderbilt University unpublished Ph.D., 1969). See also Louis Séchan, 'La Légende de Médée', *Revue des Etudes Grèques* 40 (1927), pp. 234–310. There is an excellent review of the classical roots of the legends together with a superb tabular survey of texts and a thorough bibliography (although both are uncharacteristically weak on the Middle Ages) in Duarte Mimoso-Ruiz, *Médée Antique et Moderne: Aspects rituels et socio-politiques d'un mythe* (Paris, Ophrys, 1982), chapt. 1, which is mainly a study of nineteenth- and twentieth-century interpretations, but it shares the sense that there is an identifiable, complete, and correct version of the story. He gives an overview in an article for *Companion to Literary Myths, Heroes, and Archetypes*, ed. Pierre Brunel, trans. W. Allatson, J. Hayward, and T. Selous (London and N.Y., 1992; orig. Paris, Rocher, 1988), pp. 769–78.

[2] The existence of iconographic representations which correspond to no known literary treatment is a further reminder of the variety of possible episodes and of the choices open to writers and artists in periods before the legends 'set'. See the *Lexicon Iconographicum Mythologiae Classicae* (Zurich and Munich, Artemis, 1981–) s.v. Iason, Medeia for examples. Vassiliki Gaggadis-Robin's magisterial iconographic study of the legends as depicted on the late Roman sarcophogus is organized by morphological unit: *Jason et Médée sur les sarcophages d'époque impériale* (Rome, Ecole française de Rome, 1994).

for a preservation or modification, it is important to be aware of each contribution, each major addition, suppression, modification.

A paradox in the argument of this book may appear to lurk in this assertion that there is no one Medea, because the multiplication of representations which derive from 'Medeas' became a claim that there *was* something essentially female in her, or their, behaviour. Medea, like other women in the grip of irrational passion, such as Clytemnestra, is a danger and a threat: she kills. The more characters, under many names, who appear to imitate her behaviour, the more she and they can be alluded to as evidence that *all* women are capable of what Medea, exceptionally, did.

If all classicizing writers are to some degree backward looking, all had choice about selection; the ways they looked and selected, and their degrees of choice, the constraints of their own talent, genre, society – all these help to explain the modifications they brought to legends which they understood as belonging to a past which had itself to be defined and understood. Nevertheless, I am not a classicist, and this is not a work of classical scholarship; it is going somewhere, but the journey is not teleological: going to the middle ages in western Europe to consider once more the inexhaustible subject and endless analysis of the classical heritage and its beneficiaries. This focus governs my own selection and interpretation. It may be asked if another rehearsal of Graeco-Roman mythology is necessary; the argument of chapter one must be the answer to that.

When Euripides conceptualized his *Medea* in the tragic mode, he invented one at least of the most famous actions of the play, her murder of her children; yet, in referring back to events not of his own inventing which were presumed to have happened before the play itself, as well as forward to Medea's escape to Athens, he connected the events to other times and places, to historical and to tragic stories, to other (and equally plausible) versions of what might have brought about what might have happened. His inventions were consistent with incidents which already existed and with ostensibly irreproachable ideals of sheltering the defenceless, of keeping one's oath. To discover a tragic pattern of events in the flux of the past is to recognize, believe, and inscribe the belief that there are patterns, that human history is not chaos, that certain patterns repeat, and that they are tragically inevitable, and inevitable in a way which corresponds to the shape of works of art.[3]

There are concomitant correspondences: 'historical' stories appear to

---

[3] I shall discuss the claims of allegory below, Chapter Three. It will be clear that issues of reference must engage with Walter Benjamin's distinction between the history-conscious 'play of sorrow' and 'Tragedy' itself.

claim that they represent a version of actual events, whose plausibility depends not only upon connection to other stories equally self-defining as historical, but also to their repeating patterns. Something which appears to have happened many times is the more, not the less, likely: as we shall see, Virgil's borrowings from Apollonius Rhodius reinforced beliefs about the historical likelihood of their characters' deeds and characters, even when there was, simultaneously, a tradition that Virgil's heroine was a fiction, if not entirely his own invention. I shall be discussing an attitude to true stories about the past which assumes a core of similitude within great latitude of invention.

Nevertheless, there is the sense of something out there to be known and maintained. As the writer of King Richard's deeds and journeys (cited as one of this book's epigraphs) asked in the fourteenth century, how *would* Jason and Hercules, Alexander and Caesar have been known had it not been for such as he? The temptation to search for origins, which will be one of the focal points of Chapter Four, arises at the beginning of this book, too. A legend is no more restricted to its first telling than the meaning of a word is to its etymology. Were there an originary text, it might have special status, or at least a status to be determined. But there is not; or at least, the text in which we see the beginnings of what became the legends is not about them. With the exception of the genesis of Medea's murder of her children, there is no single definitive version of any part of the legends, and the status of this or that one changes depending upon its audiences and readers. The first 'rationalizing' attempt to write one comprehensive version came with Apollonius Rhodius in third century BC Alexandria. Before that separate treatments may have been episodic, but they were not yet 'episodes'. It will be useful to be able to think of some of the segments as if they were morphological units.[4]

Before the beginning of this story, there is a story of the remarriage of King Athamas to Ino, who persuaded his people to sow wheat which she had parched, so that it would not sprout; when famine resulted she

---

[4] Propp helps us to understand why certain motifs and combinations of motifs appear convincing (because familiar and expected), but it remains important to remember that a Proppian analysis ignores not only the historical and cultural context in which the folk-tale motifs are told or written, it ignores the way they are told or written. So, similarly, Bernard Mezzadri's comparison of Jason's 'sins' ('fautes') and Indian epic disregards the cultures in which the legends were being told and rewritten and falls into the trap of treating 'the legends' as one inevitable story; 'Jason ou le retour du pêcheur: esquisse de mythologie argonautique', *Revue de l'Histoire des Religions* 208 (1991), pp. 273–301.

claimed that the gods demanded a human sacrifice in order to rid herself of Athamas's children by his first marriage. (Legitimate succession is at issue.)

1 Aeetes, King of Colchis, receives as his guest the fleeing Phrixos (he and his sister, Helle, escaped from the plot of their step-mother, Ino, and fled on the back of a flying, golden, ram; before reaching Colchis Helle fell from the ram and drowned in the Hellespont, which bears her name). In some versions Phrixos marries Aeetes' older daughter, Chalciope, while in others Phrixos is murdered (by Aeetes, who thereby offends against hospitality).

2 In Thessaly, Pelias dethrones the king, his brother, Aeson, which ought to deprive Aeson's son (who has been sent to be educated by the Centaur, Chiron) of his legitimate succession to the throne. The Oracle warns Pelias to beware of the arrival of a stranger wearing only one sandal. When the predicted one-sandalled Jason (he lost the sandal in the river when he helped carry an old woman across it – the 'old woman' turned out to be Hera) appears as Pelias's guest, the king tries to ensure his disinheritance by sending him to recover the Golden Fleece. The vehicle for Jason's 'flight' is the Argo.

3 Heroes gather to accompany Jason. Here can be inserted numerous adventures for the heroes (among the best known are Calais and Zeetes and the Harpies, Hercules and Hylas). Two incidents connect this voyage to the Theban and Trojan stories:

3(a) The Argo stops at Lemnos, an island inhabited solely by women, because they have murdered their husbands, who returned from a war with concubines. Their queen, Hypsipyle (who secretly saved her father from death), falls in love with Jason and bears him a son (in some versions twin sons). After Jason leaves Lemnos Hypsipyle is banished (because her trick to save her father is discovered) and eventually becomes a slave discovered by her now-grown sons on their way to the siege of Thebes.

3(b) The Argo stops at Troy to ask for fresh water, but the king, Laomedon, believing they are hostile Greeks who wish to conquer his city, refuses to allow them to land. Hercules swears to return and avenge this slight, which he later does, achieving the first destruction of Troy. In some versions he presents the enslaved princess, Hesione, to his friend, and allows her to preserve one Trojan alive; she chooses her infant brother, Priam. (Here a sister saves a brother.)

4 Jason arrives in Colchis as Aeetes' guest, but Aeetes plots Jason's

death by encouraging him to attempt the impossible task of gaining the fleece by harnessing fire-breathing bulls, sowing dragon's teeth, and then killing the soldiers who grow from them. Medea, under the influence of Aphrodite, decides to give their guest her aid, but thereby betrays her father.

5 With Medea's help (she gives him unguents which make him fire-proof and instructions which enable him to trick the soldiers born from the dragon's teeth), Jason succeeds in winning the fleece. He escapes, taking Medea with him, and flees on the Argo. Either Jason (with or without Medea's knowledge or aid) plots to stop Aeetes' vengeance by killing her adult brother, Apsyrtos, or Medea, seeing that the Colchian ships are faster, dismembers her young brother (Apsyrtos) and throws the pieces into the sea. In this version Aeetes stops to collect them and the Argonauts escape. Aeetes now has no legitimate successor because he has no son.

6 Jason and Medea return to Iolchos, where Pelias pretends to welcome them. In some versions Medea rejuvenates Jason's father. Medea understands Pelias's evil intentions, and persuades his daughters that she can rejuvenate him (as she rejuvenates a ram which she dismembers, boils, and then produces as an intact lamb from her cauldron). The daughters (with the honorable exception of Alcestis) dismember Pelias, whom Medea refuses to resuscitate. Jason can now become king, in legitimate succession to his dethroned father, Aeson (whom Medea rejuvenates in some versions, but who, in others, is already dead). But the people rise at the murder of Pelias, and Jason and Medea have to flee, once more on the Argo.

7 Jason and Medea live in Corinth. Jason plans to marry the daughter of the local king. Medea sends poisoned gifts to her, but when she dies, the people rise (this is the pre-Euripides tradition) and take their revenge by dismembering Medea's children. In some versions Medea's own attempts to make her sons immortal result in their deaths. Jason has no legitimate successor, and Medea must flee, which she does in the dragon-drawn chariot of her grandfather, Helios, the sun god. Euripides' invention makes Medea the murderer of her own children in order to deprive Jason of legitimate succession, and assimilates her to the status of a god. The Argo rots on a Corinthian beach.

8 Medea finds refuge and guest-protection in Athens by promising the aged and apparently childless King Aegeus that she will bear him a son, guaranteeing legitimate succession.

9   Time passes. A stranger arrives in Athens. Medea, who realizes that this dangerous guest is in fact Theseus, Aegeus's son by an early liaison (another seduced-and-abandoned king's daughter), and that he will deprive her son, Medus, of Aegeus's throne, persuades Aegeus to murder his guest with a poisoned drink, but Aegeus recognizes his own sword at the young man's waist and saves him in time. Medea has to flee one last time, returning to Colchis with Medus.

10   Some versions reconcile Medea with Jason, and then with Aeetes, whom Medea may restore to his throne. Medus supplies the lack of legitimate successor and founds the race of the Medes in Colchis.[5] Some versions describe Jason's death as an accident when timber from the rotting hulk of the Argo falls and strikes his head.

The associations of guest-obligation/ betrayal, legitimate succession/ usurpation, and settlement/ flight provide precisely those repetitions which only reveal themselves when a plot is stripped down to its motifs. Jason's locomotion, and his loss of movement with the loss of his own legitimate succession and the breaking apart of the Argo, contrasts with the powerful and unnatural flying ram and dragons. The centrality of 'sparagmos', the scattering which is perhaps best known in another Euripidean context, *The Bacchae*, here manifests itself in the disintegrating Argo (an inviting trope for the loss of heroic status) and in murders which are contextualized as part of dramas over inheritance. It is remarkable that the dismemberments of Apsyrtos and Pelias have been so little remarked. In *The Bacchae* the powerful figure is the new god, Dionysos; Agave, who dismembers her son, is a human woman used, unknowingly, by the god. By contrast in these legends the powerful dismemberer is Medea, a human woman who is, nonetheless, close to the gods. The source of her power is a combination of god-like control over life and death as well as her female control over children; it is that mysterious control for which men give labels as attempts to explain. That a woman should have such control is terrifying, because she uses it with the uninhibited and amoral singleness of purpose which Greek myths associate with their gods.[6]

---

5   For Pindar the status of the Medes as part of what became the Persian empire had resonances in his own experience of the Persian threat and the invasion of Thebes. If there is an implication of tyrannical rule it is by contrast.

6   This analysis, although it uses the same structuralist techniques, is quite different from that of Mimoso-Ruiz, chapt. 2, which, useful as it is, nevertheless strikes me as over-elaborated. He still sees Medea as a sorceress, implicated in the misogyny of antiquity. As Mary Lefkowitz points out, Greek writers were able to see events from women's

Thus, there is a controlling narrative of a disinherited hero who is set impossible tasks (Jason in search of the Golden Fleece, Jason recovering the throne),[7] the stories which accrued to the voyage of Argo itself, from Jason's encounter with Hypsipyle and the women of Lemnos, and *her* subsequent attachment to the story of the war against Thebes,[8] the stories of the other heroes on board Argo, and *their* adventures (which could easily be multiplied), and the motif (within the 'controlling narrative') of the young woman who falls in love with the hero, helps him, and returns to his country as his wife.[9] The aftermath of this story (her revenge upon Jason, her retreat to Athens and subsequent attempt upon the life of the son of her new husband, Aegeus) changes its geographical centre, and becomes part of the legend of Theseus, itself part of a discourse on Athens.

These are not one and the same story told from different points of view: these are reinterpretations (and inventions posing as interpretations) of material which overlaps (or is made to overlap in order to legitimate it). Authors themselves referred to 'the stories' as if they were actual and pre-existent deeds as points of reference in order to thicken the historical texture of their own fabric; that is, the sense that the stories are interconnected increases the impression of historical possibility and contingency. For an idea of a 'whole' legend had its own place in Greek ideas of – as well as plots set in – the past, whether or not the versions exploited the

points of view, and dismissing them as undifferentiated misogynists elides numerous distinctions. To define Medea as *either* a witch or a sorceress is therby to beg the question of the source of her power. The attempt to read Medea in terms of existentialism similarly elides distinctions and struggles with anachronism, as in William Sale, *Sickness, Tragedy, and Divinity in the Medea, the Hippolytus and the Bacchae* (Melbourne, Ramus Monographs, 1977). There is an excellent bibliography in Vassiliki Gaggadis-Robin, *Jason et Médée sur les sarcophages d'époque impériale* (Rome, Ecole française de Rome, 1994), chapt. 1. She modifies the traditional view that Medea is and always has been a witch by stressing the varieties of her association with magic.

7   Some of these are well-known folklore motifs which can be compared by reference to A. Aarne, Stith Thompson, *The Types of the Folk Tale: A Classification and Bibliography* (Helsinki, FF Communications, 184, 1961), vol. xxv ii, A no. 577 The King's Tasks, p. 98 and The Dragon-Slayer II, no. 300, p. 45. There are also murderous mothers: II, B, no. 765, pp. 121, 122. For detailed recountings of the legends see Pierre Grimal, *The Dictionary of Classical Mythology*, trans. A. R. Maxwell-Hyslop (Oxford, Blackwell, 1987; orig. *Dictionnaire de la mythologie grecque et romaine*, Paris, Presses Universitaire de France, 1951); it is in the nature of such reference works to make disparate classical treatments appear to be sections of longer legends which cohere.

8   Told by Statius in his *Thebaid*, which became a central classical text in the Middle Ages.

9   In these stories the woman-as-treasure may function as a commodity or an ambassador of new alliances, but she may also create motives for further strife. This pattern comprehends Ariadne as well as Helen.

chronology of when the events had taken place. For Statius, writing in the shadow of Virgil, Hypsipyle's encounter with Jason not only becomes an incident in her own tragedy; her own personal (because feminine) tragedy becomes part of the temporal connection between the heroes to whom she recounts it and the vast prehistory of the Theban public and political tragedy. Her brief public role – as ruler in succession to her ostensibly dead father, Thoas (whose life she secretly saved) – is cancelled by her private sexuality and reinforces stereotypical ideas of the irrational feminine. Statius derives Hypsipyle's love for Jason most obviously from Dido's for Aeneas, but Virgil derives his heroine from a prior Medea (whom his character transcends). The tissue of incidental references becomes a backdrop tapestry of the disappearing heroic age, in which men – and women – were close to the gods. The passing of that age is in central ways marked by derogation: Medea, the granddaughter of the sun, loses godhead and becomes a mere sorceress.

This multiplex sense of a plot influencing what appears to be an argument underpins the stories. At the heart of early references to them lies a contradictory account of male rivalry over the exchange of women. Medea's place as part of a larger historical narrative was, however contingently, recorded by Herodotus, who opens his own history with a reference to Jason and Medea which he employed in order to establish the context of East/West enmity:

> The Greeks sailed in a long ship to Aea of the Colchians and the river Phasis: and when they had done the rest of the business for which they came, they carried off the king's daughter, Medea. When the Colchian king sent a herald to demand reparation for the robbery, and the restitution of his daughter, the Greeks replied that as they had been refused reparation for the abduction of the Argive Io [by the Persians] neither would they make any to the Colchians.
> Then (so the story runs) in the second generation after this Alexandrus son of Priam, having heard this tale, was minded to win himself a wife out of Hellas by ravishment; for he was well persuaded that, as the Greeks had made no reparation, so neither would he. So he carried off Helen. The Greeks first resolved to send messengers demanding that Helen should be restored and atonement made for the rape; but when this proposal was made, the Trojans pleaded the rape of Medea, and reminded the Greeks that they asked reparation of others, yet had made none themselves, nor given up the plunder at request. . . .
> For my own part, I will not say that this or that story is true. . . .[10]

---

[10] Herodotus, ed. and trans. A. D. Goodley (London, Loeb Classical Library, 1921), I.5–7,

The apparent specificity of the chronology (two generations), the report of the negotiations, even the disclaimer at the end, disarms scepticism while establishing the priority of the Argonautic voyage. What we see less readily is the imitation of Homer's epic reference to the story which everyone knew.

The beneficiaries of the classical tradition were constrained in some parts of their interpretations more than in others; none of them was free of previous interpretative habits and assumptions. In the high and late middle ages, classical texts, as is well known, offered a high-status alternative to the stories of the religious traditions, tempting their readers and reinterpreters with all the seductive power of literature to consider different attitudes to the world and threatening that ideologically Christian world with ideas about sexuality, ambition, and conquest which ought to have been anathema – but never were. Their authority, both in the sense of an author's responsibility for a text and its events as well as in the sense of providing alternatives to Christian society, was a vexed question, a site of cultural conflict, an invitation into forbidden territory. In terms of poetic authority, the ancient world's deference to Homer was to be questioned by Christian writers for whom he was essentially a Greek defending Greeks.

Priority conferred status. What gave these legends power was their claim to represent an originary moment in secular history: the voyage of the Argo was the first secular adventure, the first time a prince sets off in search of those prizes which validate his status upon his return. But in the middle of Jason's stories are Medea's, which do not conform to a pattern of successful patriarchal legitimation. Betrayal, murder, and revenge may seem the common coin of many classical and medieval tales, subjects common enough to be trivial, but where the central actor is female, difficulties abound. A study of one group of classical legends which claims to represent historical events not only implicates other legends (which may or may not claim a similar status); it reveals ambivalences and contradictions about medieval readers' attitudes to, desires for, a secular past. Medieval writers' arguments over how these legends were to be read reveal cognitive dissonance about their understanding of historical representation, and offer promising parallels to interpretation of their own histories of the European past. The range of selection and interpretation, allusion and intertextuality, reveals central anxieties about loyalty and

9. On Herodotus' treatment of the Argonautic legends, see A. Momigliano, 'The Place of Herodotus in the History of Historiography', in *Studies in Historiography* (New York, Harper and Row, 1966), pp. 127–42. Plot here functions as one possible causal explanation, from which Herodotus can distance himself even as he employs it.

10

betrayal, inheritance and power, legitimacy, and, perhaps above all, about the place of the cunning intelligence of women who are unscrupulous as well as knowledgeable.

Herodotus's implicit allusion to Homer already takes a shared past for granted. When Homer refers to the Argo and the heroes who sailed with Jason as 'of interest to all', he is already referring to a known pre-history of the Trojan War; he is also exploiting, or creating, epic *topoi* and webs of association which became challenges to his imitators.[11] He may be referring to actually existing poems, but, of course, he may not; he may be giving the illusion of authoritative reference. There have been, he implies, conquests of Troy before this one; the rape of Helen is part of a sequence. Nothing survives of pre-Homeric poetry on the pre-history of the fall of Troy. The first extant text also preserves the first reference backward and outward to other versions, other authorities. Herodotus had nothing to invent, when he connected East-West enmity to the theft of women, because Homer had established the idea: we may wonder how far the historian was moved to take account of a body of received ideas which 'everyone knows' because everyone knew Homer, how far Herodotus's urbanity was a way of not contradicting, while not affirming, Homer's legendary world. He, too, may take advantage of an illusory epic reference. The idea that the poets, including Homer, manipulated material which was at base historical was common and unquestioned. Powerful associations between the poetry and the history led to generalizations about cyclic patterns, while creating (however they appeared merely to appeal to) ideas about cyclic patterns in human behaviour, not only as a generalization about human behaviour both individual and collective (e.g. injury inspires revenge, and counter-revenge), but within a single human life (someone who murders once is the more likely to do so again).

---

[11] Homer refers often to aspects of the Argonautic adventures, but whether that means that complete cycles predated his own is not clear, e.g. *Iliad* VII.467–69, where Hypsipyle's son is the originary trader whose ships are loaded with wine; XI, scholia on line 741; *Odyssey* XI. 235, 238, 254–9, XII. 69–72, where Circe describes the escape from the Symplegades: 'Only one ocean-going craft, the far-famed/ Argo, made it, sailing from Aiêta;/ but she, too, would have crashed on the big rocks/ if Hêra had not pulled her through, for love/ of Iêson, her captain'. Quoted from the translation by Robert Fitzgerald, (New York, Doubleday, 1961). Strabo thought that Homer used an earlier 'Medea' as the model for his Circe, but there is no evidence to suggest that this is anything but a literary strategy, using a reference to create the impression that Homer's story can be attached to other, familiar ones. See *The Cambridge History of Classical Literature*, ed. P. E. Easterling and B. M. W. Knox (Cambridge, Cambridge University Press, 1985), I, pp. 106–8.

Homer's reference (or 'reference') immediately raises four questions. First, there is a question of chronology. The sequences of history could remain unanchored as long as particular stories were treated independently. This happened 'before' that. It must be remembered how late it was before there was an attempt to make a comprehensive, coherent chronological account of them, although, second, poets often give the impression that if such an attempt were to be made it could be successful. That in turn implies, third, that the references do not only *appear* to anchor themselves in actual happenings in an unspecified, or unanchored, past, they do belong to the past, and are not mere invention. Nevertheless, the status of the interpretations is contestable. Even invention comes in the context of a poem, an author, a circumstance, and these stories were never static; if epics claimed representative and unchanging authority, it was because the epics were by Homer (and even Homer nods). Other versions (with less authority) presented themselves as versions. Authorial concern with authority marks a number of the poems written about the heroes. To write about these (or other) legends, an author would have to consider how to place them in the past, how to relate them to other events and retellings of that past, what to claim as a known action (or actor), and upon what authority to present his own (not *her* own for some centuries yet) interpretation.

Homer's heroes were taken to be exemplary, and his epics to teach his audience how to live. Age and status were the great determinants of excellence, *aretê*, and his poems are full of young men learning *aretê* in many areas of life from their well-born elders, who are prompt to remember and to recall their own exploits. The appropriate behaviour for heroes might contain both the courage of Achilles and the cunning of Odysseus. What, however, of Homer's women? They will seldom exhibit physical prowess (with the strange exception of the Amazons), but they do know things, and knowledge may be power. Knowledge of herbs, of plants as drugs, for healing, metamorphosis, or poison, was one of the outstanding arts – and one of the most dangerous.

The power of immortal women, such as Circe, daughter of Helios, the Sun, suggests another, deep-seated, set of concerns: that of knowledgeable, and therefore powerful, women as agents of disruption. Anthropological structuralism suggests that we pare the plot down to a sequence of binary polarities in order to discover those conflicts which societies could not temper.[12] One may be too tempted to find that the liminal and the

---

[12] Thus Françoise Desbordes, in her brilliant study, thinks the legends mediate the ideas of here and elsewhere, Europe and Asia, home and foreign, exogamy and endogamy,

dangerous answer all needs, but it is unquestionably true that the women associated with these legends use their power to palliate or overcome positions of 'natural' social marginality and weakness. Circe's powers of metamorphosis will reappear in the powers of the granddaughter of Helios, Medea, who is the daughter of Circe's brother, Aeetes. Their point of view, their attempts to manipulate men to their own ends, are seen by the men who cheat them as untrustworthiness, as evidence of sorcery or access to the supernatural. Women imitate men at their peril – because they imperil men as well. The association of feminine power, drugs and sexuality with the sea, which probably antedates Homer, nevertheless finds authoritative expression in his verses.[13] Odysseus, like Jason before him (that is, before him in assumed time, after him, perhaps, in poetic composition), uses trickery against trickery, travels and escapes by the sea, understands drugs and conquers sexual temptation. His own imperviousness to seduction appears to redeem his willingness to use it. There is an implication that Odysseus' tricks are in some way *decent*, as others' are not. In theory, he embodies the Greek virtues of Justice, Intelligence, Self-Restraint, and Courage. A hero who seduces a petty king's daughter in order to preserve his life (or accomplish his tasks) is not castigated for lowering her value; on the contrary, he has made her the mother of a potential hero whose own adventures will begin with the search for the missing (or absconding) father. Difficulties arise if she disagrees about the plot and her place in it. Odysseus, like Jason, has the goddess's help to make him handsome, but Odysseus is not the bearer of political implications for an imperial Ithaca. Virgil will remember this moment for Aeneas, but handle it in his own way. The etymology of Jason's name, perhaps

hospitality and war. This is too thin, and covers too many of the subjects of epic. Nevertheless, there *are* important structural repetitions which she was the first to identify and suggest unifying explanations for. See her *Argonautica: Trois études sur l'imitation dans la littérature antique* (Brussels, Latomus, 1969). I suggest below a different and more specific set of inversions. Certainly Euripides used the Symplegades, the Clashing Rocks, as a symbolic border between the Greek and barbarian worlds. That the Euxine Sea is inhospitable marks one of the standard binary polarities which forms these legends.

13 Françoise Desbordes' analysis of the boundaries inscribed in the legends is powerful. She argues that not only are the rocks rooted in the sea, disrupting usual boundaries, but the story also contains a flying ram and a dragon chariot, which transgress the usual restraints on possibility and voyaging, travelling without roads. 'Mais, à l'opposé, le diasparagmos, degré extrême de la perte, foisonne dans les histoires argonautiques où interfèrent la lignée de Minyas et la lignée de Cadmus; membra disiecta, *sparsa per agros*, Apsyrte dépecé, Pélias dépecé, les dents qu'on sème, Créuse et Créon dont la chair se détache en lambeaux: atomisation des objets, éclatement de la personne, négations irrépressible du même' (38).

bestowed upon him by his teacher, Chiron the centaur, meant 'healer', but any use of drugs or medicine by Jason is not mentioned in the legends as we have them.

If we move from thinking about plots and plot-repetitions in a structuralist mode, to a feminist one which invites us to invert the 'phallogocentric' point of view, a different description becomes available. There is a familiar pattern in stories about exchange of women where the motive is theft and counter-theft; that is the pattern which is our point of departure. Medea appears to offer a complex contradiction. But let us begin with 'normal' theft in the more famous cycle of legends: Paris steals Helen and is killed by Menelaus.[14] This is a pattern many times multiplied, and abduction in association with marriage is strikingly repeated. The question of 'ownership' of the women, of kinship responsibility, is only one of the disputes. The women's subjectivity is itself another. At the beginning of the Trojan war, Agamemnon 'steals' his daughter (on the pretext that she is to marry Achilles) to sacrifice her to Artemis and is subsequently killed by his wife (in some versions her lover, in others the two of them together), who is condemned by all parties for the crime; during the war Aegisthus 'steals' Clytemnestra and is killed by Orestes, who is condemned but pardoned (elevating the status of Athens); after the war is long over Orestes marries Menelaus's daughter, Hermione, but she is 'stolen' by Pyrrhus, whom Orestes also kills. As Herodotus points out, it is hard to speak of the abduction of Medea as theft, since she abetted her seducer, but Jason certainly did not obtain her from her father by honest means. Already our 'normal' expectations are transgressed: Jason succeeds. The young outwit the old, but the marriage is not the plot's ending. So far from Aeetes catching the lovers, they evade his navy by a murder in which a body is desecrated (*sparagmos*): Medea kills and then dismembers her young brother. (This potentially brings the House of Aeetes to an end, but some versions of the legends repair this apparent breach.) If the gods do not immediately avenge this transgression of their prerogatives, they do not bless Jason's marriage. He regains his kingdom, but, in many versions, must leave it because of the manner of his – or, rather, Medea's – disposing of the usurper, Pelias. Like Medea's brother, Pelias is dismembered, hacked

14 Mihoko Suzuki, *Metamorphoses of Helen: Authority, Difference, and the Epic* (Ithaca, Cornell University Press, 1989) follows Helen's fortunes in the epic. Suzuki stresses the importance of the victim as Girardian sacrifice or scapegoat, and sees 'woman' as an object of desire yet conceived of as valueless. As will become clear, I wish to argue that Medea is an exceptional case for a number of reasons. There is a study of that other prelude to the Trojan war in *The Judgment of the Trojan Prince Paris in Medieval Literature* by Margaret Ehrhardt (Philadelphia, University of Pennsylvania Press, 1987).

apart by his own daughters. Now, the manner of this murder is gratuitous: all that was apparently necessary for rejuvenation was the replacement of aged blood by revivifying drugs. The dismemberment is an excess stimulated by its expressive qualities; it enacts the dis-jointing of the patriarchal family and state. In an analysis like this, however, it it important to remember that before it is a symbol it is also deeply horrible.

It is at the point of Jason's remarriage, about which many versions are silent, that the inversion of the pattern of theft and revenge manifests itself. If the spouses' genders were reversed it would be easy to understand an outraged husband avenging himself upon his wife's new alliance. Medea might be thought of as avenging a theft, but it is hard to think of her husband as 'stolen'; she kills Creusa (and Creusa's father, thus ending the House of Corinth) and not her own offending spouse, Jason. However, if revenge is a matter of hurting one's enemies more than one is hurt oneself, and finding a safe haven from which to exult over their defeat, then Medea has succeeded beyond the 'normal' revenges of the men, because she has destroyed Jason's house. It is banal, but nonetheless true, to say that she has usurped a male prerogative: her usurpation is a multiple offence. It is a scandal. It is difficult to overemphasize just how unusual she is. The legends go on to make her, unlike Jason, still fertile, still powerful, still capable of exerting her not-quite-human will. With the exception of Euripides' metaphorical and lexical allusions to heroism, none of them see her behaviour as 'like' what men do; none legitimate her revenge. The final *sparagmos* is Medea's dismemberment of Jason's sons. The endings supplied for her are attempts to repair her disruptions and dismemberments.

When the Argo first appears, Jason is clearly there, but Medea's presence is more problematic. The epic poets shared legends, but changed them. Cyclic patterns appeal to the audience's sense of the likely, the possible, the necessary. Some scholars believe that Homer may have used earlier epics, and based his Circe on a pre-existing Medea, though, as will become apparent from later discussion, this is unlikely.[15] It is more probable that Homer himself is the source of the character who later became Medea. In *Iliad* 11, when the aged Nestor recalls his first battle, to protect his father's lands against marauding Greeks (nothing of Eastern barbarians here), he mentions the name of the first man he killed, and identifies his family, 'He was Moulio the spearman, a son-in-law of Augeias and married to his eldest daughter, fair-haired Agamede, who knew all the drugs that the

---

15 See Apollonius Rhodius, *Argonautica Book III*, ed. Richard Hunter (Cambridge, Cambridge University Press, 1989), p. 14n. There is *no* evidence that Homer borrowed, only speculation supported by the belief in a primitive and complete version of 'a' legend.

broad earth grows' (lines 739–41).[16] This Agamede, a grand-daughter of the sun, is a Greek, not a foreigner, knowledgeable in an art, neither a sorceress nor a witch.[17] Hesiod's reference in the *Theogony* knows a hero winning a bride by completing difficult tasks.[18] Pelias is there as an unreasonable king, but Hesiod gives no explanation for his wrath. The Argonautic voyage, which includes a war at Troy, precedes that city's more famous destruction by at least one generation. Or, at least, one generation of human heroes, since among the Argonauts were Castor and Pollux, twin sons of Leda and Zeus, whose sisters, born from the same egg, were Helen and Clytemnestra. Already the impulse to rationalize runs into positivist sands.

The impression which the legends create *en masse* is of a lost civilization of Bronze Age heroes whose stories survive not simply, as Homer has it, 'to make a song for men in days to come', but which survive in ways which are recoverable, discoverable by deduction and inference. The heroes on the Argo, like the heroes at Troy, represent their descendants, the citizens of this or that Greek *polis*, legitimate them by their precedence, and reflect glory upon them. That is, they exist both as *poetic subject* and, concomitantly, as *historical explanation*. Because they exist in what we now call a liminal space, that mythical Bronze Age onto which Athenian literature could project its own concerns, they remain estranged from Athenian customs; their own status remains strange.

Because authors themselves looked back to find the roots, origins, and causes of the legends they wished to retell, scholarship needs to follow their gaze. But retelling is a Janus-faced activity. In what follows I shall be attempting to describe numerous ways of understanding, misunderstanding, that is, interpreting, a changing group of stories which sometimes use, but sometimes challenge, contemporary assumptions.[19] The shadow of

[16] *The Iliad*, trans. Martin Hammond (Harmondsworth, Penguin, 1987), p. 211.

[17] See also *Pausanius*, ed. W. H. S. Jones, R. E. Wycherley, and H. A. Ormerod (London, Loeb Classical Library, 1918–35), V.xvii. 9–10. The *Naupaktia*, a lost epic, is supposed to have dealt with the Argo, and the *Kypria* referred to it. The early Greek poet Epimenides is also supposed to have written his own Argonautic voyage about 600 BC. See G. L. Huxley, *Greek Epic Poetry from Eumelos to Panyassis* (London, Faber and Faber, 1969), Duarte Mimoso-Ruiz, *Médée antique et moderne: aspects rituels et socio-politiques d'un mythe* (Paris, Ophrys, 1982), chapt 1, and Edith Hall, *Inventing the Barbarians* (Oxford, Clarendon Press, 1989), p. 35 and nn.

[18] *Works and Days* 992–1002, *Theogony*, ed. M. L. West (Oxford, 1966).

[19] That there is an iconographical tradition which does not correspond to *any* of the extant literature of the legends is a further reminder of the sometimes arbitrary 'success' of one version over another. For a detailed list of the representations (e.g. Jason in the dragon's mouth) see Vassiliki Gaggadis-Robin, *Jason et Médée sur les sarcophages d'époque impériale* (Rome, Ecole française de Rome, 1994), pp. 88ff.

universalism hovers, because there are always husbands and wives, parents and children, hosts and guests, power and obedience or revolt, but even the most constant constants are modified by the cultures in which they are found, and our best defence against Idealism may be our alertness to its dangers.

The plan of this book is as follows. Chapter One looks at a series of classical works in Greek by Pindar, Euripides, Apollonius Rhodius, and in Latin by Virgil, Ovid, and Seneca. 'Medea' was not only a succession of characters recreated by poets, she became, by process of imitation, a kind of literary parthenogenesis, a succession of *different* characters. Chapter Two situates the Argonautic voyage in a different discourse: the history of the world. Chapter Three considers another way of using the legends, as literal narratives ripe for allegorical interpretation. Chapter Four discusses one striking fifteenth-century attempt to offer a comprehensive, coherent account of the hero, Jason. But Jason's adventures are embedded in a political narrative which is meant as a Mirror for Princes. The peculiar circumstances which gave rise to Lefèvre's fifteenth-century book offer an opportunity to look at a late-medieval invention in which different kinds of narration combine to create an unusual amalgam. Chapter Five selects 'Medea' from the complex tissue of the legends, and considers her as one among the medieval Ovidian 'heroines'. A brief Conclusion suggests the ways that the legends changed after the end of the middle ages, and indicates where a consideration of the masculine/historical and the feminine/allegorical strands might lead into the seventeenth century and indulges in some speculations concerning our own.

ONE

Medeas of Antiquity

This chapter discusses the earliest versions of the legends in Greece and Rome, considering different kinds of time and attitudes to the past as much as individual authors. It describes the interpretations and inventions of, in particular, Pindar, Euripides, Apollonius Rhodius, Virgil, Seneca, and Statius. Forward references to medieval interpretations, or to the drama of Corneille, or the libretto of his son for the composer Charpentier or the operatic collaboration between Hoffman and Cherubini must not come to seem goals to which earlier versions tend, far less to which they ought to have aspired, any more than Euripides' play represents a perfect form. Ovid's Medeas, and the imitations they inspired, will be postponed to chapter three. Far from there being a platonic Idea, or even canonic texts of the legends, the characters and events I shall discuss change constantly, and change according to the contexts and societies in which they are written. From the outset, authors and texts take advantage of reference to a known past which is remembered outside themselves.

Two ideas recur: first, in the context of who Medea is arises the problem of whether or not she is a witch. If we believe that this is not a question, we need to consider when a witch might not be a witch: when she is already a supernatural figure, or when she is not a woman. I have already referred to the innocence of 'witchcraft' of men such as Odysseus who take advantage of medicinal herbs. That must also be true of Jason, who benefits so dramatically from Medea's knowledge of *pharmakon*. But Jason is a man, a Greek man. Medea is a woman, and not Greek. These issues are intertwined, and not usually argued, but they suggest views about women and foreigners to which poets alluded. Second, in the process of re-telling, they create, emphasize, and multiply examples of a female type, a *topos* which becomes a claim upon the real.

Most of the post-Homeric treatments of the legends avail themselves of a part of the Argonautic adventures. They all, at the same time, take advantage of the idea that somewhere else (not necessarily in writing)

19

there exists the memory of a whole history, even if it appears, for good reason, to be an indecency to be avoided. In the rest of this chapter I shall consider those interpretations and show how they became accretions upon a possible – but un-told, even non-existent – narrative. That is, they suggest, but do not describe or account for, a large-scale Greek past in which memories of dynastic rivalries, competition for trade, even large-scale migrations, as well as the outlines of contemporary interests can be discerned.

The mastery of Medea's power, and the transformation of her story, is crucial to many retellings. It is banal now to stress the importance of women's enthusiastic obedience in the reproduction of society, generation by generation; it is nonetheless unavoidable. Medea's desire to be that obedient, fruitful wife, providing heirs to royal houses, is constantly frustrated in the versions which were written in classical antiquity. She uses drugs and cunning to abet Jason in his tasks; as his dependant, she flees with him intending to marry him in Greece. If she is the murderer of Apsyrtos, her murder of her brother is a human murder. That some versions make Jason responsible for the murder of an adult Apsyrtos reminds us that story-tellers differed in their ascriptions of cunning in ways that change ideas of responsibility and blame.[1] She possesses the great gifts of *metis*, the ability to use 'premeditation, deceit, the surprise attack and the sudden assault'.[2] That is, she does not use the power she inherits from her grandfather until, despoiled of her status as Jason's wife, she finds herself a foreign woman, in a doubly foreign country, with no possibility of appeal to her own or her husband's human kinship group. Her supernatural inheritance gives her the means not to revenge (that she accomplishes with the earlier mixture of cunning and craft) but escape. A technique of juxtaposition, which allows the author to avoid explanation or rationalization, presents a Medea whose status need not be discussed.

---

[1] Lost plays on these subjects by, e.g. Sophocles are known only from fragments, but it would seem that they preserve a tradition, which Apollonius followed, that Jason or the other Argonauts were responsible for murdering Apsyrtus. The temptation to displace blame onto Medea is too obvious to require explication. For a succinct summary, see Howard Jacobson, *Ovid's Heroïdes* (Princeton, Princeton University Press, 1974), chapt. six.

[2] Detienne and Vernant, *Cunning Intelligence*, p. 21. It is hard to see how one can avoid the assumption that any woman whose knowledge includes drugs can escape the label 'witch'.

Greek Poetry to Pindar

It may have been Eumelos who first linked the Corinthian cult of Medea with the Argo in his eighth-century heroic epic, to which there are references in Pausanius (II.iii.8–11) and in the scholia on Apollonius Rhodius. Eumelos was himself Corinthian, and in his Argonautic poem seems to have linked the Argo to Corinthian worship, identifying (or 'recognizing') Aeetes as a Corinthian who migrated to Colchis. Pausanias says that late in the poem Medea was invited to return to Corinth (2.1.1, 2.3.10). At this point she and her family are still Greek; perhaps the Corinthians were trying to legitimate their own expansion into the Black Sea by insisting upon a prior historical connection to a Greek city.[3] The 'explanation' of a cult is only one use of precedent, and a relatively straight-forward one; like imaginary etymologies, it adds more than it satisfies about what needed to be explained. There are associations which disappear once the poem is removed from the Greek language, since the pervasive ideas of 'craft' which are associated with Medea appear to be part of her name, 'metis' and 'Medeia'.[4] That is, in Greek the word 'Medea' sounds like 'intelligence', 'knowledge', 'cunning'.

---

[3] *Cambridge History*, I.108 and Denys Page, ed., *Medea* (Oxford, 1938), p. xxii. Moving Medea (an exchange of women) is one way of creating a kinship relation; moving her back legitimates a link to the throne of Aeetes. See, for a fine example of this kind of rationalizing explanation, E. Will's argument for Aeetes as a chthonic deity. Even if there were a cult of Medea's children in Corinth, that does not make *her* a goddess. Despite his insistence, the evidence is at least ambiguous, and susceptible of several interpretations. The problem may be the fashion for hypotheses which begged the question by assuming the widespread existence of Great Mother cults. See E. Will, *Korinthiaka: Recherches sur l'histoire et la civilisation de Corinthe des origines aux guerres médiques* (Paris, E. de Boecard, 1955), esp. pp. 85–129. This kind of argument builds on the fantasies spun by Bachofen, in his work on 'mother right', to which I will return below. A more rationalizing hypothesis is explored in R. Drews, 'The Earliest Greek Settlements on the Black Sea', in the *Journal of Hellenic Studies* 96 (1976), pp. 18–31 which argues for poetic interest in Aeetes to serve Corinthian expansionism.

[4] For the semantic field, see Detienne and Vernant. Referred to by Jason in Euripides' *Medea*; see Page, p. 102. Zeus had an affair with Metis (her name means 'craft' or 'cunning intelligence'), who became pregnant. Zeus was told that she would bear a daughter, then subsequently a son who would be greater than his father and would conquer him. Zeus swallowed Metis to prevent this, but could not stop the birth of her daughter, Athena, whose apparently motherless parturition is familiar from other Greek stories. One of Medea's sons, Medus (the father is usually thought to be Aeson), is a prophet, and ancestor of the Medes – but of course this resemblance may have worked the other way, pulling Medus into the orbit of the Medes. See Pierre Grimal, *The Dictionary of Classical Mythology*, trans. A. R. Maxwell-Hyslop (Oxford, Blackwell, 1987; orig. *Dictionnaire de la mythologie grecque et romaine*, Paris, Presses Universitaire

This evocation of a possible past is nowhere more endowed with strangeness than by Pindar in the fourth Pythian Ode, where the legends are fragmented so as to resist precisely that explanatory reconstitution. This long celebratory poem is often dated to about 470 BC, and associated with a dynastic reconciliation. As Charles Segal puts it, 'By skillfully mixing fullness and brevity, Pindar surrounds the events of the tale with an aura of numinous mystery. By selecting intense moments and rendering their quality of the marvellous through strong metaphors, he impels the hearer or reader to share the imaginative recreation of the mythic past in its elusive beauty and remoteness'.[5] Segal goes on to show how the structures of the poem appear to evoke contemporary concerns from the past with such abstract and general issues as the status of the hero, the question of origins, and the trammels of male/female conflict. The association of these legends with these questions (like the renaissance love sonnet with male sexual and artistic frustration) gives them a double hold upon the writerly imagination. Pindar's Jason navigates between crafts, craft, and craftiness; finds his way between potions as protection and as poison; is aided by but must control love. Pindar works more by the powerful poetic strategy of juxtaposition than by argument. In calling attention to his ode as an ode, he asks us to attend to his authority, his relation to earlier poetry, his account of some events of the past.

There is a displacement here: by concentrating on *a* hero, and situating him in historical events which are themselves contextualized in the largest terms of 'primitive' male/female conflict, Pindar turns our attention to the great cycles of human experience, and poetry becomes one of the mediations of reflection upon that experience. To repeat the cliché ''twas ever thus' is to open oneself to derision, but to evoke it is to allude to the powerful authority of what everyone knows, while avoiding the very political questions the poem threatens to raise.

Segal shows how Pindar's Ode asks us to consider the poet's own crafty craft, the poet's wisdom and trickery, his healing or danger. It is the poet

---

de France, 1951), who refers to Diodorus Siculus and to Pausanius. Cp. the discussion in Mary Lefkowitz, *Women in Greek Myth* (London, Duckworth, 1986), 31–2.

5 *Pindar's Mythmaking: the Fourth Pythian Ode* (Princeton, Princeton University Press, 1986), 4. See also R. Lattimore, *The Odes of Pindar* (Chicago, University of Chicago Press, 1947). Deborah Steiner points out in passing the use of Jason as a metonym for the hero's fleeting youth, a pattern to which the aged Pelias appeals through the metaphor of the fast-fading flower (IV. 157–8) in *The Crown of Song: Metaphor in Pindar* (New York, Oxford University Press, 1986), p. 31. It is worth attending to omission: the 'flower of youth' type, so common as to be almost a universal trope in literature, is seldom invoked for Medea.

who chooses what to memorialize and how, whose navigation through heroism and sexuality controls our access not only to the past but to understanding it. 'Cunning intelligence' is, after all, an ambiguous gift; the young hero is normally renowned for his behaviour in open combat.[6] Wily Odysseus, honey-tongued Odysseus, is by those very epithets unusual. Like drugs or love, words change our behaviour, they change what it is to be *us*. Odysseus is *polymetis*, multi-cunning. Words as drug for good or ill are judged by how they are used, but also by whom and to whom: in the mouth of the hero they are likelier to be well used than in that of the usurping uncle (or a woman, or even a poet). The truth, like other possessions, may be hidden. Where the arts of persuasion are employed *in* a text, they also constitute the success of the text itself. That is, the poet colludes with the ideal audience, who both are and are not susceptible to his suasions.[7]

There is, on the surface, an odd association which merits what may appear to be a digression. The heroic straight path is often contrasted to the twists and turns resorted to by weaker characters (such as younger brothers in folk tale) who must work by guile rather than by force. While in the case of Odysseus there is no question of a lack of physical prowess, that assumption of brute strength is not always associated with clever heroes. Oedipus, the most famous of the puzzle-solvers, is linked by his name to limping. Jason, too, has a sobriquet, 'monokrepis', which appears to suggest the uneven gait which belongs to the 'feeble' hero rather than the strong one. Pelias, his uncle, has been told to beware of a man who arrives wearing only one shoe; Jason loses a sandal on his way to Corinth and arrives to fulfill the prophecy. Older scholarship associated this shoelessness with a loss of rights; whether that is true or not, there appears to be a deeper association with mental compensation for physical

---

6   For the discussion of verbal entrapment as opposed to war, see Marcel Detienne and Jean-Pierre Vernant, *Les Ruses de l'intelligence: la Métis des grecs* (Paris, Flammarion, 1974); translated as *Cunning Intelligence in Greek Culture and Society*, J. Lloyd (Chicago, University of Chicago Press, 1991; orig. Brighton, Harvester, 1978), pp. 279–326 on the 'circle' and the 'bond'.

7   The association of drugs (sometimes sorcery) and poetry became a familiar literary *topos*. It will reappear in Chapter five below in Christine de Pizan's juxtaposition of Medea with ideas of prophecy (Manto) and poetry (Cornificia, Proba, and Sappho) in her *Livre de la Cité des Dames* I.28–31. There are perhaps questions to be raised about the gendering of such ideas as 'charming' one's listeners: no one suggests that Orpheus is anything more than gifted. In addition, the generic appropriateness of ambiguous oaths or prophecies may be more important than the speaker.

disadvantage: the 'crooked paths' are represented by a metaphorically crooked hero.[8]

Medea's desire to unite herself with a Greek may have seemed entirely plausible to a Greek audience, and Pindar stresses that aspect of Greek ideas of social – or ethnic – mobility. Pindar's Colchian princess desires Greece as his Greek heroes desire fame. However the hero controls sexuality, Pindar's heroine is its victim. The rhetorical skills of seduction are unnecessary, since Medea is a prey to Aphrodite. As Segal is only one of many to point out (p. 56ff), combining the theft of a bride and a sea journey is part of the pattern of male maturing; Jason returns to claim his kingdom. By a dangerous vessel he imports the dangerous vessel of his descendants. One might add first that this contextualization, by disarming his audience into recognizing an assumed world of folklore motifs, concomitantly distracts his listeners from applying other kinds of analytic criteria to the narrative (the theft from Aeetes' point of view); and second, that in these legends nobody escapes by land: they flee either by sea or air.[9] Jason's use of the power of Aphrodite to win Medea is subsumed by Hera into the legitimacy of stable rule and orderly generational succession. Jason may have benefited from Medea's fire-proof drugs, but it is his strength which yoked the magical bulls, his courage which won the magical fleece. Pindar controls the possible reading beyond his own use of the myth with references to oracular prophecy and by arranging the narrative

---

8 The distraction appears to come from the semitic custom of using the shoe to cede male rights (or obligations), particularly to marrying a widow, as in Ruth or Deuteronomy XXV 9, 10. The work of scholars such as J. Brunel, 'Jason [monokrepis]', *Revue Archéologique* (Paris, 1934), pp. 34–43 has now been superseded by J. P. Vernant, 'Le Tyran boiteux: d'Oedipe à Périandre', many times collected, perhaps most conveniently in his and Pierre Vidal-Naquet's *Oedipe et ses mythes* (Paris, Editions la Découverte, 1986), which unites their work on the legends; this essay is translated as 'From Oedipus to Periander: Lameness, Tyranny, Incest in Legend and History', in *Arethusa* 15 (1982), 19–38; and in *Le Chasseur Noir* (Paris, Maspero, 1981) where he develops an iconographic picture of Jason as a double figure representing man and boy, outsider and king, hero and seducer. See also Segal, p. 58n. The emphasis on walking as metaphor for journey, exile or life itself, is apparent. Discussed by Desbordes, chapt. one. The crooked way (of cunning) is briefly referred to by Euripides' Medea when she describes her use of poison as the direct, or straight, way – in one of those parodies of 'heroic' speech in which the play abounds.

9 At the risk of being accused of the solecism of counting Lady Macbeth's children, I should like to suggest that when Medea flees from Colchis with Jason, as Jason's subordinate, in the human scheme, she is a passenger on his ship, and uses human solutions to escape the faster ships of her father. (So much for the superiority of the first sea-going Greek adventurers.) It is only when she needs her inherited supernatural power to combat human patriarchy that she takes to the air. In addition, of course, in that flight she has only herself to save.

24

sections of the Ode in ways which break continuity and paradoxically discourage any views of the legends after the end of the poem. This poetic coherence is anti-historical. Like the past alluded to, but not described, by the poets of the epic cycles, this is a strange place which is never brought together as a whole; the past is not dis-membered, because it was never unified.

The establishment of a legitimate dynasty, with the king as *basileus* and not *tyrannos*, is at the heart of the occasion for the Fourth Pythian Ode. Pindar's gift to his patron is part of the healing of a political rift, and suggests the healing power of poetry as *pharmakos*. That these legends should be associated with dynastic concerns from so early on may seem merely coincidence. It is no such thing. The political subjects of legitimate dynasties and of expansion co-exist with the surface narrative of the legends, and will be reused, spontaneously, despite differences in country, political organisation, religion, and literary types (as, for example, by Valerius Flaccus). If, however, we once again turn the insights of structural anthropology upon the repetitions in the stories, thinking about the 'appropriateness' of a core of legitimate succession as the fulcrum upon which its episodes turn, we can extend Segal's reading until Pindar's insights assume prophetic aspects. The desire for continuous and coherent narrative, or for consistent characterization, will raise problems about who Medea is which were of no concern to Pindar.

Euripides

They were, however, the centre of Euripides' interpretation in his extant play, *Medea*, produced probably in 431 BC, with a *Philoctetes* and a *Dictys*.[10] This was not Euripides' first play on an Argonautic subject, but it is dangerous to try to generalize about the plays, because the summaries and

---

10 I follow Page, in his introduction to *Medea*. It was he who first established the evidence for Euripides' innovative emphasis on Medea as a barbarian, as shown in post-*Medea* vase painting (pp. lvii–lxviii, and see *Lexicon* and Hall, p. 35). Athens was at the precipitous height of its power, and, though it will not concern us further, at the height of trading interests with Corinth. Charles Segal, 'The Two Worlds of Euripides' Helen', *Transactions and Proceedings of the American Philological Association* 102 (1971), 553–614. Twentieth-century syntheses are beyond the scope of this book, but associations between Medea and her literary offspring, Ariadne and Dido, recur in, for example, Hélène Cixous's essay, 'Sorties', in her and Cathérine Clément's *The Newly Born Woman* (St Paul, University of Minnesota Press, 1986 [orig. *La Jeune Née*, 1975]), esp. pp. 107ff. The authors' psychoanalytic orientation leads to a contrast between sorceress and hysteric. See also Anne Burnett, 'Medea and the Tragedy of Revenge', *Classical*

fragments of the earlier plays are sometimes obscure, leaving it unclear what consistency Euripides may have drawn from play to play. *Peliades* seems to have been the first, produced in 455 BC (just three years after *The Oresteia*); it concerned the daughters of Pelias and their dismemberment of their father. *Aigeus*, about 440 BC, seems to have been a 'recognition' drama about the return of Theseus to his father. From the extant 'hypothesis', or summary of the play, it seems possible that Medea was portrayed as part of an older generation, trying to protect herself and her child or children by Aegeus against the claims of the legitimate heir who has suddenly appeared.[11] If so, this would connect her once again to dynastic concerns.

Medea is one of the most famous as well as most-interpreted of Greek tragedies. Traditional critical misogyny and ethnocentricity have dismissed her as a barbarian witch, one of Euripides' 'bad women' who, although provoked, undoubtedly goes 'too far'. Recent studies of women and barbarians, as well as attention to structures of analogy and reference, have done much to address the problems of understanding Euripides' play.[12] In particular, they have freed it from a sequence of charges from sordidness to extravagance. Nevertheless, traditional interpretations of Medea and *Medea* are part of the concern of this book, and although I shall propose a reading which would not have been available to many of the historical interpreters of the play, mine is not intended as any sort of 'corrective'; rather, I wish to call attention to those places where stereotypes are in the process of creation. The recognition by generations of critics that Medea's complaints are legitimate does not always identify which claims or how they are legitimate. This sense of Medea as herself a model for other, subsequent, dangerous women is important because (as a literary character) she sets precedents for other, even more famous, ones, above all, Dido. It is too easy to slide from admiration of Euripides' ability to compel

---

Philology 67 (1973), 1–24; Bernard Knox, 'The *Medea* of Euripides' in his *Word and Action: Essays on the Ancient Theatre* (Baltimore and London, Johns Hopkins University Press), pp. 295–322.

[11] For these two plays see the descriptions in T. B. L. Webster, *The Tragedies of Euripides* (London, Methuen, 1967), pp. 32–6, 77–80. A fourth play, *Hypsipyle*, belonged to a trilogy on the Theban cycle; the fragments are published by G. W. Bond, ed. *Hypsipyle* (Oxford, Oxford University Press, 1969), now supplemented by W. E. H. Cockle, ed. *Hypsipyle: Text and Annotation based on a Re-examination of the Papyri* (Rome, Anteneo, 1987).

[12] Synnøve des Bouvrie, *Women in Greek Tragedy: an anthropological approach* (Oslo, Norwegian University Press, 1990) VII. pp. 214–39; Edith Hall, *Inventing the Barbarian* (Oxford, Clarendon Press, 1989); Simon Goldhill, *Reading Greek Tragedy* (Cambridge, Cambridge University Press, 1986).

admiration for her to characterizing her as expressing an essential aspect of woman's fate. Loss of status and civic rights is not gender specific.[13] But from the outset it should be stressed that – at least in Euripides – untrammelled irrational passion is not female in any simple or straightforward way, since it is associated with Dionysos. When Pentheus sees the 'Asiatic' Dionysos as 'effeminate', he shows an instance of the way the exotic is feminized by contrast to ideas of rational and self-controlled Greek manhood. The nexus irrationality, vindictiveness, and unrestrained passion became gendered by association. Once gendered, the nexus encouraged the interpretation of Medea's desire for revenge as profoundly irrational. But it is.

As with 'heroic' women from the creation of Aeschylus's Clytemnestra, independent action (that is, beyond the behaviour appropriate to a wife sheltering in her husband's house) usually means action which usurps male prerogatives, beyond what is sanctioned by (even permitted to) men. Medea is partly exceptional because of the ambiguity of her identity. Of course, she is the daughter of Aeetes, the king of Colchis, himself the son of Helios and the brother of Circe and Hecate. Like her aunts, she is skilled in the use of drugs, a skill which also raises issues of gender. For example, in *Iliad* 10, Odysseus and his sailors find themselves on Circe's island, where the sailors are transformed into swine by the beautiful and dangerous goddess (who is explicitly linked to Aeetes); Odysseus is protected by 'moly', a flower given to him by the gods' messenger, Hermes. The gods' aid emphasizes the limits of human intelligence against the double treachery of deception (false guest-welcome, false words) and drugs, and marks Odysseus out as worthy of the advantages bestowed by the gods' favour. If the words which are normally used to describe Circe carry implications of sorcery or witchcraft, that is because of her gender: no such suggestion is implied for the user of 'moly'. Odysseus's cunning is a superlative gift of intelligence, not a supernatural power. The herbal antidote remains a plant. That is, we may wonder if, to outwit Odysseus's great cunning, a woman requires an explanation other than even greater cunning.[14] Medea appears

---

[13] Thus, for all the subtlety of George Steiner's appreciation of Euripides' Medea's expression of the 'incensed hurt of women', he, too, sees her predicament largely in terms of her gender. He is, in context, stressing the importance of the Greek myths as points of references. To Steiner's emphasis on 'the truth and variousness' of Greek tragic women one might add conditions of power and powerlessness associated with, but not exclusive to, women. See his *Antigones*, pp. 129, 237. It is to Medea's advantage in persuading (or manipulating) the Chorus to emphasize her gender – the truth of her assertion of the dangers of child-bearing does not make her statement less rhetorically calculating.

[14] Later analyses of this incident accuse Odysseus's companions of responsibility for their

to be a mortal woman, if not an ordinary one, whose exceptional intelligence (emphasized by Creon's fear of her, Jason's knowledge, and her own self-estimation) and knowledge of drugs (which, as is now well known, can be healing or poisonous) is assumed to assimilate her, too, to sorcery or witchcraft.[15] Indeed, one constant in modern interpretations of Medea is her supposed status as a witch. Witches, of course, forfeit human sympathy without inspiring the awe which comes from recognition that super-human powers may stem from closeness to the gods. Medea is one of those dangerous figures between gods and men, whose exact status is unclear. She appears to be wholly human when, as a young girl, she falls in love with Jason and uses her knowledge of drugs to protect him, but appears to be something other when she begins to employ that knowledge which is her inheritance.[16] Medea is a play much closer to the Bacchae than has always been realized: the tragic monstrosity of the protagonist's actions themselves make her transcend the very categories of good and evil which she recognizes. Her revenge for Jason's injury – four deaths and the destruction of two houses – exceeds all expectation. Unusually, there is no suggestion that her behaviour is stimulated by Ate, the madness visited

own entrapment by interpreting them as gluttonous when they trust their hostess, lower their guard, and eat what she offers. If drugged wine, and the drunkenness which ensues, take away male advantage, the threat they pose to themselves by their failure to maintain control is partly transferred to the female deceiver. The underlying idea that men are only beaten by women when the women either trick them or poison them (through their cunning) is here supplemented by the criticism that only a glutton or a fool allows himself to be so seduced. The companion who remains a pig, dehumanized by the extent of his low desires, is another of the literary constants: Spenser remembers that 'Gryll will still be Gryll'.

15 Derrida, 'Plato's Pharmacy', in his Dissemination, trans. Barbara Johnson (London, Athlone Press, 1981, pp. 61–171. Bernard Knox covers the accusations (Word and Action, pp. 308–10, esp. 320 n.60). Denys Page immediately spots Medea's 'sorcery' when she decides that poison is the best method for killing her enemies: 'n.b. 1) Medea the sorceress' (note to lines 364ff, p. 99). Criticism by Webster, as by D. J. Conacher, Euripidean Drama: Myth, Theme, and Structure (Toronto, University of Toronto, 1967) may be taken to exemplify the unthinkingly misogynistic assumptions of Medea as guilty witch-woman. By contrast, see M. Shaw, 'Female Intruder', Classical Philology 70 (1970), pp. 255–66. Even Simon Goldhill, with whose concise and impressive analysis I am otherwise in complete agreement, calls her a sorceress, Reading Greek Tragedy (Cambridge, Cambridge University Press, 1986), p. 117 and 'a great and violent witch' in The Poet's Voice: Essays on Poetics and Greek Literature (Cambridge, 1991), p. 303.

16 In the course of the play Helios is invoked more frequently as Medea comes closer to murder. Knox stresses her appearance in the dragon-chariot as a parallel to the place in the theatre where the gods appear (Word and Action, p. 303). Aegeus swears by Helios and is echoed by Medea, who shortly afterwards describes the poisoned dress as part of her inheritance from Helios. The invocations of Helios are associated in the play's imagery with gifts and oaths.

upon human beings by gods. Her escape in her grandfather's dragon chariot assimilates her to those who have what Jean-Pierre Vernant has called
'la mort dans les yeux'.[17]

Throughout the play Medea's intelligence (her *sophia*) is emphasized as a
dangerous attribute; it is dangerous because intelligence is power, and she
is an intelligent woman. Creon is afraid that she might 'think of something'. This could not sound more rational. Jason, of course, is certain,
although neither of them (less intelligent, as they suspect) can anticipate
what it might be. In the world of epic the hero invents his escape, his defeat
of more powerful enemies, precisely by his cunning, his ability to outwit
them. Magical assistance might be one thing which would help the weak
hero to kill his enemy; if the end, however, is murder, and murder by a
woman, that is something else. At the beginning of the play the nurse says
little of why Medea is doubly-exiled and without the support of her own
kin, though we may assume that Euripides' audience would have known of
the murders with which those exiles were associated. Characters refer to
the murders in the course of the play. But in the event Medea's kinship
group *does* come to her aid, as demonstrated by the arrival of her grandfather Helios's dragon chariot. Knox showed that Medea's heroic anger
(*thymos*) is an interpretation of Sophoclean tragedy. Whether there is a
larger nexus of reference (e.g. to other plays of Euripides) is impossible to
determine, but one may notice how often Euripidean revengers are anti-
heroic.[18] One of the things which is unfortunately unclear in the summary

17 In the book of that name Vernant's argument restricts itself to goddesses, but the
extension is inviting: not only Medea's constantly repeated status as 'barbarian' (which
disappears in modern translations), her invocation of Artemis as legitimater of her
revenge, and herself as an imported curse, but in her own metaphoric association of
childbirth and war. *La mort dans les yeux: figures de l'Autre en Grèce ancienne* (Paris,
Hachette, 1985). It is possible (attested by Macrobius in the *Saturnalia*) that Medea was
identified in Rome with the cult of Bona Dea, which included, in its temple, a herb
garden from which priestesses concocted medicine. But this would be a projection
backwards, and could be an imaginary association due to literature rather than actual
cult practice. See John Scheid, 'The Religious Roles of Roman Women', in *A History of
Women in the West*, I. *From Ancient Goddesses to Christian Saints*, ed. Pauline Schmitt
Pantel, trans. Arthur Goldhammer (Cambridge, Mass., Belknap Press of Harvard
University Press, 1992), pp. 377–408. For the association women/medicine/love
philtres/Venus, see p. 400.
18 Adrian Poole associates Medea with Alcestis as well as with Phaedra in his discussion of
wronged women in *Tragedy: Shakespeare and the Greek Example* (Oxford, Blackwell,
1987). There is an extra irony in this juxtaposition when one recalls that in some
versions Alcestis was the one daughter of Pelias who refused to acquiesce in the dismembering of their father.

of *Peliades* is whether or not Medea actually could rejuvenate the ram she showed the daughters of Pelias; it may have been a trick. That is, although there is no question of her skill with drugs, the limits of that skill are never explicit. She herself dismembered her brother; Pelias was murdered by his daughters on her instigation – or persuasion. The legendary rejuvenation of Aeson, Jason's father, which was a use of drugs to a good end, is nowhere mentioned or referred to. I have called Medea's terrible revenge 'murder', because she is already a murderess. The social context of those murders was to change profoundly with the end of the ancient world, and was to invite new interpretative condemnations.

The underlying metaphors of the play turn on the sea-journey through the Symplegades, the voyage which is exile, Greek v. barbarian, and the tensions between force and persuasion (in which drugs play a mediating role, as we have seen in Pindar). Above all, characters are concerned with the health of the *oikos*, the house. What appears to be a domestic, private, scene is *also* evidence of Medea's isolation. She, who was a Colchian princess, and then the wife of Jason, is surrounded now only by aged slaves. *Medea* opens with her nurse blaming the pines of Pelion for the events which have brought them to this day, and the second character to appear is the tutor of Medea's and Jason's sons. A slave, loyal to her mistress, speaks to another slave about the injuries to their house (77); both are doubly marginalized by their status as slaves and foreigners (as the Corinthian messenger is also a slave who identifies with Creon's house). Both are honest (even if the old man is an eavesdropper), both – like Medea herself, heard from within – fear for the house. Both, of course, as traditionally with minor characters, simply disappear from the play, though we might wish to find in them reminders – at the 'low' level of society – reminders of parental, protecting relationships.[19] This emphasis is often overlooked; societal claims of the house upon its members are precisely what Medea will attack, as she formerly attacked her father's house in killing her brother (166–7). The chorus – of Corinthian women – recall the tight unfolding of events in a metaphor which stresses opposites: that rivers (like time or events) should flow backwards, that men are deceivers, that Medea sailed to find a home, but found exile where good faith no longer exists and Greek men break oaths.

The performances of great actors can illuminate texts beyond the reader's expectations: Diana Rigg's 1994 Medea, which evoked a vaguely

---

[19] As they were depicted in post-Euripidean art. See Vassiliki Gaggadis-Robin, *Jason et Médée sur les sarcophages d'époque impériale* (Rome, Ecole française de Rome, 1994), chapt. 17.

Balkan setting, mixed the high register of musical *vocalise* from its tiny chorus (one of whose members was an operatic singer) with a spoken register which was strikingly colloquial. In a moment of pure *anagnoresis*, Rigg's Medea *realised* 'I'm going to kill my children' and, from that moment, with powerful ambivalence, pursued the revenge which would remove her from ordinary experience. There was a fatalism about her act which was perceived as a choice already made, and nothing mad or emotionally extravagant about the doing of it. Euripides sees her both as an impersonal curse (at line 608 Medea describes herself as the curse called down upon Creon's house – and Jason's) and as a blessing to Aegeus, who will be a harbour for her – still, a refuge is not a home; she will go into one further exile. The Chorus will recall the Symplegades once more, as inside her house (the physical house) Medea is killing her children (and ending the kinship house). In the second part of their ode, they labour to recall the Greek woman, Ino, the only instance they can remember of a mother killing her children.[20] This reference has been taken to belong to the nexus of contrasts (and ironies) of Greek v. Barbarian, but that assumption is one more instance of the accusation it pretends to describe: only a barbarian would do such a thing. It belongs to the web of metaphors which includes wandering, curse, and necessity that pervade the play. More importantly, since it was Ino's attack on her step-children, Phrixus and Helle, which was the origin of the blight which is *Medea's* subject, Ino belongs in the play as surely as does the pine of Pelion (because Ino persuaded the local women to sow parched grain, which could not germinate). When the chorus name Ino, the woman who attacked her step-children, she who could be said to have initiated (far more than the pines of Pelion) the curse which has worked itself out through the play, they invoke the ancestral attack on children. That original tearing apart of the *domos*, that dismemberment of the house, is present in each generation.[21] To look

[20] When Charles Segal emphasizes the normality of Medea's language, he points to an important feature of Euripides' *generalized* representation of having children, but one may wonder if the world surrounding Medea is, indeed, 'normal', unless it is 'normal' for Jason to repudiate her. See his 'Tragedy, Corporeality, and Language', in *Interpreting Greek Tragedy: Myth, Poetry, Text* (Ithaca, Cornell University Press, 1986), pp. 245–8. John Kerrigan points out the way the play is suffused by the vocabulary of jealousy and emulation in a forthcoming work on revenge which I am most grateful to have been able to read in typescript.

[21] Although the events might be considered to occur 'after' those of this play, there is *sparagmos* in the destruction of Hippolytus at his father's wish. Theseus joins the ranks of Greeks who have destroyed their own children, a rare example of a father killing his male child. His foreign wife, Hippolytus's step-mother, Phaedra, who has instigated the disaster, is herself destroyed, in some versions by Hippolytus's sword.

forward for a moment, at other murders of children, we may contrast the figurative centrality of Astyanax, murdered by the triumphant Greeks to prevent his growing up to revenge the death of his father, Hector (the Greeks execute Astyanax by casting him down from Ilium's topless towers). The death of Astyanax is also the destruction of the Trojans. Euripides leaves the child's corpse intact, but Seneca's *sparagmos* (the body fragments on impact) is a graphic illustration of the dismemberment and scattering of the city itself. *Mutatis mutandis*, dynastic concerns will continue to be part of the fabric of these legends, as will the social context of Medea's barbarian status.[22]

The lengths to which critics have gone to explain Medea's escape (apparently from punishment, thus ending the play with the 'villain' triumphant) in her grandfather's dragon chariot suggest an almost wilful refusal to understand. The desire for poetic justice, and the refusal of power to women, have often hampered critics. Wilamowitz, for example, insisted that there was a reference to the goddess of death in the appearance of the dragon chariot, a myth of which, curiously, no traces survive. This insistence upon prior conceptions of character pervades criticism of the play. Reinhardt asserted that the traditional Medea was a criminal sorceress, an 'ondine' devoured by her own love and rage. In his interpretation, Euripides' sentimental heroine becomes absurd, yet worthy of our pity, and what we see in Euripides' creations is a confused breakdown in meaning.[23] This is to desire coherence and consistency at a low level; it is to assume an ingenue who somehow metamorphoses into a witch, and gets away with it. But Medea no more 'escapes' scot-free than Marlowe's

---

[22] Those flaws by which barbarians can be defined – and thus define, by contrast, what it is to be Greek – include cunning, disrespect for age (and authority), duplicity, female freedom, lust (especially incestuous lust), power-lust, treachery. But it must be remembered that Athenians accused Spartans of some of these flaws. It is part of Euripides' genius that he manages to accuse Greeks of these faults as well. The tissue of allusions which ties this play to Aeschylus's *Seven Against Thebes*, with its own destroyed children, is one studied by Richard Garner, *From Homer to Greek Tragedy: The Art of Allusion in Greek Poetry* (London, Routledge, 1990), pp. 90–7. What he describes as 'upheaval' might be more specifically, for this play and this character, be described as 'dismembering'. Despite its title, Lena Hatzichronoglou's 'Euripides' *Medea*: Woman or Fiend' is actually about her closeness to depictions of Dionysos, and therefore her status as *theos*; in *Woman's Power, Man's Game: Essays on Classical Antiquity in Honor of Joy K. King* (Waukonda, Illinois, Bolchazy-Carducci, 1993), pp. 178–93.

[23] Karl Reinhardt, *Eschyle. Euripide*, trans. Emmanuel Martineau (Paris, Editions de Minuit, 1972), p. 305. Charles Segal stresses the simplicity and, indeed, universality of Medea's pleasure in the smell of her children's bodies, to show the contrast between her outer success and complete inner destruction. *Interpreting Greek Tragedy: Myth, Poetry, Text* (Ithaca, Cornell University Press, 1986), p. 346f.

Mephostophilis escapes Hell. The play is explicit: Medea's revenge is as terrible to her as it could be, to her as well as (perhaps more than) to Jason – but success is contingent upon her own suffering. When the play opens her 'happiness' is already irrevocably ended. It is not as if something she could now do would redeem it. Her heroism, and her *aretê*, are triumph at a revenge from which her enemies will have no room to gloat over her defeat.[24] It is calculated and rational: the gender she is performing transcends the male.

Whatever the impact of the play in the theatre, produced as part of a religious festival for one *polis* at a particular historical moment, it was the text alone – without its music or choreography – which survived. On stage, in the ritual space in Athens, even re-produced in a similar public space elsewhere, the play was contained and defined by its existence as part of a larger cultural event. In a way, a play suspends itself for the duration of its playing, and although, as we have seen, Euripides evokes Medea's past for his own purposes, there is no sense *in* the play that its events are part of a longer historical argument; although what we see in the theatre is an immediate representation of possibility, a possible past which precedes its own recording. The theatrical moment is, it goes without saying, far removed from the experience of reading a text, when one can move backwards and forwards along the scroll, comparing, contrasting, considering the annotations of the scholiasts, whose learning informs the reader of the traditions Euripides exploited, thereby connecting his play to other texts and other events.[25] That is, the drama which once isolated becomes a text which connects. As we shall see, the topics *apparently* erected by Euripides set the problems of the legends for subsequent classical poets. And the 'easy' interpretation of a dual Medea, ingenue and witch, however much it is a misinterpretation, became part of its legacy. How this retrospective interpretation established itself is in part due to changes in language and society (Medea loses her semantic association with cunning intelligence and her proximity to divine figures), but is in the main the work of

---

24 The parodic use of language appropriate to other conventions underwrites this, from Medea's 'heroic' speeches to her sudden quotation of the 'bidding prayer' which precedes sacrifice when she is on the point of murdering her children (1053). She will achieve fame for her actions.

25 There is an important article by Margaret Williamson which shows how changes in Medea's linguistic registers, which have long appeared to imitate the language of Sophocles' heroes, also correspond to political movement from private (inside the house) to public (outside, Corinthian public life) spheres. This would, of course, have been lost almost immediately. See her 'A Woman's Place in Euripides' *Medea*', *Euripides, Women, and Sexuality*, ed. Anton Powell (London, Routledge, 1990), pp. 16–31.

subsequent interpreters, including, and perhaps above all, Ovid. We shall see their concerns with dynastic legitimacy, with wandering, foreigners, the power of rhetoric, the irrational love-hate frenzy, and the control of women.[26]

And, of course, their concerns with Euripides. If his play did nothing else, it created a frightening figure in its mature protagonist. If one compares *Medea* with the *Bacchae*, a legitimate question arises: whether or not Dionysos has human conceptions of justice on his side, what he does is the kind of revenge of which gods are capable. What happens when a woman has that same capacity? Clytemnestra's heroic revenge is vitiated by her adultery, which reduces her authority. We do not dismiss Dionysos as wicked or depraved. This is no question of simple disobedience, as Antigone may be said to disobey the edict against burying her brother. Nor is it the deliberate revenge of Ajax, which miscarries through the intervention of a god. It is like the rare revenge of Procne, who also sacrificed her son to punish her husband. She, too, will come to be associated with Medea, and the association will reinforce ideas of tragic – and pathetic – women beyond control. A reader of Ibsen familiar with the stage history of his *Doll's House* will inevitably be reminded of contemporary actresses' rejections of Nora's desertion of her children on the grounds that no woman would do such a thing.

Hellenistic Poetry

Medea's ambivalence was recognized in a sequence of poems about paintings which survive as a sequence in the Greek Anthology. The poets praise the artist's ability to represent Medea's ambivalence at the moment of decision, and stress the painting's representation of the complexity of her feelings. This doubleness has, in other contexts, been associated with the

---

[26] The question arises of the transmission of the classical heritage. One of the ways Euripides' matter was preserved, for the Greekless, was in the pages of Hyginus, *Fabulae*, ed. H. J. Rose (Leiden, A. W. Sijthoff, 1934), III, XII, XIII–XXV. Hyginus himself was available in the west after the Carolingian renaissance; see M. L. W. Laistner, *Thought and Letters in Western Europe* (2nd edn, London, Methuen, 1957), p. 235. As a name, or reputation, Euripides is associated with the outstanding authors of antiquity to whom the poets devote their love, in the *Purgatorio*, when Dante meets Statius (whom we will meet below). Euripides reappears in MSS of the early fifteenth century in Italy; see R. R. Bolgar, *The Classical Heritage and Its Beneficiaries* (Cambridge, Cambridge University Press, 1954). There exists a Virgilian cento on the subject of Medea by Hosidius Geta; ed. Giovanni Salanitro (Rome, Ateneo, 1981) and discussion by Desbordes, *Argonautica*.

victim of sacrifice, the willing scapegoat whose ritual death informs so much tragedy. Only here, where we see a female criminal triumphant, is there a reflection on the earlier heroic theme of, for example, Orestes' horror at his matricide.[27] The moment of decision could only *be* a moment. To write at length was to address other difficulties.

One way around the power of Euripides' Medea was to invent the early period of her life, when she was still a young woman full of hope, full of the desire to marry and beget children, as Greek women were expected to do. Similarly, despite the notoriety of Euripides' *Medea*, it remained possible to write from the point of view of a heroic Jason; one could concentrate on *his* early life and avoid – to a certain extent – the Euripidean interpretation. The challenge of scale finally brings us to a comprehensive narrative: the *Argonautica* of Apollonius Rhodius, written in third-century BC Alexandria.[28] His establishment of an erotic Medea is important in part because of subsequent interpretations of women called by other names than 'Medea'. Clytemnestra was not sexually bound to Agamemnon. Not only the Ariadne of Catullus, but Virgil's Dido is so much the direct descendent of her epic model that the commentators delighted in pointing out the Latin poets' allusions to the altogether allusive Greek. That is, in studying Apollonius's epic, we consider the establishment not only of a 'plot', but also an immensely significant *topos* for the portrayal of women: even – perhaps one should say 'especially' – Apollonius's incoherences legitimate inconsistencies in the characterisations of later women. The more the apparent existence of such women appear to be legitimated by great authors, the more influential their depictions upon beliefs about the capacities for evil of independent women. As we shall see, by one of

---

[27] I am grateful to Dr Simon Goldhill for calling these poems to my attention; see his essay in Goldhill and Robin Osborne, *Art and Text in Ancient Greek Culture* (Cambridge, Cambridge University Press, 1994), pp. 212–14. René Girard's famous emphasis on the dialectics of the sacrifice and the scapegoat do not, it seems to me, extend to the sacrificer. Medea the wife may legitimately voice the destiny of wives, but that destiny does not commonly involve murder. See his *La Violence et le Sacré* (Paris, Pluriel, 1972), esp. chapt. 10.

[28] Studies of Apollonius have blossomed in the last fifteen years. In addition to the recent books of Richard Hunter, I have found especially helpful Charles Rowan Beye, *Epic and Romance in the* Argonautica *of Apollonius* (Carbondale, Southern Illinois University Press, 1982) and the essay by Simon Goldhill, 'The paradigm of epic: Apollonius Rhodius and the example of the past', in *Poet's Voice*, pp. 284–333. Another study which emphasizes the texture of parallels and allusions is James J. Clauss, *The Best of the Argonauts: The Redefinition of the Epic Hero in Book 1 of Apollonius's* Argonautica (Berkeley, University of California Press, 1993). For Book III the annotations of M. M. Gillies, *The Argonautica of Apollonius Rhodius Book III* (Cambridge, 1928) are still useful.

those ironies of literary history, Virgil's Dido was later to be used as a model for subsequent Medeas.[29]

Homer referred to stories which were known, linking his epic inventions to an unspecific but ever-present sense of a shared past. Whatever 'being Greek' had meant, by the time of Apollonius Rhodius that shared past was rather imbued with a shared *literary* past in which many writers could participate. Alexandrian writers were proud of their ability to recapitulate, renew, and rationalize the literary texts they inherited. Divorced from the social context of two hundred years before, the politics of trade, migration, and rivalry among Greek city-states, even the sense of danger between islands, has practically disappeared. One cult is much like another. The threat posed by Persians and Medes is a faded memory, a trope of power. Dynastic anxieties are silenced.

One does not think of the Athenian theatre as 'learned' (although perhaps one should); one can hardly think otherwise of third-century BC Alexandria. When, in that urban, backward-looking literary culture, Apollonius Rhodius revived the epic genre with his *Argonautica*, he was imbued with the results of generations of commentary and discussion, collation and collection. Richard Hunter has described that literary culture as distinguished by 'a persistent and ironic rhetoric of doubt, self-effacement, deferral'.[30] Apollonius achieves authority almost by stealth, conveying his vision through juxtaposition and allusion as much as by authorial voice; indeed, his narrator exploits an almost naive experience of the events he

---

[29] Modern criticism of the poem begins with Charles Augustin Sainte-Beuve, who returned repeatedly to Apollonius's Medea, whom he found sexually exciting. In recognizing how far Dido was based upon her, he was unaware of the importance of Catullus's own intervening repetition for Ariadne in Carmen 64. Although he saw the *literary* disunities of the poem, he emphasized the truth of its depiction of Medea as a type. See, e.g., his 'Etudes sur l'Antiquité: de la Medée d'Apollonius', *Revue des Deux Mondes* 2 (1845), esp. pp. 874–6. Beye extended this sexualized characterization to Jason, arguing that Jason's *aretê* was precisely his attractiveness – something which Euripides' character attributed to the power of Aphrodite to avoid responsibility for seducing Medea. But this involved Beye in allegorizing the golden fleece into a symbol of Medea's virginity. See his 'Jason as Love-Hero in Apollonios' *Argonautika*', *Greek, Roman, and Byzantine Studies* 10 (1969), esp. 38, 43, 54 and *The Iliad, the Odyssey, and the Epic Tradition* (London, Macmillan, 1968).

[30] Richard Hunter, *The Argonautica of Apollonius: literary studies* (Cambridge, Cambridge University Press, 1993), p. 4. Although my own approach resists his amalgamation of 'the' legend, his annotated edition, Apollonius Rhodius, *Argonautica Book III* (Cambridge, Cambridge University Press, 1989) is indispensable. All quotations are from his translation, *Jason and the Golden Fleece (The Argonautica)* (Oxford, Clarendon, 1993). It is, as Dr Hunter points out, easier for us now to read a literature of intertextuality than it has, perhaps, been in many years. See also A. R. Dyck, 'On the Way from Colchis to Corinth: Medea in Book 4 of the "Argonautica" ', *Hermes* 117 (1989), pp. 455–70.

finds himself recounting, as if his text surprised him. Whether his narrator is naive or faux-naive, his *narration* has the minimal strength of a sequence of connected episodes.

Apollonius is our first author to exhibit an ambition to flourish his own learning at his equally knowledgeable readership. The journey-motif allowed him to do so: the thread is the Argo and the heroes who sailed in her. The itinerary of the Argo provides the opportunity for him to tell the stories of her sailors whose hero-cults dotted the ancient landscape. The implications for such matters as characterization are important. Like the knights whose adventures detracted from King Arthur's precedence in the Arthurian cycles, the insistence upon the Argonauts distracts from their leader. Apollonius's rationalizing impulse elides all variety. The attempt to make the poem a comprehensive mythological source-book gives the adventures a certain breathlessness, and little sense of motive emerges, even contingently, from action. Jason's companions are there to do what they are there to do; there is not even much by way of theme: although Argos (the boat-builder) hints in the course of Book III that Pelias feared Jason, the potential themes of dynastic power or personal revenge slip away. Instead of strength or even cunning intelligence, Jason has good looks: his chief characteristic appears to be his irresistable attractiveness, which is far from *aretê*.

It is traditional to castigate Apollonius's epic achievements, as if his Jason could not be the hero who dares all, leaping forward to face certain death, if he depends upon the magical unguents (and cunning intelligence) of a young woman. There is even commentary from another character, Idas, upon Jason's dependence. The problem is partly that Jason does not have enough to do, partly that he has so few choices to make. Apollonius's invention breached epic decorum with its concentration on the erotic, but that, in the end, was the source of his success. His young Medea is indeed in the grip of an irrational passion: her love for Jason drives her to betray her father. The serious choice is Medea's: loyalty to Jason must mean disloyalty to her father, and *this* moment of decision is one much rehearsed. The great moral changes which came at the end of Antiquity made revenge an ethically parlous option; but the rhetorical debate lived on. If the god insists upon a choice which must be a betrayal of one man or the other, the human dilemma is insoluble. That aid robs Jason of the credit for his courage in fulfilling the impossible tasks of defeating the dragon, the fire-breathing bulls, and the armed men who spring from the ground in which he sows the dragon's teeth. Yet we may wonder if Jason would be so vulnerable to criticism if the aid came from another man. It is as if the whole enterprise were contaminated by a woman's presence, which includes the trickery, the cunning, by which she traps her brother so that Jason can kill him.

Apollonius's Medea is a young woman overcome by love. Because Virgil's Dido was in part inspired by her, their creations combined to become one of the great epic *topoi* for the depiction of women, a *topos* we will follow throughout the rest of this book. There had, of course, been important women in epic before Apollonius – no Helen, after all, no Trojan war. Nor did epic exist in a vacuum: heroic women were a feature of Greek drama – no Clytemnestra, no *Oresteia*. We may think of Medea as an object of exchange, but poets argued over her complicity. The first really powerful women are Circe, whom Homer presents as the demi-goddess she is, and Calypso, whose desire for Odysseus keeps him imprisoned on her island, while he longs for his ageing human wife at home. Even she, however, plays by conventional rules, and allows her lover to leave her and resume his adventures. The dilemmas are Odysseus's; the women are snares.

Even Helen, we may recall, is made the tool of destruction by gods intent upon punishing Troy (not Helen herself or her husband, Menelaus). Even Herodotus sees her as only the most important in a series of abductions. The gods' indifference to us, that tenet so central to so much Greek thought, becomes first a question, then a very different attitude under Christianity. Putting Medea in the centre of a traditionally misogynistic genre disrupts generic expectations.

This Medea is a young woman acting under compulsion: Eros makes her fall in love, protect her father's enemy, and finally betray her own house. This vitiates her sense of having a real choice. She performs her tasks not with the masculine (and potentially transgressive) courage of an Amazon, but with the misgivings and self-loathing of a guilty woman who has left her proper sphere. If she appears to be more powerful than Jason because of the magic which all the Argonauts fear, she is simultaneously weaker than he is because of her love for him: she flees expecting to marry him in his father's house and there become a respectable Greek bride. It is rather like comparing Dryden's Cleopatra or Cressida to Shakespeare's. She is titillating, but the overall effect is of contradiction. If Apollonius hints, in flash-forwards, that there can be no happiness for such a woman, he distracts from the character he has carefully designed.[31] There is a question of responsibility, and mutual responsibility, emerging which will be relevant to subsequent stereotypes of 'woman', but in Apollonius it is

---

[31] There is no question that his character is incoherent; even appeals to post-modernism *avant la lettre* cannot make this problem disappear, or turn a flaw into an achievement.

still inexplicit. It arises at first with the onset of love, and the place of that love in a wider scheme. If, for example, Aphrodite impels Helen, or Phaedra, to love because she is intent upon helping Paris or harming Hippolytus, how responsible are her victims, male or female? If women are in tutelage, is 'responsible for their actions' a question which can apply to them at all? In Greek societies, responsibility and power are allied to questions about the exceptional status of the women concerned. When that is removed, the contextual explanation gives way before newer, personal, moral assessments of blame and guilt which we will now begin to see developing. In a different culture, although some questions, as Richard Rorty puts it, simply go away, others arise and demand explanation, such as the duty to harm one's enemies, or the recontextualization of Medea as an *eastern* princess, which came to be of importance in Rome.[32]

Roman Epyllion and Epic

Given that the rediscovery of Apollonius's text came late, what matters here is his preservation and transmission of 'the' matter of Argo, his consolidation of a 'complete' narrative, and his contribution to the characterization of the woman in the grip of an overwhelming passion, the love/hate frenzy which suggests that a woman in the grip of strong emotion is a dehumanized and unbalanced threat to order.[33] An essentialist idea of woman-the-irrational becomes a cliché of disruption. The chain includes Ino who, at least in some versions, killed her children before throwing herself off a cliff; Procne, who dismembered her son and served him up to her husband in a pie; Medea. At one remove we might include Agave; at another Ariadne. Catullus's Carmen 64, now usually called 'The Marriage of Peleus and Thetis', contains a long *ekphrasis* which describes a scene embroidered on the coverlet of their bed: Ariadne on the beach at Diâ. One may think it a curious portent for a marriage, since Ariadne is

---

[32] From the Republic, and to be found as early as the works of Pacuvius, according to André Arcellaschi, *Médée dans le Théâtre Latin* (Rome, Ecole Française de Rome, 1990), chapt. 3.

[33] There was a Latin translation of the *Argonautica* by Varro Atacinus, and Ennius had translated two of Euripides' plays about Medea. Cicero knew plays about her by Accius and Pacuvius. But none of these works are extant. For details see H. D. Jocelyn, *The Tragedies of Ennius* (Cambridge, Cambridge University Press, 1967), pp. 52, 342–6; N. E. Lemaire, *Poetae Latini Minores IV* (Paris, Bibliotheca classica latina, 1825); *M. Pacuvii Fragmenta*, ed. G. D'Anna (Rome, 1967) and *Marco Pacuvio*, ed. Pietro Magno (Milan, Pegaso, 1977), pp. 96–98.

depicted in the moment of discovering that Theseus has abandoned her. Catullus imagines her aria of impotent frustration: she accuses Theseus of perjury, reminds him that for his sake (and his promise of marriage) she abandoned her kin, stresses her utter dependence upon him, and finally calls the Furies of vengeance down upon him. Catullus is adapting the angry Apollonian Medea of Book IV, but readying her for the arrival of Dionysus. Contingently, the description of the enraged and irrational woman as 'effigeis bacchantis' (64.61, like the statue of a bacchante), reminds us of the disruptions sponsored by the god.[34]

For Virgil, the examples of Circe and Calypso, Medea and Ariadne aided him in his own epic innovations, and Dido follows Homer's narrative precedent of the woman as temptation and delay as well as Apollonius's character precedent for the destructive force of passion. The complex over-determination for both Aeneas (complicit, active, responsible, and suffering from the necessities by which he admits himself bound) and Dido (ruler of Carthage) make Virgil's intertextuality also and always intensely original. Each character sees the action from his or her own point of view and with great ambivalence. Ariadne was saved on the beach at Diâ by the appearance of Dionysos; in Virgil's more morally-coercive world there is no redemption for his forsaken queen; she may have political power, but she has lost self-esteem and reputation, and suffers the consequences of actions which are no less hers, than Aeneas's, or Venus'. Those consequences, given her symbolic status, bear upon the enmity between Rome and Carthage, like Herodotus's references to East-West enmity. As a woman she can be pathetic, as a queen, important, but as a figure for future strife with Carthage, she combines character and history in a model which would have been familiar to Herodotus, who would not say that this or that story was true. Her public humiliation at Aeneas's desertion replaces the Herodotean narrative of abduction and counter-abduction. The status of Aeneas's word becomes in part a question of public duty (*pietas*) identified with male role, and male self-control. Yet we must not forget his own self-doubts, to the point of collapse, especially in Book V. It is only the authority of his father which sets him back on course. For Virgil, Dido's prior oath (to her dead husband, Sicheus, not to remarry) is a precedent which overdetermines Dido's doom. She who is overcome by desire knows

---

[34] See David Konstan, 'Neoteric Epic: Catullus 64', in *Roman Epic*, ed. A. J. Boyle (London, Routledge, 1993), pp. 59–78. Florence Verducci writes illuminatingly on Catullus's Ariadne in the context of Ovid's in her *Ovid's Toyshop of the Heart: Epistulae Heroidum* (Princeton, Princeton University Press, 1985), chapt. 6, but does not pursue the connections I am elucidating here.

no moderation, and a widow is the more susceptible because she knows what she has lost. There is another interesting question here, raised by Dido's *recognition* of the old flame. Her knowledge of passion removes the excuse or defence for the innocent ingenue's confused behaviour under an unknown stimulus.

Revenge is out of the question (though a post-death snub in the underworld is not). But 'revenge' takes us back to the explanatory urbanity of Herodotus, since part of Virgil's purpose in the *Aeneid* is to reflect upon contemporary Rome and its antecedent history.[35] Although Apollonius was intensely interested in the origins of cults, none of them were connected to contemporary Alexandria, which, founded as it was by Alexander, had its own recent history. Once again we see the introduction of an explanation of political enmity (the rivalry between Rome and Carthage) projected onto a female historical figure. Epics write their politics onto foundation stories, and Virgil's conforms to that expectation, while using his learning to innovate.

The closeness of Dido to Apollonius's Medea is remarkable, but remarkably effortless, as well as everywhere an improvement.[36] To make Dido fall in love Virgil adapts Apollonius's divine machinery, but, since the fate of Rome is in question, the intervention of Venus affords far greater dignity than what is, in effect, the mere theft of the golden fleece. Aeneas's striking good looks, which originate with Odysseus, are also familiar from Apollonius and Catullus. This time it is the human hero who is close to the gods: Aeneas may be human, but Venus is his mother. Medea sat at her father's banquet and stared; Dido is overcome at her own feast, in the course of which she persuades Aeneas to recall the Fall of Troy. Already, by allowing her maternal feelings to overcome her role as queen, and taking the apparent child she believes to be Aeneas's son into her arms, she proleptically embraces Aeneas himself. Virgil wants proximity, and Cupid,

---

35 Virgil's literary desire to fulfill or complete Homer's epic is explored in a series of books by Gian Biagio Conte, most recently *Genres and Readers: Lucretius, Love elegy, Pliny's Encyclopedia*, trans. Glenn W. Most (Baltimore, Johns Hopkins University Press, 1994). See esp. chapt. five.

36 The study of such imitations has emphasized the necessary innovations in imitation. The use of, to take an outstanding example, Lucrece as a model for later heroines, up to and including Richardson's Clarissa, serves to remind us how firmly ensconced views about women and their behaviour can become. For this series of re-interpretations of a classical story, see Ian Donaldson, *The Rapes of Lucretia: a Myth and its Transformations* (Oxford, Clarendon Press, 1982) and, on Dido, *Enée et Didon: Naissance, fonctionnement et survie d'un mythe*, ed. René Martin (Paris, CNRS, 1990) and Marilynn Desmond, *Reading Dido: Gender, Textuality and the Medieval 'Aeneid'* (St Paul, University of Minnesota Press, 1995).

disguised as the young Ascanius, can practically handle Dido's breasts as he penetrates her with his love-inducing dart. The physicality of this encounter (after all, his preferred weapon, the bow, is normally shot from a distance) eroticizes Dido from the start (and that the child stabs the woman reverses Medea's actions). Like Apollonius's Medea, Dido consummates her 'marriage' in a cave, but unlike her, of course, there are insoluble questions over the status of marriage or nuptial oaths, as, indeed, Aeneas tactlessly reminds her. The acceleration of her love for him creates a kind of 'double time' feeling, which Virgil evokes by opening Book IV with the queen's complaint. That is, her love-sickness appears after a narrative space, designated by the opening word, a gap in which she has had time to suffer. Medea's interior monologue has been replaced by the dialogue with Anna, but the complaint is the same:

> At regina gravi iamdudum saucia cura
> vulnus alit venis et caeco carpitur igni.
> multa viri virtus animo multusque recursat
> gentis honos: haerent infixi pectore vultus
> verbaque, nec placidam membris dat cura quietam.

> [But now for some time the queen had been growing more
> grievously love-sick,
> Feeding the wound with her life-blood, the fire biting
> within her.
> Much did she muse on the hero's nobility, and much
> On his family's fame. His look, his words had gone to her
> heart
> And lodged there: she could get no peace from love's
> disquiet.][37]

Like Medea, Dido is haunted by dreams, she desires to be swallowed by the earth or struck by lightning (as, in effect, she will be, penetrated by the hero's sword, burnt, and buried), her tears pour freely, love's wounds are renewed when she attempts to sleep on a familiar couch. Virgil links the desire to disappear with a sense of something much larger than human experience: a voracious swallowing and absorption by nature itself.[38] In

---

[37] P. Vergili Maronis Opera, ed. F. A. Hirtzel (Oxford, Clarendon, 1900), IV.1–5. The monumental edition of Book IV, *Publi Vergili Maronis Aeneidos Liber Quartus*, ed. A. S. Pease (Cambridge, Mass., 1935; repr. Darmstadt, Wissenschaftliche Buchgesellschaft, 1967) contains detailed evidence of Virgil's borrowings. The translation is from C. Day Lewis, *The Eclogues, Georgics, and Aeneid of Virgil* (London, 1952).

[38] The identification of the feminine with wild and untamed nature is distanced here, as the civilized woman distinguishes herself from that untrammelled force. Seneca's

addition, the internal burning anticipates what is to come. When Dido loses her self-control and strides through the streets of Carthage she is like a Bacchante, beyond the norm of female behaviour, even mad – no doubt, if she is careless of appearing in public. These assimilations of uncontrolled woman to violence in nature are an obvious stricture in a society in which self-control is a masculine and civilized virtue, as has often been pointed out.

By contrast to the innocent ingénue, of course, the mature married woman is expected to exhibit strict control, although she cannot suffer the maiden's version of shame; her *pudor* is still potent, and the internal monologue in which love and modesty quarrel is here set as a *topos* for generations to come. This appears to create a telling character for whom readers may – famously and notoriously, as St Augustine witnesses – feel sympathy (even if, geographically, one may wonder which team he ought to be supporting). But among the potentials of this juxtaposition is an emphasis on figurative representation in which the values (speaking personified as Amor or Pudor) themselves take over from the agents who experience them: that is, personification, although meant as metonymy (reifying a part of the inner life), becomes a symbol larger than the individual whose experience we watch. There is a kind of rhetorical reversal: unlike inanimate objects which speak of human suffering in *prosopopeia,* future female characters disappear into arguments over morality and courses of action. They are subsumed into the conflict between Love and Shame which becomes typical of Woman. Ethical dilemma is on the way to allegory.

One of Virgil's improvements upon Apollonius is to use dialogue, which, since one character is understanding, or misunderstanding, another, builds interpretation into the fiction. Only Euripides' Medea could vanquish Medea, but Virgil's queen is susceptible to advice and reason, seeing, famously, the right choice, but taking the wrong one. Nonetheless, even in Dido's 'ranting' speech, the poetry alludes to Virgil's models by reference to the details of her circumstances: she is surrounded by enemies and has no supporting kin, her brother is hostile, she accuses Aeneas of perjury and calls the Furies of vengeance down upon him. When she compares herself to Medea one is reminded of Virgil's daring, as well as of his place in a learned tradition, although the allusion is subtle enough not to be distracting. The image is Euripidean *sparagmos:* Dido imagines a kind of pre-emptive revenge in which she seized Aeneas's body,

---

Phaedra suffers similarly, and the metaphoric structure underwrites her position through its references to hunting, also in part derived from Virgil.

dismembered it, and scattered the pieces on the sea – as Medea did to her brother, Apsyrtus:

> non potui abreptum divellere corpus et undis
> spargere?
>
> [Why could I not have seized him, torn up his body and
> littered
> The sea with it?][39]

The idea of dismembering reappears even when scarcely appropriate, except that, of course, at a deeper level it is not only a violence beyond the norms permitted to women, it is the revenge of erasure, a denial of unity. The most famous 'Medea' is Dido.

Or, perhaps, Didos. For traditions varied about the date and even the existence of Dido. Some of the books Virgil used place her a generation or more away from Aeneas, some of them reported her suicide as a ploy to avoid an unwanted remarriage, a cunning trick of promising to marry in order to protect her city, then killing herself before the marriage could take place. The commented texts of Virgil which were popular throughout the Middle Ages preserved the scholarship which marked Virgil's reinterpretations, and were used in the later middle ages by writers such as Boccaccio for whom the authority of ancient witnesses was a prime concern. Servius explained at the beginning of Book IV,

> Apollonius wrote the *Argonautica* and in the third book introduced Medea in love: from that all this book is translated.[40]

At greater length, Macrobius commented

> Virgil's wine has not come from the grapes of a single vine, but wherever he has found material worthy of imitation he has turned it to good use for his own ends. Thus he has modelled his fourth [recte third] book of the *Aeneid* almost entirely on the fourth book of the *Argonautica* of Apollonius by taking the story of Medea's passionate love for Jason and applying it to the loves of Dido and Aeneas.[41]

---

[39] *Aeneid* IV.600–1; Day Lewis, p. 89. The *sparagmos/spargere* chime disappears in English.

[40] 'Apollonius Argonautica scripsit et in tertio inducit amantem Medeam: inde totus hic liber translatus est', *Servii Grammatici*, ed. G. Thilo (Leipzig, Teubner, 3 vols, 1881–1902), III.459. My translation. Medieval readers did not know the precedents of Naevius or Ennius, any more than they knew Valerius Flaccus.

[41] 'Non de unius racemis vindemiam sibi fecit, sed bene in rem suam vertit quidquid ubicumque invenit imitandum; adeo ut de *Argonauticorum* quarto quorum scriptor est Apollonius, librum *Aeneidos* suae quartum totum paene formaverit, ad Didonem vel

This line of imitation and emulation continues into the first century. Ovid returned repeatedly to Medea, and it was Ovid who consolidated some of the associations which link a series of dangerous women, Ovid who created a literary register which combined allusion, imitation, and serious parody. Because his work was so central to medieval readers and writers, Ovid will be the major force in Chapter Three. Here let us move to his younger contemporary, Lucius Annaeus Seneca.

Roman Tragedy

One outstanding and influential Medea play survives from Latin literature, that of Seneca, but it is important to remember one that was lost, for Ovid had also chosen Medea as his subject for a drama.[42] Criticism of this play has moved from concentration upon Seneca's rhetorical displays to Stoic ideas of morality and the self. Seneca indeed concentrates on the opportunities provided for set pieces of rhetorical display, charge and counter-charge, accusation and defence, but he is a poet, and we ignore his imagery at our peril. Seneca's *Medea* is, of course, based upon Euripides' *Medea* (but differs significantly); it is also full of reminiscences of other authors, which Seneca's first audience would have recognized.[43] Like Seneca's

---

Aenean amatoriam incontinentiam Medeae circa Iasonem transferendo', *I Saturnali di Macrobio Teodosio*, ed. Nino Marinone (Turin, Unione Tipografico-Editrice, 1967), at V.17.4 (pp. 610–11); trans. P. Vaughan Davies, Macrobius, *Saturnalia* (New York and London, Columbia University Press, 1969), p. 359. Further detailed annotation in Pease, e.g. p. 13 nn. 93–4.

[42] Only two lines survive: 'servare potui: perdere an possim rogas?' (I was able to save; do you ask if I can destroy?) and a line quoted by Seneca the Elder: 'feror huc illuc ut plena deo' (I am carried here and there, as if filled with [?possessed by] the god). The closeness of the power that saves to the power which destroys emphasizes the importance of the person who controls it. See Seneca, *Medea*, ed. C. D. N. Costa (Oxford, Clarendon Press, 1973), note at line 123. I shall return to this below, chapter three.

[43] Many scholars, especially, in recent years, those who are translating the play, have emphasized those aspects of Seneca's play which make it unfair to make a simple contrast to Euripides. See Seneca, *Medea*, trans. Frederick Ahl (Ithaca, Cornell University Press, 1986), intro.; Seneca, *The Tragedies*, trans. David R. Slavitt (Baltimore, Johns Hopkins, 1992), *Medea*, pp. 131–70; see introduction. Both translations are emphatically twentieth-century interpretations, meant to be actable, and therefore not as close as the Loeb edition by F. J. Miller (Cambridge, Mass, 1917). None come to terms with Seneca's word-play, which, as much as Ovid's, offends twentieth-century taste. In what follows I have benefited from Costa's full annotation and from the Budé edition of Léon Hermann (Paris, Les Belles Lettres, 1924), I.132–74; A. J. Boyle, 'In Nature's Bonds: a Study of Seneca's "Phaedra" ', in *Aufstieg und Niedergang des römischen Welt* (1985), pp. 1284–1347; Helen Fyfe, 'An Analysis of Seneca's *Medea*', *Ramus* 12 (1983),

Thyestes and *Phaedra, Medea* is haunted by the past and its determining effects upon the present; one of his methods of creating that sense of the burden of the past is by tying the imagery of his play to the epic and dramatic *literary* inheritance. The sense of the play as expressing a larger linguistic tissue grows from our recognition of its relation to those earlier texts. Traditionally, interpretations of Seneca have revolved around character as the expression of ethical types, how far Seneca's stoicism informs them, and whether or not his conception is vitiated by his rhetoric, from the plays on words (especially case-changes) to which Silver Latin poets were prone to his declamatory school pomps and circumstances. Nothing tends to misinterpretation more than the assurance that Seneca's opinions are known, that we have nothing to learn by attending to the poetry beyond Seneca's confused inferiority to his predecessors.

Critics have defended Jason, Creon, and Medea in turn, drawing their arguments from Seneca's presumed attitude to Euripides and, sometimes, to Horace and to Ovid.[44] If we look at the imagery rather than beginning with character, some of Seneca's intentions may become clearer. In the Introduction I referred to Françoise Desbordes' study of the *Argonautica* as a sequence of binary polarites which approach the heart of human

---

pp. 73–93; John Henderson, 'Poetic Technique and Rhetorical Amplification: Seneca *Medea* 579–669', *Ramus* 12 (1983), pp. 94–113. Peter J. Davis, *Shifting Song: the Chorus in Seneca's Tragedies* (Hildesheim and New York, Olms-Weidmann, 1993) offers the most thorough analysis of Seneca's choral poetry yet available. This last book came to my notice when my own section was already formulated.

[44] But most of the arguments use the allusions to elucidate character, in what now may seem an outmoded way. The verbal reminiscences are listed by C. D. N. Costa in his editon and in his 'The Tragedies' in *Seneca*, ed. C. D. N. Costa (London, Routledge, 1974), p. 107. So we find Gilbert Lawall, already a defender of Apollonius's Jason, attempting an apology for the male characters, in 'Seneca's *Medea*: the elusive triumph of civilization', in *Arktouros: Hellenic Studies in Honour of Bernard Knox on the Occasion of his 65th Birthday*, ed. G. W. Bowersock, W. Burkert, and M. C. J. Putnam (Berlin and New York, Walter De Gruyter, 1979), pp. 419–26. Norman T. Pratt argues that the plays are meant to form a philosophical impression, *Seneca's Drama* (Chapel Hill, University of North Carolina Press, 1983), ch. 4, where Medea is a figure of *ira*. R. M. Krill explores the 'Allusions in Seneca's *Medea*' to explicate the gods' role for the characters, in *The Classical Journal* 68 (1972–3), pp. 199–204. C. Rambeaux stresses the fear Medea inspires in the men around her as an explanation for Jason's desire to escape her; he then follows this theme through the centuries, in 'Le Mythe de Médée d'Euripide à Anouilh ou l'originalité psychologique de la *Medée* de Seneque', *Latomus* 31 (1972) 1010–36. Recent interpretations of a more psychoanalytic bent have insisted upon male power and the phallus, and seen Medea's concern with sceptres and the recapture of her virginity as a confrontation with phallogocentrism. Charles Segal interprets the names in the play, and the play of alliteration, to stress the association of Medea with monstrosity as well as motherhood in '*Nomen Sacrum*: Medea and other Names in Senecan Tragedy' *Maia* 34 (1982), pp. 241–46.

structures of order. In Seneca's dangerous city, these epic themes offer themselves as a way of treating central concerns of order and disorder. They are present throughout Seneca's play. It witnesses to his usual themes of the dissolution of the human body and the body politic, of social norms and moral behaviour, while it comments (obliquely) on the politics of tyranny.[45] Poetry is a way of negotiating contradictory and complex ambivalences; Seneca invokes more than he chooses.

Sometimes that imagery can seem too slight to be anything more than a trivial reminiscence, but the changes rung on epic similes are at the heart of Roman literary creativity and response. The comparison of Medea to a lioness comes twice in Euripides (187, 1342), and the stock epic comparison between an enraged woman and a fierce animal defending her young was used by Virgil, among others. The idea is that the wild beast is prepared to die to *protect* her young, or paces in fury searching for them when they are already dead. It was Ovid who reversed the image for his Procne, whom he compared to a tiger of the Ganges. Seneca's Chorus invoke the image in the moments before the Nuntius enters to announce the destruction of Creusa and her father, and juxtapose it to one of the plays' *leitmotifs*, the polarity of joining/severing. Within the imagery of the play, the Chorus allude to the yoked tigers who draw the chariot of Bacchus.

> huc fert pedes et illuc,
> ut tigris orba natis
> cursu furente lustrat
> Gangeticum nemus.
> frenare nescit iras
> Medea, non amores;
> nunc ira amorque causam
> iunxere: quid sequetur? (862–9)

> [She paces here and there like a Gangetic tigress, from whom her offspring have been taken, furiously courses the forest. She does not know how to rein in her hatred or her love; now the case of love and hate are joined: what follows?][46]

---

45 On this subject see, for example, Charles Segal on the importance of individualism in the face of Roman political dangers, and therefore emphasis on integrity of the self/ violation of the body as an allegory of that political danger. 'I suggest that the tragic dimension lies in the conflict between good and evil in the individual soul. In this conflict evil sometimes wins, and the hero is engulfed in his or her own inner monstrosity', 'Boundary Violation and the Landscape of the Self in Senecan Tragedy' in his *Interpreting Greek Tragedy: Myth, Poetry, Text* (Ithaca, Cornell University Press, 1986), p. 319 n. 8.

46 The word-play and in the intensity of the love/hate juxtaposition disappear in a

The dramatic ironies here, for an audience which hears the epic reference, are multiple; what appears to be a comparison about nonhuman irrationality becomes much more specific. Medea has just destroyed someone else's child, and searches for her own children to destroy them next. An English equivalent might be achieved through a tasteless pun which recapitulates a familiar Shakespearean allusion: Medea is intent on dis-jointing. She will combine the physicality of the love-hate frenzy with the idea of a world out of joint. This is, as it happens, the play's second tiger. The world created by the imagery is multiple and polyvalent. To understand the full force of Seneca's poetry the reader (not the theatrical spectator) needs to be alerted to such repetitions and reminiscences. The web of words links ideas of joining/separating, marriage/repudiation, kinship/love, oaths/betrayal, homecoming/exile, fire/water, day/night, boundaries/disorder.

The metaphors also function historically, by evoking an age already past, and, like Euripides' Chorus thinking of Ino, they tie Medea to Procne and to Althaea (both of whom took revenge by murdering their sons) through association. Woman becomes an untameable beast intent upon destruction, a man-eating tigress or lioness (perhaps also exaggeratedly exotic, through the distancing Indian reference); the direction of the danger is less clear.[47] But this is the second time the tiger has appeared, as many of Seneca's images recur in different contexts. The first one comes in the choral epithalamium which has been celebrated as an innocent rhetorical demonstration of a kind of poem not elsewhere found in Seneca. It is nothing of the sort; in context, most of its references are ironic. Images of the marriage gods abound, gods just (and justly) invoked by Medea, who calls upon them to punish the unlawful repudiation of their earlier bond. The young Jason, it will be remembered, had been a protegé of Juno, goddess of the marriage bond. The pine nuptial torches which accompany the procession are related not only to the pines of Pelion which built the Argo, but to the images of fire which suffuse the play. The day of the

---

syntactic language such as English. Slavitt compresses the lines and loses Seneca's reinterpretation: 'She ought to control her emotions,/ but she paces, mutters and mumbles,/ as if she were crazy, as if she/ weren't a human, but rather/ a tigress whose cubs have been taken (p. 163). Ahl has 'So, when her children perish,/ a tigress roams through Ganges'/ jungle: mad, obsessed with/ ritual, futile searching.// Medea does not know how to/ rein in love or anger' (p. 89).

47 This association was imitated by later writers who borrowed Seneca's Medea back for their own Procnes. Costa sees traces imitated in Gregorio Corraro's *Progne* (c.1429, printed 1558) and Fulke Greville's *Alaham* (c.1600) (p. 9).

marriage which begins with Phoebus and ends with Hesperus will, by the time the play has finished, seem a boundary transgressed by horror.

The idea of the age which has passed is related to the day of the tragedy, referred to throughout in images of Phoebus (more obviously important as Medea's ancestor) and Hesperus. The multivalency of the images is striking. Let us follow another apparently trivial example, the helmsman of the Argo, Tiphys, evoked by Medea in her opening speech, then in the second choral ode, and then again in their third ode. Tiphys rather than Jason is a metonym for the voyage, a focus of blame for the Argo's fault in broaching the high seas, offending the gods by bringing together what had hitherto been kept apart, the cities of men (335–9). If the Argo destroyed boundaries then, so Medea's fire in the palace will allow Neptune's seas on the two sides of Corinth to join as one. In the third choral ode Neptune's punishment of the individual Argonauts becomes a list of their fates which also links Tiphys (still a metonym for Jason) and Phaeton (who fell to ruin when attempting to drive the chariot of his father, the Sun). The series of deaths includes Argonauts Orpheus, dismembered by women, and Meleager, whose mother, Althaea, burned the brand on which his life depended in revenge after he killed her brothers (644). This image, too, is immediately repeated in Medea's incantation as a masterly compression of the deed which is, from different points of view, pure and defiled:

> Piae sororis, impiae matris, facem
> ultricis Althaeae vides. (779–80)

> You see the brand of Althaea's vengeance, pious sister,
>   impious mother.

This incantation, a word-painting of exceptional skill, itself recapitulates Ovid's ultimate achievement for (even definition of) a sorceress: she can make nature run backwards, including making time reverse itself. This is why Medea thinks of herself as she was before she knew Jason, why her own virginity becomes a trope of innocence lost when the Argo set off. Virginity is also intimately a trope for marriage.

At the heart of the play's poetry, in a sequence of references to the sea, and identifications with the sea, Seneca reveals his concern with order, disorder, and the web of events.[48] In the Ode from lines 300ff the Chorus

---

[48] 'In "Medea" the Argonautic expedition, to which the long central odes of the chorus are dedicated (301–79, 579–669) and which pervades Medea's thoughts . . . sits like an incubus on the play, encapsulating a series of events which proves both model for and cause of the events of the play itself. The unloosing of nature's bonds and breach of her covenants . . . by the crew of the Argo, the fear generated . . . and the death and

stresses the sea's uncertainty, the voyage as an allegory of a life, the idea of Woman as analogy with the sea's unpredictable power and disorder. Yet, elsewhere, the play reminds us that the sea is Neptune's, that the Argonautic voyage offended him by traversing (and, concomitantly, transgressing) his domain, for which he exacted punishment upon each of the heroes in turn. From this point of view, Medea is as much his instrument as Phaedra is Venus's. But Medea herself sees the sea as hostile, and as hostile to her as to anyone else; she fears Neptune's anger at Jason's offence. By moving through these analogies, Seneca can have things both ways: other characters can see Woman as disorder, while the woman concerned can see the sea as the god's. Seneca can associate the sinuousness of the sea with flames and serpents, using poetry to create the metaphoric world of the play without having to argue for the associations. One question the play asks is when disorder *is* order. The relevance of such a question to Seneca's own experience of Claudian and Neronian Rome is one which emphasizes the play's politics.

If we move to land, and to the male political structures which are invoked, Creon, the human king, becomes a source of both order and its excess. Medea can argue that she has served the male city, because she preserved its heroes; in her speech to Creon she boasts only of her aid to the Argonauts (lines 230ff). Here Medea tries to persuade us that Creon's power allusively invokes the stock *tyrannos*, making *him* an agent of disorder who is willing to dissolve a legal marriage and remove protection and reward from the Argonauts' benefactress.

It is Medea whose first words, 'Di coniugales' opens the play; Medea whose closeness to those gods is a perverted piety. It is worth recalling that Jason, who has the last word, also ends with the gods, 'deos', but to deny them. That denial is the impiety which refuses to believe that a punishment is merited, even that there is sense or a pattern in the events just experienced. Medea never blasphemes. Part of the problem in thinking about the characters of Seneca's drama is to believe that one must elevate one and denigrate another, as if tragedy were not fundamentally a demonstration that this is not so. One way in which Seneca *is* like Euripides is in

destruction which ensued . . . as penalty for the breach, are mirrored in Jason's breach of marital fides . . . in exhibited Cornithian fear . . . and in the chaos and destruction of the finale, where Medea's past actions on behalf of Jason and his comrades . . . are reenacted in her dissolution of all familial ties, the murder of her children, and her climactic serpentine flight', A. J. Boyle, 'A Study of Seneca's "Phaedra" ', pp. 1313–14 and n. 63. See also C. D. N. Costa, ed., *Medea* (Oxford, 1973). My analysis differs from Davis's, *Shifting Song*, because I see different connections between the images in the odes, pp. 78–93, 195–9.

his willingness to show men at fault and failing to understand the women with whom they are in conflict.

All analyses of the play must ask the question, as Medea and her nurse both do, What is it to be Medea? This, after all, is the key to hundreds of years of interpretation: she is *ira*, she is disorder incarnate, she is a woman in the grip of irrational frenzy. She is also a tragic human being in an insoluble dilemma, one already known to other women, such as Procne and Althaea, each of whom sacrificed her child in order to avenge herself for the sake of her sibling – each of whom, as this book argues, is a literary creation based upon earlier literary Medeas.[49] Far from being a wholly irrational creature, she could not be in better control of her language. Her agony over the murder of her children in order to hurt Jason becomes a rhetorical *suasoria* with careful balancing of the arguments for and against the slaughter. As she works herself up, however, to a pitch of frenzy, what she sees is that archaic order in which blood-feud created a never-ending series of murders and counter-murders. It is often said that the actual deed is provoked by the sudden appearance of her brother's Furies, but that is too simple; that appearance is an emphatic argument about the name of the deed. If the Furies were meant to represent Apsyrtus's revenge, rather than the gods' revenge for her earlier transgression of kinship pieties, there is an extra symmetry. First, the murder of her father's child (whose death also 'murders' her father's house) stimulates a repetition of her guilty deed which will destroy her husband's children and her husband's (thus her own) house. Apsyrtus's revenge, under this description, is Aeetes' revenge, a patriarchal destruction of the man who robbed Apsyrtus's father of progeny and the continuation of the House of the Sun.

At the same time there is a demonstration – not necessarily Stoic – of the way that lack of self-control associated with barbarians, and the indulgence of ire combine in the vulnerable to make subsequent crimes easier than the first.[50] No less than Macbeth or Beatrice-Joanna has Medea

---

[49] Both Althaea and Medea insist upon their revenge as consistent with order in the universe; although there is nothing unusual in tragic characters claiming to have right, or dikê, on their side, Seneca's moral agents are as sinned against as are such earlier women as Clytemnestra. See Thomas G. Rosenmeyer, *Senecan Drama and Stoic Cosmology* (Berkeley, University of California Press, 1989), pp. 200ff.

[50] That Medea's inability to reconcile herself to Jason's desertion had become a focus for Stoic debate dates at least from Chrysippus (and possibly Pacuvius). In Epictetus (*Discourses* II, 17) the discussion begins from the impossibility of achieving 'health' through our own efforts as an example of the need – and the difficulty – of reconciling ourselves to desiring only what is possible. At 19–22 we find, 'Medea, for example, because she could not endure this [accepting the inevitable], came to the point of killing her children. In this respect at least hers was the act of a great spirit. For she had the proper

become the deeds' creature. Throughout the play she is concerned to know what it is to be Medea. It is not anachronistic to speak of sadism, of mental cruelty, but it is important to see her self-assertion (as opposed to the self-abnegation normally required of women) as more than to do with her 'love' for Jason.[51] Medea is more than a middle-aged woman whose husband has deserted her, although this is a traditional interpretation, from the Roman Stoics onwards. The questions Martha Nussbaum asks in her important reading of the play concentrate upon the philosophical issues and implications of the possibility of experiencing passionate loving and remaining virtuous. While this approach enriches our understanding of the play, it *is* a philosopher's reading, which privileges argument over poetry. It will be appropriate to reconsider it below, in chapter four.

Nussbaum's reading also risks falling into the trap of which it is, ironically, most aware: gender. The mingling of 'justification and horror' which she notes as characteristic of Seneca cannot be abstracted either from the complex imagery of the play or from the gender and powerlessness of his female protagonists (so often, as she notes, abandoned by their husbands). Medea's position, for example, is not summed up in Jason's recent betrayal of her: she is an isolated foreigner who has already murdered twice. When she cries out 'Medea superest', the self that she has constructed, or found, is consequent upon the self she has been. The traditional interpretation is

conception of what it means for anyone's wishes not to come true. "Very well, then," she says, "in these circumstances I shall take veangeance upon the man who has wronged and insulted me. Yet what good do I get out of his being in such an evil plight? How can that be accomplished? I kill my children. But I shall be punishing myself also. Yet what do I care?" This is the outbursting of a soul of great force. For she did not know where the power lies to do what we wish – that we cannot get this from outside ourselves, nor by disturbing and deranging things. Give up wanting to keep your husband, and nothing of what you want fails to happen. Give up wanting him to live with you at any cost. Give up wanting to remain in Corinth, and, in a word, give up wanting anything but what God wants. And who will prevent you, who will compel you? No one, any more than one prevents or compels the god.' Quoted from *The Discourses*, ed. W. A. Oldfather (London and New York, Loeb Classics, 1926), vol I, p. 343. Discussed at length in Arcellaschi, *Médée*, pp. 407–13 in the context of Seneca's stoicism, where he cites also Cicero's Fourth Tusculan (69) and Persius, Satire V.

51 Some of the best criticism, as always, comes from other writers. In a letter to Jean Paulhan (16 December 1932), Antonin Artaud writes, 'Je suis en train de lire Senèque – dont il me paraît fou qu'on puisse le confondre avec le moraliste précepteur de je ne sais quel tyran de la décadence – ou alors le Précepteur était celui-ci, mais vielli, désespéré de la magie. . . . On ne peut mieux trouver d'exemple *écrit* de ce qu'on peut entendre par cruauté au théâtre que dans *toutes* les Tragédies de Senèque. . . . P. S. Dans Senèque les forces primordiales font entendre leur écho dans la vibration spasmodique des mots. Et les noms que désignent des secrets et des forces les désignent dans le *trajet* de ces forces et avec leur force d'arrachement et de broiement'. *Oeuvres Complètes* (Paris, Gallimard, 1961), III.30.

52

to see her as a woman in love. Nussbaum quotes the well-known stoic view that if Medea had been able to cease wanting Jason, all would have been well.[52] But 'wanting Jason' is exactly the misinterpretation which places the irrational woman in the grip of love/hate frenzy at the heart of theories about women. Whatever Seneca's Medea (or Euripides'), feels towards the man whose bed she has shared (and both plays are acute in their imagery of marriage), his betrayal of her denies her civic status as a person to whom oaths must be kept; it is also a betrayal of a princess, which condemns her to exile, that horror of the ancient world. Worse, it betrays the order underwritten by those 'di coniugales' with whom the play began, the chief of whom had been Jason's patron. Using women and the social bonds of marriage, as Seneca does (and as Euripides did before him) can also be a metaphor for the politics of Rome, and we ignore the political aspects of oaths at our peril. A stoicism which insists upon indifference to fortune, even in the face of exile, death (including the possible death of one's children), cannot be a triumph of love, either in Antiquity or subsequently. Some transformations of Senecan tragedy – and this central problem – will concern us below, in chapter six.[53]

---

[52] See 'Serpents in the Soul: a reading of Seneca's *Medea*', in her *The Therapy of Desire: Theory and Practice in Hellenistic Ethics* (Princeton, Princeton University Press, 1994), pp. 439–83. In an earlier article Nussbaum quotes the lines from Epictetus cited above in the course of her discussion of the place of love in the passions. But the stoic discussion, however contingently, runs the risk of categorizing Medea's 'problem' in terms of a gendered 'need' to possess the beloved rather than to see her position in political terms. In a more popular form this view persists in psychology as well: 'For the transactional script analyst, as for the play analyst, . . . if you know the play and the character, you know what his outcome will be, unless some changes can be made. For example, it is clear to the psychotherapist, as to the drama critic, that Medea had her mind made up to kill her children, unless someone could talk her out of it; and it should be equally clear to both of them that if she had gone to her treatment group that week, the whole thing would never have happened', Eric Berne, *What Do You Say After You Say Hello?* (London, André Deutsch, 1974 [orig. 1972]), p. 36.

[53] The transmission of Seneca's text is fascinating, and involves a tradition of medieval commentary, e.g. *Il Commento di Nicola Trevet al Testo di Seneca*, ed. Ezio Franceschini (Milan, Orbis Romanus, 1938), on which see also E. Courtney in *The Classical Review* 11 (1961), 166; brief extracts are printed in *Medieval Literary Theory and Criticism c.1100–c.1375: The Commentary Tradition*, ed. A. J. Minnis, A. B. Scott, with the assistance of David Wallace (Oxford, 2nd edn 1991), pp. 340–60. Seneca's efflorescence in the renaissance requires a book-length study of its own. The translation of J. Studley is collected in Thomas Newton, *Tenne Tragedies* (London, 1566, 1581). See Robert Miola's study of Shakespeare's interpretation of Seneca, *Shakespeare and Classical Tragedy: the Influence of Seneca* (Cambridge, Cambridge University Press, 1992). For the neo-Latin tradition, J. W. Binns on William Alastor's *Roxana* (1632), where Atossa, the main villain, explicitly compares herself (in competition) to Medea: 'Shakespeare and Neo-Latin Tragedy in England', *Seneca*, ed. C. D. N. Costa (London, Routledge and Kegan

Seneca's play extracts much more than murder from the large tissue of Homer's 'well-known' story. For other authors, one way of finding their own place in the literary succession (as well as protecting themselves against too lively interest from the Emperor) was to concentrate upon characters who had in the literature of earlier epochs played only minor roles, particularly by linking the men. Not only did some poets connect Jason and Theseus, but they reconsidered the horrors of fratricidal civil war under the guise of the House of Thebes, and included the ruin of the pious as contingent stories, as Statius was to do. In establishing the cluster of women which links Medea and Ariadne, I have concentrated on their anger and desire for revenge. Classical treatments of them often remarked the association of the two heroes, almost contingently upon the association of the offended women, so that Jason and Theseus, because aided by the daughters of enemy kings, were also linked as wily betrayers.[54] Statius is only one author to connect their stories, a connection which might again be traced back to Homer's ramifying references.

Statius and Thebes

As Dante climbs the mountain in *Purgatorio*, he and Virgil meet a poet who might be mistaken for a righteous pagan, but who turns out to be a kind of honorary Christian. This is Statius, who – by an invention which seems to be wholly Dante's – claims to have been brought to a knowledge of Christ through the works of Virgil himself (presumably the fourth Eclogue, taken, as it was, to prefigure the coming of the saviour). In Cantos XXI to XXV the three poets discuss the salvation of the soul, but in the context of a poet's own creative love, and Dante, in showing Statius's love and respect for Virgil (which brought him through the love of poetry to the love of God) inscribes the process of poetic deference.[55]

Paul, 1974), pp. 207–15. 'Anti-Medeas' will concern us below, but it is worth pointing out here that Judith is compared to Medea in, e.g. *Ecloga Theoduli*.

[54] I shall return to this association in chapter four, but it is worth remarking, especially after looking at Seneca's *Medea*, how *little* Jason is associated with gods, particularly in comparison to Theseus. Plutarch's human Theseus nevertheless belongs to a different kind of time from Jason.

[55] Statius alone of the great pagan poets has achieved the road to salvation. The poets after whom he asks, among them Homer and Euripides, are in Limbo. So, too, Virgil explains, are many of the characters of whom Statius wrote, thus insisting upon their own historical status just at the moment when he is inventing a Christian past for Statius. As they climb higher Dante follows the two poets and listens to their conversation about the art of poetry, of which he reveals nothing. Some of the teaching is now put in

There is no evidence that the historical Statius was a Christian, but much that he was a follower of Virgil.[56] Statius belonged to a family from Greek-speaking Naples (so he could read Apollonius). He spent his adulthood in the dangers of Rome, from the civil wars of 68/9 to the tyranny of Domitian. He had absorbed the lessons of political discussion projected onto an ancient history, not only from Virgil, but from Seneca's equally ill-starred nephew, Lucan; he shares the latter poet's deep pessimism, and his epic is informed by a tragic view of history in which the innocent along with the guilty are destroyed by civil war. His completed epic, the *Thebaid*, published probably in AD 91 or 92 shortly before his early death, recounts the slaughter caused by the sons of Oedipus.[57] Its contribution to Argonautic invention comes in the inset story of their stay in Lemnos told by Hypsipyle to Adrastus, one of the leaders of the Argive army. Statius has opened the narrative back out, and repeatedly sets personal tragedy within the exigencies of history. If he cannot make Thebes rival Troy, he can make it reinforce the anxieties over the destruction of the city. His is emphatically a civil war; the idea of colonization, or of 'foreign' women as a threat, is far from his conception of the political.

In *Thebaid* V Hypsipyle becomes the heroine of her own narrative; Jason is an incident in a long life of suffering. Slowly, and with great dignity, she tells how a queen became a slave, little suspecting that her sons by Jason are marching with Adrastus. She is an amalgam of models from Apollonius, Virgil, and Ovid, but not solely their ranting women; she is

Statius's mouth. There is a deconstructive interpretation of the figural place of Isifile in these cantos which some may find overdependent upon a particular interpretation of allusion in Jeremy Trambling, *Dante and Difference: Writing in the 'Commedia'* (Cambridge, Cambridge University Press, 1988) pp. 58–66. There is an important analysis of the *Thebaid* in the context of Boccaccio's understanding and imitation of it in David Anderson, *Before the Knight's Tale: Imitation of Classical Epic in Boccaccio's Teseida* (Philadelphia, University of Pennsylvania Press, 1988).

56 There is a short introduction to Statius in *Roman Poets of the Early Empire*, ed. A. J. Boyle and J. P. Sullivan (Harmondsworth, Penguin, 1991), which contains a translation of *Thebaid* Book X by N. J. Austin and myself. Only after long discussions, and wrestling with the richness of Statius's Latin, did we begin to understand the esteem in which Dante and generations of medieval authors held him. The story of Statius-translations and imitations is being told, largely as part of studies of the Boccaccio-Chaucer links. There is a complete translation by A. D. Melville (Oxford, World's Classics, 1992).

57 Complete text ed. J. H. Mozley (London and Cambridge, Mass., Loeb Classical Library, 1928). The poem is assessed in David Vessey, *Statius and the Thebaid* (Cambridge, 1973); F. M. Ahl, 'Statius *Thebaid*: A Reconsideration', *Aufstieg und Niedergang der römischen Welt* 32.5 (1986), pp. 2803–912; and in *The Imperial Muse: Flavian Epicist to Claudian*, ed. A. J. Boyle (Berwick, Victoria, Ramus Essays, 1990). Martin Götting, *Hypsipyle in der Thebais des Statius* (Frankfurt am Main, University of Tübingen, 1969), pp. 50–62 is useful for sources and verbal reminiscences.

also an imitation of *pius Aeneas*, who saved his father Anchises: the Lemnian woman who preserved the life of her father, Thoas, when all the other women, aroused to *furor* by the goddess Venus, slaughtered the Lemnian men. Having arranged her father's escape, Hypsipyle pretends to share the Lemnians' guilt; they make her queen. When the Argonauts arrive Venus removes their madness, but replaces it with desire for the young men, who thus repeople the island, before leaving at the beginning of the next sailing season to continue their adventures. Hypsipyle bears twin sons to Jason, but her preservation of her father is discovered and the Lemnians, unable to bear the reproach of her innocence, drive her into exile. She is captured by pirates and spends the next twenty years as the slave of King Lycurgus, where Adrastus and the soldiers come upon her, and unite her with her doomed sons, who will die at Thebes. This text was widely disseminated, and offered details of a part of the Argonautic narrative which we have not met elsewhere.[58] As an absent presence, Jason affects the narrative only in terms of the consequences of his actions.

Once again, the epic poet can only rely upon what all his readers know to connect his subject to pre-existing poetic renderings of other historical subjects. Because readers are aware of the intersection between the heroes marching on Thebes and the heroes on board the Argo, the *Thebaid* simultaneously increases its sense of belonging to history *and* epic poetry's interpretations of history. One of the claims of the plot is an argument about the past as a repository of wisdom on the subject of civil strife. We shall go on to study this association with history in the next chapter. Like Homer referring to what everyone knows, like Herodotus using an

---

[58] The medieval Statius has been illuminated by P. M. Clogan in a series of articles: 'Chaucer and the *Thebaid*' in *Studies in Philology* 61 (1964), pp. 599–615 and his *The Medieval Achilleid of Statius* (Leiden, Brill, 1968). There is a magisterial survey in Jane Chance, *Medieval Mythography: from Roman North Africa to the School of Chartres, AD 433–1177* (Gainesville, Florida, University of Florida Press, 1994) which shows the rationalizing tendency of late antique and medieval commentators at their most extended. Statius may have been competing with a near contemporary, Valerius Flaccus, whose unfinished epic on the Argonauts (which, further, remained unknown, unread, and uninfluential until the late renaissance) was in progress while Statius was writing the *Thebaid*. There is a translation of his Book VII (the seduction of Medea) in *Roman Poets of the Early Empire*, and an essay which discusses his relation to Apollonius, Catullus, and Virgil in *Roman Epic*, ed. A. J. Boyle (London, Routledge, 1993), pp. 192–217. The omission of Valerius from consideration here is deliberate, as he influenced no further classical or medieval writers. (There is an argument that Chaucer read Valerius because at one point he writes 'Argonauticon', but that is as likely to be a second-hand reference [through Boccaccio] to Apollonius). Valerius's innovations, both political and personal (Jason has been promised the fleece as a reward for his support of Aeetes against Aeetes' brother) would repay detailed study.

imitation of that reference, Statius asserts a relation between his past and other pasts and renditions of those pasts. The plausible account he represents simultaneously refers to the generic past of epic. Using Hypsipyle as his fulcrum, he transfers the weight of historical tragedy onto a contingent actor and offers a counter-proposal to the models of Dido and Medea. For the history of literature, he is one of the amalgamators of epic and tragedy, tragedy and history. For the history of the depiction of irrational womanhood in the grip of love/hate frenzy, he appears to guarantee the limits of Medea as a model, since his Hypsipyle asserts a pious alternative (although Ovid, as we shall see, made her more rather than less like Medea). Hypsipyle, who ends as the enslaved nurse, failed protectress of someone else's child, has been only the last addition to a group of women who stem from literary imitations of (or reactions against) 'Medea' to create an essential definition.[59]

The history of the legends of Jason and Medea is in part a march toward comprehensiveness, the kind of 'complete' story today to be found in the pages of classical reference texts, which treat accretions and innovations as representing actual parts of a complete story. We have seen how various aspects of that retrospective wholeness arose: Euripides' characterisation of the barbarian princess successfully emphasized her foreignness, her superior intelligence, her ruthlessness. Apollonius Rhodius offered another characterization, an ingenue internally contradictory, yet nonetheless of great attractiveness. His Jason, overwhelmed by the pressure of the competing, heroic Argonauts, introduced a further problem. With Rome, and above all with Ovid (the subject of chapter three) and Seneca, Medea becomes finally and irrevocably – whatever else she may be, for whatever reasons – a criminal sorceress. Pathos and irrational frenzy, powerlessness and revenge, the successful exchange of women and recalcitrant kinship loyalty, passivity and cunning intelligence – we have seen the growth of patterns for an essential 'woman', with all her contradictions, and all her danger. Nevertheless, however crucial to the growth of stereotypical characterization of 'woman' Medea became, it would be a mistake to consider her (or, perhaps, them) in isolation or to emphasize one role at

---

[59] It is part of Hypsipyle's tragedy that the unfortunate slave should – in the moment of regaining her own children – lose another child: in the brief period in which she reveals her past to the invading army and discovers that among her listeners are her two sons, she is distracted from her duty to her master's child. Although there are obvious reasons (such as the relative likelihood of *seeing* a beast of prey), it is surely imaginative overdetermination on Statius's part, not mere coincidence, that that baby should be stung by a snake – Medea's totemic association. None of this prevented Dante locating Hypsipyle in Hell.

the expense of other characters'. The importance of Virgil (whose Dido is the most influential of all 'Medeas') cannot be overemphasized, both in terms of literary imitation and in the context of Roman political ideas of origin and expansion. If this characterization is a characterization of literary characters, there is also a description in which certain historical and political concerns draw the legends toward views connected to a past perceived as true, or at least possible. Medea's foreign otherness is the basis of Dido's eastern attraction and threat. We shall return to the implications of these exemplary models in what follows. But it is time to connect the legends to historical time, and models of true tales about the past.

TWO

The History of Jason

> Out of these events history itself was born: the
> abduction of Helen, the Trojan War, and, before
> that, the Argonauts' expedition and the abduc-
> tion of Medea – all are links in the same chain.
>
> Roberto Calasso,
> *The Marriage of Cadmus and Harmony*

The Fall of Troy

When, in 1728, Isaac Newton's *The Chronology of Ancient Kingdoms Amended* finally appeared, it represented the last gasp of medieval ideas about the history of the world and the place of the Argo in dating that history.[1] This is to say that the date of the Fall of Troy had long preoccupied historians, and it was Newton's contention that since the Argonauts lived two generations before that fall, the solution to the first problem implied the solution to the second. Or vice versa. Had Newton argued his theory fifty years earlier he would probably have found a ready audience, but his *Chronology* succeeded the linguistic and historical advances which had already devastated belief in a historical Troy, especially one whose survivors had founded the contemporary European nations. Newton's attitude toward pagan poetry was itself an empirical reinterpretation of the

---

[1] Newton had been working on such problems for most of the latter part of his life, and had become unshakeably convinced that the named constellations marked that point at which recorded history began, because each of the major star groups commemorated a part of the Argonautic adventure. The book – Newton had died in 1727 – was vigorously attacked. See Frank Manuel, *Isaac Newton Historian* (Cambridge, Mass., Belknap Press of Harvard University, 1963), pp. 78–9. The star map mentioned in the preface to this book (p. xiii) is from Johannes Bayer, *Vranometria: omnium asterismorum continens schemata, nova methodo delineata, aereis laminis expresa* (Ulm, Sumptibus Iohannis Gorlini, 1661), which is illustrated on precisely this assumption.

uses of the past: he tried to turn to a new exactitude the old assumption that under the decorative veils of poetic representation there lurked truths available to the initiate; in his own case, the man best able to read the book of the world. His ambition was to extract evidence about exact chronology which would establish irrefutable dates, to treat poetry's connection with the stars as part of an empirical re-analysis of 'evidence' supplied (perhaps unwittingly) by an age which lived before precision.[2] On first acquaintance, Newton's views do not seem far-fetched: ancient philosophers did indeed study the heavens, and they named the constellations. Mathematical calculations could, Newton argued, correct for changes in the heavens and reveal an originary moment in man's relationship to Nature. It was the specious exactitude of Newton's mathematical house of cards which brought his chronological speculations into disrepute, rather as Stephen Hawking's musings about ultimate Creators have appeared to many readers to outdistance his scientific claims.

Newton did nothing to restore faith in the idea that Troy once existed. Not until Schliemann's excavations in the nineteenth century would the world once again contemplate a historical Troy. Newton's proposal for a benchmark for secular chronology found no favour. Yet objections to Newton's theories could not forever erase the assumption that, in some way, Greek legends had something to do with the history of mankind. The idea that the Argonautic voyage could be used as *evidence* already relocates the intellectual context as something almost forensic, beyond the psycho-social patterns of anxiety and desire to which structural anthropologists and literary critics are devoted. The impulse to account for, to rationalize, Greek legends (an impulse which begins within the traditions of telling them) is not so far removed from allegory and the cracking of other great codes.[3] Homer's categories of well-known stories leave their status free. Even in late antiquity, as is well known, readers tried to reinterpret them as veiling hidden philosophical knowledge. Newton's insistent exactitude places them under his own reflecting lenses, insisting that the correct unveiling would lead to the hidden order of the universe.

This chapter goes back to consider how the *idea* of the destructions of

---

2 In the ancient world there was a traditional date, which was expressed in the styles of a number of different, co-existing chronologies. It increases the sense of their precision to express them in modern calendrical terms: 1184.

3 The phrase is, of course, Northrop Frye's. His distinction between Biblical stories which are parallel to Biblical 'history', and the use of such stories as 'concrete illustrations of abstract arguments, in other words, as allegories' is pertinent to the use of classical legends to illustrate truths about human history and human character. See his *The Great Code: The Bible and Literature* (London, Routledge and Kegan Paul, 1982), p. 33.

Troy wove its way into the fabric of European beliefs about the secular past, and carries the story forward until the loss of those beliefs returned the classical legends firmly into the lap of the poets. It is concerned with ways of treating time, and with the construction (parallel to the Judaeo-Christian history) of a secular history of the world. It considers the effects not only of a style of narrative which claims a relationship to actual events which took place at a time remote from its readers' memories, but also of the ways that that kind of narrative imposes coherence upon interpretations.[4] By contrast to the previous chapter, it emphasizes a public, male, aristocratic, secular journey.

Strategies of coherence can be sequential, chronological, and causal; they can be based upon imagery, theme, and structure. All of them presuppose the possibility of connections which are not merely arbitrary, and that refusal to dismiss arbitrariness, to insist upon relationship, is part of the rationalizing tendency which underlies comprehensive historical narrative. In chapter one I mentioned Homer's references to the Argonautic legends, and how he assumes their prior occurrence (p. 11). The contrast to Newtonian ideas of time is clear. For Homer, and for other classical writers, sequence was not necessarily anchored in a dated chronology. 'Priority' implies causality, but it also, for ancient and medieval writers, tended to presuppose the prestige which accrued to precedence: the sooner the better, to take advantage of an old phrase. In this chapter I shall concentrate on the rationalizing tendencies which locate the Argonautic legends in a particular matrix, usually categorized as historical, both by style and content.

To look forward for a moment, beyond this book's own chronology, it is worth remembering that Schliemann's dig indeed returned the Greek epics to the status of histories, however refashioned, or fashioned in an antique mould. That epic was, finally, evidence of *something* contributed to the anthropology which made the study of 'Classics' at Cambridge part of an intellectual movement which proposed other rationalizing keys to all mythology. As Janet Ruth Bacon argued in her early study of the Argonautic route and what it might reveal, trade routes may have been as important as war in contributing to the legends; her rationality helped inspire Robert Graves's novel.[5] The politics of competition between sixth- and

---

4 Thus *ancient* history could suggest an alternative 'time' to the liturgical time of medieval history, secular and sacred. See, for example, 'The Time of Purgatory' and 'The Time of the *Exemplum*' in Jacques Le Goff, *The Medieval Imagination*, trans. Arthur Goldhammer (Chicago and London, University of Chicago Press, 1988; orig. 1985).

5 Janet Ruth Bacon, *The Voyage of the Argonauts* (London, Methuen, 1925). Robert

fifth-century Greek cities, or between Rome and Carthage, disappeared with the civilisations that needed them, and classical legends changed their aspects accordingly. The fall of Troy becomes generalized outward to a history of the world or the example of a city's destruction, while the actors in its tragedy are generalized to the roles in the plot or reduced to icons of individual fate. This interplay between chronology and genre invites – while it confuses – the rationalizing impulse. How far the 'events' of the legends were (or remained) malleable changed, as we saw in the previous chapter, as time passed and they became more and more embedded in a known and plausible history. That reinterpretation of that history was possible will be illustrated by Christine de Pizan at the end of this chapter.

The connections between the Argonauts and the legends of Troy could be assumed by later writers, and, as in the epic of Apollonius, were so connected. That urge to comprehensive explanation probably antedates Alexandrian scholarship, but it is certainly epitomized by it. It is one of the defining characteristics of a historical imagination, and related to the contextualization of epic poetry. On this approach depends an assumption that unimportant matters are defined by exclusion. This extends to unimportant characters. In Greek accounts watchmen, tutors, nurses, all unfree members of the *oikos*, disappear when no longer necessary. It is difficult, but not impossible, to retain certain asymmetries in the narratives, which immediately appear if one shifts point of view away from the adventure undertaken by the young men. Suppose, for the sake of example, a tragedy of Pelias and his daughters. The triumphalist generational narrative which assumes the heroic centrality of Jason acquiring his rightful inheritance depends in part upon the idea that Pelias was indeed an unlawful usurper, that his place in the story is, in the end, a difficulty to be overcome (and in 'a' story). The plot, expressed in tragic drama, requires a sequence of

Graves, *The Golden Fleece* (London, Cassell and Co., Ltd., 1944). This, too, is a fictional triumph of supposed rationalization, which Graves, with greater learning than artistic success, connected to his theories of The White Goddess. The apparent scientific vogue for such theories was underwritten by scholars such as E. Will, noted above, p. 21 n. 3, and contributed, in its sad way, to the European tragedies of the twentieth century. Graves's novel suffers from that overweighting of the plot with learning which so plagued Apollonius, while managing to be both repetitive and reductive. Unreadable as it now is, it was an important inspiration for other authors, such as the poet, Henry Treece, who attempted to live by writing pot-boilers, and whose *Jason* followed Graves's example (London, The Bodley Head, 1961). John Gardner, too, followed Graves, often incident by incident, for his book-length poem, *Jason and Medeia* (New York, Knopf, 1973). Neither of the latter writers acknowledges either Graves's novel nor his scholarship, and each is marked by 'boys' own' homosocial assumptions that women dangerously complicate a hero's adventures. Both attribute such 'crooked ways' as oath-breaking to the threatening uncivilized princess, Medeia.

speakers. The *epic* of Jason is threatened by countervailing points of view. By a similar (but perhaps more inviting) inversion, the dramatically expressed, embodied and enacted, point of view of the women turns 'the' story inside out, like some narrato-topological trick which reorients the agents and actions, and redefines 'the history' as something else. Certain post-modern assumptions, and the literary fashion for alternative tales, make it easier now to imagine a shift from a narrative of action impressed by men to that undergone by the women.[6] High rhetorical tragic expression *within* epic comprehends certain generic aspects of drama (especially in a culture in which reading still indicates reading aloud). As Statius introduces Hypsipyle as an icon of pathos, other authors could offer other possibilities. Emphasis on local moments of great emotion helped the poet avoid problems of narrative succession. Even if one follows the young heroes, certain chronological problems resist a comprehensive narrative (Castor and Pollux were Argonauts who belong to the prelude to Troy's first destruction, but their twin sisters, Clytemnestra and Helen, also born from Leda's egg, were at the heart of the legends of Troy and its aftermath). Nevertheless, many could be rationalized into a single narrative, even if ex post facto. If one erects genealogical tables, for example, the patrilineal houses of Helios and Erechtheus can be clearly outlined, and Homer's Circe appears as Medea's aunt; their cloudiness, their hypothetical nature, disappear under the decisive clarity of straight lines, which erases the historical accretions of writers' calculations and claims to offer authoritative versions of relationships.[7]

Yet the story which Herodotus told, quoted in chapter one, makes no mention of a series of destructions of Troy. His sequence of rapes and counter-rapes names Io, Medea, and then Helen; Herodotus, as ironic narrator, plays down the mere kidnapping of a girl as the motive for war, while as historian he half-embarrassedly acknowledges that the Greeks sailed to Troy on behalf of a young Spartan bride. The force of a quarrel over women as a motive for war is itself stressed by constant repetition, against Herodotus's own apparent expressed opinion. Another set of stories, of equal antiquity, includes another quarrel over women: Laomedon, Priam's father, promised his daughter, Hesione, to Heracles as a reward for freeing Troy from a sea-monster, then, when Heracles had done so, refused to perform his side of the bargain (in some versions the prize is

---

6 As indicated above, Chapter One, p. 26, Euripides' *Peliades* seems to have concerned Pelias's daughters, of whom Alcestis alone resisted Medea's blandishments.

7 Jane Chance, *Medieval Mythography: from Roman North Africa to the School of Chartres, AD 433–1177* (Gainesville, University of Florida Press, 1994).

a horse or horses).[8] Heracles killed Laomedon, sacked his city, and abducted the prize he had been promised, but gave her to Telamon. Hesione became the mother of Teucer. Hence Priam's readiness to send Paris to the Greeks and the continuance of East-West enmity.[9]

The 'mere' kidnap of a girl is one form of plot (Herodotus is of the urbane view that young women are not carried off without, in some sense, assenting); a second is a broken promise, and the revenge which must follow public shame. There is a third, the reprisal for direct injury to men, which follows the mistreatment of guests, of which Laomedon also was said to be guilty when he attacked the Argonauts who beached on his shores in search of fresh water. Each offers a familiar story-pattern which might be exploited by different kinds of writer to different ends. Because of their appeal not only to familiar plots with known outcomes, but also to a generalized 'human nature' they avoid both the traps of particular characters and of specific times: they do not suggest that we might meet Mrs Aesonides shopping. Story-pattern is not 'truth', however, even if we suppose a kind of positivist writer whose intention was to encompass and rationalize all the available tales. Herodotus offers us a sequence of stories which men used to explain present enmity, while himself making no investment in their status as representations of an actual past. It would not be altogether anachronistic to categorize such gestures toward 'stories which everyone knows' as an evasion posing as a deferral. A writer attempting to give a sequential account of the history of Troy might well wish to claim that his outline was, at least in the main, true, but that any

---

8 Illustrations of Heracles' bargain with Laomedon survive from the sixth century BC, and several are reproduced in Susan Woodford, *The Trojan War in Ancient Art* (London, Duckworth, 1993), pp. 45–8. The pictorial evidence, mainly on vases, is susceptible to varied interpretations, and reminds us how many interpretations persisted, as is also illustrated by the *Lexicon Iconographicum Mythologiae Classicae* (Zurich and Munich, Artemis, 1981–).

9 It is this story which is recalled in *Troilus and Cressida*, when Troilus reminds his brothers of their agreement to the kidnapping strategy:

> It was thought meet
> Paris should do some vengeance on the Greeks;
> Your breath with full consent bellied his sails;
> The seas and winds, old wranglers, took a truce
> And did him service: he touch'd the ports desir'd,
> And for an old aunt whom the Greeks held captive,
> He brought a Grecian queen, whose youth and freshness
> Wrinkles Apollo's, and makes stale the morning.
> Why keep we her? – The Grecians keep our aunt. (II.ii.74–81)

The sexual fecundity in the metaphors needs no emphasis. Shakespeare's more immediate sources will be discussed below, chapter five.

particular scene depended upon authorities who might or might not be mistaken. Any particular scene might in addition be extracted, and used in different ways, without losing its status as true, or possibly so, or in part possibly corresponding to something which might have happened. Strategies of coherence include dramatic irony, so that the addition of a detail which *will be* relevant to a later section of the narrative may emphasize the ways that apparently contingent choices have fatal consequences, thus tying history back to tragedy.[10] It is also an appeal to history as a sequence of identifiable patterns, in which we as readers are privileged in the hindsight of our expectation. Some versions of Heracles' destruction of Troy (and one much repeated in medieval accounts) contain the ironic addition that Heracles, recognizing Hesione's innocence, allowed her, when he gave her to Telamon, to choose one among the Trojan captives, who would be spared the usual captive's fate of enslavement. She chose her favourite brother, Priam.

As long as these stories can be retold in a culture which already knows them, and as long as they retain the anecdotal status accorded them by writers as diverse as Herodotus or Euripides, their actual truth status (or precise date) has little consequence. What it is to tell such a story, to claim legendary figures as founders of a city or ancestors, is to make a connection, but to leave its exact status indeterminate.[11]

Only when historical narratives begin to claim exclusive representative and interpretative truth do their contents assume a different kind of correspondence, one that opens possibilities of exactness within historical representations of the world which were predicated upon certain unavoidable inexactnesses. That the Christian god appeared when and where the stories said was not only Revelation, it revealed a new kind of necessity about history (that there should be a locatable, demonstrable historical moment) and erected a new criterion. Not only can 'prophecy' be read back into

---

[10] This may appear to coincide with certain ideas of Hayden White, but it is restricted to the case where *only* certain kinds of narrative are available and only *certain kinds* of narrative are written. In the conceptual space which precedes modern historiography, the questions themselves are defined in terms inappropriate to current categories. I have dealt with some of these issues in 'Telling the Truth with Authority: From Richard II to Richard II' *Common Knowledge* 4 (1995), pp. 81–98.

[11] The long tradition of allegorical interpretation of Homer co-existed with the belief that some of his stories were true. Origen preserves this attitude in his *Contra Celsum* of the early third century, in the course of a plea for reciprocal open-mindedness about the interpretation of the Gospels, which also attempts to 'prove' that Moses was anterior to Homer. See Robert Lamberton, *Homer the Theologian: Neoplatonist Allegorical Reading and the Growth of the Epic Tradition* (Berkeley, University of California Press, 1986), pp. 80–1.

pagan poetry, but the re-interpretation of earlier poetry *as* prophetic introduces a question-begging claim about the status (and usefulness) of poetry. The idea of 'figural' representation has a historical aspect within an assumption of cycles, or of repeated circumstances, which can be secular as well as religious, as I shall discuss in the next chapter.[12]

The authority which set the fall of Troy at the core of secular history was not only its existence at the heart of classical literature (for that might have been undermined by medieval ideas about the non-Christian past), nor even its strange status as the ancestral city (so important to Roman self-description), but its location in an early Church history and its approval by Augustine and Jerome.[13] Despite the claim that the word of god supersedes the competing words of classical legend, classical legends survived and throve. One must underline the plurality of those legends, since the pagan world not only tolerated, but rejoiced in a variety of versions without apparently needing to posit one as a sole truth. In the new Christian world in which one could know when a god appeared, one could ask questions about when legendary journeys took place: to prove their existence was part of one kind of competition, to disprove them another. And despite the Christian insistence that there is only one history, the salvation history of mankind, the double status which I have already remarked, of story and history, is established from the earliest times. No history of the world written in the middle ages would ignore the Greek Chonicle written by Eusebius and translated by Jerome, or the Latin history written by Orosius and authorized by *The City of God*.[14] These early historical texts set a

---

[12] For example, more than one sixteenth-century writer still saw Seneca as foretelling modern explorations of the world, including Columbus's son, Ferdinand, who annotated his copy of the plays: 'haec prophetia expleta est per patrem meum Christoforum Colon almirantem anno 1492', quoted from Seneca, *Medea*, ed. C. D. N. Costa (Oxford, Clarendon Press, 1973) note at l. 379. When Hayden White asserts that 'History is always allegorical', he elides many of the different types of allegory; history can certainly always be interpreted as illustrating patterns of event and behaviour, and, traditionally, has been susceptible of moral analysis. See, most recently, 'Historiography as Narration', in *Telling Facts: History and Narration in Psychoanalysis*, ed. Joseph H. Smith and Humphrey Morris (Baltimore, Johns Hopkins, 1992), pp. 284–99.

[13] Although the arguments of the magisterial work of J. Perret, *Les Origines de la légende troyenne de Rome (231–81)* (Paris, 1942), and 'Rome et les troyennes' *Revue des Etudes Latines* 49 (1971), pp. 39–52 have been the subject of severe reservations, it contains the best collection of material on the subject. Erich S. Gruen, *Culture and National Identity in Republican Rome* (Ithaca, Cornell University Press, 1992), chapt. one emphasizes the cultural legitimacy which Trojan roots lent the expanding Republic. This insight about colonial expansion will return at the end of this book. Léo Mallinger, *Médée: étude de littérature comparée* (Louvain, 1897) also preserves early testimonies to the connection to Roman 'prehistory'.

[14] Eusebius/Jerome dates the beginnings of the Trojan War to 820 years after Abraham.

precedent which had the opposite effect to their intention. By emphasizing the parallel foundation histories (Troy/Rome) which it was Christianity's task to counter, fulfill, and supersede, they not only located Troy at the centre of any historical consideration, but ensured the appeal to precedence through their subscription to the poetic immortality of that city.

If Orosius's *History Against the Pagans* did nothing else, it established the *topoi* of world history, and further legitimated depictions of the fall of Troy as a paradigm of secular disaster. As a *paradigm* it could survive outside a world of proof and disproof. As an event it suggested an alternative genealogy of importance. Even when medieval historians, such as Matthew Paris, dissented from the truth of their Trojan representations, they still included them, since they were the established beginning of any world chronicle.[15] Although neither Augustine nor his disciple, Orosius, could have foreseen it (or would have approved it if they could), the preservation of the story of Troy affirmed the importance of this-worldly values, and especially the prestige which accrued to the martial, aristocratic quest for glory. European aristocrats imitated the Roman fashion for erecting genealogies which linked Rome to Troy, and the European 'nations' found Trojan refugees whose descendants they could claim to be. As long as Orosius's original selection of human misfortunes retained authority, so did Troy; as long as chronicles attempted to begin at a worldly beginning, the prelude to the war over Helen, the Spartan bride, would be among the first events recounted.[16] Like Augustine's tears over Dido, rejections of Troy inscribed it the more deeply in the centre of historical accounts.

Authority, legitimacy, and exemplarity reinforce each other. Each time the stories (whatever their status) are retold, their association is confirmed

Margaret Ehrhart, *The Judgment of the Trojan Prince Paris in Medieval Literature* (Philadelphia, University of Pennsylvania Press, 1987); Augustine, *City of God* III.ii. Orosius, *The Seven Books of History Against the Pagans*, trans. Roy J. Deferrari (Washington, DC, 1964). Orosius studied with both Jerome and Augustine; the history, his last work (AD 418), was a development of *The City of God*, and a defence against the accusation that Rome's recent disasters were the fault of the Christians. He dates the abduction of Helen and the Trojan War to 430 years before the foundation of Rome.

15 'De raptu Helenae et fabulis poetarum' Matthew calls this section in his *Chronica Majora*, ed. H. R. Luard (London, 1872), I.15–16. Vincent of Beauvais follows this inclusiveness in his *Speculum Historiale* (first printed edition, Augsburg, 1474), II. f. 57r. The section is dealt with at length in the widely-used *The Universal Chronical of Ranulph Higden*, ed. John Taylor (Oxford, 1966), one of the most important historical chronicles for fourteenth- and fifteenth-century Britain. I hope to deal with medieval 'ancient history' in *Imagined Histories*.

16 See Mihoko Suzuki, *Metamorphoses of Helen: Authority, Difference, and the Epic* (Ithaca and London, Cornell University Press, 1989).

almost by inertia; that confirmation confers 'historical' status upon stories which come into their orbit. The style in which the mutually-confirming histories are told becomes *less* important where they belong to a recognizable narrative, although there remains a large space for conflict. This contentious co-existence of 'poetic' interpretations with 'historical' chronicle was a source of anxiety for the defenders of both history and fiction. Thus, to take the key example for these narratives, the link between the histories of Jason and the pre-history of the fall of Troy was legitimated by the survival of two curious fictions which purported to be the work of two eye-witnesses to the Trojan War, one from each side. Until 1702, these two short Latin texts were considered to be genuine.[17] To inertia one might add a kind of circumstantial attribution, by which 'authority' grows. Homer mentions both authors: Dares the Phrygian and Dictys of Crete. When the author of the *Itinerarium Peregrinorum et Gesta Regis Ricardi* (which forms one of the epigraphs to this book) claimed that only historical writers save the past from being lost, he cited Dares as one of his exemplary authors, while making no scruple among the different kinds of historical writer.[18] In the sixteenth century Sir Philip Sidney was typical in assuming their authority as 'true' while elevating the *moral* precedence of Virgil's 'feigned' Aeneas over the 'right' one depicted by 'Dares', acknowledging the distinction while changing the usual rules of preferring truth to untruth.[19] But other authors were less scrupulous in accepting the distinction between 'history' and 'fiction'.

That the paired histories themselves appear to invite choice (either between the two authors, or between their versions and Homer) further narrows the range which describes the contents and continuities of the stories. The texts of Dares and Dictys were normally printed together, to give a pair of supplements to the narrative which could be extracted from Homer. Perhaps written in Greek in the first century AD (but translated into Latin centuries later), they seem to have originated in the fashion for 'Greek romances', but, once the cultural context changed, to have appeared actually to be what they perhaps never meant to pretend to be: eye-witness accounts which could be used to correct the partisan poetry of

[17] It was J. Perizonius who, using recent advances in linguistic and historical analysis, first demonstrated that the texts must be far later than they pretend, in his edition, *De Bello et Excidio Troiae* (Amsterdam, 1702), and that the accounts are therefore false, and likely to be forged in order to deceive.

[18] Ed. William Stubbs for the Rolls Series (London, 1864), I.3, 4.

[19] *An Apology for Poetry*, ed. Geoffrey Shepherd (Manchester, 1973; orig. 1965), p. 110 and n.; Shepherd points out that doubts were already being expressed about Dares, as by Vives. Sidney further contrasts the 'true' Justin, who will concern us below, to the more poetic kind of history, but he appeals to exemplarity as an ultimate justification.

Homer.[20] The urbane recital of Herodotus, which depends so much on an informed audience capable of interpreting his archness of tone, referred to stories told but did not underwrite their truth – or otherwise. It is the triumph of Herodotus's urbane voice to make masterly allusions without spelling them out, to appeal to stories everyone knows. Dares' alternative history opens Homer's authority to question, but question is neither rebuttal nor refutation. It need not even be doubt, but a way of introducing another, co-existing, possibility.

For Dares, after all, Jason's voyage matters only insofar as it provoked the first destruction of Troy under Priam's father. The Argonauts pause at the shore of Troy to take on fresh water (as they pause, in other accounts, at Lemnos), but so far from showing them any hospitality, the Trojan king, Laomedon, who takes them for Barbarians invading his kingdom, threatens to destroy them all. Faced with a superior force, but swearing revenge, they return to their ship, then:

... Colcos profecti sunt, pellem abstulerunt, domum reversi sunt ...[21]

The golden fleece is a contingency. Less than a single sentence binds Jason to Troy, yet it is a sentence of consequence, especially for a culture with a firm allegiance to *amplificatio*. Although this opening records Jason's heroic status, its main function is to make room for Hercules' subsequent

---

20 There are numerous studies of Dares and Dictys, several by Chaucerians, e.g. Robert M. Lumiansky, 'Dares' *Historia* and Dictys' *Ephemeris*: A Critical comment', in *Studies in Language, Literature, and Culture in the Middle Ages and Later*, ed. E. Bagby Atwood and A. A. Hill (Austin, University of Texas Press, 1969), pp. 200–9. See also N. E. Griffin, 'Un-Homeric Elements in the Medieval Story of Troy', *JEGP* 7 (1907–8), pp. 32–52. See the summary in C. David Benson, *The History of Troy in Middle English Literature* (Cambridge, D. S. Brewer, 1980), chapt. 1. Further on Dictys, Stefan Merkle, 'Telling the Story of the Trojan War: The Eyewitness Account of Dictys of Crete', in *The Search for the Ancient Novel*, ed. James Tatum (Baltimore and London, Johns Hopkins University Press, 1994), pp. 183–96. Merkle dates the Latin translations to the fourth (Dictys) and fifth (Dares) centuries.

21 The whole narrative, from the beginning, follows the outline already mentioned. This is the opening, which gives a vivid impression of the style: 'Pelias rex in Peloponneso Aesonem fratrem habuit. Aesonis filius erat Iason, virtute praestans: & qui sub ejus regno erant, omnes eos hospites habebat, & ab eis validissime amabatur. Pelias rex ut vidit Iasonem acceptum esse omnibus, veritus est ne sibi injurias faceret, & se regno ejiceret. Dicit Jasoni Colchis pellem arietis inauratam esse, dignam ejus virtute, ut eam inde auferret, omnia se ei daturum pollicetur. Iason ubi audivit, ut erat fortis animi, & qui loca omnia nosse volebat, atque clariorem se futurum existimabat, si pellem inauratam Colchis abstulisset, dicit Peliae regi se velle eo ire, si vires sociique non deessent.' The Jason section occupies a paragraph or two in the course of a short work. Quoted from *De Excidio Troiae Historia*, ed. Ferdinand Meister (Leipzig, Teubner, 1873). Trans. R. M. Frazer, *The Trojan War* (Bloomington, Indiana, University of Indiana Press, 1966).

attack upon Troy and his rescue of Hesione. Medea is never mentioned. The existence of works of art illustrating Hercules' adventure at Troy may go some way to explaining his inclusion. But one must acknowledge the impulse to place and frame the narrative, to supply its omissions. In retrospect it is tempting to guess that *because* the heroic status of the heroes is what is at issue, no deviation has a place. Omission, like the silencing of Medea which we shall see elsewhere, is the simplest way to maintain that heroic mode. To focus on Argo's relation to Troy is to maintain epic heroism within the attempt to supply a comprehensive, comprehending, and correcting account of Homer. Nevertheless, silence, too, can be an invitation, and the existence of Hesione suggests yet one more repetition of the plot first adumbrated by Herodotus. The architectonics of medieval structures expanded the roles of the women.

Jason's career depends at several points upon Medea's assistance, assistance more interventionist, and more powerful than, say, Ariadne's thread. This contrast is instructive, since Theseus sloughs off his obligation to Minos's daughter, abandons her on the beach at Diâ, and returns home alone, ready to undertake further heroic exploits. Ariadne's own loose thread is picked up by the arrival of Dionysos, who rescues her for a new, and no doubt superior, liaison. Jason, however, brings Medea home to his father's house (where she continues to intervene in his cause), and marries her. His marriage (in some versions) inhibits (and excuses) him from joining Hercules to participate in the retaliatory first destruction of Troy, and thereby removes him from the public heroic sphere to the more domestic or at least localized wrangles over succession. Unusually, Jason declines from heroism, with its external adventures.

Jason rapidly disappears from many of the so-called histories of Troy, but even his brief and contingent part authorized his presence in those texts. The *apparent* 'historical' heroism was bound to raise questions whenever the narrative extended itself to follow his career, because his decline is so striking, and so unusual. Underelaboration is one solution to the loose ends associated with the Argonauts and their leader. But there was another solution to the problem of Jason's later life, unlooked for, and – for modern readers – a surprise: an overelaboration. As has already been referred to above, some versions returned Medea to her father's kingdom. Others offered the idea that Jason and Medea were reconciled. The narrative of his adventures was expanded in another of the 'universal' histories which survived to be used by medieval readers, the so-called 'Epitome' of the *Historia Philippicae* of Trogus Pompeius, attributed to 'Justin'. A chief source for Ranulph Higden, referred to by writers such as Antoine de la Sale, translated into English by Arthur Golding, 'Justin' was one of the sources of the reconciliation between Jason and Medea[22]. Even here, however, the causes of the rupture are inexplicit:

> King Pelias, wishing to procure [Jason's] death from dread of his extraordinary ability, which was dangerous to his throne, despatched [him] on a prescribed journey to Colchis to bring home the fleece of the ram so celebrated throughout the world; hoping that the man would lose his life, either in the perils of so long a voyage, or in war with barbarians so remote. But Jason, having spread abroad the report of so glorious an enterprise, at which the chief of the youth from almost all the world came flocking to him, collected a band of heroes, who were called Argonauts. Having brought his troop back safe, and being again driven from Thessaly by the sons of Pelias, he set out on a second voyage for Colchis, accompanied by numerous trains of followers (who, at the fame of his valour, came daily from all parts to join him) and by his wife Medea, whom, having previously divorced her, he had now received again from compassion for her exile....[23]

Such a surprising modification of the later lives of the protagonists may appear to be an eccentric late accretion. It is not, however, unprecedented in the history of myth and legend. Helen was in Egypt while a simulacrum was at Troy. Orpheus the monotheist had appeared as early as Hellenistic times, against the prevailing descriptions of him as hero, musician, prophet, establishing a stratum from which later Judaeo-Christian allegories could mine arguments for pagan 'recognition' (by reading the book of the world) of their god.[24] By late antiquity, a 'whole' history was emerging.

---

22 *The abridgment of the Histories of Trogus Pompeius*, collected by Iustine (London, 1564).

23 *Justin, Cornelius Nepos, and Eutropius*, trans. J. S. Watson (London, 1833), pp. 278–80. '. . . Iasonis Thessali comite, quem cum perditum propter insignem periculosamque reno suo virtutem Pelias rex cuperet, dementiata militia in Colchos abire iubet pellemque arietis memorabilem gentibus reportare, sperans interitum viri aut ex periculis tam longae navigationis aut ex bello tam profundae barbariae. Igitur Iason divulgata opinione tam gloriosae expeditionis, cum ad eum certatim principes iuventutis totius ferme orbis concurrerent, exercitum fortissimorum virorum, qui Argonautae cognominati sunt, conparavit. Quem cum magnis rebus gestis incolumen reduxisset, rursum a Peliae filius Thessalis magna vi pulsus cum ingenti multitudine, quae ad famam virtutis eius ex omnibus gentibus cotidie confluebat, comite Medea uxore, quam repudiatam miseratione exilii rursum receperat . . .', M. *Ivniani Ivstini, Epitoma Historiarvm Philippicarum Pompei Trogi*, ed. Otto Seel (Stuttgart, Teubner, 1972), p. 284. The second campaign in Colchis was in some versions attributed to Medea alone, who restored her father to his throne.

24 John Block Friedman, *Orpheus in the Middle Ages* (Cambridge, Mass., Harvard University Press, 1970), chapt. 2. Orpheus, too, became grist for chronographical arguments (see p. 23) upon which were hung the precedence of Moses (or other Old Testament figures). And the story of Orpheus's descent to the underworld was supplied with a happy ending in the fourteenth century (pp. 114–17).

Or, perhaps, a whole 'history'. Its gaps invited research, invention, reworking, supplements which came from non-historical texts.

Medieval Secular History

The distinction between historical and other kinds of texts is one which has, once again, become a matter for debate. To say that the legends of Jason and Medea were absorbed into histories of the world makes use of terms which require some careful definition for the conceptual space of the Middle Ages. They may otherwise appear to invoke categories apparently familiar to modern readers of histories. To look at the spectrum of texts which might invite the category 'historical' to medieval readers and writers is, perhaps, to cover ground familiar from those recent debates, but some summary will be useful.[25] I shall begin with some general remarks about 'history' before moving to 'ancient history'.

Medieval historians worked under a variety of constraints which they acknowledged both explicitly and tacitly. One of the severest of these was the justification of writing secular history at all. Because throughout the medieval cultures it was difficult to write a text on one's own authority (though obviously less so as precedents multiplied), authority was often projected onto another text. As dozens of prefaces attest (or appear to attest: prefaces, too, had their *topoi*), no author takes it upon himself to guarantee the truth of a narrative set beyond the reach of memory. He defers. What historian, classical, medieval, or modern, would be likely to discredit his rhetorical *ethos*, that creation of a trustworthy voice, by opening with a claim to have falsified the past, by departing, even in little, from the strictest canons of true representation? To cue one's preface by invoking a 'Breton lai', for example, would be to affiliate oneself to traditions of story-telling and rescension which tacitly accepted invention. By contrast, the memory of the *ancient* past calls up the prestige (in history *as well as* other modes) of its achievements. One might, however, play with the cues, claim to write history, and invent from whole cloth.

Free-standing secular history depended for its existence on the strictest fidelity to the 'true law of history', as Bede (whose status as authority

---

25 See Lee Patterson, *Negotiating the Past*, who extends the discussion to recent philosophical arguments (Madison, University of Wisconsin Press, 1987). These are the central concerns of Bernard Guenée, *Histoire et culture historique dans l'Occident médiévale* (Paris, 1980). There is an elegant discussion of these issues in Gabrielle Spiegel, *Romancing the Past: The Rise of Vernacular Prose Historiography in Thirteenth-Century France* (Berkeley, University of California Press, 1993), pp. 55–69.

rivalled his ancient predecessors) defined it; it could be legitimated by the command of a high-status figure like a prince or pope, magnate or bishop; its utility was justified by the agreement that history was not only a piety towards one's ancestors' memory but also an example for the future; and it was further authorized when the writer could claim either to have been an eye-witness or to have had access to reputable eye-witnesses or to authorized earlier texts.[26]

This is not the place to explore either the transmission of the historical heritage of antiquity or its establishment of a range of *topoi* but perhaps one or two reminders may suffice.[27] One part of the inheritance was a style of presentation; this has been described as part of Roman rhetoric, which analyzed literature, or stories, less for their own sake, than as they supported the moving and persuading of an audience in order to argue a case. The kinds of narration which orators such as Cicero described were means of defending deeds done, or deeds which might have been done. Plausibility, therefore, is forensic, and part of what makes a narration plausible is – once again – the trust which the speaker creates for his ostensible truthfulness.[28] In a court of law, or government, 'historia' is a plausible account of something which actually happened.[29] But in court making something appear to be a plausible account of what actually happened can be just as important, and Quintilian is only one rhetorician to suggest that imputing opinions to someone absent is a useful technique.[30] 'Plausibility' must, of

---

26 See Roger Ray, 'Bede's *Vera Lex Historiae*', *Speculum* 55 (1980), 1–21 and, on the rhetorical heritage, his 'The Triumph of Greco-Roman Rhetorical Assumptions in Pre-Carolingian Historiography' in *The Inheritance of Historiography*, ed. Christopher Holdsworth and T. P. Wiseman (Exeter, University of Exeter Press, 1986), 67–84.

27 See Alastair Minnis, *Medieval Theory of Authorship* (2nd ed., Philadelphia, University of Pennsylania Press, 1988), and *Chaucer and Pagan Antiquity* (Cambridge, D. S. Brewer, 1982). I have analyzed this inheritance and its augmentation in *Truth and Convention in the Middle Ages: Rhetoric, Reality, and Representation* (Cambridge, Cambridge University Press, 1991), where a detailed discussion can be found in chapt. 2. See my 'Telling the Truth . . .', from which this section is adapted.

28 Cicero was one of many to assert that the good orator *is* a good man. There is a parallel in the history of historians' prefaces which insists that no historian worthy of the name would deviate from the truth.

29 This is stressed repeatedly in classical texts, e.g. Cicero, *De Inventione* I.xix (on *narratio* – but see *De Legibus* I.i–iii for the distinction, in another context, between history and poetry); *Ad Herennium* I.viii; Quintillian *Institutio Oratorio*, X.i.31–4, 73–5, 101–12). These lessons were repeated by medieval encyclopedists, if out of context. Janet Coleman insists upon the distinction between the generalizing powers of the poet and the particular exemplification of the historian in medieval thought, but it is part of my contention that the apparently particular depends upon and underwrites generalization about human possibility. See her *Ancient and Medieval Memories: studies in the reconstruction of the past* (Cambridge, Cambridge University Press, 1992), chapt. 1.

30 This is a subject explored in detail by ancient historians, who are agreed that rhetoric

---

course, vary with the times; dragons and fire-proof ointments might well lose plausibility with time. Nevertheless, they retain a hypothetical status (sometimes called 'argumentum' in rhetoric texts) which, like a heuristic device, allows the rehearsal of a possible past.

If content is one obvious way of recognizing 'history', since its events are those remote from our memory, another part of the inheritance designates the variety of texts categorized as 'histories' from Livy to Statius. The double definition is inscribed early: 'history' is a narrative of something which happened, or a story which is told *like* stories which happened. By convention, the focus is upon public events which concern the political life of cities or nations; that is, questions of power, expansion, and continuity: supremely, war. Confusion over whether something happened or not is a problem, but it does not imply that the problem cannot be solved; cannot be solved in all instances; cannot ever be solved. And even if it turns out to be true that there will always be a spectre of doubt, that does not discredit the attempt to efface doubt, any more than the impossibility of speaking like a native stops one trying to speak another language as best one can. There is, throughout these texts, a *deferral* of authority which may be expressed in apparently opposite assertions: some texts imply that although doubt and uncertainty may be the fate of the text currently being read, nevertheless authoritative texts do exist, even if elsewhere. Others claim that they have resolved the uncertainties of other texts. The deferential voice of the particular historian assumes that somewhere 'truth' exists and 'truthful' renditions exist. This also presupposes rational analysis as a means of distinguishing the plausible and possible from the 'fabulous'. A 'known' historical account, such as Dares', which includes apparently supernatural power, is a special challenge to these distinctions. The assertion that poets cloaked wisdom in fables could be extended to the interpretation of ancient histories: where a historian represented something implausible (because against possibility in Nature), perhaps he was cueing the

triumphed, and oratorical display became an end in itself, that is, the sophists were more influential than the philosophers. This helps account for the popularity of *prosopopeia*, practice exercises in inventing speeches for a particular voice. See, for example, the essays collected in M. I. Finley, *The Use and Abuse of History* (London, Hogarth Press, 1986); Nancy Streuver, *The Language of History in the Renaissance* (Princeton, Princeton University Press, 1970); and, magisterially, Arnaldo Momigliano, *The Classical Foundations of Modern Historiography* (Berkeley and Los Angeles, University of California Press, 1990). For an argument of another kind, which begins from the idea of a 'plasmatic narrative', a narrative which can be moulded within the assumptions of historical presentation, see Ben Edwin Perry's Sather Classical Lectures, *The Ancient Romances* (Berkeley and Los Angeles, University of California Press, 1969) e.g. pp. 74–5.

narrative to indicate a veil, a deliberate difficulty of interpretation. That would in effect elevate the importance of the implausible. Multiple styles of reading might be *incumbent* upon the alert interpreter.

Neither the plain nor the embellished styles, neither one genre nor another, guarantee truth or falsehood, not in their terms nor in our own. Teasing out what constituted those terms is peculiarly difficult, because of the pervasive ironies by which words suggest that they may not mean what they say, and because the terms themselves were manipulated in different circumstances by different kinds of writers in pursuit of arguments or ideas of their own, including the ambiguities which fictions-in-the-guise-of-history allow readers to enjoy. That is, jokes, parodies, pastiches, and fictions all depend upon sliding terms, gaps in delineation, and unclear demarcations between semantic fields and literary genres (insofar as that is a useful term for the middle ages). Medieval 'ancient history', because it was *so* long ago (remote from our memories), as well as *so* far away, allowed (and invited) a greater degree of invention than recent history could do. The invention which supplemented surviving classical accounts belonged to the idea of *amplificatio*, the expansion necessary to fleshing out any account, and its affiliation to a rhetorical hypothetical was one of the ways of avoiding 'harder' categories. Nothing, or very little, was likely to hang on the amplification of an ancient historical account, be it of Alexander and his conquests, or Jason and his. 'Very little', however, might turn out to be the subject of history itself.

The great medieval historians – among them Bede, Notker, Orderic Vitalis, William of Malmesbury, Froissart – were all aware of the author's shaping voice and hand and crafted their prose accordingly to create convincing, verisimilar accounts of the past, within conventions that are broadly classed as rhetorical, from the invention, or finding, of a subject, to its presentation through the medium of familar *topoi*, in the style recognizable as the historical.[31] Whether or not the accounts were also veritable, under whose description, is another question.[32] They co-existed not only with historians about whose works doubts were expressed, but also with

---

[31] See Nancy Partner, 'Making up lost time: writing on the writing of history', *Speculum* 61 (1986) 90–117. Many of these issues have been explored by Bernard Guenée in a series of essays most easily accessible in his *Politique et Histoire au Moyen Age: recueil d'articles sur l'historiographie médiévale (1956–1981)* (Paris, Publications de la Sorbonne, 1981), esp. 'Y a-t-il une historiographie médiévale?' (pp. 205–20) and 'L'Historien par les mots' (pp. 221–38).

[32] The phrase is a translation of 'le vrai et le vraisemblable', which were the terms of a seventeenth-century debate among literati for whom Corneille's *Le Cid* became the focus of arguments over whether something ostensibly 'historical' could be used if it appeared implausible.

court historians whose long verse compositions claimed to be authorized narratives for men and women who expected to be entertained in the vernacular. The twelfth-century vogue for ancient history, in the form of highly embellished ancient historical fiction, took as its point of departure texts such as Dares' and Justin's which appeared to be authorized, and expanded the acceptable 'subject of history'.

As I have argued in *Truth and Convention*, the preliminary step for modern interpretation is to recover tacit assumptions about the expression of meaning, what have been called the conventions of unspecified invention. So familiar were many of these *topoi* that they needed no signal. Invention began with the choice of words to convey an argument, but spread to include much more. Speeches are persuasive because dramatic.[33] Dramatic representations might be written with the assumption that their readers would recognize them as being speeches written to move and persuade, as arguments, and therefore as essentially hypothetical, neither as representations of what a character actually said, nor as conveying that character's 'character'. This is why speeches, for so long, appear so little the spontaneous outpouring of the human heart, and so much the variation on pattern-books of conventional speech-making. Such texts seem to be neither acceptable history, nor inviting poetry. Yet they offer keys to contemporary opinion on a wide range of topics.

There are two arguments to follow: the truth-status of history, and the impact created by the style of history. Readers looking for sources need to avoid an anachronistic approach to medieval historiography as a decodable source of 'facts'.[34] On this kind of modern interpretation of medieval historiography, it appears self-evident that in the course of the western Middle Ages many so-called (and self-styled) historians had 'literary' or 'romance' 'values', and that they embellished their narratives; nevertheless, an astute modern historian develops a sense, through years

---

[33] This approach, by asking what controlled or legitimated invention, avoids the 'hard' distinctions between 'history' and 'fiction' from which, to take an influential example, Hayden White begins. There is as serious a danger of anachronism in positing universal categories such as 'romance' or 'tragedy' as in 'history' or 'fiction', as evidenced in his 'Historical Text as Literary Artifact', *Tropics of Discourse: essays in cultural criticism* (Baltimore and London, 1978). Two recent discussions of these problems are particularly useful for *modern* historians: Richard T. Vann, 'Louis Mink's Linguistic Turn' in *History and Theory* 26 (1987) 1–14, which is devoted to historiographical questions, and Andrew P. Norman, 'Telling it Like it Was: Historical Narratives in their Own Terms', *History and Theory* 30 (1991), 119–35. Although all these essays concentrate on post-sixteenth-century history, their analysis of the terms of the debate put White's arguments in perspective.

[34] These issues are discussed in similar terms in Gabrielle Spiegel, *Romancing the Past*, chapt. 5, esp. p. 372 n. 1 on the problem of 'fact'.

of dealing with the narratives and the documents, of who can be trusted under what circumstances. 'History', (like perspective in the old accounts of the development of western painting), remains a known category towards which certain medieval historians aspired. That is, we acknowledge that the cultures are different, but believe that we can use their writing in our own ways, which will uncover 'what really happened'.[35] We can discern the truth, our truth. The trouble with this is the double assumption that not only do we know what we mean by 'truth', but also that we simply trust some medieval historians to recognize and tell it. Despite all the suspicion modern historians try to muster, they seldom apply literary or rhetorical analysis to those medieval narratives about the past; they are constantly susceptible to the illusion that 'realism', especially when that of a self-proclaimed or apparent eye-witness, appears precisely to be a guarantee of truth. In this, of course, they are remarkably like medieval historians themselves.[36]

Further, one generation's 'realism' is the next generation's tedious stylization. For medieval readers, the more a sequence appears to conform to expected concatenations of events, the more plausible (rather than the less, because stereotyped or clichéd) its plot appears. While conformity to expectations of what heroes (or women) do, underwrites their depictions in 'historical' texts, *difference* opens a range of possibilities which remind readers of the distance of the pre-Christian past. That sequence of events (which may or may not be plausible) necessarily introduces historical agents whose behaviour creates possible actions that themselves contest acceptable actions: whether immorality, in the behaviour of Jason or Aeneas, to take two crude examples, was rewarded or not. Arguments about the value of history arise from their status as moral example of a special kind: moral example believed to be true. The plausible, moving,

---

[35] The contemporary debate over the status of historical 'objectivity' and its textual representations is well-known. To the historians of nineteenth- and twentieth-century Europe one must add such medievalists as Gabrielle Spiegel, whose 'History, Historicism, and the Social Logic of the Text in the Middle Ages', *Speculum* 65 (1990), pp. 59–86 is a timely reminder of the insistent changes in cultural spaces which studies of the earlier periods emphasize.

[36] And this helps to explain why the study of medieval ancient histories, those preliminaries to so many chronicles, has only recently preoccupied historians. This lack in modern historiography was remarked by Walter Goffart in his *Narrators of Barbarian History* (Princeton, Princeton University Press, 1987). Spiegel's new, ground-breaking study, which concentrates upon the narratives about Caesar in thirteenth-century France, *Romancing the Past*, suggests how fruitful such attention can be. As she elegantly demonstrates, these texts are a rich source for the study of medieval attitudes to the past. In what follows I shall stress a kind of experimentation in a historical 'place' exotic by time, and the creation of stereotypes about women.

'realistic' example which claims a connection with what actually happened has, therefore, a special status, if a contestable one. Well-written (i.e. like 'poetry') history rivalled philosophy as a source of *exempla* for medieval readers. From Plato to Caxton, this great defence of secular writing is also a hostage to criticism, because the reader is free to assess and interpret the actions included. No moralist has ever succeeded in controlling the emotional reaction of readers.

Although in historical prefaces the moral implications of arguments over history were articulated in binary terms, historical writing was not a matter of *either* a true report *or* a falsification. We might succumb to the temptation to follow the terms of the medieval historians themselves, and posit that the easiest delineation of an idea like 'truth' in medieval *history* would be to contrast it with its obvious opposite, and that ideas of falsehood or forgery would provide us with limiting cases. Modern scholarship has attended to various aspects of the problem of defining 'telling the truth/lying', 'genuine/specious'. So, after all, did Augustine, who wrote two essays about mendacity; and Dante famously put the fraudulent in the eighth *bolgia* of hell, close to the Father of lies himself. As ever with binary divisions, the first term immediately constrains our observations, the polarity hardens the opposition and excludes third (or fourth) terms which may bear upon all the available definitions. When we look closely, the subjectivity of 'false' has to be taken into account: false for whom, to whose advantage, under what circumstances?

Nevertheless, let us follow this line for a moment. For taxonomies and morphologies of falsification we are indebted to recent work by scholars such as Umberto Eco and Giles Constable, who have studied the range and breadth of literary and historical forgery in the western Middle Ages, and who have both emphasized the subjectivity of the status of truth or falsehood for medieval interpreters.[37] Medieval laws and literatures recognized the offence of deliberate deceit by means of creating, claiming, or substituting fakes or copies in place of genuine or authentic articles for the sake of individual gain. The penalty for counterfeiting money suggests the

---

[37] 'Non è la falsificazioné singola che maschera, naconde, confonde, è la quantità delle falsificazioni riconoscibili come tali che funziona come maschera, perché tende a rendere inattendibile ogni verità. Non sappiamo come i medievali, con la loro concezione "ingenua" dell'autenticità, avrebbero giudicato questa nostra concezione cinica della falsificazione non ingenua', Umberto Eco, 'Tipologia della falsificazione', *Fälschungen im Mittelalter* (Hannover, 1988–90) I. 69–82. In 'Forgery and Plagiarism in the Middle Ages', *Archiv für Diplomatik* 29 (1983) pp. 1–41, Giles Constable analyzed the 'fact/fiction' divide mainly in twelfth century history; and his 'Forged Letters in the Middle Ages' considers the use of invented letters as sometimes 'a legitimate literary device', *Fälschungen* V.11–37.

seriousness of the crime: mutilation as a punishment for coining was not an empty threat. (That mutilation is also a horrible pun by which the emasculated body represents the offence reminds us of the allpervasive force of analogy in medieval thought. This, too, is a 'true representation'.) But these are examples where interpretation of a text may have serious and immediate consequences for its readers. In secular law or church doctrine, in inheritance or feudal loyalty, the liens are clear. It may at this point be worth inserting a reminder that texts were of too many kinds to allow for 'a theory of everything', as the physicists now put it. Interpretations varied with their readers, competed with custom, memory, and other texts on many different grounds, and it is rare to find one medieval author accusing another of *deliberate* falsehood or *intentional* dishonesty.[38] A narrative embellished in order to promote a good end would hardly be judged and condemned dismissively as, say, 'lying'. Interpretations by chancery clerks, or clerics inside or outside the cloister, lawyers, magnates were themselves hardly consistent; even the 'categories' by which the texts might be classified implied decisions rather than recognition. Medieval bureaucrats of all kinds supplied invented written evidence from oral tradition and claimed that it was authentic. The subjectivity of the status of 'true' is inescapable, and cannot be unravelled from the status of 'authority'.

It may be objected that whatever the embellishments of a text, a bedrock of truth remains, and remains verifiable through other sources (such as accounts, or archaeological remains, or coins, if not the names of constellations). One need not abolish the 'fact', although even for us 'facts' have become at least more difficult to ascertain, even if we are secure in their status as a possibility.[39] After all, the probability that Caesar crossed the Rubicon is at least as high as is the probability that the man we call William the Conqueror crossed the Channel.

No one event in secular history can by itself guarantee its own status, but, then, we do not interpret individual incidents independently. They are

[38] The *locus classicus* is the outrage caused by Geoffrey of Monmouth's *History of the Kings of Britain*, that marvel of invention. But one cannot fail to remark how many subsequent medieval writers used Geoffrey's accounts, with or without protestations. For an exploration of twelfth-century historians in terms of a theory of memory, see Janet Coleman, *Ancient and Medieval Memories*, chapt 14.

[39] Recent scholarship is opening up this area, e.g. Luis Castro Leiva, 'The Idea of the Fact in English Law' unpubl. Ph.D. dissertation, Cambridge University, 1976. The interplay of law and history has been explored for the early modern period by Donald Kelly, *Foundations of Modern Historical Scholarship* (New York, Columbia University Press, 1970) and J.-Ph. Genet, 'Droit et histoire en Angleterre: la préhistoire de la "revolution historique" ', in *L'Historiographie en occident du Ve au XVe siècle, Annales de Bretagne et des Pays de l'Ouest* 87 (1980), pp. 319–66.

always contextualized, if not by the book in which we read them, then by our knowledge of the world of books, as well as by our experience of the world. In medieval texts, warning 'falsifiers' are often built in to the narratives which offer methodological hints on how to read them. The Daliesque moment at the end of the *Paradiso* (xxxiii) in which we watch the astonishment of Neptune as he looks *up* to see the shadow of the Argo passing overhead presupposes Dante's knowledge of 'Neptune' as a pagan error. But, more profoundly, it is in this moment of beatific vision that Dante encompasses all history in his momentary allusion: his vision comprehends the chronology of everything, from the first quest to the goal of the ultimate, salvific, journey. As a trope for time, the historical status of the Argo disappears into its metaphoric function. The beginning of pagan history implies its own end, as well as the deaths of the pagan gods; in context, it implies the final end.

The idea that there are, at bottom, bedrock facts does not go away; indeed, it is one of the stories we need to tell ourselves while we get on with embellishing them out of recognition. As I shall discuss below, the selection of ostensible 'facts' depends upon a prior picture of how things happen in the world, such as the idea of the Fall of Princes, which may itself stem from a prior distinction between ruler and tyrant, or such apparently inevitable pairings as 'crime and punishment', 'offence and revenge', even 'loyalty or betrayal'. When truths about human nature or human events are known, 'truth' takes on a different colouring. Modern historians of the Middle Ages incline to the view that contemporary audience (or reader) memory set a limit on embellishment, but even memory is notoriously subject to omission, correction, and dispute. If much depends upon which side one is on, so one's 'side' may be constructed by ostensible truths which have suggested lines of debate, affiliation, or even the limits of possibility. It makes a difference who poses the question, as the Wife of Bath's 'What do women most desire?' differs from Freud's 'What does Woman want?' The question is not discredited because Alisoun of Bath is an invention, and the exasperation of Freud's dismissively derogatory 'das Weib' conveys expectations through his tone. Both implicitly raise the problem of female subjectivity. Alison's plural is less essentialist than Freud's singular. In this, medieval ancient history is an exploration, projected onto a plausible past, of a range of moralized (but seldom, as I shall argue below, allegorized) human actions, of ambition licensed by its distance from contemporary Christianity, and the contradictory assertion of a rationalizable past in which a succession of irrational acts are central. It is a kind of travel literature, which embeds an 'exotic' in a past remote from our memory, but recoverable. Its possibilities suggest that it may not be only in memory that that exoticized past is recoverable, but that we may look for it beyond the known world, where it may have survived. Because what has happened may happen, and what has been be, for good or ill.[40]

Medieval Ancient History: Benoît de St-Maure

The historiography of medieval ancient history is a complex web; what concerns me now is the strand which preserved the destructions of Troy, and with the city, the voyage of the Argonauts. The historical precedence, and therefore prestige, of that voyage, established by Dares and Dictys as much as by Orosius, put it at the beginning of many medieval world chronicles.[41]. Into that structure, in the context of its claim to represent historical time, and the sequence of secular events to which the Romans – and their imitators – traced their beginnings, medieval writers let in, with careful stitching, a long series of amplifications. Since medieval writers borrowed the *matter* of their chronicles from a variety of different kinds of texts, according to ideas of decodable, plausible, and extractable historical representation, they regularly included material written in a variety of *styles* of expansion without distinguishing those expansions which belonged to the imagination of individual poets from an astringent and limited history of Troy. That is, an account of the Argonautic voyage and its aftermath which appears to be controlled by the assumptions of 'history', absorbs (in the course of its drive to be comprehensive and preserve 'the whole story') a sequence of inventions, some of which contradict the heroic thrust of the original voyage. They reorient the narrative from its public, male, political focus to one that comprehends the dangers posed by women. In what follows two kinds of medieval history will be of interest. Their mutual influences help explain remarkable changes in the history of the first destruction of Troy.

A fashion for ancient history (as opposed to the routine inclusion of a

---

40 As narratives which helped legitimate crusading voyages, the ancient histories were of use to preachers and travellers. The importance of underlying memory and expectation is part of the argument of Mary B. Campbell, *The Witness and the Otherworld: Exotic European Travel Writing: 400–1600* (Ithaca, Cornell University Press, 1988).

41 The introduction to this history in N. E. Griffin, *Dares and Dictys: An Introduction to the Study of Medieval Versions of the History of Troy* (Baltimore, J. H. Furst, Co., 1907) is still useful. For Dictys, see Stefan Merkle, *Die Ephemeris belli Troiani des Diktys von Kreta*, Studien zur Klassichen Philologie, 44 (Frankfurt am Main, P. Lang, 1989) and his article in *Die deutsche Trojaliteratur des Mittelalters und der Frühen Neuzeit*, ed. H. Brunner (Wiesbaden, Reichert, 1990).

classical prologue in Latin universal history) is associated with the twelfth-century historians who wrote for the Anglo-Norman court of the Angevin kings of England. It emerges as one part of a vogue for secular and vernacular historical texts written to uphold the values and ideals of an increasingly worldly order, interested in tracing its own origins. To the creation of long poems such as *Le Roman de Rou* (which celebrated the founder of the Anglo-Norman House) or vernacular translations of Geoffrey of Monmouth's History of Britain was added a return to Latin sources with the anonymous, and trend-setting, *Roman d'Eneas*, the first of the so-called 'romans antique'.[42] The greatest of these, in size and ambition as well as influence, was the *Roman de Troie* of Benoît de Ste. Maure.[43]

The circumstances of composition of the 'romans antique' are not known. If, as seems probable, they were written for the Angevin court, Benoît's work may have competed with the historiography of Wace, who had already translated Geoffrey of Monmouth, and whose work on a Norman foundation history, the 'Roman de Rou', Benoît may have taken over.[44] Arguments as to the function of these narratives are similarly speculative, and circular, but Benoît's own thematic (and political) concerns appear through his structural repetitions and the interpretative cues

[42] In what follows I am indebted, as all scholars must be, to the elegant discussion in Barbara Nolan, *Chaucer and the traditions of the* Roman Antique (Cambridge, Cambridge University Press, 1992). I agree entirely with her analysis of the intrigue between Jason and Medea, which comes as part of a study of the *Roman de Troie* as an innovative literary 'mode'. There is a fine introduction to the problems raised by 'roman' and the twelfth-century roman by Jacques Le Goff, 'Naissance du roman français' in *La Nouvelle Revue Française*, 238 (1972), pp. 163–73.

[43] I have used the single-base text (BN f.f. fr. 2181) edited by A. Joly, Benoît de Sainte-More et le Roman de Troie, in *Mémoires de la Société des antiquaires de Normandie* 27 (1869–70) rather than the composite text edited by L. Constans, S.A.T.F. (1904–12), which was heavily criticized by Edmond Faral in *Romania* 42 (1913), pp. 88–106. A new edition is a *desideratum*. These texts have been studied mainly by literary scholars interested in the growth of romance. M. Wilmotte, 'Observations sur le *Roman de Troie*', *Le Moyen Age* 27 (1914), pp. 93–119; Jean Frappier, 'Remarques sur la peinture de la vie et des héros antiques dans la littérature française du XIIe au XIIIe siècle', in *L'Humanisme médiéval dans les littératures romanes du XIIe au XIVe siècle*, ed. A. Fourrier (Paris, Klincksieck, 1964), pp. 13–51; R. M. Lumiansky, 'The Story of Troilus and Briseida according to Benoît and Guido', *Speculum* 29 (1954) and his 'Structural Unity in Benoît's *Roman de Troie*' *Romania* 79 (1958), pp. 410–24; Rosemarie Jones, *The Theme of Love in the Romans d'Antiquité* (London, 1972). *Eneas* is the main focus in Jean-Charles Huchet, *Le Roman Médiéval* (Paris, Presses Universitaires de France, 1984). On Benoît himself see G. A. Backmann, *Trojaroman und Normanchronik: Die Identität der beiden Benoît und die Chronologie ihrer Werke* (Munich, Max Hueber Verlag, 1965).

[44] See Emmanuele Baumgartner, 'Ecrire disent-ils. A propos de Wace et de Benoît de Ste. Maure', in *Figures de l'Ecrivain* (Actes du colloque d'Amiens, mars 1988) (Amiens, Presse Universitaire de Picardie, 1989).

he gives the reader, above all with flashes forward which indicate the later consequences of particular incidents (without, however, ever foreclosing on interpretation of the current incidents).[45] That the narrative assumes a certain distance because it is the exotic recital of ancient history offers a range of interpretative possibilities to medieval readers. As Barbara Nolan astutely summarizes his enterprise,

> In an important sense, Benoît's entire poem may be viewed as a complex of causes or arguments, both public and private. Again and again, the audience are called upon to judge the moral actions of the pagan characters in a variety of specific (and for them, hypothetical) situations. Their final judgment will encompass the largest questions about human conduct and ethical value: public honor and reputation *versus* private passionate love; the roles of prudence, reason, and rhetoric in the rule of nations and the making of history; the place of Fortune; the changeable character of women; the transient nature of the world's goods. These questions, as they are presented in *Troie*, bear precisely and specifically on *secular* aristocratic life. The poem as a whole invites its public to examine those values which are especially appropriate to the good moral life of medieval rulers.[46]

Benoît opened his long poem with a spirited (and conventional) defence of the value of history, and of knowledge generally, which Solomon tells us it is our responsibility to preserve and continue, for good deeds inspire readers to emulate them. Like Geoffrey of Monmouth before him, Benoît took this moral imperative as a legitimation of his additions. First, he rationalized his sources according to unstated, but common, criteria of plausibility, verisimilitude, and moral example; second, he expanded, adding 'missing' details from his reading in other texts (and other types of texts); third, he modernized his material, transforming his pagan subjects

---

[45] The hypothesis that the behaviour approved in these long narratives was a strategic encouragement of courtliness by clerics who were attempting to civilize their masters, meets the objections that there are serious contradictions between the secular values which the text celebrates and the Christianity of the Angevin court. Benoît's approval is harder to pin down than one might think. See C. Stephen Jaeger, *The Origins of Courtliness: Civilizing Trends and the Formation of Courtly Ideals 939–1210* (Philadelphia, University of Pennsylvania Press, 1985), chapt. 12. Recently, Emmanuèle Baumgartner has argued for a more utopian projection of an idealized city of love, functioning as a societal fiction, which Benoît directed to his patron, Eleanor of Aquitaine, in Emmanuèle Baumgartner, 'Benoît de Sainte-Maure et le modèle troyen', *Modernité au Moyen Age: le défi du passé*, ed. Brigitte Cazelles and Charles Méla (Geneva, Droz, 1990), 101–11. Nolan's emphasis on the multi-vocality of literature is important here.

[46] *Chaucer and the* Roman Antique, p. 70. Nolan's superb analysis of the *romans antique* has emphasized Benoît's innovations; I shall try to supplement her account by contextualizing some of his continuities with historical writing.

into idealized knights and ladies. In the vernacular, he included all the set pieces, the *topoi*, of historical literature: antecedents, physical descriptions, descriptions of cities, armings of knights, analyses of character and motive through agonizing decisions and defences; individual actions and scenes of battle. Above all, he turned his long poem into a carefully structured sequence of repeated patterns within a chronological narrative.[47] The most important of these is the pattern of betrayal which he focusses not on male, public, political events, but on four love intrigues. This has been taken to suggest that his audience contained women, and that some of them were powerful women; that the occasion for the recital, or performance, was an elite court of considerable literary, especially rhetorical, sophistication, and that he expected the courtiers to discuss the issues he raised. But it might equally well be argued that it is less threatening to focus discussions of betrayal and disruption on women (as Pindar shifted his male/male political discussion to the eternal verities of male/female conflict); it displaces anxiety over male responsibility onto the gender expected to be guilty while allowing the thematic issues full range. Like Pindar's displacements (and unlike the epics of revolt), Benoît's rewriting turns attention towards a partisan and potentially woman-blaming (although not misogynistic) analysis. There is, in addition, as much as with a short text such as *Gawain and the Green Knight*, a manifest focus on the narrative, while it introduced difficult – and perhaps irresolvable – thematic content in its plot-situations. It is history as tragedy, emphatically appealing to known patterns of human events, above all injury and revenge, loyalty and betrayal.[48]

Jason betrays Medea, who is the daughter of a hostile king; Briseida betrays Troilus for an enemy of Troy; Achilles is betrayed by his love of an enemy, although he has, ironically enough, tried to make peace; and Paris and Helen, faithful as they are to each other, each betray their city, and, of

[47] His sources include not only other 'romans antique', but also such recent successes as 'Piramus' and 'Tristan'; see Faral's review of Constans' edition, *Romania* 42 (1913), pp. 88–106. See also J. L. Levenson, 'The Narrative Format of Benoît's *Roman de Troie*', *Romania* 100 (1979), pp. 54–70 on the importance of deliberation (represented anachronistically as medieval councils) in the rhythm of the narrative.

[48] When Walter Benjamin identifies this connection as one of the sources of German baroque tragic drama, he emphasizes the paradox that the salvation drama of the whole Christian history nevertheless contains the tragedy of tyrant, martyr, and intriguer. *Origins of German Tragic Drama*, trans. John Osborne (London, New Left Books, 1977), pp. 76–8. The medieval elision of legendary figures (closer to the Greek gods) with human historical time might, in Benjamin's terms, be taken as a necessary anti-tragic circumstance, especially as there can be none of the atoning sacrifices which open the way to the establishment of new communities that he identified as integral to the tragic death.

THE HISTORY OF JASON

course, destroy hundreds of innocent lives. This shift to the love interests may appear to be the triumph of romance over history, but in the more flexible generic conventions of the Middle Ages, Benoît's book is a brilliant modification of history as a 'serious entertainment': a moralized rhetorical account in the course of which his expansions explore (as it were by stealth) precisely those public and political moral problems which might be treated directly in other kinds of book.[49] One need hardly emphasize the dangers of foreigners, especially when they are young women. The love-intrigues are implicated in competing political worlds: even when the lovers agree, those worlds conspire to destroy them. The four situations ring changes upon the possibilities of love in countries at war, and to restrict our view of the loves as due to the presence of women who were interested in 'courtliness' is to mistake Benoît's intentions. It is Benoît's great success to illustrate without explicitly drawing the lessons.

But nothing of this is apparent as the plot begins. A reader alert to the shifts from Dares may assume that Benoît's expansions are the kind of *amplificatio* which supplies from other texts that which is lacking. Yet, if we consider the connection of the Argonautic story to that of Troy, we may recall that it was Laomedon's refusal of hospitality which provoked a punitive expedition and the first destruction of the city. Benoît's interest is in the cause: Laomedon's fear of the young Greeks who have arrived unannounced on his shores. Benoît assures us that they had no aggressive intentions, and that they did no harm; he gives no explanation for Laome-don's mistaken judgement, and lets Hercules, Jason's companion, threaten revenge for the insult which forbids them to remain. The word repeated again and again is 'engin', which refers to that cunning which no ruler can be without. Pelias has it, when he anticipates Jason's threat to his throne. Medea has it, as she thinks through what is necessary to protect Jason from the fire-breathing bulls and herself from the risks Love makes her run. It is a kind of cunning intelligence.

Benoît's craft as a narrator is partly revealed in what he does not say; he works by juxtaposition and repetition rather than by explicit commentary on the events of the text. He cannot have known Herodotus, yet in his own interpretation of the history there is not only much of Herodotus's urban-ity, there is a strong perception of the pattern of abduction and counter-abduction, of injury and revenge, which lies at the root of the Trojan War. His knowledge of the *Eneas* is clear: he has borrowed the love-intrigue of Lavine for his own Medea, who watches Jason set off for his trial from a

---

[49] The phrase is Nancy Partner's. See her *Serious Entertainments: The Writing of History in Twelfth-Century England* (Chicago, University of Chicago Press, 1977).

tower, full of assurances to herself that she loves him 'de fine amor' (1850). The heights of courtly loving, however, do not occur in a political vacuum.

Multi-vocal, as well as multi-focal, Benoît's narrative begins where one might think, where Dares begins, by following the Argonauts, whose arrival in Colchis appears as a splendid procession. It is only slowly that the narrative point of view shifts to Medea, who has seen, and fallen in love with, their leader, Jason. It is plausible that the judgement of a young ingenue should be overcome by love, and thus Benoît's own narrative seduction works on his reader without reservation. Like Lavine, but unlike Dido, Medée is surprised by her emotional turbulence. He makes Medea the only child of her father, thus simplifying the history, by writing Medea's first murder out of it, and attributes those qualities of mind to her which can be used for good or ill. The section of the text in which the two become lovers is almost entirely told in 500 lines of dialogue or straight narration of what Medea did or thought; the narrator disappears behind the narration. Although Medea is Ovid's skilful sorceress, she is also the fair maid of tradition, rich as the bed which contains her:

> El lit se coche la pucele,
> Qui molt est sage et gente et bele,
> Bien estoit digne de tel lit,
> Qu'onques nus hom sa per ne vit. (lines 1555–8)

> [The maiden, who is wise and noble and beautiful, lies down
> in the bed. She was well worth of such a bed, whom no man
> had ever seen her equal.]

We might think of this as the height of temptation were it not that the narrative is following Medea's point of view here; she is as worried about her honour as she ought to be, and insists that Jason swear an oath to guarantee his promise of marriage. His terms are those feudal categories which assume a single loyalty, unshared by any other.

> Dame, gie sui li chevaliers,
> Qui vostre quites sans partie
> Serra toz les jorz de sa vie.
> Vos prie et requier dolcement
> Que'l recevez si ligement,
> Que nol jor mès chose ne face
> Que vos seit grief, ne vos desplace. (lines 1588–94)

> [Lady, I am the knight who will be yours – freely and indivis-
> ibly – all the days of his life. I ask and request you gently to

accept him so utterly [i.e. as her vassal] that he never does
anything to cause your grief or displeasure.]

Readers of other romances, including Chaucer's *Troilus and Criseyde*, will
recognize this as the courtly lover's fealty oath. Medea makes Jason swear
on an image of one of the gods (1611) to be her loyal lord and lover. Only
now does Benoît flash forward:

> Jason issi li otreia,
> Mes envers lie se parjura,
> Covenant ne lei ne li tint;
> Espoir por ço li mesavint.
> Mes gie n'ai or de ço que faire,
> Del reconter, ne del retraire,
> Assez i a d'el a traitier,
> Ne vos voil or plus ennoier.   (lines 1621–28)

> Here Jason consented, but he perjured himself to her: he
> kept neither law nor oath – perhaps that is why she came to
> grief. But I have nothing to do now with telling this nor
> relating it. There is plenty to be said about other matters, and
> I do not wish to irritate you any longer.

Benoît puts them into bed together, because, he says, they both desired it;
so there is no blame apportioned.[50] And yet, of course, they are both at
great fault, since Jason is betraying his host and Medea her father and lord.
Such a clandestine marriage offends the order of society.

Jason's impossible tasks require courage, and he completes them well,
aided by Medea's fireproof ointment and magic ring. His great companion, Hercules, waits on the shore to celebrate his return (an association
which is important to Benoît for Hercules' later revenge expedition, but
also important for Benoît's imitators, who found their friendship there). If
the king is distraught at Jason's success, the anonymous crowds believe
that the gods must have intended it, because no unaided man could otherwise have 'engignié' such a victory. But 'engin' is not enough, and never
guarantees power and continued control. Although Benoît leaves the lovers celebrating for a month, he tells us

> Grant folie fist Medea:
> Trop a le vassal aamé,
> Quant por lui let son parenté,

---

[50] Cp. Nolan, pp. 96–102. Some of my textual readings differ slightly from Nolan's, because I follow Joly's text.

Son père et sa mère et sa gent;
Puis l'en avint molt malement.
Car si com li auctors reconte
Puis la lessa a molt grant honte:
Elle l'ot gari de la mort,
Puis la lessa; si fist grant tort.
Trop d'engingna, ço peise moi,
Ledement li menti sa foi.
Les Deu vers lui s'en corocièrent
Qui trop asprement la vengièrent.
N'en dirai plus, ne nel voil faire
Car trop ai grant ovre à retraire.[51] (2014–28)

[Medea made a great mistake when she loved the vassal too
much and left her family for him, her father, her mother, and
her people. Her fortune then turned to great evil, for, as the
author says, he later left her most shamefully, she who had
saved him from death. Then he left her; he did a great wrong.
I regret to say that he deceived her, and despicably betrayed
her. The gods were aroused against him and avenged her
most terribly. I shall say no more and wish to say no more,
for I have a very long tale to tell.]

There is nothing of the lovers' clandestine escape, yet there is, nonetheless,
a textual deferral which connects this story to events which can be read
elsewhere. Benoît signals these by retreating behind the authority of Dares,
who tells no more of Jason (though he gives no indication of his earlier
dependence upon Ovid and the *Eneas*), but moves on to the punishment
of Laomedon's discourtesy (lines 2045–62).

Among the repetitions which one might miss at this early stage is the
theft of Oetes' gold in addition to his Golden Fleece. The association of
woman and treasure here is much less equivocal than it will later be, when,
for example, Paris's followers pillage the temple from which they carry off
Helen. The climax of these associations will be the theft of the Palladium,
the female image upon whose possession the safety of Troy depends.
Thefts which Benoît's readers may have greeted with unreflective pleasure
at a first occurence become more and more problematic – and nothing
explicitly asks them to reconsider their own experiences of sacking, although, in an Angevin court, there might be a reminiscence of the experi-

---

51 Joly's text is inferior to Constans' at lines 2021–2, where Constans reads 'Elle l'aveit
guardé de morir/ Ja puis ne la deüst guerpir'. Like 'engin', 'guerpir' [abandon, reject] is
one of Benoît's important repetitions. It has already appeared several times in this
section, as Medea's anticipated fear of deception, cheating.

ence of the voracious crusaders. Benoît's vocabulary is consistent, building from the beginning those insoluble problems of 'engin' and physical force, loyalty and betrayal (through 'engin' and its failures), the desire for glory and for riches (the wealth of the cities is constantly emphasized) which are the themes of history.

As Barbara Nolan has pointed out, the *romans antique* introduced a gendered shift in the *kinds* of rhetorical argument which inform the public debates of traditional historical works. When women speak they may be offering new ways of thinking about public events: for example, they may argue that love may over-rule political agreement, as in the *Roman de Thebes* or the *Eneas*.[52] We may think of this as a vernacular contribution to a new kind of historical writing, or of the contribution of history to a new kind of vernacular fiction; whether we emphasize romance or history will depend upon our context and definitions.[53]

But a version which includes extended direct speech, especially in the form of *suasoriae*, those internal debates over a course of action yet to be taken, opens the text to interpretation by inscribing precisely that self-reflexive interpretation *by the characters* within the text. By giving the word to women, in contexts of decision, Benoît contributed – perhaps unconsciously – to an important shift in literary representation whose roots may be traced back to Dido, and to Augustine's tears over her. He projected the texts' larger problems (of loyalty and betrayal, of the behaviour of guests, of the legitimacy of rulers and rule) onto women, who ought to be the most private of citizens; he showed those private citizens as participating in public events, which they see from their own points of view. He emphasized not only the role, but the possibility, of female subjectivity by putting his sequence of female agents into dilemmas in the course of which they express opinions. To stress this innovation (not just on Benoît's part, of course) may appear to belabour the obvious contributions of imaginative literature, but the very idea of imaginative literature is one of those anachronisms which we forget at our peril. The dangerousness of Benoît's creations is nowhere more criticized than in the interpretation of Guido delle Colonne, and it is in his criticism of Benoît that we can most see Guido's own emphasis on women's place.

---

52 Lee Patterson, 'Virgil and the Historical Consciousness of the Twelfth Century: the *Roman d'Eneas* and *Erec et Enide*', in his *Negotiating the Past: The Historical Understanding of Medieval Literature* (Madison, University of Wisconsin Press, 1987), pp. 157–95.

53 Michel Zink, 'Une Mutacion de la conscience littéraire: Le langage romanesque à travers des exemples français du XIIe siècle', *Cahiers de Civilisation Médiévale* 24 (1981), pp. 3–27, discusses this question in the early romances-as-history.

But it is less Benoît's own poem itself than the adaptations of it that transmitted Benoît's inventions – however controversial – to other medieval writers. There are two interwoven threads: the historical or chronicle and the free-standing history of Troy. Like Geoffrey of Monmouth's fictional history of Britain, which found its way into succeeding historical texts, Benoît's Troy was adapted without comment almost immediately. That familiar medieval attitude to the text which rejected (or pretended to reject) the retelling of the events (yet preserved the events themselves) depended on authorial confidence that it was possible to separate invention from core material. The idea that one could recognize truth through verisimilitude and plausibility simply ensured that many of Benoît's imaginative successes came to be thought of as true.

The story of Benoît's clandestine authority is in part a chapter of accidents, but it is a chapter which illustrates the ways in which apparently independent texts might come to reinforce one single original. Call them epitomes, redactions, translations, or adaptations, the textual descendants of Benoît's inventions appeared to underwrite their own status as history because they continued to appear in unimpeachable contexts. Medieval 'ancient histories' connected a series of poems, epitomes, and histories into a connected secular narrative which would give at least a parallel history of the world that could be read alongside Biblical events.

They are a marked feature of the encyclopaedism of the thirteenth century, the same period in which Peter Comestor, among others, collected sacred histories which transposed the events of the Old Testament into a readable account of the Christian past.[54] That soubriquet, the 'eater', suggests the ambition and scope of the 'digest' he produced, and its slightly ironic compliment registers the admiration for (and slight incredulity at) the amount of work the book represents. In its emphasis on voracity, it also locates a desire for textual comprehensiveness which would take account of everything, with which an author might, once and for all, submit the chaos of the past to his own control. One important aspect of this is a narrative control by which, through a sequence of repetitions, human history falls into patterns and parallels to which historians and moralists (insofar as they can be distinguished) could refer. History was coming to seem a sequence of cycles, in parallel, which were winding down towards the end of time. Their *narrative* teleology was to

---

54 The sense of eras is also to be found in the *Ovide moralisé*. There is an acute discussion of Peter Comestor's interlocking chronology in Paule Démats, *Fabula: trois études de mythographie antique et médiévale* (Geneva, Droz, 1973), pp. 89f. Jephtha and Hercules are contemporaries, and the rape of Helen took place shortly thereafter.

teach men how to understand the past in order to understand the present, its never-resolved, ever-contradictory claims upon men's ambition, and their supposed aspiration to despise the world and its works. But the lessons of history, because they focussed on the adventures and glories of high-status characters, always re-emphasized, and legitimated, the very acts and values which, in other kinds of texts, were supposedly under attack. The reader's desire for similar experience, for similar glory, were never proof against the seductions of the world.

History (or, perhaps, 'history') appeared to offer an unassailable status as true tales about that past. That there is 'a' past, which can be acquired, extracted from classical texts, and re-presented in the vernacular, suggests a renewed genealogical impetus among the rising *upper* classes, those members of the medieval elites who came to rule secular states, for whom an unbroken line of descent that could be traced back through Rome to Troy was an important legitimation of their power. Since Jason and Medea are pulled into this ambit, and since the presentation of their story or stories is contextualized by assumptions regarding the patterns indicated by Troy and its fall, some attention to the trajectory of the histories of Troy must occupy us, however briefly. The vicissitudes of Benoît's inventions may stand as an extreme example of the multiplication of ostensibly 'independent' testimonies.

Not only was Benoît's *Roman* often copied, and often in the context of other 'ancient histories', it was much adapted.[55] I shall briefly sketch the fate of these versions, beginning with four translations into French prose. The *Roman de Troie en prose*, in a northern dialect, was followed by a southern French version.[56] The first probably dates from the middle or third quarter of the thirteenth century. By and large, it follows Benoît's poem, but it exhibits a familiar tendency to fill gaps and supply omissions from other texts. To complete Benoît's mere reference to Medea's fate, the author has created a pastiche of the legends of Ariadne and Hypsipyle: his

---

[55] In an important early article Brian Woledge underlined the shift from verse to prose and the new tendency to descry 'accuracy' where rhymes did not need to be found. 'La légende de Troie et le début de la prose française', *Mélanges de linguistique et de littérature romanes offerts à Mario Roques* (Paris, Editions Arts et Sciences, 1950–1953), vol. 2, pp. 313–24.

[56] *Le Roman de Troie en prose*, ed. E. Faral and L. Constans (Paris, Champion, 1922), is incomplete, and no critical apparatus was ever published. The text is based on BNf. f.fr. 1612. Clem C. Williams, Jr. identified another, more expanded, prose translation, in 'A Case of Mistaken Identity: Still Another Trojan Narrative in Old French', *Medium Aevum* 53 (1984), pp. 59–72. This expanded version adapts a series of *Heroïdes*, as for example in BL Royal 20.D.I. See below, Chapter Five. There are similar variants in Trinity College, Cambridge MS 1257, which also contains additions adapted from Ovid's *Heroïdes*. See Spiegel, *Romancing the Past*, pp. 107–17.

Medea is abandoned on a beach (as Theseus abandoned Ariadne in Catullus's *Carmen* 64) pregnant with twins (the fate of Hypsipyle in Statius's *Thebaid*), and Jason returns alone to Pelias. The reinforcement of the Ovidian pattern of seduction and abandonment also appeals to historical repetitions of the fates of unfortunate women. The unfortunate women repeat the association I have already identified, and to which I shall return in the next chapter. Further combinatory texts are to be found in a textual tradition represented by manuscripts such as BNf. f.fr. 24396 and Bodleian Library MS Douce 353, which expand the Argonautic section to give a 'complete' narrative as well as translations of parts of Ovid's *Heroïdes*. The southern translation, independent of the northern version, also survives in several manuscripts; the modern edition is based upon Bodleian Douce 196 (of perhaps 1323), originally written either in southern France or in Italy.[57] It is close to Benoît, whom it names three times. It must have been complete by 1270, because, as Chesney showed, it is the main source for Guido delle Colonne. We can say nothing, in considering the reception of Benoît's inventions, about the belief or scepticism of the majority of his readers. Still another prose adaptation, translated directly from Benoît, is to be found intercalated in a Grail-cycle extant in a late-thirteenth-century manuscript, which suggests the force of the desire for historical comprehensiveness.[58]

The single most influential interpretation of Benoît was, however, not one of the amalgamated ancient histories, but the Latin translation and critical reconceptualization of it in prose by Guido delle Colonne, the *Historia Destructionis Troiae*. Because Guido was the direct source of so many medieval interpretations of the legends (and because of the emphasis of his moral interpretations), it will be convenient to discuss his work in chapter five.

It is, however, clear, that at least two of Benoît's readers took exception to his amplifications, and retranslated Dares in close French prose without interpolations. Such reactions are reminiscent of the reception of Geoffrey of Monmouth's Arthurian extravagances: his survived and flourished, while his critics were little read or heeded.[59]

---

[57] First identified by Kathleen Chesney, 'A neglected prose version of the *Roman de Troie*', *Medium Aevum* 11 (1942), pp. 46–67. Two other manuscripts, BNf. nouv. acq. fr. 9693 and Grenoble 861, appear to represent similar versions.

[58] *Le Roman de Troie en prose (version du Cod. Bodmer 147)*, ed. Françoise Vielliard (Geneva, Fondation Martin Bodmer, 1979), intro. pp. 12–23.

[59] *Li Rommans de Troies: a translation by Jean de Flixecourt, 1262*, ed. G. Hall (University of London unpub. Ph.D. dissertation, 1951). The context of this text is a collection of narratives on the history of France. Jean's objection is 'Pour che que li roumans de Troies rimes contient molt de coses que on ne treuve mie ens u letin, car chis qui le fist

In the early thirteenth century an unknown scribe dedicated a prose adaptation of classical histories to Roger, Chatelain de Lille, which came to be called *L'histoire ancienne jusqu'à César*, in the course of which an abridgement of Dares represents the fall of Troy.[60] But there is a second redaction, which substitutes an early version of a prose epitome of Benoît's poem, and which thereby assures the link between Jason, Troy, and the foundation of Rome.[61] The history of *this* text, which was later copied together with *Li Fait des Romains* (itself a vernacular version of the histories of Livy, Sallust, and Suetonius) connected Benoît's invention to unassailable and apparently independent authorities. It is one more reminder of the penetrability of 'historical' and 'romance' texts, despite the authors' claims that their prose adaptations are somehow more truthful because written in prose: as verse became associated with recognizable fiction, and thus discredited as a medium for true stories, prose defined itself as dedicated to accuracy.

Verse, however, could still be a medium of historical representation. Jehan Malkaraume, who translated the historical books of the Old Testament into French octosyllabic couplets, inserted Benoît's Troy history into the events which took place in the time of Moses. This typically thirteenth-century encyclopaedism created one more place where an uninstructed reader would come upon Benoît's inventions.[62]

ne peust autrement belement avoir trouvee se rime, je, Jehans de Fliccicourt, translatai sans rime l'estoire des Troiens et de Troies du latin en roumans mot a mot ensi comme je le trouvai en un des libres du librairie Monseigneur Saint Pierre de Corbie ... (p. 2). That he knew of the expansions of the Argonautic section, but followed Dares, is also clear (p. 7). The second, discussed by Woledge in the article cited above, n. 55, was made between 1270–1300 by the learned Dominican Geoffrey of Waterford with the help of Servais Copale. Neither translation seems to have had any attention.

60 The text, which has an exceptionally complicated textual history, is still unedited. Bibliographical details are to be found in Brian Woledge, *Bibliographie*, nos. 77–9. The first, and still important, discussion, is Paul Meyer, 'Les premières compilations française d'histoire ancienne', *Romania* 14 (1885), pp. 1–18. The first redaction dates from the 1220s, and its Troy-history is adapted directly from Dares; in the second, the Troy-section follows Benoît. See Spiegel, *Romancing the Past*, pp. 353 n.20.

61 There are parallels between the transmission of these legends and other interpretations of classical history. See M. I. Finley, 'Myth, Memory, and History', *History and Theory* 4 (1964–5), pp. 281–302. On verse moralizations inserted into the text, see Renate Blumenfeld-Kosinski, 'Verse and Prose in the *Histoire ancienne jusqu'à César* (in BNf. 20125)', *Zeitschrift fur Romanische Philologie* 97 (1982), pp. 41–6.

62 The modern edition acknowledges the place and importance of Troy, but omits the whole Troy section in its translation of Exodus, because Jehan reproduced Benoît. *La Bible de Jehan Malkaraume (Ms Paris, Bibl. Nat. F. Fr. 903) (XIIIe/XIVe Siècle)*, ed. J. R. Smeets (Amsterdam, Van Gorcum Assen, 1977–8), note at l.6571. See Jean Bonnard, *Les Traductions de la Bible en vers français au moyen âge* (Paris, Imprimérie Nationale, 1884).

Medieval Ancient History: Christine de Pizan

Benoît's inventions were to be treated as an independent source for the Trojan history by, among others, Christine de Pizan, in her *Mutacion de Fortune*.[63] With *La Mutacion* Christine makes the first of a series of appearances in this book. Time and again we will find that her approach, because of her engagement with male-dominated historiography and the actual position of women, appropriates and recuperates her sources in order to argue that, however tragic the outcome for individual women, they are not the monsters of duplicity, sexual incontinence, and irrationality that they are traditionally accused of being, and she uses history to make her demonstration. She has an unusually strong sense that laws as well as mores change with changes in society, and that before the Christian dispensation, people (she always insists on not taking 'woman' as a special case) made their decisions in ignorance of what is truly right or wrong. It is class or status to which Christine's hierarchical loyalties tend, not gender. She wants the contribution of high-status women to be recognized.

This long work (of 23,636 lines) has often been categorized as a universal history in verse (or mainly in verse, since one section is in prose), perhaps inspired by the *Histoire ancienne*. Although its largest section (lines 8075–22090) is indeed a recital of ancient histories, it is much more than a verse adaptation of any chronicle.[64] Probably begun at the very end of the fourteenth century (Christine mentions, among other

---

63 *Le Livre de la Mutacion de Fortune*, ed. Suzanne Solente, Société des Anciens Textes Français (Paris, Pinard, 1959–64). See also P. G. C. Campbell, *L'Épitre d'Othéa: Étude sur les sources de Christine de Pisan* (Paris, Champion, 1924). Recent work on the progress of Christine's texts is transforming our understanding of her authorship. In a series of articles J. C. Laidlaw has demonstrated her working methods. See, for example, 'Christine de Pizan, the Earl of Salisbury, and Henry IV' *French Studies* 36 (1982), pp. 129–43; 'Christine de Pizan: an Author's Progress', *MLR* 78 (1983), pp. 532–50; 'Christine de Pizan: a Publisher's Progress', *MLR* 82 (1987), pp. 37–75; 'L'unité des "Cent Balades" ', in *The City of Scholars: New Approaches to Christine de Pizan*, ed. Margarete Zimmermann and Dina De Rentis (New York and Berlin, Walter de Gruyter, 1994), pp. 97–106.

64 Joël Blanchard is alert to Christine's seizure of authority by stealth: what seems to be a compilation is, nonetheless, Christine's structure and selection. M. Blanchard has been an important critic of Christine's work, who has indefatigably demonstrated its political content. See his 'Christine de Pizan: Les Raisons de l'histoire' *Le Moyen Age* 92 (1986), pp. 417–36; 'Compilation et légitimation au XVe siècle', *Poétique* 74 (1988), pp. 139–157; and 'Christine de Pizan: tradition, experience, et traduction' *Romania* 111 (1990), pp. 200–35. See also Kevin Brownlee's demonstration of the ways that Christine adapts earlier, male strategies of authority in 'The Image of History in Christine de Pizan's *Livre de la Mutacion de Fortune*', *Contexts: Style and Values in Medieval Art and Literature* (New Haven, Yale French Studies Special Issue, 1991), pp. 44–56.

contemporary events, the overthrow of Richard II by his rebellious subjects), it is unusually autobiographical, allegorical, and moral in its preliminary orientation, as a way of addressing princes on the subject of the city of mankind.[65] Christine presented copies to her royal patrons in January of 1404, which makes it contemporaneous with her other allegories about human political society, including such works as her *Epistre d'Othea* and the *Cité des Dames*.[66] The structure of its seven sections shows the emphasis on the book as something not entirely removed from, yet not to be identified with, a mirror. Its original nature is clear from the outset. She begins with her own experience of Fortune, expressed in an allegorical (but transparent) story of herself and her family on a ship, attacked by Fortune as a storm which injured her life-journey by robbing her of her husband, Estienne de Castel (washed overboard by a wave), and left her to head her own household. The evocation of a double sequence of classical parallels (she rejects the fate of Ceyx and Alcyone and lives on) raises her own status to something approaching the dignity of classical figures whose lives were rendered worthy of note. Fortunately, her father had given her gifts of which Fortune could not deprive her: 'science', learning. Her allegorical father, then, is 'science', and her mother is Nature, in the sense of the great creatrix of the world. This allegory already lifts her to an unusual plane. Christine's preoccupation with gender and rule expresses itself by an uneasy, but fascinating, Ovidian metamorphosis, which claims authority by turning her into a man, capable of rule and writing. Christine achieves this shift of narrative allusion in an original and unanticipated manner, full of risk for a Christian narrator: she juxtaposes in sequence a second set of classical parallels: characters whose sex the gods changed. The daring of this move is to use the fable, clearly fiction, clearly not to be believed, to insist upon *inner* qualities (through allegorical interpretation) which a woman may achieve. 'Science', learning, is a self-reflexive theme throughout the poem: writing it demonstrates her learning, as she

---

65 There are summaries of what is known about Christine's life in Suzanne Solente, 'Christine de Pisan', in the *Histoire Littéraire de France* 40 (1974), pp. 335–422. Enid McLeod's *The Order of the Rose* (London, Chatto and Windus, 1976) is a popular work, but with interesting reflections on Christine's influence in England. Christine also speaks of her own autobiography in, for example her 'L'Avision Christine', ed. Mary Louis Towner (Washington, DC, Catholic University Press, 1932).

66 Christine had a great burst of creative energy, spurred perhaps by need, about 1400–03. The *Epistre d'Othea*, which will be discussed in the next chapter, belongs to that period, as do a number of other moral compilations, including the allegorical *Livre du chemin de lonc estude* as well as the *Mutacion*. They share a profound concern with society and its injustices. See H. D. Loukopoulos, *Classical Mythology in the Works of Christine de Pisan, with an edition of* L'Epistre Othea *from the manuscript Harley 4431* (unpublished Ph.D., Wayne State University, 1977).

describes the lessons of history; reading it will bestow learning upon the princes to whom it is addressed, from the example of her own persever-ance and participation in the rule of a family, to the more public historical examples she describes. Throughout Christine's career she preached – by example even more than by precept – her vision of a just society which treasures its members. In fictional city after city, she illustrates those gen-der-neutral virtues to which all persons may aspire, by which justice reigns and humanity flourishes. In Sections two and three she describes Fortune's Castle, as a walled city surrounded by gates and streets and the fates of those who live in it, which becomes in turn an Estates Satire, criticizing the faults of men in power, of whom she excepts those who have learned from Philosophy, and Philosophy and learning form the beginning of section four.[67] Almost casually, and in passing, she has stressed the virtue of women (6617–6674). Then there is a curious transition from knowledge to the foundation of the world, the fall, early civilizations, and a summary of the history of Babylon and, in prose, that of the Jews. When she returns to her theme, she begins with a disquisition on Covetousness. Section five follows ancient history to Athens; six is a parallel recapitulation of the history of the Amazons and of Troy; seven describes the Romans and Alexander the Great. There is nothing innocent about this sequence. Her historical examples, modestly disguised as the compiler's craft, also correct a masculine vision which excluded and blamed women in all times and places. Far from being a rhymed universal history meant as an easy or attractive read, the *Mutacion de Fortune* is a stealthy demonstration of the compiler's art.

The compiler's options are complex. Christine can change the story by rewriting it (a) on her own (i.e. by changing the facts, suppressing them, recasting them, offering new interpretations of motive), or (b) by choosing one version over others (and suppressing the rejected ones); she can reproduce the story in the old way but reinterpret it or offer counter-

---

[67] Christine seems usually to have depended upon translations of classical texts. Her 'Ovid' is the *Ovide moralisé*, which will be discussed at greater length in the next chapter. She has the now-familiar view of *poets* that poetry may correspond to true history, and that one may use other poet's narratives in historical writing:

> Les poëtes, qui l'aviserent,
> en poësie deviserent
> Ses fais; Ovide en recorde,
> Qui a la vraye histoire accorde
> A parler selon methafore.
> Tout ne pense a recorder ore! (13913–17)

[Poets who knew about it recorded his deeds in poetry. Ovid, who speaks metaphorically in agreement with the true history, recalls this. I do not think of recalling all of it now.]

96

examples (as fickleness of men against inconstancy of women); reorient it (by seeing it from another character's point of view, absorbing it in another story); recontextualize it, (a) by its position in a sequence or (b) by the permutations available by contrast to other stories told in the same sequence. She uses style to achieve some of her effects: register, metaphor, semantic field – all the resources of poetry in order to change the tone.

One brief example merits attention. One section of the *Mutacion* is in prose; Christine tells us that illness was responsible, and that as soon as she recovered she returned to poetry. This is, on the face of it, plausible enough. But, when we look closely, there is no reason to think 'illness' a sufficient explanation. Rather, we should look at the contents of the prose section (which, in any case, she could have rewritten had she wished). First, there is a *captatio benevolentiae* about her illness as a rhetorical move. Then, there is another explanation for the shift to prose for the *particular* section of the history: it is the few pages devoted to the history of the Jews. By a Gresham's law of style, the shift to 'romance', and 'romanced historiography', in the course of the twelfth century introduced doubt about history in verse; prose, by contrast, claimed a higher relation to a true report about the past (also specious). Christine shifts to prose for the section of her history sanctioned by the Bible, the study of the Church Fathers, the least doubtable part of her history. Furthermore, it is into this section that she has slipped, without comment, two of the greatest heroines of the Old Testament: Esther and Judith (the dangerous Biblical heroine most often, through her cunning intelligence and fatal courage, linked to Medea). At the heart of her history lie active and dangerous married women, women who successfully bring death to men in power yet survive themselves.

Christine's Books V and VI reorient the male, public, secular history along lines which are subtly but surely shifted toward the idea of female participation and aid. By mixing the secular and sacred histories she introduces an implicit argument about the nature of cooperation in all times and places. Some of her women are powerful rulers, others work by influence, e.g. in her Bk V: Semiramis (9087–9174), Judith (9803–10432), Esther (11244–11692), Ariadne (13357–13456). This is an innovation upon the inherited Ovidian list. Section six begins with the Amazons (13457–13704), before moving to the long history of Troy, taken largely from the second redaction of the *Histoire ancienne*, which adapted Benoit; she begins with the Argonautic voyage and the insult from Laomedon which led to the city's first destruction, then explains the aid given to Jason by the Princess Medea (14153–14734).

The section is disproportionately long. Christine's Medee is a model of learning, but she is also a demonstration of the limits of learning. Christine constantly associates her with 'science', that theme of her book:

> Li roys Ostes ot une fille,
> Sur toutes les femmes soubtille,
> Sage clergece et es .VII. ars
> Apprise, et adés, tost et tars,
> Estudioit plus en magique
> Qu'en la science de logique.
> Si en avoit l'experience
> Et en sot toute la science.
> Ne lui fust impossible a faire
> Riens qu'on peust par science faire. (14301–14310)

[King Ostes had a daughter who surpassed all other women: a wise and learned woman skilled in the 7 Arts, and who constantly, early and late, studied more magic than the art of logic. She was well practised in it and thoroughly knew its lore. Nothing that it was possible to do by such means was impossible for her.]

There is no suggestion of witchcraft, sorcery, or malign intention. Medee has been dedicated to learning, and has disdained marriage, because none of her suitors have seemed able to compete with 'science'. But all the learning in the world is no proof against the combined forces of Love and deception. Medee sees Jason and is overcome by love (or by Love) and pity for the young man who faces certain death. That *sens* which is good sense becomes the vulnerability of those *sens* which are the senses. At her father's command she speaks to Jason at a banquet,

> Mais ce parler lui fu trop chier
> Vendu, car lors lui volt tranchier
> Amours un si divers morsel,
> Dont puis soustint pesant faisel.
> Jason, qui fu d'eulx tous le chief,
> Premier aregna, par meschief
> Et Fortune, qui l'ordena,
> Qui puis maint ennui lui donna. (14355–14362)

[But he [the king] bought this conversation too dearly, for then Love chose to cut him so spiteful a portion that afterwards became a grievous burden. By bad luck and by Fortune, who later arranged it and caused him much trouble, he spoke first to Jason, who was the leader.]

98

'Love' and 'Fortune' overcome Medee, despite all her learning, and she, who knew so much, did not know enough to protect herself from folly. This is the same accusation that earlier writers made, but changed by the narrator's exigent sympathy. Christine's imagery has shifted to something akin to a romance, with allegorical labels for inner conflict, and a sense of the self devoured, but her theme is tragic. The allegorical personifications yield to Medee's own self-deception:

> Or lui couvient un estrangier
> Amer, malgré sien! Bien vengier
> S'en scet Amours, qui tant rebelle
> L'ot trouvee! Adont, comme celle
> Qui tant de science comprent,
> A elle meismes se reprent
> De ceste folour et chastoie,
> Et dit que n'est droit qu'elle doye
> Consideré son grant savoir,
> A Amours laisser decevoir
> Son cuer, n'ainsi estre surpris,
> Qui tant avoit de sens compris;
> Si s'en blasme trop durement,
> Mais n'y vault nul murmurement,
> Car, d'autre part, Amours l'estraint
> Si durement qu'a cuer contraint
> Couvient qu'elle obeïsse a lui;
> N'y vauldroit chastoy de nullui.   (14419–14436)

[Now it befits her to love a foreigner, despite herself. Love knew well enough how to take revenge on the one found so rebellious. Thus she, being one who knew so much of art, had only herself to blame and reproach for this irresponsible conduct and says that it is not right that she, considering her great knowledge, should allow her heart to be deceived by Love, nor to be thus overcome – she, who had such deep understanding of the senses. She criticizes herself very harshly, but complaints are in vain, because Love, on the other hand, so crushes her that her heart, in thrall, must perforce obey him – no one's remonstrance would have the slightest effect.]

The warning in the last two lines, which repeats the necessity of the first, reminds the reader of human vulnerability, and its graphic physical compulsion emphasizes Love's constraining power. When Medee offers Jason her aid she is torn by conflicting emotions, and makes him swear an oath

99

with which she threatens him should he deceive her. In an unusual attribution of motive Christine is explicit that he knowingly did so:

> Adont, gemi
> Jason, par faintise, en semblant
> Que, par fort amer, voit tremblant
> Et moult parfondement soupire,
> Encor deist, mais plus ne peut dire.
> Si recoppe adont son lengage,
> Et celle, qui seult estre sage,
> Adés pert et sens et savoir,
> Et n'apperçoit que decevoir
> La veult cellui que mentira,
> Sanz faille, de quanque il dira,
> Mais bien cuide que verité
> Lui dye ... (14528–14540)

[Thus Jason groaned dissemblingly, as if, by the strength of love, he is trembling, with the deepest of sighs, would have liked to say more, but cannot utter it. And so he refrains from speaking, and she, who was usually wise, now loses both sense and knowledge, and does not perceive that he is trying to deceive her, he who will lie without fail, whatever he says, but really believes that he is telling her the truth.]

But she reads the episode as a tragedy of Love's power, which overcomes even the most learned, and repeats the lesson again and again:

> (Si fait a noter comme Amours,
> Meismes aux sçavens change mours
> Et avugle si et deçoipt
> Que le plus sage n'apperçoit
> Sa follie, par trop amer;
> Dont ne fait le simple a blasmer,
> S'en tel cas hors raison se boute,
> Quant le plus sage n'y voit goute.) (14685–14692)

[Thus it is to be remarked how Love changes the behaviour even of the knowledgeable, blinds them and deceives them so much that the wisest does not perceive his folly, because of loving too much. So one cannot blame the simple for behaving unreasonably in such a situation, when the wisest is blind.]

Christine exploits the technique of using the negative in order to suggest (because lexically, the word is present although denied) the positive,

100

particularly to deal with the gendering of virtues. The rhyme on 'apperçoit' (not noticing, not perceiving), is repeated within a few lines in this section: learning is not knowledge. 'Le plus sage' chooses the masculine, which is exemplary, rather than the feminine (which would be appropriate either with 'personne' or with Medee herself) to universalize the generalization about Love. Jason persuades Medee to flee with him by night, stealing all her father's treasure (an association remarked above). Christine marvels that Love's power made Medee abandon her father and all her family for a foreign knight. While the other Argonauts return to Troy to revenge themselves upon Laomedon, Jason stays at home. She, who had not made a reference to authority hitherto in the section, gives the end of their story, but makes it doubtful:

> Ains le parjure et desloyal
> La changia pour une autre dame
> Et la laissa, et prist a femme
> La fille d'un roy, qu'il ama,
> Dont Medee si s'enflama,
> Quant elle sot le mariage,
> Que mourir le fist plain de rage
> Et deux enfens, qu'ot eus de lui,
> Sanz estre rescoux de nullui.
> Aucuns dient qu'après s'occist
> Et autres dient que non fist.   (14770–14780)

> [Instead, the disloyal perjurer exchanged her for another lady with whom he had fallen in love, and left her, and wedded the daughter of a king. Medee was so enraged by this when she knew of the marriage that in an insane rage she killed him, and her two children by him, with no one to save them. Some say that she afterwards killed herself, but others say she did not.]

It is Benoît's story, but it is not.[68] Medee is a victim – a pagan victim – of love and deception who suffers in the course of her choice, who is abandoned by the man who owed her his life. Christine's comments throughout have made it an instance of the overwhelming power of love rather than the threat of powerful women, and she makes the end doubtful.

---

68 Most of the scholarship on this section records Christine's sources as a combination of the *Histoire ancienne* and other, unspecified, reading, but none emphasize the originality of her presentation. See Solente, III.274ff; Loukopoulos, 119ff, and Marilynn Desmond, *Reading Dido: Gender, Textuality, and the Medieval Aeneid* (Minneapolis, University of Minnesota Press, 1994), chapt. 6.

Christine is never one to restrict her female characters to private life. *Even Medea has become grist to Christine's mill.*

The rest of the Troy history is much as in Benoît, and although abridging, emphasizes the positive roles of the women. Christine has Hesione and Helen, Briseida and Polyxena, even the Amazon, Penthesilea, and then Penelope, as figures integral to the events and their outcome. By the time she comes to the 'modern instances', which are very short, she has set up a model of parallel princely fortunes which emphasizes morality throughout, but not in the standard style of the universal chronicle nor the Mirror for Princes. It is a vision of society in which women play an active part in the pursuit of virtue. This was, after all, Christine's argument throughout her career, and it is worth remembering that such an unusual interpretation of the historical past was possible, and achieved some currency in the fifteenth century. We shall return to her again in the chapters that follow.

The association of the Argonauts with Troy shifted the representations of Jason and Medea from what we might categorize as mythographical material to the highest-prestige medieval historiography, the great and initiating European tragedy. That depiction emphasized secular concerns (adventure, oaths, power, inheritance, marriage, revenge) and insisted that however embellished by the poets, the story was, in essence, true. The patterns which inform the compositions of writers such as Benoît and his adaptors inscribe ideas of the true knowledge of history into ideas about its cycles, as well as about the behaviour of pagan men and women. There are universal claims in the writing of history which we can see as much in the writers who take them for granted as in those who question or oppose them. Because the Argonautic voyage was the benchmark of secular chronology, Jason appeared in many – if not most – histories of the world, in narratives which we have seen traced back to Benoît, but which seemed to arise from independent sources. This multiply legitimated fiction posing as history could be assimilated to a series of arguments, not only in the context of the destruction of Troy, about usurpation and rightful inheritance (through Pelias), about failures of hospitality and treatment of foreign knights (through Laomedon), but also about the position of women, of adventure, loyalty, and the conflict between East and West. The history of Jason which was still alive in the eighteenth century was not only to be found in historical (or pseudo-historical) writing; as we shall see, it re-entered medieval mythographic writing under the guise of interpretations of Ovid.

THREE

Medea sparagmos

> For whoso can discovre and take away the veyle
> or shadows fro the fables, he shall see clerly
> sometyme poetrye and somtyme right hye phy-
> losophe; under other polytique; under other he
> shal fynde geste or hystorye comprysed, yf he wil
> entende and employ hys tyme by aspre diligence.
>
> William Caxton
> Prohemye to 'Metamorphoses'

This chapter has a dual focus: it is about Ovid, and it is equally about some significant interpretations of Ovid's *Heroïdes* and *Metamorphoses* to the end of the fifteenth century. This latter focus may appear to be a familiar part of the well-known story of the ways in which a succession of classicizing friars found history within classical legends. Classical material, some of which was discussed in chapter one, was often legitimated by medieval readers as part of a larger argument about pagan wisdom secreted under fables. Studies of Graeco-Roman myth in the main medieval period, of the survival of classical legends, stem from histories of Ovid-commentary, from the rediscovery of the *Metamorphoses* in the twelfth century to the last waning gasp of the fifteenth.[1] As we have already seen, the legends of Jason and Medea are not myth, although they may be closely allied to the gods and their myths.

---

[1] The bibliography on the subject is extensive and well-known. There are overviews in John Block Friedman, *Orpheus in the Middle Ages* (Cambridge, Mass., Harvard University Press, 1970), esp. pp. 118ff and nn. pp. 230–33); Judson Boyce Allen, *The Friar as Critic: Literary Attitudes in the Later Middle Ages* (Nashville, 1971); Ann Moss, *Poetry and Fable* (Cambridge, Cambridge University Press, 1984) chapt. 1; Leonard Barkan, *The Gods Made Flesh: Metamorphosis and the Pursuit of Paganism* (New Haven and London, Yale University Press, 1986); Margaret J. Ehrhart, *The Judgment of the Trojan Prince Paris in Medieval Literature* (Philadelphia, University of Pennsylvania Press, 1987), chapt. 3.

Whatever the genres of Ovid's own compositions, the commented texts which preserved and legitimated them for medieval readers recuperated them as wisdom literature. In classifying the rewriting of Ovid as 'commentary', scholars already distinguish such texts from texts of disparate kinds; they decide the categories in which they are to be interpreted. The medieval mythographers whose apparently fanciful allegories on Ovid this chapter considers believed they held a method (recognition of parallels and analogies) for deciphering ancient mysteries which veiled moral and anagogical truths otherwise opaque. But they never interpreted in a vacuum; they believed that part of what they read represented history. As the epigraph to this chapter suggests, sometimes the wisdom they uncovered included what actually happened at some point in the past. The historical context of certain legends about human actors links Ovid, Ovidianism, and the historical texts discussed above.

Medieval commentators elevated themselves, and, concomitantly, their texts, by their demonstrations of skilful 'reading'. Their writing, at one extreme of creativity, re-author-izes precious, specious, dangerous classical texts. As we shall see, making Ovid safe for posterity becomes a way of keeping Ovid difficult, a text to which readers (and writers) may continue to aspire. What appears to be an attempt to *control* the reading of Ovid becomes a Foucauldian delirium, making textual interpretation an unstable category, as it destabilizes classical 'literature' itself. Free-standing poetry is implicated in history, and vice versa. Ovid in translation became an amplified account which was sometimes not translation at all. The twin impulses of historical fusion and mythographical fission interact in a number of ways which had unlooked for repercussions beyond the apparent purview of either kind of text. As 'Ovid' becomes 'Ovidianism', certain aspects of his poetry underwrite attitudes to history, and the depiction of Woman, a double theme introduced in Chapter Two.[2]

In what follows I shall be exploring the assumption that the 'literal' legends of Jason and Medea include aspects which are true and part of the history of the West. The mythographic impulse, in all its profusion, coexists with a historical impulse; how closely it is to be identified with the historical impulse (towards comprehensiveness) depends upon the uses to which a particular author wishes to put the text he is interpreting or his own, free-standing text. If the interpretations of medieval mythographers sometimes appear to be incoherent, that is sometimes because of their

---

[2] Ovidian imitations, that is, free-standing new compositions on the model of Ovid's *Heroïdes*, will return among the subjects of Chapter Five, including the proto-feminist appropriations of Christine de Pizan, which use Ovid to argue against him.

concurrent, and contradictory, purposes: to rescue Latin poets, to find morality in their texts, but also to trace the descent of the European nations and trace the timeless patterns of their political experience. It is also a way of saving the cyclical theory of history for Christianity. That is, coherence at any one level may control a creativity which is limited only by one subject, be it moral, historical, mythic, or a combination. The contingent understanding of human possibility (what human beings are essentially *like*) underwrites these interpretations throughout. But habit is not hegemony, and dissenting readings were always possible, as in Christine de Pizan's reinterpretations of Benoît. In this chapter the challenge of reading Ovid now is complicated by the consideration of actual historical readings of Ovid.

One early question is the status of the fable as Ovid tells it. Certain kinds of allegory presuppose the truth of the literal meaning, and assume that it covers, or hides, meanings which require interpretation, meanings which are also true. As Leonard Barkan has so eloquently demonstrated, the change from Ovid's own drawing of metaphors from his fictions (which was an optional addition to the poetry) became, in the hands of Christian mythographers intent upon maintaining the purely fabulous nature of those myths, something much more compulsory.

> For Ovid metaphorizing is optional: that is, he is free to take the story literally or figuratively or both. Christian writers are not so free; and, once metaphor is compulsory, then the very nature of metaphor is different. Here again the experience of Old Testament typology is relevant. The events of the Jewish Bible (somewhat like the pagan myths to Ovid) were both literal and figurative. As such they inspired the creation of great systems of parallels and correspondences. Ovid's *Metamorphoses*, the Bible of the gentiles, denied a literal level, must be metaphorized not casually and occasionally, but in a grand and complex system. The turning of individual metaphors into systems produces allegory.[3]

We might now also want to argue that the movement from historical particularity into the general claims of poetic, mythographic representation becomes a claim to systematic depiction. The rich attitude to allegory which so characterizes the Middle Ages grows from this necessity, as Barkan shows, referring to Boethius's allegorization of Circe and

---

3 *The Gods Made Flesh*, p. 108. The section I shall be discussing is 'Demystification, Allegory, Integumentum', pp. 103–17. Ovid was not always denied a literal level, as Caxton points out. The existence of the Biblical system not only creates a model for the Ovidian system, it underwrites its style and inter-systemic reference. The semiosis itself is parallel.

Ulysses. In some ways, an obviously 'mythic' narrative is less problematic for Christian recuperation than a narrative which is not so obviously fabulous. Even here, however, some distance from the truth or falsehood of the literal representation leaves room for a parallel metaphoric interpretation posited upon recognizable analogy. Barkan brilliantly traces the philosophical difficulty about identity, and the way that in the course of the Middle Ages writers began to change their attitude to the meaning of the mythic representation. They came to believe that the parallel text (commentary either within a composition, or in a subsequent reading), was no longer simply drawing a lesson from the Ovidian (or Boethian) poem. Rather, the commentary becomes a demonstration which elides the distinction between an interpretation which claims that the poem 'means' that, for example, the glutton becomes bestial and an interpretation which 'recognizes' that the glutton *is* a beast. For Barkan, the drama of the moral metamorphosis legitimates not only readings of pagan texts, but allegory itself. The more distant from the text the commentary became, the more its own parallel narrative connected itself to absent texts, becoming also a commentary on, for example, the life of Christ or the ascent of the soul.[4] At the same time, the coincidence of representations between 'poetry' and 'history' also elides the truth-distinctions between them.

And yet another kind of interpretation remained possible: that which recovered historical events from what had become myth, in a familiar impulse of interpretative euhemerism which returned gods to men.

Ovid's Heroïdes *and Heroinism*

Ovid's poems were themselves always ambitiously intertextual challenges in amalgamation and interpretation. His competition with his predecessors is characteristic of his self-conscious retellings of mythographic material, and one can hardly imagine his Medeas in the absence of Virgil's Dido or Catullus's Ariadne. Modern scholars have often dismissed the medieval insistence that the *Heroïdes*, for example, could be made safe for schools because they could be taught as if Ovid were intent upon demonstrating what is to be avoided.[5] This is neither a foolish nor an impossible reading.

---

4 One might, in this context, reconsider the impulses towards identification discussed by Joel Fineman in 'The Structure of Allegorical Desire', collected in his *The Subjectivity Effect in Western Literary Tradition: Essays Towards the Release of Shakespeare's Will* (Cambridge, Mass., MIT Press, 1991), pp. 3–31.

5 *Heroïdes and Amores*, ed. Grant Showerman, rev. G. P. Goold (London, Loeb Classical Library, 1914; 1977). The sources of the letters are explored in Arthur Palmer's still-

His collection of women driven beyond the bounds of reason established once and for all a rhetorical *topos* of the irrational woman articulating love/hate frenzy which (because it was multiplied and embodied in numerous women in Ovid's own work as well as in such successors as Seneca) appeared to prove the truth of the depiction of 'woman'. Ovid's 'Medeas' radiate out to emphasize woman's threats to order, not simply because she is a foreigner, a barbarian from the East, not because of injustices done her (as Euripides or Seneca ask us to consider), nor even because of conflict between the family into which she marries and her own kinship group. Woman is a threat because she deceives men under the impetus of erotic passion, not only her husband or lover, but her own kin: she cannot be trusted to be loyal, cannot be assumed to obey her father. The logical conclusion is that women in control of knowledge destroy the patriarchal house. The limits – and limitations – of the Girardian idea of sacrifice appear here, because the idea of 'sacrifice' or 'scapegoating' implies a public and ritual event. The parodic quality of the murders we have seen may evoke the idea 'sacrifice', but they are emphatically *not* sacrificial. In addition, none of the murders are of female children, and the contrast to the deaths of either Iphegenia or Penthesilea illustrates the their distance from murder.

The importance of parallelism in Ovid's work has often been remarked by modern critics, although it was not one of the characteristics commented upon by many medieval ones, and it is a powerful method of analysis.[6] Ovid is, of course and preeminently, a repository of classical myths and legends, and he tells them as a repositories, collections of stories which is one of the great frame-tale compositions. As stories they can have

valuable edition (Hildesheim, 1967; orig. Oxford, Clarendon Press, 1898). *Amores* XI.1–6 recapitulates the idea of tracing back to first causes: the familiar pine on the mountain of Pelion which tempted men to go down to the sea. The recent translation by Harold Isbell contains useful annotations (Harmondsworth, Penguin, 1990), but he thinks the characters rather more characterized (as well as more moralized) than my own reading suggests. André Arcellaschi's section on Ovid traces his roots in earlier literature, and finds Medea central to Ovid's career as a writer of love and of exile, *Médée dans le Théâtre Latin* (Rome, Ecole Française de Rome, 1990), chapt. 6.

6   The *Vulgate* commentator of the mid-thirteenth century is an honourable exception. See Frank T. Coulson, 'The *Vulgate* Commentary on Ovid's *Metamorphoses*' *Medievalia* 13 (1989), pp. 29–61. There are two outstanding modern commentators whose criticism of Ovid has brought the *Heroïdes*, and the traditions it inspired, back into serious consideration. See Howard Jacobson, *Ovid's Heroides* (Princeton, Princeton University Press, 1974) chapts five and six; Florence Verducci, *Ovid's Toyshop of the Heart*: Epistulae Heroidum (Princeton, Princeton University Press, 1985), which is a model of what comparative literature can be. She discusses Hypsipyle and Medea at length in chapter two. Both these heroines, as Ariadne (see her chapt. 6), stress their betrayals of their fathers.

no political repercussions, and Ovid appears to have removed both politics and history, placing both his letters and his metamorphoses in an unspecific 'past'. His stories of gods and men assume, at least for the purposes of his fiction, knowledge of the Olympian deities, but they do not assume contemporary Roman belief in those deities. The past to which he assigns them is also the past of poetry, where 'epic' can be parodied as it is celebrated. To think of Ovid as transgressing religious pieties would be to impute to him assumptions which he did not have. There are, nonetheless, assumptions throughout his collections which might be thought of as social in the broad sense of a concern with power and gender, love and magic. He traces patterns of *human* behaviour which do not change (although the particular circumstances change) because human nature itself does not change. Again and again he explores the problems of keeping one's word, of inheritance, and of the dangers which arise when loyalties are torn between kinship and marriage, and he emphasizes, through a sequence of associations, the risks which accrue upon desire. This is important to medieval interpreters, because so much of what their analyses extract in terms of exemplary human behaviour is, indeed, as they insisted, already there. When Ovid creates, through his relation to his literary predecessors, a canon of *auctors* whose genres and styles, as well as subjects, offer models of uncertainty, of interpretations and re-interpretations, he encourages subsequent authors to make poetic choices *between* classical authors which also imitate the choices those authors had themselves made.[7] He establishes authority and insists upon its limits, upon its necessary contradictions.

In his *Heroïdes* he invented an epistolary world in which suffering became a show, but not the whole show: the letters are multiplex in their effect. They are the apotheosis of the rhetorical exercise in which the student creates a speech to be put into the mouth of a historical character. But they neither argue the case for action to come nor defend a course of action taken; they are something new. Their complex tone – which discomfited so many generations of critics – is precisely a self-referential game. Critics' demands for consistency and decorum (tragic characters expressing themselves in high and dignified language) now appear one of those aesthetic rules which was a period critical requirement, from which

---

7   See Gian Biagio Conte, *Genre and Poetic Memory in Virgil and Other Latin Poets*, trans. Charles Segal (Ithaca, Cornell University Press, 1986), esp. pp. 60–64 on Ovid's use, in his creation of Ariadne (*Fasti* 3), of Catullus's Carmen 64. As Conte argues, the poet's dependence for his effects on an audience well-read enough to recognize the allusions plays upon the fictionality of fiction *for the reader* which anticipate both Romantic Irony and a kind of Derridean 'free play'.

postmodern taste for parody and pastiche releases us. There is no straight-forward mimesis. Most of the letters are from women to men, but the last six are three paired with letters from the men.[8] They assume an audi-ence/readership fully cognizant of the legends in which the heroines act, and aware of the collection *as* a collection, so able to scroll from one letter to another. In the insistence upon rehearsing the course of events which has brought the heroine to her present pass, the audience cannot miss Ovid's voice within the apparent mimesis of the writers, because the wit and the puns which suffuse their letters act as arch reminders of poetic artifice. They also suggest the multiple interpretation of historical events. Their connections to the legends of Troy lends them further importance, because the insistence upon their legendary (rather than mythic) status pulls them into the ambit of the high historical.[9]

Four of the twenty-one letters underline the nexus of legends which concern us: VI (Hypsipyle to Jason), XII (Medea to Jason), and, more obliquely, but no less importantly, VII (Dido to Aeneas) and X (Ariadne to Theseus).[10] Medea's and Hypsipyle's letters grow in irony when they are considered to be a pair of another kind, in which the predictions of the earlier verge upon fulfilment in the later. The order of the letters matters: it is dramatic. Ovid's short tragic speeches dramatize without the necessity to place the heroines in a plot, which can be supplied by the knowledgeable reader (in this there is some similarity to the implied narrative of a sonnet sequence). The rhetorician may be at one with his subject in these letters, in which Ovid thought he was creating a new kind of text, but the net effect is to repeat over a dozen times the pathos of a woman in the grip of overwhelming passion, and to create, through the establishment of this display, a *topos* which insists upon a rhetoric of impotent frustration asso-ciated with the powerless, and therefore with women.[11] That is, the heroines'

---

8   These are usually taken to be a later composition which became attached to the first fifteen individual epistles. Howard Jacobson is among many scholars to assume this separateness, in his *Ovid's Heroïdes* (Princeton, Princeton University Press, 1974). The second group are, in any case, irrelevant to the heroines who concern us.

9   With the exception of the only 'historical' figure, in the modern sense, Sappho, whose story is well told by Joan DeJean, *Fictions of Sappho, 1546–1937* (Chicago, Chicago University Press, 1989). One may ask how far the 'character' of Sappho, with its as-sumed passion for a lost male lover, itself recapitulated and reinforced the stereotype I have been discussing.

10 There is an important corrective to the view that the letter-writers are simply women in love in Mary Lefkowitz, *Women in Greece and Rome* (Toronto, Samuel-Stevens, 1977) and *Women in Greek Myth* (Baltimore, Johns Hopkins University Press, 1986).

11 E. K. Rand: 'We should regard them not as unsuccessful attempts at tragic monologues, but as thoroughly competent studies in women's moods', *Ovid and his Influence* (Lon-don, George Harrap and Co., 1925), p. 22. Jacobson summarizes older views, while

apparent psychological verisimilitude rests in part on the intensity of a kind of abstract confusion, an unbalanced disturbance which gains in emphasis from its brevity, as Shakespeare's technical use of disturbed syntax indicates a character whose mind is unbalanced (Lear on the heath, Othello before his fit). In part, though, Ovid convinces because of the gender of his most hysterical characters (here one might evoke Lawrence's oft-repeated depictions of women in the throes of sexual passion.) Even if one considers (invoking realistic criteria of motivation and explanation) that the women are in the grip of an *âte* inflicted by Aphrodite, they are still distanced from the civilized self-control which is the mark of *male* achievement. Ovid stylizes passions; he does not describe individual persons. This appears to lead to a kind of allegory, in which woman equals the passions which conquers her. But it is not. The passions appear convincing in part because they illustrate an argument about Woman. They also elevate her to a strangely contradictory dignity. Gender stereotypes encourage readers to generalize from these women to all women, with further distrust. That is, the net effect of the multiplicity of the same reaction achieves an almost grotesque denigration, almost comedy, since although one hysteric (especially one endowed with the glamour of mythological status) may move our sympathy (or fear) while she threatens her lover, a crowd becomes at once ridiculous while dangerously threatening patriarchal order.[12] The group who suffer begin to be recognizable as part of a group which becomes, in turn an argument about Woman, along with the patterns of their power. On the surface, the passive sufferers form an associative *topos* of love betrayed; in the full flower of their pathos they can be iconic (or exemplary) for a 'right' (that is, morally acceptable to men) scheme of women's suffering. If the symptoms which all such sufferers display become conventional, 'conventional' in this context also means 'assumed to be true'.[13] In terms of decorum, it might be argued that so extreme are the circumstances in which they find themselves that *only*

---

insisting on his own psychological one, pp. 371–76. It is curious that he sees the heroines as sometimes 'bizarre', but nevertheless convincing.

[12] Attempts to assess the variety of classical attitudes are complicated by the nature of the evidence, both literary and historical. In addition to the scholarship noted above, chapter one, see Sarah Pomeroy, *Goddesses, Whores, Wives, and Slaves* (London, Robert Hale, 1975), esp. pp. 66ff on marriage to foreign women; Mary Lefkowitz, *Heroines and Hysterics* (London, Duckworth, 1981), chapter one. This is not the place to offer a study of Ovid's male ranters, but it would be worth making a detailed comparison. It might be suggested that they are young, misguided, and often effeminate.

[13] The discussions of Ovid as a depictor of woman were summarized by J. M. Frécaut in *L'Esprit et l'humour chez Ovide* (Grenoble, 1972), pp. 205–6. Like so many, Frécaut concluded that Ovid had excellent psychological insight. Arthur Palmer's view that the

concomitantly extreme reactions are appropriate, in deed or in word. It may be suggested that physical passivity reaches its apogee of feminine pathos in Philomena's dismemberment, that loss of her tongue which prevents her from revealing who has raped her. Speech, and activity, are displaced in her story onto her sister, Procne, who, as a Jungian double, acts out both Philomena's revenge, and a counter-dismemberment itself displaced onto Tereus's (and her own) children.

Dido, whose self-betrayal in her perjured oath to her dead husband, Sichaeus, condemns her beyond anything Aeneas has done, therein was appropriated to exemplary status (and such interpretations were likely to have been less complex than modern ones would be). Ariadne is less guilty, because although she betrayed her father to help Theseus, she caused no harm. Hypsipyle, the pious protector of her father, was seduced and abandoned. Yet each of these women has disrupted a kingdom, each threatens violence to the beloved. The limits of the group can be tested by thinking of Thisbe, who, like Juliet long after her, is one of those unfortunates for whom the fatality of love is its own explanation: bad luck rather than bad behaviour. There is no sense of *her*, at least, as a threat. Underlying the list of Love's victims are women prepared to take a more active role: Medea, Procne, and Ino.[14] Ovid identifies the conventions of suffering with a list of particular women; to mention one invites comparison to the others, who also offer themselves when an author wishes to create a contrast.

These are implicit comparisons, but there are also parallels within the first section which invite readers to see another kind of pairing, as do the letters from Hypsipyle and from Medea. They both, of course, address the same recipient; they both deal directly with Argonautic material (mainly from Apollonius, but drawing also upon Euripides).[15] Given the assumption that readers know the legends of Troy, the propinquity of the Matter

women personify situations not character seems more convincing, in his Introduction to P. Ovidius Naso, *Heroïdes*, p. xiii.

14 As we have already seen, Ovid did not invent these associations, which occur in passing in, e.g., Horace's *Ars Poetica* 123: 'Medea ferox inuictaque, flebilis Ino' (let Medea be savage and indomitable, Ino weeping'). Other antique poets seem to have felt the rightness of the association without, perhaps, reflecting upon it explicitly. Agave is excepted from this list of dismembering mothers because she acts upon the command of Dionysus and not according to her own will. Ovid has another revenger in *Metamorphoses* Book VIII in Althaea, who burns the brand which protects the life of her son when he has slain her brothers. Ovid's speech for her, like Euripides' reversals of epic heroism in *Medea*, refers generically to the *suasoria* and *controversia*, the rhetorical exercise for a character in the throes of a difficult decision. See above, pp. 27–34, 48–9.

15 Letters VI, *Hypsipyle Jasoni*, and XII, *Medea Jasoni*. There are casual allusions which link 'perfidious' Jason to Theseus in *Ars Amatoria* III. Jacobson is particularly sensitive to the repeating parallels between the myths as part of larger mythic kinship bonds, pp. 378ff.

of Argo to the fall of the city reinforces this association, as the collection, including Hypsipyle, Medea, Dido, Ariadne, reinforces the nexus of suffering women. Without an audience learned enough to recognize the allusions there can be no dramatic irony.

Hypsipyle insists upon Medea's status as a barbarian, but she is not far from wishing to do what barbarians do. As both Jacobson and Verducci have pointed out, the traditional depiction of Hypsipyle is as the pious, passive (except in her preservation of her father's life), accepting daughter and mother. Ovid's treatment of her is a new interpretation, the creation of a self-deceived victim of her own desire for Jason. It implicates her in the violence which Euripides' chorus thought of as unGreek (although they invoked Ino as their sole example). For this Hypsipyle thinks of what would have happened to that barbarian interloper had the Argo returned to Lemnos, and how she would have torn her apart, and splattered Jason with her blood. Now, helpless, she hopes that Jason will be cursed, as she was, by the loss of spouse and two children. She wishes to act out, therefore, what Medea accomplishes; had she the power, she would be another murderess.[16] Are we to think of this letter as a psychological characterization, suffused, as it is, with material its ostensible author cannot know, ironized, as it is, by events available only to its readers? Only if we accept the arch doubleness at which Ovid excels, though perhaps not even then. If we suspend our *belief*, Ovid's bravura performance becomes an interpretation of a legend he need not tell. Such an interpretation moves the argument from plausibility and verisimilitude to analysis of the rhetorical performance and concentrates on the word.

These women appear to have the word, to have the power of speech, in their letters, but it is Ovid who speaks through them, Ovid who calls attention to himself, while simultaneously through his doubleness arguing for the same picture of Woman-in-the-grip-of-passion. The women appear to be empowered, but Ovid makes sure that their rhetoric betrays them, like Volpone's ostensible seduction of Celia in a song which builds in its own refutation. What is empowered is *Ovid's* skill at weaving an idea of female subjectivity. He creates a forensic illusion which will engage and

This seems to me evidence that Ovid has a view about the similarity of the behaviour of women, not that he is psychologically acute to individuals.

16 Verducci, who sees Hypsipyle as a more realistic and convincing depiction of a possible character than I do, points out the parallel between Hypsipyle's desire for revenge upon her husband and the earlier Lemnian uprising against the unfaithful men who deserted their wives for Thracian slave-concubines. This similarity can be extended to a threat posed by Women who object to any husband's infidelity/betrayal, but it is also limited by Hypsipyle's desire to revenge herself only upon the active seductress, Medea, and not on her so-called 'husband'. See pp. 64–5.

persuade any reader who already knows 'what is known to all'. Like Homer or Pindar, he can allude to familar events, even when he is choosing between versions. Outside her letter, Medea, grand-daughter of the Sun, will carry out what Hypsipyle anticipates and we validate from our prior knowledge.

The opening words of Letter 12, 'Medea Jasonis', begin, as Latin syntax allows, 'At tibi Colchorum memini'. Like 'Nay but this dotage' at the beginning of *Antony and Cleopatra*, we are *in medias res*, or at least, in the middle of something not much like a letter: 'But/and', 'for you', 'of Colchis', 'I remember' (the whole line will read something like 'yet I remember how I, regal Colchian, found time for you'). This is a speech against, although against what or whom (beyond Jason's forgetting) is not immediately clear. This openness, this engagement, implies a relationship, above all, with the reader, upon whose power to choose its effects depend. Memory appears to be invoked against question or accusation. Medea characterizes herself as guilty, guilty of the murder of her brother, of the terrible slaughter of Pelias by his daughters. Her memory of their shared past is both acceptance of that guilt and a desire for Jason to erase it by returning to her: if he remembers correctly, as she remembers, he will come back. Implicitly, however, her argument works counter to its claim upon memory, since what she now remembers, and calls by another name than 'love', condemns her. But what she is really guilty of takes us right back to Pindar's association of poetry, rhetoric, and drugs: for it is Medea's credulity which she most holds against herself.[17] The woman of cunning intelligence has been its victim. Jason deceived her with his promises, with the rhetoric which is a woman's main weapon; now her words recreate their history, and she repeats the act of remembering, in which they both become guilty. Ovid's Medea, unlike Euripides', condemns herself and sees her guilt as the reason for Jason's desertion, as if he had been suddenly overcome by a distaste for her murders. Out of her own mouth comes self-condemnation. Hypsipyle saw herself as a potential threat; Medea is an actual one. In her frenzy, she does not know (but any informed reader could tell her) what horrors she will perpetrate. Unlike many of the other women, Medea, grand-daughter of the sun and accomplished priestess of Hecate, has the power to carry out what the others can only wish. As

---

17 Verducci has a completely convincing defence of the manuscript 'credulitas' against the emendation of generations of editors to 'crudelitas', pp. 68–72. Harold Isbell also accepts this reading: Let the sentence/ we deserve catch us at sea, you for deceit/ and me for my eagerness to trust' (p. 110). Yet the emendation exemplifies the interference of editors who believe they know what the poet must have meant: here a certain conception of the cruelty but not the intelligence of Woman.

Jacobson has stressed, Ovid blackens her character; there is no room for taking her side against perfidious Jason, no sense that she is the victim of Jason's goddess-backed seductiveness (Jacobson, pp. 114–15). This time her barbarian ancestry has been foregrounded, by Hypsipyle, who reiterates the accusation. Although Medea has the word in her letter, she has no power there. The disruption of her speech, like that of so many of the heroines, indicates the fragmented, and fragmenting, female self, shapeless, unstable, and consistently inconsistent. Like Pindar's poetry, this is poetry about itself, about its own position vis-à-vis other poetry, other Medeas.

What Ovid has, supremely, is sensual description which comprehends earlier poets without competing with them on their own terms. Objections to his irony are misplaced, because they assume canons of taste and an authorial desire for the independence of his characters he does not share. Like Dickens's interfering narrators, who constantly call attention to themselves as tellers of the tale, Ovid places himself, through his improbabilities and ironies, at the centre of the letters. His parody is serious, a challenge to the past, without ever forgetting its own textuality. His heroine presents herself as if she were still the demure maiden of Apollonius's epic, but the self she describes is far from that girl. Arguments over verisimilitude cannot reach the letter's intense literariness. Nevertheless, if for Ovid his achievement was dramatic, rhetorical, and intertextual, for generations of his readers it was, in some sense, a depiction of the truth, the truth that women who appeal through their pathos also threaten through their power. Loving or hating, women are the same irrational, unpredictable, contradictory creatures of complaint and passion. These are the dangers which made Ovid appear to medieval readers profoundly a moral master warning his readers against love, and especially women in love. One need not invoke a deconstructive reading to see the heroines simultaneously condemning themselves precisely where they evoke most pathos, and Ovid condemning as he invites sympathy.

As the previous chapters have shown, the ancestress of this dangerous and irrational woman is the literary creation named Medea. The *topoi* were reinforced in one of the texts which had immense currency in the Middle Ages, and the multiplication of 'Medeas' further reinforced the stereotype of the ranting, irrational, eroticized, and dangerous woman. It is extraordinary what currency she – or they – had. The truth of the depiction, which builds up a literary convention, was assumed, both as a model of female characterization and as plot. That the texts were genuinely preserved as dire warnings of the risks of passion unrestrained by manly self-control does not preclude their also being preserved because they are titillating. In the *Heroïdes*, when women threaten the men who have abandoned them with their own revenge or the force of their curses they combine rhetoric and *eros*, sexuality and the word. Even when they have no other weapon, they have rhetoric, and the threat which comes with intelligent speech.[18] As much as Pindar's emphasis on the universal conflict between male and female, Ovid's orators make themselves the dangerous adversaries of male power.

Medieval students of the *Heroïdes* were to be in no doubt: the collection castigated illicit, foolish, or otherwise unacceptable love.[19] It described the trajectory of affairs as surely as did Ovid's other amatory writings, but the threat was clearer. From the Accessus to the annotation, commentators emphasized Ovid's ostensible 'intention' to teach and warn. We shall return to the medieval interpretations of Ovidian heroinism in chapter five.

Ovid's Metamorphoses *and Some Metamorphoses of Ovid*

The Medea of the *Heroïdes* was not the only Medea whom Ovid treated, and it is largely to Ovid that we owe the establishment of Medea as sorceress.[20] In the *Metamorphoses* her story is one of the longest, and well as the longest-lived.[21] Ovid's poetry is inter- and intra-textual in association and allusion, and there are implicit links among dangerous women which amount to an important and influential nexus. An obvious parallel would be the ways that the depiction of the ostensibly childlike, irresponsible, and ultimately untrustworthy colonial subject functioned to legitimate imperial rule (whether Roman about barbarian Gauls or French about

[18] See Mary Lefkowitz, *Women in Greek Myth*, chapt. 5, esp. pp. 91ff for a study of women's access to rhetoric as a threat. There is detailed discussion of the rhetorical background to Ovid's compositions in H. Fränkel, *Ovid: A Poet Between Two Worlds* (Berkeley and Los Angeles, 1969), pp. 5–6, 36, 190.

[19] I rely throughout this section on Ralph Hexter, *Ovid and Medieval Schooling. Studies in Medieval School Commentaries on Ovid's* Ars Amatoria, Epistulae ex Ponto, *and* Epistule Heroidum (Munich, Münchener Beiträge zur Mediävistik und Renaissance-Forschung, 38, 1986), III. *Epistulae Heroidum* (pp. 137–204), which has transformed our knowledge of Ovid and the medieval Ovid.

[20] This association is remarked in passing by Macrobius, *Saturnalia* I.12.26, but he, of course, may be making a plausible reconstruction in the light of his own literary experience. See John Scheid, 'The Religious Roles of Roman Women', *A History of Women in the West* I. *From Ancient Goddesses to Christian Saints*, ed. Pauline Schmitt Pantel (Cambridge, Mass., Belknap Press of Harvard University Press, 1992), p. 400.

[21] Jonathan Bate, *Shakespeare and Ovid* (Oxford, Clarendon Press, 1993) has a long section on Medea's importance. This is an exceptionally useful literary account, although Bate is perhaps more convinced by Ovid's consistency than I am.

uncivilized Africans). Of course women must be kept in tutellage – and away from sharp objects. The nexus is ultimately one of female disorder, of their social dis-memberment, of the risks men run because of the uncontrolled desire/sexuality of their daughters and wives, and of the social upheavals underwritten by the god Bacchus, or Dionysus, under whose terrible influence women may tear men's bodies asunder and bring civilised organisation to an end. Men are not innocent in this sundering, but women are always guilty.

I want to look briefly at five stories which are important in the continuity of the central books of the *Metamorphoses*, before returning to Medea herself. Ovid's poetic techniques of juxtaposition and allusion have in recent years attracted considerable commentary which has illuminated the structure and rationale of the poem, coherence which is thematic through the use of repeated (or related) words and images. The atmosphere which the poem creates depends in part on a tissue of apparently contingent allusions and associations which make its events appear consistent and inevitable. Aerial – Gods' eye – views connect the events as things observed from above, replacing the whole journey-motif on which the *Odyssey* was built. Another structure is the repeated recourse to Bacchus (in the destructive manifestation of Bacchic disorder). In Book III in the course of a sequence of stories about the destruction of the House of Cadmus (already familiar to us from Euripides' *Bacchae*, discussed above in chapter one), Ovid's nameless narrator tells how Pentheus was torn limb from limb by his mother and aunts. There is an allusion to Acteon (torn apart by his own hounds), and those female relations are named. One of these, Ino, is also familiar to us from Euripides, where she is the only example the chorus can think of of a Greek woman who attacked her children (it will be remembered that it was her attack on her step-children, Phrixus and Helle, which began the legends of the Golden Fleece). The thread which ties together the larger context of the story, the worship of Bacchus, continues intermittently in the following books. Bacchic rites are the essence. In Book VI Procne is able to free her raped sister, Philomela, under the cover of Bacchic worship. The sisters take a terrible revenge upon Tereus, Procne's husband, who is guilty of raping his sister-in-law and of tearing out her tongue (an unusual dismemberment of a woman), by feeding him a pie baked from his son's body, which they have dismembered. Within Book VI there are verbal reminiscences between Procne's kissing her son, who resembles his father, and Euripides' emphasis on the sweet smell of the children's bodies in *Medea*, and I shall return to this section in my discussion of the *Ovide moralisé*. That discussion will encompass Book VII, as well. But it is difficult to isolate and disentangle the poetic sweep of

116

the narrative, which constantly refers, through its imagery, both forward and back. In the course of Book VII, for example, Medea compares herself as a disobedient daughter to Scylla, whose betrayal of her father is one the subjects of Book VIII. There, Scylla falls in love with Minos, who is besieging the city of her father, Ninus, and cuts off the magical lock of hair upon which the safety of the city depends. When she takes the lock to Minos he is horrified, will have nothing to do with her, and sails away without her. Through Minos Ovid moves to Theseus's escape from Minos's Labyrinth and his betrayal of Ariadne, who aided him with her long thread. This story is briefly told, and there are no speeches.

This sequence of women is associated through Bacchus, the theme of *sparagmos*, disobedience to fathers and, by implication, destruction of patriarchal houses.[22] Within the fiction itself, characters refer back to parallel situations in which other characters, whom they categorize as historical, find themselves in relevant repetitions, not just of human behaviour, but also of social circumstance. In the classical world references to Dionysiac disorder built questions of civilization and its discontents into a world-view which encompassed principles of divine destruction: divinely ordered disorder. The characters reflect upon their relationships with the gods. With the changes concomitant upon Christian monotheism, divine responsibility for social dismembering was displaced, and partly legitimated, by the apparent evidence of these stories: displaced onto Medea, and women like her. The paradoxical mixture of divine interest in particular human beings and terrible indifference to humanity was no longer part of the Christian idea of godhead; actions are human actions. If Jason's voyage is the benchmark secular adventure, Medea's revenge is a landmark in secular, female disobedience. She and the women 'like her' form a kind of image cluster, and where one of them is invoked, poets are likely to invoke the others. As characters, they themselves recall the others. Where they represent women overcome by too much love the nexus is usually Medea, Dido, Ariadne and Hypsipyle; where revenge is in question one finds Medea, Procne, and sometimes Agave and Althaea (who burned the brand which protected her son's life after he killed her brothers). The implications of this constellation for an anatomy of Woman will occupy us below.

Let us now turn to look in more detail at the two incidents which

---

22 The *Vulgate* commentator notices the associations and verbal reminsicences, as Frank T. Coulson remarks in his 'The *Vulgate* Commentary on Ovid's *Metamorphoses*', *Medievalia* 13 (1989), pp. 44, 46, but for which he offers no explanation.

concern her in *Metamorphoses* VII.[23] This – it is worth reminding ourselves – is the first time we have seen her power actually metamorphosing
someone; in previous versions she took advantage of the willingness of the
gullible to believe her power sufficient to restore youth. Ovid gives us
scenes from a narrative more than the narrative itself. Critics have been
alert to some, but not all, of these associations. The most obvious, of
course, is the line of descent which ties Ovid's Medea to Virgil's Dido.
Ovid's focus encompasses that earlier creation, as if he expects his audience to use a kind of peripheral vision which will allow them to interpret
his Medea against her predecessors. Ovid gives Medea an internal monologue, adapted from Dido, and with Dido's debate between *amor* and
pudor (VII.1–73), full of the flames of love and the beauty of the beloved.
Both women speak of flames and invoke the beauty of the man:

> Dido: Multa viri virtus animo multusque recursat
> gentis honor: haerent infixi pectore vultus
> verbaque . . .
> Quis novus hic nostris successit sedibus hospes,
> quem sese ore ferens, quam forti pectore et armis!
> credo equidem, nec vana fides, genus esse deorum.
> *(Aeneid* IV.3–5, 10–12.)

> [. . . Much did she muse on the hero's nobility, and much
> On his family's fame. His look, his words had gone to her
> heart
> And lodged there. . . .
> This man, this stranger I've welcomed into my house –
> what of him?
> How gallantly he looks, how powerful in chest and
> shoulders!
> I really do think, and have reason to think, that he is
> heaven-born.]

> . . . agnosco veteris vestigia flammae *(Aeneid* IV.23)

> [I feel once more the scars of the old flame.]

> Medea: excute virgineo conceptas pectore flammas,
> si potes, infelix. si possem, sanior essem;

23 Quotations from P. *Ovidii Nasonis, Metamorophoses,* ed. W. S. Anderson (Leipzig, Teubner, 1972). Translations from Virgil by C. Day Lewis, *The Eclogues, Georgics, and Aeneid
of Virgil* (Oxford, Oxford University Press, 1966) and from Ovid, *Metamorphoses,* trans.
Mary M. Innes (Harmondsworth, Penguin, 1955). See also Brooks Otis, *Ovid as an Epic
Poet* (Cambridge, Cambridge University Press, second edn, 1970), pp. 167–73.

sed trahit invitam nova vis, aliudque cupido
mens aliud suadet: video meliora proboque,
deteriora sequor! quid in hospite, regia virgo,
ureris et thalamos alieni concipis orbis?

Quem nisi crudelem non tangat Iasonis aetas
et genus et virtus? quem non, ut cetera desint,
ore movere potest? Certe mea pectora movit
(*Metamorphoses* VII.17–22, 26–8)

[Unhappy girl, rid your inexperienced heart of the flames
that have been kindled there. Oh, if I could, I should be more
like myself! But against my own wishes, some strange influence weighs heavily upon me, and desire sways me one way,
reason another. I see which is the better course, and I ap-
prove it; but still I follow the worse. Why do you, a princess,
burn with love for a stranger? Why dream of marriage with a
foreigner? . . . Who but a monster of cruelty could fail to be
stirred by his youth, his noble birth, his valour? Though he
had none of these virtues, who would not be moved by his
words? He has certainly touched my heart . . .]
(pp. 155, 156)]

Ovid has little interest in the Argo or in the events in Corinth as part of an
alternative narration, and it is the concentration on the mechanics of
metamorphosis (and not any inhibition about repeating himself), and the
place of the incident in the balance of his epic plan, which explain his
choices. To two acts of magic used to protect and preserve, Ovid adds two
which are threatening: the murder of Pelias and the attempt upon Theseus.
In each of these incidents he follows Medea. There is no plot continuity,
and no consistency of characterization; what plot or characterization there
may be are contingent upon his interest in change. His emphases in this
section continue the emphases of what has preceded it. The restoration,
the re-membering, of a 'complete' narrative (which will, of course, wreak
its own havoc with his poetry) comes from another impulse.

The narrative bridge from Book VI to the beginning of Book VII is
through the winged Argonauts, Calais and Zeetes, who 'joined the Miny-
ans in sailing over the unknown sea, in the first ship ever built, in search of
the shining golden fleece'.[24] Only at VII.74 does Ovid turn to magic, to

---

[24] The sceptical may at this point wish to point out that despite the emphasis on the Argo's
priority as first sea-going ship, Aeetes appears to have faster ones in his fleet. As far as I
can see, no one has ever raised this as a problematic contradiction, or defined 'first' as
'first Greek'.

Medea's power with the fire-proof ointment which will protect Jason from the dragons who guard the golden fleece. Jason succeeds and carries off his bride; the whole episode takes only about as many lines as Medea's subsequent rejuvenation of Aeson. Ovid's third and fourth incidents narrate the murder of Pelias and the attempt upon the life of Theseus. If one spoke of point of view, a cinematic analogy would help: Medea appears to be flying throughout this section, as she looks down from her dragon chariot, and Ovid tells us what she sees, continuing the theme of 'winged' characters from the previous book. Medea is in no way a reflector, because the narrative's point of view does not absorb her inner life or thoughts about experience; Ovid's description are curiously objective. This gives further weight to familiar stereotypes. Calais and Zeetes adventure under their own physical power; Medea is carried by the dragon-drawn chariot of her grandfather, the sun. Her power is knowledge which can control, cunning intelligence, not physical strength, not a gift beyond the human with its normal bodily limitations, nor self-metamorphosis. It is commonplace to say that medieval interpreters were not slow to repair Ovid's omissions, pointing to habits such as the medieval taste for *amplificatio*. There are other reasons.

As Samuel Levin has pointed out, there is no basis in the *Metamorphoses* for serious allegorical interpretation; although Ovid turns humans into non-human things, plants and animals above all, those are actual physical changes, not symbolic ones.[25] Ovid's is not that kind of figural representation which is divinely coded so that men may recognize that prophecies are fulfilled.[26] Ovid's use of mythic or legendary time is typical of much ancient writing: it is selective, it is concerned with other matters than straightforward plot continuity or consistency, and, where it concentrates upon Medea, it is fictional (in a conceptual space which understands 'literary'). He creates a strikingly *literary* space, in which there is great distance between his literary creation and any events that might be taken as a representation of the actual past. Throughout, his structures depend upon reader recognition of allusion and intertextuality, rather than a strongly chronological connection. Ovid was interested in the rhetorical

---

25 'Allegorical Language', in Morton W. Bloomfield, *Allegory, Myth, and Symbol* (Cambridge, Mass., Harvard University Press, 1981), p. 26n., and his *Metaphoric Worlds: Conceptions of a Romantic Nature* (New Haven and London, Yale University Press, 1988). See also Bloomfield, 'A Grammatical Approach to Personification Allegory', collected in *Essays and Explorations* (Cambridge, Mass., Harvard University Press, 1970), pp. 242–60.

26 The *locus classicus* is Eric Auerbach, '*Figura*', in *Scenes from the Drama of European Literature* (New York, Meridian, 1959), pp. 11–78.

representation of acute psychological states – not in the portrayal of an idiosyncratic *character* under stress whose language creates the sense of her particular experience. He was more interested in the process of meta-morphosis than in the persons responsible or their victims. Unlike many of the earlier treatments, Ovid's are not concerned with central questions of human political power, and he is extremely careful to avoid historical or actual dynastic anxiety. Lest we be tempted to imagine that that is not to be expected under Augustus, we may remember that projecting civil strife onto earlier periods was a possible way around Caesar's suspicion and that Seneca was to find ways to consider human order. Ovid's way is perhaps more distant, more oblique, but he did propose that his *Metamorphoses* would be a '*carmen perpetuum*'. How different our assessment might be if his tragedy, *Medea*, had survived, we cannot know.

Mythography as History as Exemplum

A study of the end of Book VI and the beginning of Book VII of Ovid's *Metamorphoses* and the interpretations of these sections may exemplify patterns which are true of the poem (and its interpretations as a whole), but it runs the risk of distorting a number of medieval readings, written in different times and places, for different purposes, into one mould. The pattern, at least, of the medieval Ovids, is one that is likely to distract from detailed attention to such texts as the *Ovide moralisé*. In principle, an exhaustive reading would take the time to analyze the many nuances of reinterpretation, as in current analyses of Gower's *Confessio Amantis* that analyse the architecture of the whole, but here a more attenuated sequence will have to suffice. Above all, I shall try to attend, as many medieval commentators urged, to the letter.

In practice, one story prevails, a version of the history already adum-brated in the previous chapter. But the interpretations, not to say misread-ings, of that story, change it. Much depends, of course, upon the ambitions of the 'commentators', for whom the preservation and interpretation of Ovid was both a means of revealing the classical poet's moral secrets, but also an emphatic demonstration of legitimate reading. Looking at their interpretations may suggest a school of patristic criticism before D. W. Robertson's, but, as scholars from Erich Auerbach to Leonard Barkan have shown, the attempt to make Ovid safe for Christianity (even at its most astringent) was limited both in its audience and in the extent to which it transformed its texts. Under cover of 'commentary', too, other ambitions emerge.

'Rationalization' of the literal meaning might mean changing it, 'completing it', or re-orienting it, in an attempt to turn it into something interpretable as interior and hidden wisdom. It could not deny the ambition of the first secular quest. What 'complete' readings of Ovid do, however, is, by sheer weight of numbers, insist upon the fundamental virtues and vices true of all mankind in all times and places. When this emphasis is explicitly upon the individual and his quest for salvation it has a number of implications, among them the familiar anachronistic or de-historicizing of the narrative to remove Ovid from his own political society. The power relations which Ovid examines, that stem from an archaized series of 'Greek' societies, reproduce ideas of inheritance, of patron/client relations, of the dangers of absorbing women into husband's families, of the interwoven families who form his subjects. One of the obvious features of the medieval moralizations of Ovid, above all the *Ovidius Moralizatus*, is their refusal to deal with Ovid's text as a social representation. By contrast to the *romans antique*, the representations are often curiously timeless. Although I shall concentrate on the section of Ovid's Book VII which concerns Jason and Medea, these extracts are typical of a larger context of readings. Their survival assured readers into the seventeenth century of a stratum of reference books from which mythological material could be extracted, material which was rational, complete, and treated the legends as if they were a single representation. The allegorizers repeat the impulse of Alexandrian scholarship and anticipate modern mythographical works of reference which elide all historical accretions. By precisely these elisions, additions to the 'literal' sections once more built in – this time to a supposed mythographical text – that view of the secular past which we saw building in the previous chapter.

Connections between *some* of the poetic material and the history of Troy, that high-status event in the secular past, placed the mythographers in a position from which the 'fable' could not be dismissed as only fiction, or even only euhemeristic inventions. Again and again the emphasis on the historical status of some of the stories pulls them back into a possible European past. This distinguishes what we might prefer to categorize as the *legends* of Troy from *myths* which recount natural events in order to give large-scale explanations of the natural world or human society in its fundamental organisation.[27] The voyage of the Argo may be associated with the heavenly constellations; unlike many of the creation or nature

---

27 Thus the classic accounts of the *Ovide moralisé*, which concentrated on depictions of the gods, were scarcely interested in amplifications about the history of men, as, for example, Jean Seznec, *The Survival of the Pagan Gods: The Mythological Tradition and Its Place in Renaissance Humanistic Art* (New York, Pantheon, 1953) or Erwin Panofsky,

myths, it plays no part in an understanding of astrology or the planetary gods. Its protagonists are human, but the medieval stories turn Ovid's fascination with instability, the ambiguities of sexuality, with metamorphosis and change, into something less safely male-oriented, less stable, less limited by the authority of previous texts.

Strictly speaking, of course, allegorical commentaries that discover moral demonstrations within classical stories are a special kind of interpretation, one that imposes particular ethical meanings foreign to the original author and society in which he wrote; for example, when medieval readers 'discover' Christian mysteries in pre-Christian texts. In the long history of writing about such interpretation, scholars have come to agree that some such allegories, however alien to the originals, become part of the history of reading (and misreading), and are integral to our understanding of texts as cultural objects expressing cultural translation and appropriation. The Greek word, metaphor, which originally means transfer, reminds us of the almost physical sense of the way that poetry is a kind of carrying a meaning from its literal to its assumed sense, or senses. That the accent should fall on the carrying, and therefore, contingently, on the authority of the carrier, makes allegory a dynamic process, both for the poet and his reader.[28] The accretions acquire a dignity of their own when generations have read Abraham and Isaac as a 'figure' of God's sacrifice of his only son, 'completed' by *post hoc* readings of the events reported in the New Testament.

This is not the place to reconsider in any detail the functions of medieval allegory, about which there is now an extensive, and powerful, literature. From Quintillian to Robert Frost, writers have identified the trope 'allegory' as when authors say one thing but mean another in an extended and translatable way. This presupposition assumes not only that the intention to 'mean another' is integral to the work, to its 'intentio operis', but also that the relation between the work and its meta-language is a straightforward one of parallelism.[29] From Aesop to Dante, texts which invite

---

Renaissance and Renascences in Western Art (London, 1970; orig. 1965). Similarly, Jane Chance's detailed survey of pagan gods is largely about *gods*, in *Medieval Mythography: From Roman North Africa to the School of Chartres AD 433–1177* (Gainesville, Florida, University of Florida Press, 1994).

28 Douglas Kelly called attention to the deliberate ambiguities of which medieval poets take advantage when one need not distinguish whether something is meant as a metonym or as a full-blown allegory. See his *Medieval Imagination: Rhetoric and the Art of Courtly Love* (Madison, University of Wisconsin Press, 1978), pp. 24–5.

29 These definitions are perhaps too well known to require citation, but Donatus or Isidore are among the school-texts to define allegory in this way. There is a compact over-view of the Latin tradition in the notes to Martin Irvine, 'Cynewulf's Use of

single, or multiple, equivalences, have used metaphor to create a sense of connection between what is represented and what is implied. An animal, or a sinner, is first of all literally a beast or a bad man before he is bestiality or badness. In the literal sense both are usually possible in nature, but what they are represented as doing may not be so. Personification allegory, which characterizes medieval allegorical imagery, is a dramatic instance of the limiting case in which abstraction is concretized, instead of the usual, opposite, tendency. In some ways, personification allegory is the least *allegorical* representation of all, because there is no room for transfer or translation. If we interpret Seneca's Medea as embodying (the metaphor is itself revealing) *Ira*, that is still a long way from a depiction of Wrath in personification allegory. There is nothing to 'recognize' about Boethius' Lady Philosophy, Spenser's Shamefastness, or Bunyan's Christian. Nevertheless, embodied qualities, or personified abstractions, may by their depiction (in this opposite direction) contingently define the behaviour appropriate to characters of particular age, status, or gender.[30] An impossible, abstract character has the advantage that it requires no authority beyond a dream or a vision. In the most 'fabulous' allegorical representations, there is no claim to represent 'real' men or 'actual' historical events which would need legitimation beyond the text.[31] Once that escape from authority is established, it becomes a way of re-authorizing, and re-legitimating, texts which hitherto fell into categories which required extensive defence, because pagan, or representing actors behaving wickedly, or simply in a non-Christian way. A further, usually unstated, requirement, is that an allegorical interpretation should be consistent within its own narrative, and should preserve its analogy to the literal meaning, so that 'good' characters *usually* generate 'good' meanings.

Calling something allegory therefore worked as a way of authorizing by stealth. Imposed allegory is when the intention was projected onto classi-

---

Psychomachia Allegory', in Morton W. Bloomfield, *Allegory, Myth, and Symbol* (Cambridge, Mass., Harvard University Press, 1981), pp. 39–62. The idea of allegorical interpretations as a series of laminations is one way around a demand for consistency.

[30] For a recent discussion of personification allegory, see James Paxson, *The Poetics of Personification*, chapt. one. On grammatical gender and its implications for allegory, see Helen Cooper, 'Gender and Personification in *Piers Plowman*', *Yearbook of Langland Studies* 5 (1991), pp. 31–48.

[31] Here I follow the illuminating work of Maureen Quilligan, *The Language of Allegory: Defining the Genre* (Ithaca and London, Cornell University Press, 1979). See also Carolynn Van Dyke, *The Fiction of Truth: Structures of Meaning in Narrative and Dramatic Allegory* (Ithaca and London, Cornell University Press, 1985). The psychoanalytic approach to allegorical interpretation no longer has the hold it once did, but the pioneering work of Angus Fletcher is still important. See his *Allegory: the Theory of a Symbolic Mode* (Ithaca, Cornell University Press, 1964).

cal texts, as happened as early as serious and well-meaning interpreters of Homer from before the days of Plato – who condemned them.[32] This argument about whether or not an author meant his inventions to carry allegorical meaning is always with us. We may think of imposed allegory now as typical of centuries of bad interpretation, but we need to attend to the ways the literal texts may have been arranged or reinterpreted to make it possible to impose upon them.[33] Imposed allegory, moreover, never wiped out the multifarious other ways of interpreting a text which is subjected to figurative or allegorical fantasies, or even ones from which examples of human behaviour have been drawn.

There is, however, a less astringent interpretation of allegorical readings: from personification allegory (which is, under this description, hardly allegory at all) to the recognition that certain characters demonstrate virtues and vices which can be separated from who they are. Ovid's heroines exemplify irrational passion, which is greater than they are; because they 'embody' it, act it out, they may be thought of as a metonymy, of a double representation of the passion, and of woman. Not only kings have two bodies. This distinction between character and characterization is easier to see than to define. As soon as emotions are reified (her pride spoke, or, her Pride spoke) there appears to be an opening for allegorical interpretation, as if personifying an emotion authorized global personification, and psychomachia (struggle in the character's mind, with thought represented as speech with speakers) legitimated further allegorization of the speaker him- or herself. But there is another, metonymic interpretation in which individual behaviour exemplifies universal and timeless metamorphosis ('that's the gin speaking' – however variable the name of the alchohol – where 'gin' remains firmly lower case). As far as Mr Hyde extracts a permanent substratum of unbridled will from Dr Jekyll he represents the first impulse; as a metamorphosis caused by 'science', the second. That the two co-exist is a profound tribute to the quality of Stevenson's invention, as well as to the age-old argument about human moral qualities.

---

[32] The phrase, of course, is Rosemond Tuve's in *Allegorical Imagery: Some Medieval Books and their Posterity* (Princeton, Princeton University Press, 1966). See also Judson Boyce Allen, *The Friar as Critic* (Nashville, 1971); Alastair Minnis, *Medieval Theory of Authorship* (Aldershot, Scolar, 2nd edn 1988).

[33] When Northrop Frye, in a famous short essay on allegory, insisted that 'allegorical interpretation, as a method of criticism, begins with the fact that a[llegory] is a structural element in narrative: it has to be there, and is not added by critical interpretation alone', he took account of centuries of accretive imposed commentary on numerous innocent texts while simultaneously ruling it out of court. In the *Princeton Encyclopedia of Poetry and Poetics*, ed. Alex Preminger (Princeton, Princeton University Press, 1974), pp. 12–15.

Even where Medea appears, in the classicizing texts, to be central, she is often displaced by the Argonauts, or re-centred by Jason's connection to Troy, or by his association with heroism. In the Middle Ages, however often poets claimed an *exemplification* of false loving, the main *allegory* imposed upon Jason himself was often the journey of the soul, the simplest of anagogical paradigms. Almost always, the temptation of the individual soul is a story of female seduction in which surrender becomes an issue of *male* sexual betrayal and defeat, almost always an analogy to the Fall itself. Dido (and before her the Homeric minor goddesses) set a paradigm of temptation and delay. The soul (masculine virtue, both in the sense of strength and power) is corrupted by sensuality, embodied (and 'bodied' is the operative term) in a female figure. That is, the man, Jason, is allegorized, but the woman, Medea, remains a woman, because woman's embodied sexuality is an allegory of herself. That is, inscribed within the anagogical trajectory is a trope of misogyny. At the most apparently abstract level of allegory, the history of female seduction (with all its terrors and destructiveness) is grounded in blameworthy events. In medieval texts Medea, however pitiably seduced and abandoned, is the author of her own fall.

Detailed commentaries of heterogeneous approaches avoided any global interpretation of classical poems, and encouraged *inconsistent* projections of 'meanings' in the course of a reading of those texts. Too much meaning threatens to overturn interpretation into no-meaning; interpretation ceases to be controlled by the text and becomes a means of assimilating the text to known moral patterns. Too fine-grained divisions scatter a comprehensive retelling of the legends into a dismembered mise-en-abîme. But this is far from Derridean free play. Unlike the variety of the male characters, a female one potentially exemplifies the essential abstractions in which she participates. Medieval writers sometimes took one approach to classical texts and stories, sometimes others. Particularly when their intentions were to demonstrate the moral utility of such texts, the urge to write comprehensive and consistent interpretations took second place to individual readings of characters or events. Competing ideas of the moral patterns demonstrated by classical stories, combined with competing literary genres and the authority of named classical authorities, supplied abundant variations for retelling and reinterpretation. Often the same author uses the same material in a number of ways, with no explicit sense that one version may undermine another. Even the status of texts as representing 'historia' or 'fabula' appears to shift disconcertingly from true tales about the past to truths about human experience and back again, in a superabundance of authority.

But there can be insufficiencies, too, too-littles and absences which help determine how texts shall be read. The disappearance of Homer from the Latin West is an important case in point.[34] The unknown text becomes the most known in terms of content and interpretation. Readers and writers might categorize him as a controversial pagan poet, as a theologically-mystically-minded teacher, as the greatest of epic writers.[35] They could refer to him as an authority, as an authority brought into doubt by the true histories of Dares and Dictys, as a pagan poet inspired by virtue to hide moral mysteries under a frivolous exterior. What they could not do was read him. They could not experience or test the inheritance of questions and topics which they found in the commentaries, or on books which referred to Homer or to his stories.[36] He had immense, if troubled, prestige, with which there was no way to engage. The ostensible habits of reading allegorically, which stemmed from commentaries on Homer, could scarcely be questioned in the absence of the text from which those habits had developed. There is thus a further distinction to be made between text and interpretative context. Hidden in questions about the authority of Homer himself (historian? poet?) there is a further question over the authority of the *approaches* to texts like Homer's (are they historical, and, if so, how far? are their characters moral types?). Medieval readers could not contextualize either authors or commentaries. The loss of a historical sense of the growth of commentaries gave not only no map of misreading, but no archaeology of interpretation, either. The parallel to the erection of genealogical tables, including the anti-historical genealogies of the commentators, is one more example.

Medieval allegory/integumentum often appears to suppose that the surface narrative (its 'literal' meaning) is neither true nor particularly linked to the allegorical meaning, which is itself a parallel fiction, requiring

---

[34] See on this subject Robert Lamberton, *Homer the Theologian: Neoplatonist Allegorical Reading and the Growth of the Epic Tradition* (Berkeley, University of California Press, 1986), chapt. 6, pp. 249–97.

[35] On Boethius's use of Homer as a touchstone for Philosophia in his *Consolatione*, see Lamberton, pp. 274ff. He takes as his example Circe's drugs, and Boethius's distinction between corruption of the body, and of the mind (*Consolation* 4.3, and 4.7 [poems], from the *Odyssey*). This is a touchstone of examples, as Rosamund Tuve pointed out long ago, and which Barkan uses as well (see *Allegorical Imagery*, pp. 225f). That, contingently, it emphasizes the danger of knowledgeable women, is precisely our concern. Most of these examples, as with many of the art-historical studies of interpretation, focus on figures of gods.

[36] Any teacher of literature will have experienced the shock which comes with rereading a familiar text one has taught for many years. As its renewed impact dislodges memory (false *or* true) of it, one's teaching suddenly reveals itself as the specious patter it has become.

neither consistency nor truth, and sometimes that surface meaning conveyed, through its own tissues of metaphor, a further poetic mood.[37] If
history tried to make Medea safe by writing her out, or into silence, allegory writes her in, by overinterpretation. Allegory can be a method of
denying action: the ascription of a label (badness) marks the end of analysis. Any literary representation can do that by acting out (in words), as we
think of the parallel verbal world as a kind of mimesis. There is another,
and more common, method in allegory, by describing a thing done, not
mimesis but description, not the imitation of the murder of children, but
the description of a potential (but unrealizable) imitation.

Two texts often classed as commentaries which came to have the status
of reference books will concern us first, both by French authors, both
composed in the fourteenth century, but one in the vernacular, the other
in Latin. Both retain the narrative emphasis given by following the *Metamorphoses*, but the power and sweep of Ovid's poetry disappears under the
rationalizing impulse and the weight of learning. Studies of mythographic
Ovidian texts have concentrated on their 'imposed allegory', examining
the interpretative moves which appeared to save Ovid for medieval readers. That concentration has tended to insist upon the dichotomy fable/al-
legory, where the interpretation supplies the real, or philosophical, truth
which the fabulous (that is, false) narrative appears to suggest. But, as
Caxton indicates, in the epigraph quoted at the head of this chapter, Ovid's
integuments can also cover history (that is, true narratives about the
past).[38] We need to look once more at the literal narratives.

At some time in the early fourteenth century a vernacular version of
Ovid was 'translated' by a learned Franciscan writer, perhaps a Burgundian, who was working in Paris. But to call his text a 'translation' is
to extend the usual meaning of the term. The *Ovide moralisé* consists
of 72,000 lines of *rimes plats* which repeat, expand, and gloss Ovid's

---

[37] Peter Dronke points out the importance of what might be called 'distant' allegorical
meanings: such is the arbitrariness of the connection that the 'poetic' consistencies of
the text-to-be-interpreted cannot interfere with the wisdom which the text is presumed
to convey. Once this originally medieval neo-platonic assumption gained currency, any
interpretation could be projected onto any text. See *Fabula: Explorations into the Uses of
Myth in Medieval Platonism* (Leiden, Brill, 1974).

[38] There is a extended analysis of this assumption that allegory usually recuperates a 'false'
narrative in the context of thirteenth-century poetry in Armand Strubel, *La Rose,
Renart, et le Graal: La littérature allégorique en France au XIIIe siècle* (Paris, Champion,
1989). This book is an important contribution to the understanding of the varieties of
allegorical interpretation which emphasizes the process of reaching interpretative
categories in any reading. Readers, medieval or modern, regularly treat the representations in a text as hypothetical and susceptible to multiple analysis.

Metamorphoses.[39] The anonymous author demonstrates a sequence of strategies of comprehensiveness; first, there is the attempt, familiar from the historical texts discussed in the previous chapter, to reconstruct as much of the 'history' of the interconnected legends as can be recovered. Second, there are several different kinds of interpretation, foremost among them allegorical.[40] There is a third strategy, which is an attack on the kind of popular vernacular historical romance typified by Benoît de Ste.-Maure, an attack which contingently aggrandizes the Franciscan's own authority (and ambition); like many writers reacting to the romanced inventions of his predecessors, he insisted upon his own truth. That the Franciscan quotes Benoît, and Chrétien, too, when it is convenient, is a reminder of the inconsistencies of legitimate reading: if part of their narratives corresponded to what was known to be true, they extracted that part or those parts. What this reveals is that under the guise of a 'commentary' legitimated by the authority of Ovid lurk the anonymous author's (not 'commentator's') historical and epic ambitions.

This vernacular 'replacement translation' is thus a multiply corrective book which threatens to supersede the text it ostensibly elucidates. In pursuit of information, he has availed himself of Ovid's other work, notably the *Heroïdes*, but also a library-full of well-known medieval texts on mythological themes. In addition to the *Integumenta Ovidii*, he knows the commentators, the *Ilias Latina*, an earlier retelling of one of the most famous of the metamorphoses, a *Philomena*; he cites the *Vulgate*, and, from classical 'historical' traditions, previous adaptations into the vernacular, the *Roman de Troie* and the *Histoire ancienne jusqu'à César.*[41] These he

---

[39] The modern edition is in five volumes; the section on Jason and Medea falls in the third (1931). *Ovide Moralisé: poème du commencement du quatorzième siècle publié d'après tous les manuscrits connus*, ed. C. de Boer, Martina G. de Boer, and Jeannette Th. M. Van 'T Sant, in *Verhandelingen der Koninklijke Akademie van Watenschappen* 15, 21, 30, 37, 43 (Amsterdam, 1915–38). De Boer suggests a date of composition of c.1316–28 (I.9–11). This is supported by J. Engels, *Etudes sur l'Ovide Moralisé* (Groningen, 1943), pp. 46–8. See also E. Panofsky, *Renaissance and Renascences in Western Art* (London, 1970; orig. 1965), p. 78n. There are comprehensive bibliographies in Strubel and in Barkan, *Gods Made Flesh*.

[40] When John Block Friedman calls it 'not really a commentary but an anthology of allegories' he is recognizing the distance of the commentary from Ovid, as well as its independence; *Orpheus in the Middle Ages* (Cambridge, Mass., Harvard University Press, 1970), p. 131. Supriya Chaudhuri stresses the shift in interpretation through the history of medieval commentaries from a 'moral' Ovid (still interested in metamorphosis) to a 'moralized' Ovid (now the raw material for interpreted fables). See her 'Medieval Ovids: Myth and Allegory', *University of Calcutta Journal of the Department of English* 22 (1986–7), pp. 5–24. I am grateful to Dr Chaudhuri for sending me an offprint of this article.

[41] Engels, pp. 70–2; De Boer, I.23–4. See also Rosemond Tuve, *Allegorical Imagery*, chapt.

paraphrases, rewrites, or appropriates. The pretence of his text is that it is intended as an accompaniment to Ovid's own (for readers who knew Latin), or a commented replacement text (for those who did not), but the unstated assumption is that the Franciscan's extraction of the historical events together with a guided tour of their interpretations, sanitizes Ovid's poetry. It elevates 'historia' over 'fabula', correcting the events according to the criteria of the former and the interpretation according to the latter. So extensive are his changes that, in fact, the claim to coherence and comprehensiveness reorganises and replaces the original structure and content of the *Metamorphoses* with the 'historical' structure established by Dares and expanded by Benoît, authorized by Homer, which reorients *Le Roman de Troie* as a whole. The attack on (and appropriation of) Benoît recovers the work for serious consideration.[42] And, above all, it is frequently *not* allegorical.

The changes in structures suggest the extent of the reconceptualization, the daring corrections. Ovid, it will be recalled, had begun his Book VII with a poetic link, moving from one image to the next. His epic style sees the Argonauts already launched on their journey, and he uses the break between books as one of those narrative gaps which lead the reader to expect something new. His compression refers to their many adventures, but pauses only at the metamorphosis of Phineus and the harpies. In terms of the Argonautic sequence this stop was a relatively minor event (the winged heroes, the Boreides Calais and Zetes, were able to free the king from the harpies' constant visitations because they could chase them), but it made a link to the previous book, which ended with Boreas's wooing, and the prediction that his sons would be winged. There is a further tacit link in the genealogical assumption that the reader recognizes and can supply the relationship between the house of Erectheus and that of Helios.

Here Ovid's witty juxtaposition and association is replaced by the his-

---

six, and, for a more sympathetic account, Meg Twycross, *The Medieval Anadyomene: a study in Chaucer's Mythography* (Oxford, Medium Aevum Monographs, *n.s.* 1, 1972). It is difficult to be precise about the Troy sources, because Benoît's text had already been absorbed by other authors. With the insertion of the prose *Roman de Troie* (and the *Heroïdes*) into the second redaction of the *Histoire ancienne jusqu'à César*, an ostensibly independent source appeared which further authorized Benoît's inventions. See Paul Meyer, 'Les premières compilations françaises de l'histoire ancienne', *Romania* 14 (1885), pp. 1–81 and Léopold Constans, 'Une traduction française des *Heroïdes* d'Ovide au XIIIe siècle', *Romania* 43 (1914), pp. 177–98.

42 This situates the Franciscan in the subversive line identified by Barbara Nolan in the context of the twelfth-century *romans antique*; see *Chaucer and the Tradition of the Romans Antique* (Cambridge, Cambridge University Press, 1992), p. 6.

torical urge which believes that the story itself, that is, the literal meaning, is a cover for another kind of extractable information, which is a historical representation. The translator/author suffers no aporias, and changes the structure of Book VI, adding the whole *Philomena* (attributed to Chrétien de Troyes), then expanding the association with the house of Erectheus, before finally ending with the story of Phineus, and a sequence of supposedly allegorical additions. That is, genealogy has superseded poetry. The large structure is by mythological house, not by metamorphosis. The smaller-scale structure is Chrétien's story of male betrayal, informed by images of trickery and repeated motifs of cages and caging, underwritten, of course, by the final metamorphoses into songbirds. If genealogy has superseded Ovid's imagery, it is perhaps because history has subsumed poetry in a manner which erases 'literature' and the idea of a free-standing fiction told in the style of history and difficult to distinguish from a true tale about the past. Genealogy is one more recourse to order.

Nevertheless, the nexus of women which includes Ino and Procne, is apparent here (if arbitrarily, following Ovid), together with a reference to disorder. The story of Phrixus and Helle had already been introduced, not here, where one might expect it, but as a preface to the story of Hero and Leander in Book IV, where it expands Ovid's reference (*Metamorphoses* IV, 416–562, but also *Fasti* III) to the madness of Athamas, their father. This story, too, is connected to a sense of a historical past.[43]

The expansion of the section on Tereus seems to be reproduced from Chrétien for the purpose of the compilation, and the Franciscan defers to Chrétien's authority for the translation and its truth:

> Mes ja ne descrirai le conte,
> Fors si com Crestiens le conte,
> Qui bien en translata la letre.
> Sus lui ne m'en vueil entremetre.
> Tout son dit vos raconterai
> Et l'alegorie en trairai.
>
> . . . Or dirai l'exposition
> De ceste variation,
> Si porrois entendre l'estoire
> Qui sans mençonge est toute voire.[44]

---

[43] So also Paule Démats, in her excellent discussion of history and fable in the *Ovide Moralisé, Fabula: Trois Études de mythographie antique et médiévale* (Geneva, Droz, 1973), chapt. 2.

[44] *Philomena: conte raconté d'après Ovide par Chrétien de Troyes,* ed. C. de Boer (Paris, Paul Geuthner, 1909), pp. 138, 141 and in the complete edition Book VI.2217–3840 pp.

[The story is not to be described except as Chrétien tells it, he who translated the text so well. I do not want to place myself above him. I shall tell you all he says and draw out the allegory. Now I will give you an account of this version, thus you will be able to understand the story, which I assure you is entirely true.]

If he vouches for Chrétien's translation, he implies that he has compared Chrétien's version to its original. What makes one version superior to another is its truth, its truth to its own authorities. But Chrétien was not translating Ovid; he was retelling Ovid's tale. In Chrétien's narrative almost all the stress is placed on the circumstances and surroundings of Tereus's betrayal of his father-in-law, wife, and sister-in-law. Indeed, more of the tale takes place in Pandion's palace, where Tereus persuades the king to allow Philomena to visit her sister, than in Tereus's own kingdom. Tereus's inner debates receive more attention than either Philomena's or Progne's. Progne's revenge is the suggestion of the devil she worships and her own pride, and the horrors of her sister's rape and the slaughter of her son are briefly recounted. Itys suffers for his father's 'felenie' despite Progne's love for him:

> Tant la beisa et conjoï
> Que Progne deüst estre ostee
> Del panser ou ele iert antree
> Si con requiert droiz et nature
> De tote humainne creature
> Et si con pitiez le deffant,
> Que mere ne doit son anfant
> Ne ocire ne desmanbrer.   (p. 87, lines 1312–1319)

[He [Itys] kisses and embraces her so much that Procne ought to have been lifted from the thought into which she had entered, as Law and Nature require of all human creatures, and as mercy forbids them: that no mother should kill or dismember her child.]

337–69 (see above n. 39). The first extract is the prologue to the story, the second to the allegory, both added by the Franciscan, which de Boer separated from the text. I follow his lineation and pagination. At the beginning of *Cligès*, Chrétien de Troyes mentions that he has already written a story 'de la hupe et de l'aronde/ Et del rossignol la Muance' so it is plausible that he is the author of this text. For my purposes it does not matter who actually wrote *Philomena*, since the Franciscan believed Chrétien did and legitimated his own retelling by Chrétien's authority, and I shall not distinguish Chrétien from a 'Chrétien'.

'Pride' may be a Christian concept of how men are led astray, but it is a far cry from any idea of the requirement of blood-kin revenge. Although I have quoted an emotionally satisfying moment from Chrétien's narrative, it is important to stress that in the main it follows Tereus, and is his tragedy. This shift of emphasis, from Ovid's allusions and associations to a sequence of tales which begin – at least – by focussing on kings and kingship, is one of the things the Franciscan has imitated not from Ovid but from Chrétien.

The so-called 'allegory' reads the text quite differently, tracing the soul's straying from God's grace because of fleshly temptation. We may think, with the editor and Gaston Paris, that nothing could be more absurd, but we must remember that this constant discovery of human sin, located in lust, was the ultimate lesson that human beings could learn, that no reminder of the need to transcend the flesh could be untimely. It is, in fact, also a masculinist reading. The soul may be feminine, but it is the soul of a man tempted by woman. It need hardly be repeated that the concomitant association of desire with the temptations posed by women powerfully and consistently reinforced the stereotypes of misogyny.[45] The fissiparous allegory projects different aspects of humanity onto the separate characters of the story, in a way typical of a medieval psychology which separates the inner life into independent and conflicting aspects. So far from allegorizing different aspects of human experience, this kind of projection reifies human subjectivity into competing and contradictory essences. The soul, too, suffers dismemberment. Nevertheless, what is most striking about the allegory here, and in the following section, is how little allegorical it is in relation to *Philomena*. For the style of allegorical interpretation, too, was a style, and one which could be exploited to insert important moral lessons *in the guise of* allegorical explication. It is scarcely 'imposed' at all, but forms a parallel text which creates the opportunity for homily rather than homology. The 'allegorical interpretation' is, rather, an allegorical-style story.

In the *Philomena* section the 'interpretation' comes at the end, but in the section on Jason and Medea the narrator divides the narrative, calling attention to his other message at suitable points of tension, so that the reader is interrupted and cannot simply follow the history. Thus, although the alternating sections may be allegorical in flavour, they have none of the consistency usually associated with commentary and interpretation. This

---

45 Gaston Paris quoted de Boer, p. 146 from his article in the *Histoire Littéraire*, 29, p. 517. The allegory is much more ingenious than mere lust of the eyes, but it is wildly inconsistent either in terms of the narrative or of tone.

has been thought to be the victory of *allegoresis* over literary unity. Yet they are far from incoherent, and might be seen as a kind of apparently uncontrolled free association normally confined to psychoanalytic studies of dreams. A comparison to a Rorschach test is not inappropriate. Medieval allegorizors claimed to 'find', when, like dream analysts, they were constantly creating; like dream analysts, they were often released from any kind of consistency of interpretation. But, like the individual analysand, they create in a language which is consistent, and which offers a series of identifiable patterns and repetitions. The limits of the analogy must be immediately clear, since the individuals concerned are authors speaking to a public, in a shared language which, however creatively they used it, was still publicly accessible. How 'Philomena' means is not dependent upon individual interpreters, and the subjective lexical and associative language they speak. The interpreter must link the interpretative language to *other* texts, so that the parallel narrative addresses a recognizable meta-text, in this case the absent Passion of Christ and the familiar story of the struggle for the human soul. As Barkan has described the relationship, the pre-existing system of allegorical interpretation of the Bible provides another area of reference, a template, to which the Franciscan can move at ease. There is a sense in which the new interpretation wrests authority from the publicly readable text, not to interpret it, although that is what it has to pretend to be doing, since that is the public language of legitimation, but to intercalate a different series of narratives which repeat in short bursts the stories of Christ's passion, God's grace, and familiar anagogical lessons of the soul's ascent. The allegory on *Philomena* is short, and restricted to the end, which perhaps suggests the strength of Chrétien's authority. By contrast, the next section is broken up by 'allegorical' interruptions.

Ovid's Book VII opens with the Argonaut's arrival in Colchis, and Medea's immediate susceptibility to their leader; her interior monologue is one of those delicious moments when the poet can explore apparently psychological eroticism.[46] His much-quoted epigram, 'video meliora proboque/ deteriora sequor' (I see the better course, but I follow the worse, VII.20–1) asks us to remember Dido.[47] It is literally reproduced in the French: 'Je voi le bien et le mal prens' (line 349). In Ovid there is a profound intertextual recuperation, establishing, by compression, a

---

[46] Ovid's section on Medea occupies the first 424 lines of Book VII. Ovid's constant contrast of civilization and barbarism appears in Medea's desire to leave Colchis for Greece.

[47] Brooks Otis, *Ovid as an Epic Poet* (Cambridge, Cambridge University Press, 2nd edn, 1970), 60–2 and 167–73 traces the borrowings and allusions in detail, but has a more moral view of their interpretation than is suggested here. See pp. 118–19 above.

betrayal-plot in which the active agent is the woman. Medea's thoughts rush ahead to marriage, and Ovid's dramatic irony rehearses the betrayals to come in Medea's denial of their possibility. Deceived by a fantasy of herself as a Greek wife celebrated as the saviour of the Greek heroes, she distances herself from her own betrayal of her kin and country. In this instance her status as a barbarian woman, although inherited from Euripides, is not prominent. Ovid's Jason does not speak, although Ovid tells us that he swore an oath to Medea.

The brilliance of Ovid's structuring depends upon a readership well acquainted with the legends, since his anticipations and references are oblique. Ovid suppresses the murder of Absyrtus by skipping the return voyage, and merely refers to the murders in Corinth as having happened before the dragon-drawn chariot takes Medea on to Athens. Thus the hero remains heroic despite the concentration on Medea. It is Medea who drives the story forward, once she is Jason's Greek wife, Medea whose idea it is to murder Pelias by the hands of his daughters. Working by juxtaposition, Ovid sees no contradiction between the ingenue who gives herself to Jason and the wife who destroys his enemies. Ovid's tonal control is manifested by narrative reference and by the careful balance of summary to speech. He analyzes no motive; draws no lesson; points no moral. In all this Jason speaks only once, with the pious request that his powerful wife take days from his life in order to add them to his father's. This introduces Ovid's focus: the metamorphosis which rejuvenates the aged Aeson, and includes the famous lines about her power over nature (VII.179–219) which were to become Prospero's.[48] In Ovid's world of power over nature, of constant metamorphosis, one does not feel the force of human suffering. It is all rhetorical show, all held at a distance by the narrator's voice.

The anonymous redactor has different interests.[49] He has learned, perhaps from Chrétien, or perhaps from the numerous historical models of the voyage of Argo, a structure which is public, focussed on kingship, and the male-centred adventure (something he also does for his long interpolation for the Theban war). Jason, who begins as a gentle hero, is as perfidious as Tereus, and we are in no doubt from the start that the man who could abandon and forget Hypsipyle could do the same once Medea had fled. This orientation continues throughout this long section, and Medea's role is in part to create a transition to the story of Theseus. The

---

[48] Medea's speech and Golding's free translation are quoted in *The Tempest*, ed. Stephen Orgel (Oxford, 1987), Appendix E.

[49] There is an excellent discussion of his historical manipulations here and at the other points at which he touches on the destruction of Troy in Démats, *Fabula*, pp. 80–9.

relative straight-forwardness of the narrative should not hide its skill. The narrative is well told, carefully marked for the listener or reader, and abruptly punctuated by allegory. His own Book VII begins:

> Dessus aux fables fu retrait
> Comment Yno fist le faulz fait
> Dou blé cuit qu'ele fist semer;
> Comment Helle noia en mer,
> Et comment Frixus mer passa
> Si vint en Colche, et la lessa
> Ou temple Martis la toison.
> Or orrez pour quele achoison
> Jason ala la toison querre.
> Et comment il la pot conquerre.
> Tout par ordre le vous diroi.
> En Arges ot un riche roi,
> Fel tirant, qui ot non Pelie.
> Grant terre avoit en sa baillie.
> Un neveu ot le riches rois,
> Moult preux, moult sages, moult cortois.
> Moult debonaire, moult proisie,
> Moult apert et moult envoisie.
> Humble estoit et servicables,
> Debonaires et amiables.
> Li damoisiaux ot non Jason.
> Niez fu Pelie et filz Heson. (VII.1–22)

[The fables above told how Yno evilly made them sow parched seeds of wheat, how Helle drowned in the sea, and how Frixus crossed the sea and came to Colchis, and left the fleece in the temple of Mars. Now you shall hear with what motive Jason went to seek the fleece. I shall tell you everything in order. There was a powerful king in Argos, a wicked tyrant called Pelias who ruled over large territories. This powerful king had a nephew, very brave, very wise, very courteous, very well-mannered, very well-reputed, very fit and very good natured. He was modest and helpful, charming and loveable. The young man was called Jason, the nephew of Pelias, and Aeson's son.]

Ovid's 424 lines become over 2,000 lines of octosyllabic couplets, including the interpolation on the related adventures of Theseus which expand and explicate what in Ovid was merely an allusion. Since the Franciscan has suppressed some of Ovid's catalogue of places and herbs, one might consider that under 400 Latin lines have contributed to his *amplificatio*. Some of the amplifications emulate Benoît, by replacing reported with direct speech, or enlarging the rhetorical scope of something said or felt. But he includes more than Benoît did. He gives Medea monologues, and, for the first time, a dialogue with the daughters of Pelias to persuade them that she can rejuvenate their father, thus introducing an element of decision. This is the first time we have had this scene fully realized. Throughout, there is a concentration on the inner life, and upon motive, which was alien to Ovid's style in the *Metamorphoses*.

The central paradoxes of a 'complete' retelling are inescapable; the Franciscan describes Jason's flight from Colchis with the fleece and Medea, and her strategem for eluding pursuit: 'Son frere Assirtim emportoit./ De grant cruauté le membra./ Piece à piece le desmembra' (660–662). The Argo returns home to plaudits for their noble victory. We may consider that there is a tacit ironic criticism of these benighted pagans; there is certainly criticism of Medea, who advised Jason on the best means to steal the fleece and abduct her. He replaces Ovid's juxtaposition of the ingenue and the sorceress by imputing to Medea a desire to murder Pelias for Jason's sake (lines 1247–63). The criticism sometimes becomes explicit, as when the narrator comments that Medea had more pity for Jason than her own father or brother (862–65). She *is* both healer and destroyer. Female desire leads to murder by poison, both of Pelias and of Creusa (lines 1365–1506), where the concentration on Medea's aggression moves toward a condemnation of all women. But Jason is not spared: after the murder of Pelias Medea fled, and no sooner was she gone than he forgot her and prepared to marry again. It is this insult which makes her return to kill his new wife and father-in-law. We will meet this return again in the next chapter.

The allegorical interruptions come at three places and constitute the parallel story of Christ's descent to save us after the fall of the angels brought disobedience into the world. First, in lines 690–820, after the Argonauts return to Greece, the Franciscan uses metaphoric (rather than narrative) resemblance to attach the long-sought prize to the Lamb of God who took human flesh for our salvation, Jason's ploughing the soil to Christ's harrowing, but above all the magical metamorphoses to Christ's transformations which save humanity. Second, after the section in which Jason begs Medea to restore his father's youth, the story continues in lines 1081–1246, where the allegory concerns Christ's assumption of human flesh and repeats the image of the 'cage', which had begun in the previous story of Philomena. Third, after Medea's Corinthian revenge, the allegory (lines 1508–1672) concentrates on Christ's passion (the cage image

137

reappears) with practically no reference to the literal narrative. When it does come, Creusa (as the deceiver) is the enemy whom God must destroy with everlasting fire. This is so perplexing as to be easily dismissed. But if we consider it no longer an allegorical commentary, but the occasion for a parallel narrative, then it matters little that there is no narrative or character similarity, because the literal narrative is important only insofar as it *is* an occasion for a different story to be told. The Franciscan's moral commentary has often been criticised as incoherent, his amplifications a betrayal of his professed intention to translate Ovid. Yet I would enter a plea for attention to the literal sections.

'Replacement translations' have other intentions than those they express, and this compendium deserves the attention we now give to the *romans antique*. The *literal* sections are often as well narrated as those *romans*. In this section, the Franciscan's rendition of the legends combines the structures of Benoît and Chrétien (in the *Philomena*) in a style which we may think of as characteristic of earlier vernacular verse histories or romances. He has strong views about authority, which he manipulates in order to make a space for himself. There is a coming together here of mythographical and historical ideas because the narrative material coincides. Caxton's view that Ovid's apparent fiction cloaks true tales about the past was not new with him.

Throughout, one of the important legitimations of Ovid-commentary is that

> Toute ceste fable est histoire
> Et de Pelye et de Jason
> Fors solement de le toison.   (VII.690–2)
>
> [All this fable is history, both of Pelias and Jason, excepting only the fleece.]

That 'history' should be the claim to legitimacy, in a text which 'moralises' throughout, should seem less odd than it once did; in a culture which could read the past as manifesting the will of God, events, too, were interpreted as text. The anonymous author, who has absorbed (and redistributed) Benoît's text, carefully reproaches him for preferring the 'wrong' authority, and states his own elevation of Homer over Dares, but his method of discrimination is implicit. When he turns to the great destruction of Troy he explains,

> Des or comenceront, sans faille,
> L'ocision et le martire,
> La grant estoire et la matire

Que traist le clers de Sainte More
De Darès, mes ne m'en vueil ore
Sor lui de gaires entremetre
Là où bien translata la letre.
Moult fu le clers bons rimoierres,
Cortois parliers et biaux faignierres,
Et moult fu bien ses romans fais,
Mes nequedent, sauve sa pais,
Il ne dist pas en touz leuz voir
Si ne fist mie grant savoir
Dont il Homers osa desdire
Ne desmentir ne contredire
Ne blasmer oeuvre qu'il feïst
Chose que dire ne deüst
Et que de verité ne seüst.
Ja nel deüst avoir repris,
Quar trop iert Homers de grant pris,
Mes il parla par metaphore.
Por ce li clers de Sainte More,
Qui n'entendoit qu'il voloit dire,
Li redargua sa matire.
Tuit le Grejois et li Latin
Et cil qui onques en latin
Traitierent riens de cest histoire
Tesmoignent la matire à voire,
Ensi com Homers la traita
Et cil qui son grec translata.
Neïs Darès, de quoi fu fais
Le romans Beneois et trais,
N'est de riens contraires à lui,
Quar l'un et l'autre livre lui,
Fors tant que plus prolixement
Dist Darès le demenement,
Les assamblees et les tours,
Les batailles et les estours
Qui furent fet par devant Troie.
Ne sai que plus vous en diroie,
Mes cil qui l'un et l'autre orra
Croie celui qui miex vaudra.   (XII.1712–54)

[Here begins, without fail, the death and martydom, the great history and matter which the clerk of Ste.-Maure took from Dares, but I do not now want to say much about him where he translated the text correctly. The clerk was a very good rhymer, a courtly speaker and good craftsman, and his

139

narrative was well done – but that notwithstanding, saving his peace, he does not tell the truth all the time. He did not act very wisely when he dared to refute Homer, to deny or contradict or criticize the work that he made, for he then said what he should not and spoke of things of which he did not know the truth. He should not have criticized him, for Homer was too worthy – but he spoke in metaphor. Because of this the clerk of Ste.-Maure, who did not understand what he meant, challenged what he had written. All Greeks and Romans, and those who ever wrote about this history in Latin, attest the truth of the matter just as Homer described it, and so did he who translated his Greek. Even Dares, from whom Benoît's narrative is made and drawn, is in no way contradictory to him, for I have read both books, except that Dares treats the situation at greater length, the assemblies, the strategies, the battles, and the encounters that took place before Troy. I do not know what more to say to you, but let him who hears both believe the one which better merits it.]

The contradictions and complexities are clear. What controls the value of those sources which one must compare and choose between (Homer, Dares, Benoît)? What has elevated the 'right' 'historical' account over Ovid's poetry? How is it that he praises Chrétien's expanded account but derides Benoît's? When a text is both literal and metaphorical, how does one discriminate? Who would know that the version of the legends which has now solidified is in essence a combination of historical and mythographical texts which are interdependent? The Franciscan's method is consistent with what we have seen in the first two chapters; he says nothing, but makes his own tacit decisions. First, he rationalizes, discriminating the historical from the fabulous. He offers parallel 'historical' and 'allegorical' readings. The readings are not explanations; they are additional layers. If the stories are historical, one might think that their magic would need some degree of rationalization, but he has a way around this problem: the double appeal to the authority of earlier books and the inalienable status of the Fall of Troy. *Those* recitals of the story are themselves grist for allegorical interpretations which legitimate the whole enterprise by denying the importance of the status of the events. The place of Troy in the European imagination offers a long sequence of patterns of historical betrayals.

Are these events thought to be figural, in any sense? Not on the Biblical model by which chronologically later events, by recapitulating the earlier ones, 'complete' them. Nevertheless, as heuristic devices, yes, precisely.

Particularly where part of the justification of *Jason*'s adventures is their priority, one might expect some sense of the repetitive patterns of history as tragedy, with Troy foremost among historical examples.

By contrast to the epic ambitions of the *Ovide Moralisé*, the contemporary commentary known as the *Ovidius Moralizatus* presents a relatively more straightforward example of the freedom and constraints experienced by a Latinate author intent upon explicating a classical text.[50] In fact, as is well known, explicating Ovid is only one of the many ambitions of this text; the whole *Repertorium Morale* is one of those huge encyclopedic impulses which characterize the scholastic impulse at the end of the Middle Ages. As a reference book, Bersuire's text is keyed to the *Metamorphoses*, so that the searching reader can find his place. It is intended as an accompaniment rather than a replacement text. The explanatory notes follow the pattern established from the earliest times, and give etymological and historical information, expand allusions, and include related stories. For example, in elucidating Nessus' burning garment, Bersuire refers to the authority of Fulgentius and Pliny. For the historical status of the Argonautic voyage he is content to add the history of Troy to Ovid: 'Et sic vellus aureum habuit: & cum Medea furtim ad propria remeavit: sic ponit Ovidius. Et ponitur in principio Historiae Troiae', although no version is specified.[51]

The Christian emphasis manifests itself in a sequence of independent moral allegories. Here, too, it would be an error to expect one line of

---

[50] There are two versions of Bersuire's Latin commentary; all of the A-text and the introduction to the P-text were printed by J. Engels in his *Werkmateriaal*, 1–3 (1960–66) [reviewed M. Twycross in *Medium Aevum* 37 (1968), pp. 320–3 – Mrs Twycross kindly called this review to my attention]. The material on Jason and Medea is in the A-text, Bersuire's original composition, before he had reference to the Franciscan's text. He did not change it significantly, and only that first text is considered here. On Bersuire himself, see the series of articles by Fausto Ghisalberti, 'Medieval Biographies of Ovid', in *Journal of the Warburg and Courtauld Institutes* 9 (1946), 10–59 and 'L'"Ovidius moralizatus" de Pierre Bersuire' *Studi romanzi* 23 (1933), pp. 5–136. J. Engels, *Etudes sur l'Ovide Moralisé* (Groningen, 1943), chapt. 2. See also his 'Berchoriana: I' in *Vivarium* 2 (1964), pp. 62–124; 'L'Edition critique de l'*Ovidius Moralizatus* de Bersuire' *Vivarium* 9 (1971), pp. 19–24 and 'Les Commentaires d'Ovide au XVIe siècle', *Vivarium* 12 (1974), pp. 3–13. There is a book-length biographical essay by Charles Samaran in the *Histoire Littéraire de la France* 39 (1962), pp. 259–450, which supersedes the older one by Gaston Paris 29 (1885). Extracts in *Medieval Literary Theory and Criticism c.1100–c.1375: The Commentary Tradition*, ed. A. J. Minnis, A. B. Scott, with the assistance of David Wallace (Oxford, 2nd edn 1991), pp. 366–72, but, once again, emphasizing gods.

[51] *Werkmateriaal*, 2, p. 113. A collation of pp. 107–17 with the corresponding section of BNf. lat. 16787 (the revised version) shows revision in some detail, but nothing of significance. The substance of Ovid's story, and of Bersuire's original commentary, is intact.

narrative consistency, since this is a reference work intended for use by preachers. Any Latinate priest could use this collection as a source from which to select examples for sermons or homilies. There is no obligation to be comprehensive, or to use more than one from the cornucopeia of allegories offered. Although Bersuire makes no attempt to rework Ovid's hexameters into a coherent historical narrative, as did the anonymous Franciscan, he does see the story as Jason's, rather than as examples of magic, metamorphoses, or Medea's fate. If he interpolates Pelias's designs upon Jason's life, it is only to remind us how God turns men's evil to good. There is no attempt to match the succession of incidents or the development of character to any kind of moral unfolding.

He has, nevertheless, predictable responses to the idea of the hero, and imposes only 'positive' allegories upon Jason himself. The fecundity and energy of these associations reach the heights of stream-of-consciousness (or perhaps free-association) interpretations. Jason figures alternately God, Christ, and the virtuous prelate at different points, while Medea is reduced to an object (in some versions the Golden Fleece is turned into Medea). As for the outline of the 'plot', Bersuire's memorizable crib runs as follows: 'Exinde enim sequitur famae perditio: parentum conturbatio: invidiae stimulatio: proditiosa machinatio: homicidiorum perpetratio: & finalis separatio'.[52] If Bersuire has noticed difficulties about Jason's marriage to Creusa, he makes only a reference to mankind in general.

However far each of these two fourteenth-century 'commentators' thought his readings could control access to Ovid, what in effect they each did was propose a protocol for absorbing Ovid. That is, their own freedom sets an example of freedom; so far from reining interpretation in, it liberates it. The value of their moralized Ovids is manifested by the number of translations, modifications, and modernizations which were made for more than a century after theirs. Epitomes in prose were produced by various publishers, including both William Caxton and his associate, Colard Mansion. In Bruges, Mansion combined Bersuire's opening with a prose version of the *Ovide Moralisé* to create *La Bible des Poetes,* the kind of reference book to which no one could object.[53] The filiation of reinterpretations is complex, even for as vexed a subject as medieval mythography. A clear and concise analysis of redactions of the medieval Ovid,

---

[52] *Werkmateriaal,* 2, p. 109.

[53] Mansion's edition is of 1484, e.g. BL IC. 49428 and was reprinted by Vérard. Such descendants last into the seventeenth century, often with sumptuous illustrations, e.g. M. Renouard, *Les Metamorphoses . . . traduites en prose françoise* (Paris, 1618).

including a guide to parts of their contents, is to be found in Panofsky's *Renaissance and Renascences in Western Art.*[54]

Caxton's version represents a number of the conflicts which tied the historical and the mythological Ovids. His prose translation (of the Burgundian prose version printed by Mansion) exists only in manuscript, and there is no evidence to suggest that he ever set his text in type.[55] Caxton's attitude to 'authority' encompasses his vernacular reading: Gower apparently provides Iris with her 'rayny cope' and Morpheus with his bed made of 'Hebenus that sleepi tree'.[56] He sees his book as part of a textual enterprise, and refers his reader to other authors for further information, such as Chaucer for the description of the House of Fame, Lydgate, and even his own earlier translation of Raoul Lefèvre.[57] Multiplication of authorities can be a form of retreat, of muddying the waters until no one authority is any longer paramount. In Ovid, Caxton says, history and fable are intertwined; the pleasure which leads the reader to wisdom lies in his penetration of the veiled text.

And thenne emong the Latyn Poetes Ovyde of Sulmonence is to be preysed and honoured hyely . . . his werke is ryghte excellent and notable. Of whyche because of the peryce and subtilte of the fables wherin is conteyned grete and prouffitable wysedom to them that knowe and understande theme, he imposed the name Metamorphose, which is as moche to say as transmutacion of one fable into another, or interpretacion of theym. For he, seeing as wel the Latin Poetes as the Poetes of Grece that had ben tofore hym and hys tyme, hade touched in wrytyng many fables and them passed superfycyelly without expressyng theyre knowledge or entendement. The sayde Ovide hath opend unto the Latyns the way as wel in the fables of Grekes as in other, and hath them

---

54 (London, 1965), esp. p. 78n. See also Jean Seznec, *The Survival of the Pagan Gods: the Mythological Tradition and its Place in Renaissance Humanism and Art* (New York, Bollingen Foundation, 1953; orig. 1940).

55 Half of Caxton's text (Books X–XV) survives in the Pepys collection, Magdalene College, Cambridge MS 2124. Two early editions of this part of the text are George Hibbert, ed. *Six Books of Metamorphoseos* (London, 1819) and Stephen Gaselee and H. W. W. Brett-Smith, eds, *Ovyde: Hys Booke of Metamorphose* (Oxford, 1924). The first part of the manuscript was discovered in 1966, among the 'rubbish' in Sir Thomas Phillipps' collection. The whole was beautifully reproduced in a colour facsimile: *The Metamorphoses of Ovid: translated by William Caxton 1480* (Nork York, George Braziller in connection with Magdalene College, Cambridge, 1968). The specific original from which Caxton was translating is not known, but is represented by exemplars such as BL Royal 17.E.iv or BNf. f.fr. 137.

56 See J. A. W. Bennett, 'Caxton and Gower', *The Modern Language Review* 45 (1950), pp. 215–16 and his introduction to Kathleen Scott *The Caxton Master and his Patron* (Cambridge, The Bibliographical Society, 1976).

57 Gaselee, *op.cit.*, p. 77.

tyssued and woven by so gret subtyltee of engyne, charge, and solicytude in such wyse that it myght be sayde very semblably that they depended one of another and that by such ordre that frome the creacion of the world unto hys tyme he had ordeyned hys sayengis, some by fable and some by hystorye only. And otherwyse tyssued and medled with fable and hystorye togidre, which is a thyng right subtil. And his dittes or syengis ben not to be repudyed ne reproched ther as they ne conteyn but fable only.

For over and above theloquence whiche is right swete, under veyle or shadow hyd, he compryseth the scynce and advertysement of grete partye of thingis comen or at leste by possybylite ben for to com. And yf the chronyclers of hystoryes had wryten by so cler and lyght style and gestes and feates of the noble and valyant men or of thyngis possible to come, then eche man might at the first sight have conceyved and comprised theym, where they hade be holden thenne more for Phylosophers than for Poetes.... (ff. 13r–14r)

These are unusual claims, as if Ovid's text were to be set up, indeed, as a kind of poet's Bible, based on Ovid's understanding of a parallel pagan interpretation of the world, from creation until his own day. There is, almost inaudible, a reference to the *translatio studii* embedded in this passage, since Ovid's achievement parallels the previous successes of Greek poets, which he subsumes. History itself becomes a kind of allegory, which extends even to prophecy. If we look twice at this never-edited passage, it becomes curiously discordant, making claims for Ovid which belong, or should belong, only to more sacred, Christian texts. The epigraph to this chapter, which is taken from the next paragraph of Caxton's prohemye, promises poetry, philosophy, politics, and history. The true interpreter can extract numerous kinds of 'scynce' – but what *is* the key to all mythologies?

Resisting single, comprehensive explanations, whether they are primal scenes, mother goddesses, or originary acts of ritual sacrifice, is important in the analysis of the complex and contradictory social and literary inheritance of the west. Terms such as 'myth' – or, indeed, 'woman' – run the risk of elevating concepts into Ideal Types which have always been the same. To appeal to a nexus of female characters who appear to threaten patriarchal order runs the risk of elevating another essentialist concept in turn. But to restrict Ovid's variety in this way is to succumb to reductiveness. A question such as 'what is magic, in the sense of potential metamorphosis, meant to symbolize' cannot be asked without asking who is asking, in what society. Ovid's urbanity depended upon concepts such as free-standing fiction, experienced within a reading culture which was knowledgeable about earlier texts and prepared to enjoy intertextuality. Where fiction loses status and history takes its place, free play disappears. A growing nexus of dangerous women, underwritten by the status of the Argonautic voyage and the history of Troy, could be appealed to in order to establish the possibility of generalizable beliefs about 'woman'. It is a cliché well worth remembering that fictional representations by Auctors, with all their authority, contributed to (but did not create, decree, or determine) ideas of human nature, although their status also opened inconsistencies of interpretation (before the Christian dispensation, in poetry, 'fabulous') for medieval readers and writers, inconsistencies which remained contestable. Ovid's view of the irrational feminine is his description and not a necessity of essentialist misogyny. There is still space for other interpretations.

This chapter has discussed allegory and commentary as habits of reading and interpretation rather than automatic or mechanical beliefs, of, if I might mix my critical terminologies, structures of feeling in different conceptual spaces. If characters were read as representing historical agents, any particularities of 'characterization' were broad-based and only emerged from the deeds in which they were implicated; further, the emphasis was on deeds and the consequences of the deeds for social units. For example, Laomedon's suspicion and refusal to allow the Argonauts to take on fresh water, interpreted as churlish bad manners, eventuated in the first destruction of his city; the irony by which the conqueror's mercy spared the child who was to become Laomedon's successor is a historical one which appeals to ideas about unforeseen (and unforeseeable) large-scale consequences. On this kind of interpretation, the cycles of history reveal constants of behaviour which eventuate in political acts, and connect private virtues and vices to their public consequences. One way in which Laomedon (or Jason) may escape stereotype is because of his connection to the large-scale history of Troy in which he plays a part; having a specific name, too, is a feature which contributes more to specificity than we may always remember. Although such a conclusion as 'rulers should be generous' may be a moral worthy of the Duchess in *Alice*, it is nonetheless part of what Mirrors for Princes commonly preached.

If, not necessarily on another hand, the characters were read as fictions created in order to illustrate traits of human behaviour, they could be interpreted as contributing to equally constant cycles of individual experience in patterns such as loyalty and betrayal, love and hate, injury and revenge. Where these experiences are allegorized to those of a Soul they need not be gendered, but, as we have seen, certain occurences or combinations (love/hate as irrational passions) tended to become associated

145

with women, and thereby feminized. Some of these virtues or vices promise to be asymmetries: the public male vices of perjury, disloyalty, and ambition, as opposed to the unbalanced partisanship of women prepared to sacrifice their families for the love of a husband. If the fictions, in a reading culture in which 'fictions' are not condemned out of hand, display rhetorical excess, they are easier to assimilate to states of mind to be emulated or avoided. Where the fictions have become more problematic (because pagan, secular, or dangerous) they could be dealt with by *in bono* or *in malum* allegories. Where rhetorical representation passed beyond mental state and passionate speech to action, rhetoric itself opened those actions to the analysis of motive, the defence of a course taken, the *judgement* of the audience. To ask why something happened is not the same as questioning why someone did something. To ask further if the thing done, or the figure doing it, represents a cycle, a type, a category of deeds or characters, forms one of the issues of literary and historical interpretation.

The Medeas we have seen are tragic figures caught by love in a series of dilemmas. It would be unwise to see any of these characters as heroines to be elevated in a straightforward sense; they may be sinned against, but they are never suffering innocents. If they are betrayed, there are reasons for those betrayals. There are questions to be asked about whether the tragic figures of history are ever also historical figures of Tragedy, and about how far they must be reinterpreted in free-standing literary artifacts before they can assume tragic status. Thus far, only Euripides and Seneca have offered us that, a solution which extracts 'tragedy' from Benjamin's 'play of sorrow'. The inconsistencies which arise with awareness of a 'whole' story, an awareness which is implied by the existence of a historical imagination, cannot be rationalized, cannot be made to go away. It may be that the questions Medeas raise are more social, more political, than has hitherto seemed likely. The trajectory of heroic conquest in which Jason seems to be moulded is undercut by the development of the idea that there is a story, one complete and comprehensive legend. At the heart of European history, the prelude to the story of Troy is a scandal of betrayal, murder, betrayal, and murder. The allegorical Medeas and Jasons we have met in this chapter grow from the historical ones we met in the last. The fission of *diasparagmos*, of dismembering, is the central essentialism of any fusion of the legends.

In the next two chapters the road bifurcates, and I shall continue to take leave of chronology to look first at one extended work, an attempt to tell the whole 'histoire' in a culture not altogether clear about its attitudes to 'history' or 'romance'. The book we know as *L'histoire de Jason* attempts to deal with inconsistencies of character and motive, to return Jason to his heroic status within the context of the political romances of mid- and late-fifteenth-century Burgundy. Then, in Chapter Five, I will return to the varieties of Medeas who remained available, and to readings of different kinds.

FOUR

The Romance of Jason

If we begin by considering the legends of Jason and Medea as a story, one which comes from ancient history, but which may or may not be of itself 'historical', the questions which arise take their departure from the patterns of fiction. One of the risks of a comprehensive account of a 'whole' story is the virtual impossibility of making it coherent. The concentration of so many poets on the figure of Medea can amount, in effect, to a condemnation of Jason. There do not seem to be many choices: a man who is a virago's companion is a weak man, her accomplice is worse, and should he be her dupe or her victim he is additionally a fool. By contrast, the folktale figure who accomplishes impossible tasks with the aid of the ogre's daughter is a hero; he is politically neutral, because situated in the context of imaginary time and space. *His* story ends happily ever after. This appears to be true even if, perhaps especially if, he has many amorous adventures. The accretions and repetitions which his tale attracts are usually consistent, and consistently heroic. He travels outwards, defeats his enemy, and returns to assume his rightful place in society, accompanied by the most important amorous adventure: the bride who has brought him wealth and status, whose place now is as his consort and mother of his children. But that becomes another story.

The sequence of events in many Greek tales involves individual adventures and acts of heroism, including sexual exploits.[1] This is relatively easy for the gods. The trail of seduction and abandonment left by immortals is only to be expected; they have the advantage, moreover, that their victims have no redress against them. To a certain extent this is also true of human

---

[1] This has recently been emphasized by Roberto Calasso's interpretations of the repetitiveness of seduction and betrayal throughout Greek mythology in *The Marriage of Cadmus and Harmony*, trans. Tim Parks (New York, Knopf, 1993). He sees woman's chief act of reprisal as sexual betrayal.

heroes.[2] As we noticed in the previous chapter, even as renowned (and successful) a seducer as Theseus escapes contumely. His status as a foundation-figure for the city of Athens may help explain his reputation, but it may also be that *his* success survives the purely rhetorical attacks of his mistresses. *His* tragedy, when he calls the god down to punish the son he believes has offended his wife, is supremely *his*. In the only serious retaliation in his story, Phaedra may herself be the god's victim and, to a degree, the god's accomplice, but it is not her curse, but Theseus's power, which acts. Theseus is heroic, active, and close to the gods. His relationship is with them more than it is with his wife. As time passed the events of Theseus's life remained near-mythic, from the Minotaur to the bull from the sea, even in the euhemerizing hands of Plutarch.[3] Like attitudes to revenge, views of male sexuality change with changing contexts. The seducer may appear to be a perjurer (rather than merely a philanderer) if women's status rises.

But suppose we contextualize the fictions which are near myth as part of the history of Europe. Many features distinguish Jason's tale: Jason himself, of course, as constituted by his deeds (but also by his motives for those deeds) and his human vulnerability, the succession of incidents which concern the Argonautic voyage, but additionally his setting in a kind of historical time. Folklore heroes are famously short of 'character', and Euripides dealt not with a folklore hero, but with one of his self-deceived deceivers, in a play which became one of his critical looks at 'heroism' itself. As we have already seen, the sum of parts which became set or hardened with the inventions of Euripides, the scholarship of Apollonius, and the brilliance of Ovid burden any sense of a whole with the weight of their possible truth. There may be little sense of a hero who can be characterized by his *aretê* or his gifts. As I remarked above in comparing Apollonius and Virgil, Jason's connection to an immortal patron faded early from most versions. Even where Hera's favour is mentioned, his support from her disappears after he has borne her across the river where he loses his

---

2 One of the many differences between stories told in the ancient world and those of the western Middle Ages is the assumption of female stasis in the former; there is little or no assumption that women will move or travel unless summoned by or escorted by men. By the medieval period heroines begin to travel, with or without leave.

3 There is an overview of Theseus and his legend in R. Flacelière, *Thésée: Images et récits* (Paris, Boccard, 1958); a more modern, and symbolically complex study is Claude Calame, *Thesee et l'Imaginaire Athenien: légende et culte en Grèce antique* (Lausanne, Payot, 1990), esp. chapt. 6. For the medieval figure, see Simon Tidworth, 'The Roman and Medieval Theseus', in *The Quest for Theseus*, ed. Ann Ward (New York, Praeger, 1970). For Chaucer Theseus has become the stern (but monogamous) king of *The Knight's Tale*.

sandal. The accretions which Jason's story attracted created problems for anyone who wished to retell it because the once-subsidiary companions effectively distracted attention from their leader (similar to late versions of the story of Arthur). Since Apollonius, Jason has been overwhelmed with assistance; he is not outstanding among his companions. He is short of conquests or solutions to puzzles. Unlike Theseus's, Jason's seductions are insufficiently redeemed by his heroic achievements or the necessities of kingship: and even the seduction of Hypsipyle is denigrated by the sex-starved desperation of the Lemnian women. However that easy conquest may tend to ridicule, it has a darker thematic link which should not be ignored: the 'conquered' women are already murderers of men. Here, too, the adventures of Jason's companions require attention: Heracles leaves the Argo in search of his beloved Hylas, who has been drowned by the nymphs who desired him. In the end, it is Jason's powerlessness which encumbers him. In classical versions, even if Aphrodite gives him a sexual advantage, he cannot keep it, and no goddess makes him invulnerable.

A Jason ruled by Medea is a character who has ceded man's duty to head his household, located in time and space. He is a man who would be king – but never achieves his kingdom. At the point in Corinth when Creon fatally chooses Jason as his son-in-law, Jason is chosen, passive, and on the point of acquiring rule through another woman. If one looks back to folktale, the asymmetries of gender are clear, since a woman married to a wicked husband can retain some air of innocence or even virtue if she obeys her lord against her will. This problem, in which the beleaguered wife sometimes outwits the evil man to whom she is bound, is also familiar enough. There is a further problem in the story's episodes of deceit. *Both* hero and heroine lie and deceive to their own advantage. There is a related folk-tale dilemma which is found from the *Ramayana* to the rhetorical exercises invented for Roman schoolboys, to varieties of western legend: that of the ruler who makes an overgenerous promise which allows him to be taken advantage of by the character to whom he has made it. If the request is against custom or the law, his granting it affects his kingdom, while the failure to keep his word destroys his integrity. The unscrupulous character who takes advantage of a good man's unwillingness to break his word is always condemned, but that does not mean that his or her victim is absolved of blame.

The history of Jason and Medea as it coalesced by the end of antiquity leaves very little space for any such manipulations. The story of *Jason* which begins with Pelias's fear of his nephew (and motivates the journey of the Argo) continues beyond its expected end to become an unusual succession of deceptions and revenges. Radiating out from this narrative

150

is, first, the antecedent story of the Fleece, beginning with Ino's threat to her step-children; second, there is the link to Thebes through the sons of Hypsipyle; and third, there is Heracles' first destruction of the city of Troy. The story of *Medea* carries on through Aegeus to the Athens of Theseus, but also doubles back to Colchis through her reconciliation to both Jason and Aeetes. Euripides' astonishing ability to turn attention and, to a degree, sympathy, to Medea's plight changed the way his successors told the story, and created an ambivalence too successful to ignore. The desire for revenge which is integral to Ovid's vision of his solitary letter-writing heroines, as well as his Medea's ability to act it out, established and emphasized the power and immorality of the witch freed from the constraints which are the positive power of love. Its negative pole, the hatred which arises from love betrayed, were a subject which located fear *and* desire in audiences for hundreds of years. What women do (for the beloved) when they can, that powerful women are free of the scruples which bind most moral agents, are two of the fantasies to which a sequence of Medeas, and their imitations, contributed. The woman who rescued the Argonauts and rejuvenated Jason's father is the woman who betrayed her father and killed his son, tricked the daughters of Pelias into murdering their father, consumed in a poisonous fire both Jason's new bride and her father, then killed her own children. The emphases here are gendered: where a woman is the centre the politics of her exile, loss of civic status, or establishment of a kingdom take second place to her experience of private love and hate.

It is always salutary to remember how much imaginative possibilities change with different times and places. In Euripides' fiction of a Bronze Age Greece harming one's enemies was not simply a live option, it was an obligation; by contrast, in Christian Europe revenge was a contested activity which, even if it remained a kinship obligation, had become a mark of the limits of accommodating the actions of Christians to Christian belief. It could be interpreted as a sign of barbarism, even if the barbarity was interior to the culture and frequently practiced. Euripides' emphasis on Medea's foreignness made her appear stranger and more dangerous while at the same time more convincing; it is too easy to see in this geographical otherness a fantasy about the dangers of the East – foreigners are capable of undreamt of things. Euripides' Medea is not simply foreign, unGreek, she is famously close to godhead; by the time she reached Rome her supernatural powers had declined to the worship of Hecate and to the witchcraft associated with that Goddess. If Dido's Carthage, that hereditary enemy territory, shares the splendor of Medea's Colchis, it has no Eastern mystery, although it perhaps introduces some dynastic questions. But there are limits to foreignness: it should be remembered that the characters have no trouble understanding one another because of a difference in language. Even if the original impetus for the voyage of the Argo arose out of trading ambitions or the desires of Corinthian story-tellers to make Aieetes a Black-Sea Greek it is not clear how far there is anything politically imperial or expansive in Jason's adventure, at least in antiquity or the Middle Ages. Phasis on the Black Sea is neither China nor India. If the Medes are called after the descendants of Medea's son by Aegeus that is no more than another possible etymology of little consequence. In Antiquity when Jason repudiates his foreign bride he breaks his oath, but not the law. Marriage is a contract, not a sacrament; his behaviour may be shabby and dishonest, but it is not, in his eyes or those of his prospective father-in-law, wrong. If Creon banishes Medea, he is within his rights not simply as *tyrannos*, but as *basileos*, because he perceives her as a danger to his kingship. She is without recourse either to law or to her human kin, and can only appeal to Jason's debt to her. Medieval writers from Benoît onwards agree that *she* was doubly in error, first in not foreseeing that Jason would betray her, then in counting upon his word, though he swore upon the image of a deity.

Imaginative possibilities also change their expression. The classical writers we have considered worked either in known genres, or – Ovid's *Heroïdes* are the most obvious example – in generic manipulations of great sophistication and self-consciousness. Whatever interpretation of the legends they represented, their literary artifacts refer constantly to other known fictions in known and celebrated forms of expression. Euripides exploits the language of heroism as his rival tragedians established it. In the classical and late-classical interpretations we see versions of legends expressed in genres of fiction. Even if Tragedy becomes disconnected from the theatre, its texts survive. The resources of epic, known and reinterpreted, made the *Aeneid* possible – as well as what it is. In that antique context of story-time, the relationship between the Argonautic voyage and the Fall of Troy placed Jason and the heroes who accompanied him in the same special category enjoyed by the heroes of two generations later: they belong to a fictional world which is nevertheless situated in a possible historical time. As that literary-historical manipulation became more problematic, so did the problems of interpreting the status of the heroes and heroines who belonged to it. As we saw in chapter two, the status of the true depiction of the past raised problems in the Middle Ages which had not been part of the experience of pagan Antiquity. And, as we saw in both chapters two and three, some of the new kinds of writing which emerged changed the expression of pagan legends.

This chapter concentrates upon one work, written in fifteenth-century

Burgundy toward the end of the period of medieval belief that the events before Troy were true, and truly reported by a succession of what appeared to be (but, as we have seen, were not) independent authorities. If we look at Raoul Lefèvre's *Histoire de Jason* in its specific synchronic context, we see the way historical or pseudo-historical material could be turned to the purposes of political romance in a culture which included a much broader social span than we have hitherto seen. While claiming to reveal hitherto unknown evidence which would defend Jason's reputation, this pseudo-classical story – in which less than half the narrative is recognizably part of the legends as we have seen them grow – could serve as the occasion for disquisitions on personal and political morality. As medieval ancient history which could be interpreted as one among many Mirrors for Princes, *L'Histoire de Jason* occupied a curious place in a context of extended historical fictions. To understand this new expression will require some description of the long prose narrative as practiced in mid-fifteenth-century France and Burgundy.

One of the bumper crops of the Harvest of the Middle Ages was the large number of prose romances which emanated mainly from the court of Philippe le Bon of Burgundy, most magnificent as well as most powerful of the Valois dukes to reign (1419–67), and the one who came closest to establishing an independent kingdom for his heirs, a concentration which appears in many of the books commissioned by and for him. His politics combined territorial- and self-aggrandizement, and his patronage for the arts was part of his claim to outdo his royal rivals.[4] His high bourgeois subjects and the mass of the populations of his cities further complicated matters. Since the nurse and tutor of Euripides' play we have not seen much of history's spear-carriers, but now, as we shall see, the mob emerges. Philippe's competition with the English and French kings was complicated by his own desire for revenge, since although the English were invaders, the French king was responsible for the death of Philippe's father.

This chapter considers the context of late-medieval long prose fictions which have sometimes been categorized as 'romans de chevalerie en

---

4 There is an ironic subtext to this chapter which will be apparent from the date and provenance of the scholarship on Burgundian culture cited in the notes. An efflorescence of Belgian aristocratic pride manifests itself in the romantic nationalism associated with nineteenth- and early-twentieth-century imperial expansion. Not, perhaps, surprisingly, many of the scholars who disinterestedly collected historical material on the great days of Burgundy themselves belonged to the Order of the Golden Fleece, and were part of the aggrandizements which – briefly – suggested that Belgium might reestablish its former glories in the imperial theatres. That is, late-nineteenth and early-twentieth-century Belgian scholarship searched for ancestors and precedents in ways not completely dissimilar from the objects of their study.

prose', particularly associated with Philippe le Bon. At the 'centre' of Burgundy, the Ducal court stimulated literary productions of many kinds, among which extended prose narratives of more of less verisimilitude were particularly prominent; 'history' held an important, perhaps a pre-eminent, place as the prime secular subject as well as genre, or genres.[5] For 'history' was still the umbrella term which sheltered narratives of widely varying relationships to the events of the past. Sources of greater or lesser reliability, from verse *chansons de geste* to *chroniques*, provided the stock from which hybrid, synthesized prose narratives were modernized and rewritten. With few exceptions, these books are still largely inaccessible today, despite their importance in the cultural history of the fifteenth and sixteenth centuries; they remained staples of publishers' lists (if that is not too anachronistic a term to use of early bookmen) for generations, and peddlers carried some of them through the countryside well into the nineteenth century, when the romantic revival brought them renewed popularity in high cultural circles as reprinted in the Nouvelle Bibliothèque Bleue and as plots for grand operas.[6]

The Duke paid writers to furnish his library just as he paid artists and sculptors to furnish his apartments, with different scenes to suit different moods, but the moods were those of a magnate, a great prince whose self-fashioning was highly self-conscious. He was not alone in this: the French king was one of many to support writers, and the success of individual authors such as Christine de Pizan in the early years of the fifteenth century expanded the range of available genres and renewed styles such as allegory and dream vision. Court chroniclers provided posterity (and

5   Georges Doutrepont, *La Littérature française à la cour de Bourgogne* (Paris, Champion, 1909) and *Les Mises en proses de épopées et des romans chevaleresques du XIVe au XVIe siècle* (Brussels, Palais des Académies, 1939) are the two best guides to this literature. His *Inventaire de la "librairie" de Philippe le Bon (1420)* (Brussels, Kiessling and cie., 1906) is a supplementary guide. I have discussed this genre in 'Historical Fiction in Fifteenth-Century Burgundy', *The Modern Language Review* 75 (1980), pp. 48–64; see also Joseph M. Levine, 'Caxton's Histories: Fact and Fiction at the Close of the Middle Ages', in his *Humanism and History: Origins of Modern English Historiography* (Ithaca, Cornell University Press, 1987).

6   In the scholarly debate over the origins of Romance which began in the eighteenth century (and which became so important as an underpinning of natonalist debates in the nineteenth), the so-called 'classical romances' offered a compromise position between the Germanophile and Francophile positions. As early as Thomas Warton's *Observations on the Fairy Queen of Spenser*, the Jason romance was recruited to the classical-origins cause (London, 2nd edn, 1762, I.178) and, slightly later, Thomas Dibdin, *Bibliotheca Spenceriana* (London, 1815, vol. IV, pp. 195–210). See also A. Johnston, *Enchanted Ground* (London, Athlone Press, 1964), chapt. 1 and Maurice Olender *Les Langues du Paradis: Aryens et Sémites: un couple providentiel* (Paris, Gallimard-Le Seuil, 1989).

foreign courts, since many of their books were much copied and much travelled) with official versions of the history of the world and particularly of Valois glory, following the innovations of historians such as Froissart. If it seems anachronistic to call this propaganda, there is still something willed about the picture of Burgundy which the Duke publicized. Against the realities of wealth built upon rich dominions and trade, and power exercised in the balance between the monarchs competing around him, Philippe created a picture of opulence that was rooted in a vision of hierarchy and romance in order to evoke the impression of royal authority and stability, a kind of radical conservatism which turned the language of ritual into an assertion of an equality with, even superiority to, the actual monarch. If for most of Philippe's reign the Duke of Burgundy played a difficult game of negotiation between a weak French monarch and a weak English one, he never actually denied his own (or his royal cousins') subordinate position. Stories about the past appealed in part because of their analogies to the present, and, as we shall see, political lessons about benevolent rulers might be inserted anywhere. For the territories of 'le grand duc de l'Occident', which included speakers of over half a dozen languages, were bound to him – but not to each other; loyalty to the prince was a message he could hardly hear too often, as long as that loyalty could be contained.

It is difficult to place the political role of the duke's historians: among them an aristocrat such as Jean de Wavrin was both author and collector. Raoul Lefèvre, the author of the *Histoire de Jason* (as well as a long prose History of Troy), is a more anonymous figure. The role of a David Aubert was different from that of a Jean Wauquelin, and both differed from the court chroniclers whose competing versions of recent events were often couched in the style of Froissart.[7] The French romances which were popular not only in Philippe's territories but elsewhere in what was to become a unifying France were often the so-called epics of revolt, in which medieval barons defended their rights against an unjust central monarchy. The histories which Lefèvre attached to the Fall of Troy were more sympathetic to just rulers. But that in France there was a high king, a central monarch, and a ruler to whom fifteenth-century dukes owed homage was never in doubt. Histories set in contemporary or near-contemporary Europe were likely to be more equivocal than those set in earlier times, but their

---

7 I have dealt with some of the problems raised here in ' "This Vague Relation:" Histori-cal Fiction and Historical Veracity in the Later Middle Ages' *Leeds Studies in English* 13 (1982) pp. 85–108 and, in more general terms, in *Truth and Convention: Rhetoric, Representation, and Reality* (Cambridge, Cambridge University Press, 1991), chapt. 2.

'sources' were earlier poems, epic poems in long *laisses* and in octosyllabic couplets not dissimilar from the adaptations of classical poetry that we saw in the previous chapter and will see again in the next. Poetry may make nothing happen, but it is tempting to see in the Duke's encouragement of a large literature exploiting the ability of 'history' in the guise of 'romance' to offer hypothetical pasts a series of encouragements to a specifically Burgundian culture. This Burgundian 'historical' literature in turn under-wrote the unity of its diversity in an attempt to create a recognizable, enviable sense of identity for Philippe's high-born subjects. That it failed is part of another kind of history. In looking at one work written by one of Philippe's authors, it is worth remembering why Raoul Lefèvre, among so many others, might have chosen the inventions and adaptations which he did. The fictional space of the Burgundian long prose fiction engaged the imagination, but the degree of belief it compelled was varied.

Just as the period in which the 'histories' were set involved an author (or putative translator) in different kinds of presentation, so, too, the status of the subjects of the plot implied different possibilities and respon-sibilities. Insofar as the 'truths' to be grasped from the historical romances were the picture of what the individual knight should individually be, do, and attain in what kind of hierarchical society, the texts provided both a cultural fantasy and an education. A 'private' knight, that is, one free of the burden of great hereditary lands and the burden of government which accompanied them, could ride out in search of adventure as his fictional forebears had done for three hundred years. Even a great war leader, such as Boucicaut, might remain in this category, and a Jacques de Lalaing was ideal for it.[8] As 'characters' they might aspire with the safety of knowing that the limits of their aspirations were set at a level of reward in terms of lands or an heiress which threatened no actual order. The limit was where memory extended to the last serious 'crusade', which had resulted in the terrible defeat at Nicopolis, from which Philippe's father had had to be ransomed back to France at great cost. An imagined past could take advan-tage of a number of 'places': it could connect with Charles the Great and his vassals, whether in rebellion or in expansion against the infidel; it could be Arthurian and exploit a fictional place in which many different kinds of adventure could befall a known cast of knights. A different world could be evoked in the Mediterranean and its experience of crusade, but also of sultans whose daughters aid individual heroes. Each of these

8 Romances about each of these men were written: see Brian Woledge, *Bibliographie des romans et nouvelles en prose française antérieurs à 1500* (Geneva, Droz, 1954 et suppl. 1975), e.g., no. 83. I discuss these romances in 'Historical Fiction'.

fictional places is simultaneously implicated in complex and contradictory Christian ideals of renunciation and ostensible rejection of worldly ambition. Where such tales exploited the supernatural they belonged in the category of romances which treated the unlikely as part of a possible world. An antique prince carries a special cachet; the space before Troy, before nations, before Christianity, allows maximum invention and possibility.

Earlier courts had espoused chivalric ideals, and later ones were to cause unnecessary deaths in the tilt yard, but only Philippe le Bon risked the extravagant publicity of the Vows of the Pheasant at a huge banquet in 1454 at which 'Jason' was one of the displays brought before the diners. He and his courtiers enjoyed their collective imaginative make-believe posing as pseudo-historical figures who had perhaps once done what fifteenth-century men could do no longer. The defeats of the early fifteenth century, not only in the Near East, but at Agincourt, when the 'professional' armies of English longbowmen overcame vastly superior numbers of mounted French knights were already indications that the position of the aristocracy would hitherto have little to do with their soldiership. When the distinction between hierarchy and strategy conflicted, a man like Charles le Téméraire – like his grandfather, Jean Sans Peur – could lead his men to disaster. But it would be wrong to imagine them as always deceived by their own games and pastimes. Both Philippe and Charles were too good at the difficulties of international as well as internal politics for that. The histories and romances which had been among the luxury goods of aristo-cratic courts and courtiers held their own ground only into the early sixteenth century, and already by then they appear to have been well launched on their own derogation in status. Too little is known of late fifteenth century readers to generalize.[9]

Some things are clear: 'Burgundy' survived Philippe le Bon for only a further generation. The unity he tried to encourage had no impetus of its own. The swift disappearance of the political entity disconnected much Burgundian prose from the centres of power, and texts which had been symbolic supports of Philippe's prestige lost their hold, drifting first into bourgeois libraries and then down the social scale in the packs of peddlers. His son's death without a male heir is one of the explanations for the loss of Burgundian literature. One might speculate that in addition the end of

---

[9]   H. S. Bennett, *English Books and Readers: Being a study in the history of the book trade from Caxton to the incorporation of the Stationers' Company* (Cambridge, Cambridge University Press, 1989; orig. 1969), vol. I 1475–1557; and, for the earlier period, Janet Coleman, *English Literature in History 1350–1400: medieval readers and writers* (London, Hutchinson, 1981).

the Burgundian branch of the Valois family as well as the new impetus towards religion that so dominated sixteenth-century French life rendered that literature as frivolous, even wicked, as Ascham's denunciation of the *Morte Darthur* suggested. Changes in education, too, had their impact, as did the mechanical multiplication of books. It is worth remembering that Ascham's characterization of the long prose fictions as replete with sex and violence is, on the whole, correct, and that the ability of some medieval writers to encompass open manslaughter and bold bawdry may be to their credit.

Texts which had been sought after as beautifully illuminated manuscripts for the great collectors of the mid-century, such as the Duke of Berry or Louis de Gruthuyse, continued to be supplied by the new art of printing, but the printers themselves seem almost to a man to have gone bankrupt in pursuit of profits from the new business. If we know the names of many early printers in France, the Low Countries, and England, we know little of their customers. Despite the manuscript illustrations of authors presenting their books to their aristocratic patrons, the reading communities for which the books were written, then printed, are difficult to reconstruct. William Caxton, the first of the English printers, tells us something in his dedications, but all we can see beyond his attempts to attach his books to high-status patrons is a dim world of wealthy commoners with whom he discussed them. Caxton never ceased to refer to the wealth of Hesdin or other castles in the Duke of Burgundy's domains which he had himself seen. He celebrated the Worthies and the ancient world with a publisher's enthusiasm to promote his wares.

In his youth, though, the business of literary celebration throve. Some of the tales had reinforcing political or social pictures of 'a' court, some established – or attempted to establish – a classical genealogy for the house of Valois.[10] The tenuous connections between Philippe's ancestors and Hercules were more than a playful pose, though no doubt less than a legal claim. As Huizinga showed long ago, the group fantasies which eventuated in the Duke's theatrical displays were integral to his politics as well as his self-definition.[11] The idea that one of Hercules' mistresses was a

---

[10] A. Bossuat, 'Les Origines troyennes: leur rôle dans la littérature historique au XVe siècle', *Annales de Normandie* 8 (1958), p. 189. This claim inspired the *Débat des hérauts d'armes de France et d'Angleterre*, ed. L. Pannier and P. Meyer (Paris, Firmin Didot et Cie., 1877). Occasions for display are not simply truth claims, but their claims blur.

[11] Jacques d'Armagnac, Duke of Nemours, owned a Hercules-romance which is now Vienna Statsbibliothek Codex Vindobeonensis Palatinus 2586. The scribe, Johannes Leodegrensis, left spaces for miniatures which were later filled in by a mediocre artist. If this romance is the first version of what later became Lefèvre's Trojan history, it might

Burgundian princess is laughable on the face of it, but it means to be a kind of legitimation by association, and is a sign of the Duke's political ambition rather than megalomania.[12] To deny that the assertion of one's claim is, in the last analysis, true (under most definitions of 'true'), is not to deny the claim. It is to think of oneself as in a position to make the claim to link the descent of one's house to Troy through Rome, to claim already to be in the position that the link suggests. That is, the public association between the Duke and the classical past created the link by arguing for it. It appropriates symbolism in an age in which the symbol itself could acquire some degree of independence.

This is not the place to discuss the complexities of Burgundian manipulations of the kingdoms of France and England, but some reminder of Philippe's position will help to situate literary production at his court in its political context. Assassination was a repeated method: Jean sans Peur, the second Valois Duke, admitted his reponsibility for the murder of his uncle, the Duke of Orléans (Charles VI's brother), and was later himself murdered at the behest of the Dauphin (who became King Charles VII). Philippe never forgot his desire for revenge, and the feud between Burgundy and Orléans (and their allies of Armagnac) helped keep the English in France for a generation.[13] In 1420 the Duke of Burgundy went so far as to change lords: by the Treaty of Troyes Burgundy became the vassal of the English King Henry V, but much diplomatic ingenuity was expended in maintaining Burgundian independence. Character-assassination was another ploy: the French Queen Isabeau 'admitted' that her son was not the mad king's, but the Duke of Orleans', when Henry V of England's marriage to her daughter was made a means of uniting the two kingdoms.

From magnanimous splendour to aristocratic patronage for writers and artists, the encouragement of translations from the classics, of histories

help to explain Hercules' unusual prominence in that collection. If, in addition, this manuscript, or one like it, was the source of the Irish *Stair Ercuil ocus a bas*, it would solve the chronological problems raised by assuming that the Irish translator depended upon Caxton's translation of Lefèvre's Troy Book. See P. Durrieu, 'Notes sur quelques manuscrits français conservés dans des bibliothèques d'Allemagne', *BEC* 53 (1892), pp. 117–8. The Irish text is edited by Gordon Quin for the Irish Text Society, 38 (Dublin, 1939).

12 There is a detailed analysis of the political implications of these texts in Yvon Lacaze, 'Le Rôle des traditions dans la genèse d'un sentiment national au XVe siècle: La Bourgogne de Philippe le Bon', *Bibliothèque de l'Ecoles des Chartes*, 129 (1971), pp. 303–85.

13 See the series of books by Richard Vaughan, *Philip the Bold: The Formation of the Burgundian State* (London, Longman, 1962); *John the Fearless: The Growth of Burgundian Power* (London, Longman, 1966); *Philip the Good: The Apogee of Burgundy* (London, Longman, 1970); *Charles the Bold: The Last Valois Duke of Burgundy* (London, Longman, 1973); and *Valois Burgundy* (London, Longman, 1975).

which redounded to the credit of Philippe's dukedom, poetry which praised him, many of Philippe's actions can be best understood in the context of his ambition to unify and promote a collection of provinces. Territorial expansion and a royal ideal do not amount to imperialism, but there are striking similarities. His chopping and changing, however, opened him to constant accusations of oath-breaking. Sensitivity to accusations of perjury helps place Lefèvre's defence of Philippe's patron. Emphasizing an independent genealogy for Burgundy is one of those supposedly historical legitimations to which medieval men were so prone. Hence the references to Hercules. Since Hercules is chronologically earlier than Troy, his ancestor-hood suggests a foundation for Burgundy which was earlier (and therefore of higher prestige) than those of the countries who traced their ancestry to the Trojan refugees. Further connections to early antiquity encouraged that idea; the imagery is at least in part connected to this earliest period of secular history through the goal for which the Argonauts sailed: the Golden Fleece. It is, on the face of it, an attractive emblem – and it must be remembered that *as* an emblem it has had an extremely long life, and remains blazoned in churches and chapels today.[14] As the Grail and King Arthur belonged to the Matter of Britain, and Charlemagne and the *douze pairs* to the glorious past of France, so Jason and his Argonauts were intended to become symbols of Burgundy's own greatness. Tapestries illustrating the adventures had been ordered by Philippe le Hardi as early as 1392.[15] There were, however, drawbacks.

Outward celebrations of inner loyalties included the establishment of a new order of chivalry, the prerogative of kings and great magnates. Philippe did not invent this idea: his grandfather, Philippe le Hardi, had presented golden collars to his courtiers in 1404, with the idea of an order of the golden bough. No doubt 'gold' ranked high. Philippe le Bon's order remembered that allusion, while being also, according to his clerical supporters, a first step towards the organisation of a new crusade to recapture the holy places. For Philippe it was a matter of display, and in 1430/1, in

---

14 It owes much to the wealth of the Flanders wool trade, of course, although that source of prosperity is unlikely to have been what inspired the Duke to his nostalgic chivalric gesture. See J. Calmette, *The Golden Age of Burgundy* (London, 1962; orig. *Les Grands ducs de Bourgogne*, Paris, Albin Michel, 1949) and K. Fowler, *The Age of Plantagenet and Valois: the struggle for supremacy 1328–1498* (London, Elek, 1967).

15 Although the details of the scenes are not recorded, the tapestries are called 'Jason à la conqueste de la Thoison d'or', and may have helped inspire Philippe's choice of emblem and patron. They are singled out as precious in inventories of the Duke's possessions, e.g. in Laborde, *Les Ducs de Bourgogne: Etudes sur les lettres, les arts et l'industrie pendant le XVe siècle et plus particulièrement dans les pays-bas et le duché de Bourgogne* (Paris, 1849–52).

the course of celebrations of his marriage to the Portuguese princess who was herself the grand-daughter of John of Gaunt, he chose the Golden Fleece as its name and device.[16] This ostentation, which copied, sometimes extravagantly, court rituals elsewhere considered outmoded, was one more assertion that Burgundy's status was equivalent to that of an independent kingdom. It also tied Philippe's 'knights' to demonstrations of their affiliation to him; in a crude sense it played upon their joint ambitions.

Philippe le Bon may have been an avid collector, but no one has ever praised his learning; the choice of Jason and the fleece was an error of tact and a strategic miscalculation which made him vulnerable to accusations of misconduct by association. Extravagant display which invites ridicule instead of compelling admiration destroys what it seeks to create. From the outset his chancellor, Jehan Germain, had vainly proposed to replace Jason with Gideon. But the 'meanest in Manasses', Judge though he was, was no prince, whereas Jason was the first aristocrat to set out on a secular voyage, a voyage to that source of wealth which was the tacit goal of so many of the crusaders.[17] The Duke graciously accepted the Biblical hero, but retained his own first choice as part of the pageantry of his order.[18] There were a number of celebratory poems using the imagery of Jason and the fleece, and, sometimes, his 'amie', Medea. Michault Taillevent's Dream Vision imagines allegorical personifications of, among others, Bonne Renomée, Gideon, and thirty-one human followers (the order was restricted to that number of members).[19] The closing ballade suggests that the poets, at least, were already on the defensive:

> Jason conquist, ce racontent pluseurs
> La thoison dor par Medee s'amie

[16] The timing of the announcement seems also to have been a method of avoiding election to the Garter, which Philippe, already a vassal of the English king, and brother-in-law to the Regent, wished to avoid. The story is dramatized by the chronicler Georges Chastellain, *Oeuvres*, ed. Kervyn de Lettenhove, vol. II (Brussels, 1863–5), pp. 12, 172–3 (the formal announcement).

[17] Andrew Heron, '*Il fault faire guerre pour paix avoir': Crusading Propaganda at the Court of Duke Philippe le Bon of Burgundy (1419–1467)* (unpublished dissertation, University of Cambridge, 1992), pp. 159–82.

[18] Georges Doutrepont, 'Jason et Gédéon, patrons de la Toison d'Or', in *Mélanges Godefroid Kurth* (Paris and Liége, 1908), vol. II, pp. 191–208. Discussed in Pierre Champion, *Histoire Poétique du quinzième siècle* (Paris, Champion, 1923), pp. 285–338. In the course of a dream vision the poet sees an allegorical vision of virtuous men rejuvenated by the fame of their great reputations. No other metamorphosis is mentioned, and Medea appears only contingently in the last stanza.

[19] 'Le Songe de la Thoison dor', in Robert Deschaux, *Un Poète bourguignon du XVe siècle: Michault Taillevent (édition et étude)* (Geneva, Droz, Publications romanes et françaises, 132, 1975), pp. 59–86. See also Pierre Champion, *Histoire poétique*, pp. 285–338.

Dedens Colcos, mais pour estre plus seurs
Tant a Jason on ne s'areste mie
Qu'a Gedeon qui par oeuvre saintie
Arouse eut son veaurre doucement
De rousee qui des sains cieulx descent
Dont fut depuis dignement celebree.
Loenge a Dieu trestout premierement
Et aux bons gloire et haulte renommee   (lines 752–61)

[Many tell how in Colchis Jason won the golden fleece
through Medee, his beloved, but, to be more secure, one does
not dwell so much on Jason as on Gideon who, by his holy
work gently watered his fleece with dew which descended
from holy heaven, with which, later, the praise of God has
been celebrated appropriately ever since. Praise first and
above all to God and glory and reputation to good men.]

The classical figures could be used to write political verse for the Duke – or
against him – and continued to be so used throughout the rest of the
Duke's reign. One crudely allegorizing poem appears to flatter the Duke
knowingly, by remarking his physical good looks:

Or est ton nom par les plages marines
Et par terre bruyant et renommé,
Tes grans trésors, tes blés et tes farines,
Ta puissance que je n'ay pas nommé;
Mais quant j'ay tout ton triomphe sommé,
Pou à présent je ne quiers ochoison
Que d'exaulsier la dorée toison
Dont tu as prins l'ordre par sacrement,
Où je comprens haultes choses foison,
Sans toy flater fors que bien sobrement.
Qu'est ce Jason que de ton corps humain
Et Hercules de ton ame figure,
Qui vont ensembre a vie, son et main
Dedens Colcos qui le monde figure.
Le nef Argon ton beau temps prefigure
Dedens la mer, de fortune diverse
La Toison d'or qui en l'isle converse
Est le hault don d'onneur insuperable
Qu'on porte o soy, passant la mainte traverse
La sus es cieulx en la gloire durable.   (p. 98)

[Now your name is loudly proclaimed and renowned by
seashore and inland, your great treasures, your wheat and

flour, your might which I have not named; but when I have summarized all your triumph, for the present I do not seek to do other than exalt the gilded fleece of which you have taken the Order by Sacrament, by which I understand a harvest of high deeds, without flattering you unrestrainedly. This Jason symbolizes your body and Hercules your soul, which go together in life, voice and hand in Colchis, which symbolizes the world. The ship Argo in the sea symbolizes your happy times, the Golden Fleece, which dwells on the island, is the highest gift of unsurpassable honour which one carries within, with many a setback to the great passage which is the heaven of enduring glory.][20]

The connection between Jason and Hercules no longer surprises. Jean Miélot's commonplace book contained Latin verses using similarly allegorical interpretation.[21] Burgundy's enemies were not slow to follow where her friends led, and Jason's reputation as a perjurer was seized upon as a way of insulting Philippe, whose *realpolitik* had left him with an abundance of broken promises to live down. A broken truce is the occasion for a twenty-one stanza satire attributed to Alain Chartier, which includes the following:

> A Dieu et aux gens detestable
> Est foy mentie et traison;
> Pour ce n'est point mise a la table
> Des preux l'image de Jason,
> Qui, pour emporter la toison
> De Colchos, se voult parjurer
> *Larrecin ne se peut celer.*

> [Perjury and treachery are detested by God and men. This is why one does not bring to the table of the valiant the image of Jason, who, to carry off the fleece from Colchis, made himself a perjurer. Theft cannot be hid.][22]

---

20 From 'Rondeaulx avec ung dialogue de l'homme et de la femme au Duc de Bourgogne. Rondeau en forme de dédicace au Duc Philippe le Bon', in Baron de Reiffenberg, 'Poëme sur la Toison d'Or (XVe siècle)', *Annuaire de la Bibliothèque Royale de Belgique* 8 (1847), pp. 95–101.

21 C. A. J. Armstrong, 'Verses by Jean Miélot on Edward IV and Richard Earl of Warwick', *Medium Aevum* 8 (1939), pp. 193–7. Armstrong thought the poem might date from 1470, but it could be earlier. There is further material on Burgundy in his *England, France, and Burgundy in the Fifteenth Century* (London, Hambledon Press, 1983).

22 This is stanza seven of a 21-stanza poem on the occasion of a broken truce, c.1450. *Recueil de chants historiques français depuis le XIIe siècle jusqu'au XVIIIe siècle*, ed. Le Roux de Lincy (Paris, C. Gosselin, 1841), dated about 1450, but not in J. C. Laidlaw, *The*

Clearly, some kind of defence would be in order. One traditional guess –
but only a guess – is that the publicity surrounding Philippe's great banquet of the Vow of the Pheasant at Lille in 1454 brought Jason once more
to prominence.[23] There is some circumstantial evidence for a date not far
from this, because of the habit of medieval writers of copying texts whole-
sale, and submitting them to their own amplifications.[24] Raoul Lefèvre's
L'Histoire de Jason illustrates the lengths to which a medieval author could
go in reinterpreting and inventing new material for a known legend.[25]

Lefèvre's is a shadowy figure. His *Histoire de Jason* is also referred to as
Le Livre de la Toison d'Or. Contemporary references to a romance of
Hector do not correspond to any free-standing extant work, but may
identify extracts from the Troy History. Lefèvre says he is the author of a
romance of Hercules (which may have been amalgamated in his History of

Poetical Works of Alain Chartier (Cambridge, Cambridge University Press, 1974). Jason
continued to be used as an allegorical figure in Burgundy well after the period under
consideration here, e.g. in 'Pasquille demande de nouvelles sur les troubles du temps
present a Jehan l'ivrogne', in A. Thon, 'Analyse et extraits des documents relatifs à
l'histoire des Pays-Bas au XVIe siècle', *Bulletin de la Commission Royale d'Histoire* 77
(1908), pp. 37–133, esp. p. 68, ll. 117–20.

23 As in Georges Doutrepont, *La Littérature française à la cour des ducs de Bourgogne*
(Paris, 1909), p. 158. Vowing by a bird was a chivalric tradition and there were precedents for such an occasion. The culmination of the feast was a series of crusading vows
by the aristocratic diners. None of them, in fact, took the cross.

24 The encyclopedic *Fleur des Histoires* of Jean Mansel, who used the Ducal library exhaus-
tively, has nothing on Jason in its first redaction (chapters 7–12 on Troy follow a prose
version of Benoît), but makes large use of him in the second. The first redaction dates
from 1447–1451. The second, which draws upon both Lefèvre's *Jason* and the second
redaction of his *Recueil* (1464), must post-date the completion of the latter. This suggests that Lefèvre's Jason did not yet exist when the first redaction of the *Fleurs* was
completed. Further, since the second redaction of the *Fleurs* was presented to Philippe,
who died in 1467, a plausible date for the defence of Jason is sometime between 1447
and the early 1460s. See G. de Poerck, *Introduction à la fleur des histoires de Jean Mansel*,
in *Annales du cercle archéologique de Mons* 54 (1935).

25 Ed. Gert Pinkernell (Frankfurt, Athenäum Verlag, 1971). References will be to this
edition by page numbers bracketed in the text. The translations are quoted from *The
History of Jason. Translated from the French of Raoul Lefèvre by William Caxton, c.1477*,
ed. John Munro, EETS e.s. 111 (London, 1913), similarly identified in the text, but
silently punctuated by me. Bibliographical details in Pinkernell pp. 17–31 and in Brian
Woledge, *Bibliographie des romans et noubelles en prose française antérieurs à 1500*
(Geneva, 1954 and supplément, 1975), no. 134. Six editions in French by 1530 (one by
Caxton during his continental period), three in Dutch by 1556, translated by Caxton
himself into English in an edition dedicated to the Prince of Wales. This version was
'pirated' by Leeu (Antwerp, 1492), and copied twice (Glasgow, Hunterian 410 and
Cambridge UL Dd.3.45). For Mary Stuart's copy of the French incunable see Julian
Sharman, *The Library of Mary, Queen of Scots* (London, 1889) pp. 100–1. See also N. F.
Blake, *Caxton and his World* (London, Andre Deutsch, 1969), p. 233.

Troy, a long work which he continued to revise).[26] He seems constantly to have recast and reused his compositions and it may be that he was writing a kind of cycle of classical heroes which eventually became the history of Troy from Jason to the final catastrophe. This further contextualizes *Jason* in a hugely ambitious ancient history. In England, that extended history of Troy, the *Recueil*, through Caxton's translation, was accepted as authoritative, and was useful to Shakespeare when he came to write *Troilus and Cressida*.[27] The story of the Hercules romance is obscure, but it is possible that a manuscript in the Staatsbibliothek in Vienna, Codex Vindobonensis Palatinus 2586 (which originally belonged to Jacques d'Armagnac, Duc de Nemours), represents Lefèvre's first version, which was also later absorbed in his *Recueil des histoires de Troie*.[28] An autograph manuscript of *Jason* survives in the Bibliothèque de l'Arsenal, and both it and an early copy in the Bibliothèque Nationale contain striking illustrations, not all of which are immediately recognizable as belonging to the legends as we have become familiar with them.[29]

---

[26] Raoul Lefèvre, *Le Recoeil des Histoires de Troyes: edition critique*, ed. Marc Aeschbach (Frankfurt and Berne, Peter Lang Verlag, European University Studies, section 13; Langue et littérature françaises, 120, 1987). Caxton's translation was edited by H. O. Sommer, *The Recuyell of the Historyes of Troye. Written in French by Raoul Lefèvre. Translated and Printed by William Caxton (About AD 1474)* (London, Nutt, 1894). It was published after 19 September 1471 according to N. F. Blake, *Caxton and His World* (London, Andre Deutsch, 1969), pp. 230–1. A presentation copy for the Duke of Burgundy of Lefèvre's Troy Book signed by the author survives as Bibliothèque de l'Arsenal 5068 (Woledge no. 183); there are a variety of other versions, listed by Woledge nos. 180–5.

[27] As discussed by E. Stein, 'Caxton's Recuyell and Shakespeare's *Troilus*', *MLN* 45 (1930), pp. 144–6; Robert K. Presson, *Shakespeare's Troilus and Cressida and the Legends of Troy* (Menasha, Wisconsin, 1953). The discussion is summarized in William Shakespeare, *Troilus and Cressida*, ed. Kenneth Muir (Oxford, 1984). Other renaissance authors also referred to Caxton's translation. Robert Greene's epic, *The Tale of Troy* is printed in *The Dramatic and Poetical Works of Robert Greene and George Peele*, ed. A. Dyce (London, 1861); Thomas Heywood's *The Brazen Age* and *The Iron Age*, collected in *The Dramatic Works of Thomas Heywood* (London, Pearson Reprints, 1874); *Iron Age*, ed. Arlene W. Weiner (New York, Garland, 1979). Heywood also treated the material in the epic style, *Troia Britannica* (London, 1609).

[28] The manuscript is described by P. Durrieu, pp. 117–18. If this is correct, then this may be the source for the Irish translation, *Stair Ercuil ocus a bas. The Life and Death of Hercules*, ed. Gordon Quin (Dublin, 1939), and would solve the problem of the otherwise remarkably long life of the Irish translator.

[29] Bibliographical details in Woledge, no. 134. The four contemporary luxury manuscripts which preserve the text are masterpieces of the illustrator's art. The miniatures in Louis de Gruuthuyse's copy (BN f. 331) have been claimed for the 'Master of the Golden Fleece' by P. Durrieu. See L. F. Winkler, *Studien zur Geschichte der Niederländischen Miniaturmalerei des XV. und XVI. Jahrhunderts* (Vienna and Leipzig, 1915). See, however, L. M. J. Delaissé, *La Miniature Flamande* (Brussels, 1959); G. Dogaer and M.

The existence of a Burgundian body of prose historical romances gave Lefèvre an exploitable genre into which to pour his defence of the patron of the Duke's Order of the Golden Fleece, a genre whose relations to the idea of a possible past (and the politics of the present) allowed for expansive inventions as well as coherent amalgamations of the inherited legends. That is, exploiting this kind of narrative allowed for deferral of authority, avoidance of responsibility for the truth of the history, and, overall, the free play of ambiguity about the status of any specific section of the text. *Because* the long narrative about Jason resembles the form already shared by such diverse kinds of historical texts as the prose versions of the epics of revolt, ancient history, and invented romances such as 'Paris and Vienne' or 'Melusine', Lefèvre could propose a narrative as 'authorized' while leaving it to the reader to decide how much, and what kind, of belief to accord to the text and the events it recounted. It is not 'false' because it follows a loose genre; it is hypothetical within the baggy narrative genre. In the context of the Burgundian court at the specific moment, ambiguities about narrative status could be clear, and the narrative enjoyed both for its romantic intrigues and its political explorations. Once detached from that court, at that moment, *L'Histoire de Jason* looked quite different. None of Lefèvre's inventions long survived the brisk certainties of renaissance historiography, and the revival of classical learning together with the resurrection of actual classical texts, such as Homer's, soon relegated his books to the status of textually bizarre but artistically beautiful gothic manuscripts. The book is, by any account, bold in its invention.

Within the whole biographical frame Lefèvre amalgamated the historical sources which were available to him in French. The prose *Histoire ancienne jusqu'à César* agreed with the expansions in the rhymed *Ovide moralisé*, and both recapitulated the narrative in Benoît's *Roman de Troie* as well as *Historia Destructionis Troiae*. It is likely that Christine's *La Mutacion de Fortune* was also part of his reading, although he shows none of her elegance.[30] As Lefèvre took care to limit the narration to Jason's point of view, he defended the actions of this hero at that time, by invoking contemporary marriage law. The most important part of that defence was to minimize the sections of the story which concerned Jason's interaction with Medea, to silence her insofar as possible, to avoid the words written

---

Debae, *La Librairie de Philippe le Bon* (Brussels, 1967). The famous illustrator, Loyset Liédet, is associated with illustrations in presentation copies of the *Recueil*. See Pinkernell, pp. 18ff.

[30] But Christine became involved in the so-called *querelle des femmes* which, as we shall see in more detail in the next chapter, assimilated Medea and her wrongs to an argument about responsibility and the nature of woman.

for her as the *topos* of the stricken and abandoned woman. His Medea must not be allowed to make her case. After that, making her susceptible to Christian remorse and rehabilitation would be relatively easy. That anachronism accepted, still, less than half of Lefèvre's work coincides with the legends as we have hitherto seen them. Not only are there large omissions in the Argonautic voyage itself, but there are expansions which are entirely invented. This is the first time we have seen the insertion of entirely new (and entirely newly minted) material. Perhaps the most important invention, in the Burgundian context, is the imaginary society organised under the rule of a euhemerized 'Appollo', which Lefèvre set in the centre of his book as a way of preaching the necessity of hierarchy, obedience, and the dangers of envy which lead to civil strife. That is, the adventures of Jason lead to digressions on political society which underwrote Philippe's own concerns.

This orientation is underlined when one assesses the scenes which the illuminators chose (or were instructed) to portray.[31] In contemporary luxury manuscripts there are more pictures of Jason as a medieval knight and of the story of the civil war in Colchis than there are of the plot which involves Medea. Scenes of battles are popular. The most luxuriously illustrated of the manuscripts, BNf. f.fr. 331 contains eighteen miniatures.[32] The 'enfance Jason' receives more attention than does the whole story of Medea, and the history of Colchis about as much. Some of the illustrations seem to be representations which one might find in similar romances, and throughout their period style is apparent. Plate 1 (BNf. f.fr. 331 f. 78v) shows the news of Zecchius's rebellious attempt to conquer the fleece being brought to King Appollo, shown under his canopy on the left. Were the rest of the illustration not so eloquent, one might take the messenger to be presenting a gift to any king. And this quiet representation of the kingly order, calm, hierarchical, and attended by courtiers, is at the heart of Philippe le Bon's style, which emphasized his place at the heart of his domains, the place of benevolent rule. Simultaneously, the events on the island, with its fire-breathing dragon and bulls, the rescue boat which cannot save the life of the terribly burnt victim (supplicating hands raised out of the water), are ignored by a huge sheep, on the upper right, and overlooked by a god (perhaps Mars, who is referred to in the rubric under the picture), pointing down from the storm clouds of which he seems to be a part. The line of his pointing hand, which runs through the dying

---

[31] Details of the manuscripts in Pinkernell, pp. 17–31 and Woledge, *Supplément*, no. 134.
[32] This manuscript belonged to Louis de Bruges, Seigneur de la Gruthuyse (c.1420–1492), illustrations about 1470 attributed to Liévin van Lathem.

man to two men who are watching events from the distance, is parallel to the royal interior in which the king sits. His wealthy city occupies the centre of the picture, with a siege machine sitting on the beach beside the city. The divisions of the page are a series of golden sections, connected (and separated) by architectural features such as walls and pillars. Outside the frame of illustration and text, the marginal commentary includes six male figures: a dragon, a monkey carrying club and shields (blazoned with the fleur de lys), and a central group of four at the bottom of the page, two armed knights carrying swords and a third unarmoured figure carrying what appears to be a jawbone, all attacking an unarmed and unarmoured figure who has already fallen to the ground. The motifs of the grotesques in the margin here imply the anarchy which comes with civil strife, and which the text, too, describes.

The illustrator uses multiple representation to narrate Medea's rejuvenation of Aeson. In Plate 2 (BNf. f.fr. 331 f. 132) she appears four times, again in a series of imagined golden sections. Reading from the upper left hand corner down, then across to the largest part of the picture, we follow Medea's flight to collect herbs (her wings are the period accoutrements for such figures, including angels), her sacrifice before the image of the gods, then her return to Aeson's palace, whose brick facade she enters past a formal garden. In the main section, inside the palace, Aeson is naked, though there is the suggestion of a loin cloth, in a large bath (complete with royal canopy which tells us that this is the bath of the king). Two men dressed in Burgundian fashions look on while Medea begins her ministrations; perhaps the younger of the onlookers is Jason himself. If the figures are narrative, the other would be the rejuvenated king. This time the marginal monkeys are examining the anus of small human figure who bends over while separating the cheeks of his buttocks, perhaps a parody of a medical examination. The intimate interior is as carefully depicted, with the details of daily life in a royal bedroom, as is the garden exterior. In the small reproduction of this book it is very difficult to see how expressively the faces are painted, but the originals show care and concern.

The stiffer representation of plate 3, which is taken from Lefèvre's autograph, presented to Philippe le Bon (Arsenal 5067, f. 130), is more static.[33] Nevertheless, it, too, gives us a narrative. Aeson is in a large tub in front of a roaring fire. He is flanked by Medea, on his left, holding the instrument with which she is bleeding him (removing his 'aged' blood through a hole

---

[33] Miniatures attributed to Loyset Liédet (Pinkernell, p. 19). See also L. M. J. Delaissé, *La Miniature flamande* (Brussels, 1959) and G. Dogaer and M. Debae, *La Librairie de Philippe le Bon* (Brussels, 1967).

already made in his skull). The figure on the right, young and beautifully dressed, holds a similar instrument in his left hand, and, should we doubt what we are looking at, wears A and E embroidered on his upper garment: Aeson, once again, but now at the seeming age of thirty. There are no witnesses to this act of healing.

More spectacular moments also attracted illustration. In the thirteen illuminations in BNf. f.fr. 12570 Medea appears only twice: once when Jason swears his faith to her, and once when she dismembers Apsyrtus.[34] Plate 4 is a grisaille with Medea confronting her father (the crowned figure on the left, his hands raised in a gesture of horror) with her brother's severed head, while her nurse holds a cloth full of body parts which match those already in the sea between the two ships. The bow of the king's ship almost touches the stern of the ship which carries the lovers, and the Colchian navy (or decorative other ships) appears beyond the main focus of the picture. Although pennons move in a breeze, the figures, behind the three main actors, are static, as if they were represented as a rhythmically repeated crowd. Jason is not identifiable.

In Lefèvre's presentation copy, Arsenal 5067, this scene (Plate 5) appears to take place before the lovers have left the shores of the city of Colchis. In the top centre of the frame Medea, alone, and larger than the sailors behind her, is on the point of throwing the mutilated torso of her brother into the sea, where his head, one hand, and a foot emerge from the water, almost in the positions they would assume were he swimming. Neither Jason's ship nor her father's have set sails, and the men are all staring at Medea with expressionless faces. With the exception of the two reproduced here, the other illustrations in Lefèvre's manuscript might have served for any number of other stories.

Perhaps the most shocking of the miniatures is Medea's attack on Jason's wedding. Here (Plate 6, BNf. f.fr. 331) we see the moment after Medea's fire-breathing dragons have immolated the wedding guests, who throw their hands into the air, dead and dying. Whiffs of smoke are suggested at the rear of the picture. Servants hide under the table, or flee through door and window from the room, and the musicians fall over the rail of their gallery. Jason, in the centre, in front of the canopy between his new father-in-law and his already-dead bride, appears untouched – he, after all, is protected from dragon-fire by the unguents Medea gave him in Colchis. He alone is left to watch Medea tear their son apart: as she sits on the dragon, or dragons (there are four heads visible but the body or bodies

---

34 This manuscript belonged to Jean de Wavrin (d.1471); the thirteen miniatures are the work of the Master of the Champion des Dames (Pinkernell, p. 20).

are covered by her dress) which have brought her into the hall, she calmly pulls the inverted child's right leg away.[35] In the strawberry-filled margins with its birds and butterflies, a woman with the body of a lion plays the harp while at the bottom two men, one rich, one poor, struggle with a chained bear.

It is hard to imagine what other depictions of the period might have contributed to this scene of carnage, but it may be worth juxtaposing a moment which represents, like Griselda, a kind of opposite. In the famous Angers Apocalypse, itself inspired by the tradition of manuscript illumination, there is an illustration of the vision of Revelations chapter 12, in which the woman crowned with stars gives birth to a baby boy who is attacked by the seven-headed dragon. In Plate 7 St John looks on as the angels reach out to save the woman's baby. In subsequent frames (not illustrated) the woman is given the wings of an eagle (which look like the wings Medea wears above) in order to escape the dragon's persecution. This is not to say that there is a *necessary* connection between Medea and Mary (if we accept the identification of the Virgin with the woman of Revelations 12), but to remind ourselves of possible visual reminiscences whenever similar moments appear. The habit of interpretations *in bono* then *in malum* invite us to invert and reconsider what we see and imagine. The traditions of Apocalypse illustration have been well studied, but I have not seen another which might connect the two scenes. What may be at issue here is the sense in which 'saving' and 'destroying' women might be represented as visual opposites.

There are murders and atrocities wherever anarchy is represented in medieval manuscripts (that is what anarchy means), but the butchery of children stands out. It is, of course, most famously represented in the Slaughter of the Innocents under Herod, but there the murderers are soldiers obeying the king. Here, in calm silence, Medea's love, which covered Jason with protecting unguents, becomes the agent of her revenge; the artist has, in some ways, seen more than Lefèvre's text communicates. But here my discussion of the illustrations has anticipated that of the narrative.

Structurally, *Jason* resembles a princely biography of the pseudo-historical type, one of the more extravagantly fictionalized, to be sure, but one in which a core of authoritative reporting could be discerned.[36] Such is

---

[35] I do not think that the inversion is a negation, but a reference to other scenes of such horror (although the inverted bodies in the scenes of warfare do indicate defeat). See Michael Camille, *The Gothic Idol: Ideology and Image-making in Medieval Art* (Cambridge, Cambridge University Press, 1989), e.g. intro., p. 5.

[36] For this type of historical narrative see Richard Southern, 'Aspects of the European

the seamlessness of the anachronisms that it is as if one were reading a prose romance about medieval characters who suddenly modulate into defamiliarized classical legends. Lefèvre's accretions enable him to provide motivation for later episodes in the narrative, and his history is carefully and efficiently structured. Its politics stress the power of a conservative and utterly recognizable male hierarchy.

But the latitude of invention is constrained by what is 'known' of Jason, and Lefèvre makes every effort to accomodate the historical inheritance. There is, then, a threefold combination of circumstances to be taken into account in any analysis of Lefèvre's *Jason*: first, that it must defend Jason's character without contradicting the actions and events associated with him on the authority of earlier books; second, that in approximating to the form of the historical (or pseudo-historical) biographical romance popular in fifteenth-century Burgundy, Lefèvre could manipulate its relationship to those known actions and events so that the text remained in that narrative no-man's-land where its actual truth-content was of less concern than its consistency and coherence; third, that it must appeal to the political ideals and romantic fantasies appropriate to the anachronisms of the 'romans antique'. How far Lefèvre expected to be believed is perhaps not the point.

What Lefèvre offered his aristocratic readers was the claim that Jason's behaviour was totally consistent, and fully explained by the existence of a prior engagement (*sponsalia de futuris*); if only they had known, there could have been no question of accusations of perjury. The narrative authority for this claim is, in the first instance, a recourse to the *topos* of the vision: Lefèvre opens his tale with an apparition in which Jason appears and commands him to write down the truth, and present it to the father of writers, Philippe.

La galee de mon engin flotant naguieres en la parfondeur des mers de pluseurs vielles histoires, ainsy comme je vouloie mener mon esperit en port de repos, soudainement s'apparu decoste moy une nef conduite par un homme seul . . . . Au plus tost qu'il conceupt que je le regardoye de grant desir, il se mist en son estant et me dist: 'Homme de ruide engin, que t'esmerveilles tu? Ancre ta galee icy et prens ta plume pour mettre par escroit mes fais! Le roy Jupiter de Crete fu mon tayon et fist Eacus, l'un de ses filz, roy de Mirmidoine. Cest Eacus engendra mon pere, le roy

Tradition of Historical Writing', *Transactions of the Royal Historical Society* 20 (1970), pp. 173–96 and my series of articles in *The Modern Language Review*: 'Historical Fiction in Fifteenth Century Burgundy', 75 (1980) pp. 48–64; 'Problems of Early Fiction: Raoul Lefèvre's *Histoire de Jason*', 78 (1983) pp. 34–45; 'Medieval Biography: History as a Branch of Fiction', 80 (1985), pp. 257–68.

Eson. Je suis Jason, cellui qui le veaurre d'or conquesta en Colcos et qui journellement laboure en douleur, enrachiné en tristesse pour le deshonneur dont aucuns frapent ma gloire, moy imposans non avoir tenu ma promesse envers Medee, ce dont tu as leu la verité.' (125)

The Galeye of myn engyn floting not long syn in the depnes of the sees of diuerce auncient histories in suche wise as I wolde haue brought myn esperite vnto the porte or hauen of rest, sodaynly apperid by me a ship conduited by one man only . . . . Assone as he conceyued that I so beheld him by greet desir he helde him still & sayde to me in this wise, 'Man of rude engyn what meruailest thou? Ancre thy galeye here & take thy penne for to write & put in memoire my faites & dedes. The king Iupiter of Crete was myn olde bele fader & he engendrid Cacus King of Myrmidone. This Cacus engendred my fader Eson. I am Iason that conquerd the Flees of Golde in the Yle of Colchos and that dayly laboure in sorowe, roted in tristresse for the dishonneur that somme persones hurte & empesshe my glorie, inposing to me not to haue holden my promys anenst Medea, whereof thou hast red the truth.' (3)

The drifting boat is a multiplex symbol which suggests (and links) both the Argo and its sea voyages with the obedient openness of the writer to inspiration (including that direct dictation from an external figure of authority) and narrative desire, as well as the kind of dream vision which defers authority to a non-verifiable and unlocalizable source. 'Jason's' command, or appeal, is to the truth which is to be found in books, books which are not identified in the text. The limits of Lefèvre's authority are emphasized by his 'rude engin', a failure of cunning and intelligence which are no more than a humility *topos*. The solution is to write another book, one which anticipates by two hundred years the 'histoires secrètes' or 'galantes' of the seventeenth century by revealing Jason's hitherto unknown love for the princess of 'Oliferne', Mirro. Lefèvre's inventions build upon the geography of the eastern Mediterranean; he exploits both the known names of Byzantium (Bisance) and those of minor Biblical characters (Loth, Salathiel, Zechius and Zethephius) to give the flavour of Greece (Thessalonique, Epydanee, Corfus the Giant), Syria (Damas), and unspecified Slavic countries. It is not easy to assess the associations from which Lefèvre drew his inventions, and one can only speculate. Some of the names seem to have been suggested by Lefèvre's geographical knowledge, others by a conscious (or unconscious) sense of appropriateness. Appollo's disloyal subjects may derive from the the disloyal subjects from *Luke*; 'Oliferne' for Mirro's kingdom may come from the Biblical king decapitated by a powerful woman, an association between Medea and

Judith which occurs in the *Ecloga Theoduli.* Nevertheless, as much as Chrétien's exotic characters, Lefèvre's are recognizable local types.

In addition to Jason's betrothal to Mirro, Lefèvre further denied the legitimacy of the oath to Medea, because she had extracted it under duress (Jason was enchanted by her nurse). Second, Jason was right to leave Medea because of the wicked things she did, and we must admire him for leaving her although because of the enchantment he was unable to stop loving her. Third, he went back to her in the end. The difficulties which this contradictory welter of claims ought to have made, in fact created the space in which Lefèvre could create his coherent romance-biographical account. Lefèvre's Jason is a victim of other people's ill-will, sexual desire, or ambition; he is a steady, loyal young man, oblivious of the more complex attitudes of those around him. Above all, Lefèvre wrote *around* the history of Jason, from his fight with the giant to his inset euhemerized narrative of the history of Appollo's settlement of Colchis. As a *tour de force* of fictional tightrope walking, his book invites our own narrative desire.

As we saw when we looked at the impetus to make a coherent historical narrative of the legends, accounts usually began in Thessaly with Pelias already in position as a usurper to whom Jason appears as the prophesied one-sandalled stranger who threatens his power. Lefèvre will have no threat to legitimacy: his book opens with the aged Eson making his brother regent of his kingdom and guardian of his son in a testament of good advice to the young Jason, one of those collections of precepts which were intended to instruct a young prince in virtue.[37] The style is overtly Christian, and Lefèvre's metaphors familiar:

> 'Hellas! or fauldra il que je laisse l'arbre que j'ay planté, premier que voye quel fruit il aportera. Mon filz, tu es l'arbre, le fruit que tu apporteras seront tes oeuvres. . . .' Le roy Eson l'endoctrinoit tousjours et l'admonnestoit a faire oeuvres de noble homme, disant que cuer aorné de vertu rent l'homme noble, non pas sa noble rachyne. (126–7)

> 'For hit behoueth that I leue the tree that I haue planted to fore I see what fruyt he shal bringe forthe. My dere sone thou art the tree and the fruyt that thou shalt bringe forth shalbe thy werkes. . . .' The noble king Eson endoctrined him alway & admonested him euer to do vertuous werkes, saying that the herte adourned with vertue rendrith the man noble and nothing the noble stok or progenye. (4, 6)

The private virtues which were the subject of the Mirrors for Princes were,

---

37 Lefèvre has, understandably enough, conflated two characters in Greek stories who have similar names: Jason's uncle, Pelias, with Achilles' father, Peleus of Mirmidon.

of course, safe advice for clerics to proffer to their rulers. In addition, the insertion of good advice is a distraction from the truth or falsehood of the narrative. It also lengthens it.

Lefèvre translates the political situation into medieval terms, so that Pelias is the regent for his aged brother's son, something not unheard of in fifteenth-century France or England, where the royal Valois or Plantagent dukes competed for power over their infant nephews. Knowing he must give up his power eventually, Pelias takes on the role of Jason's companion and mentor, so that he can watch his nephew. It is the sequence of Jason's precocious triumphs that arouses Pelias's fear and hatred, and Envy which corrupts him. This is at an important remove from treason and deposition. The values of kingship are intact; the men agree.

Jason demonstrates his nobility first in his friendship with that other hero of the Burgundian court, Hercules, already, perhaps, the protagonist of Lefèvre's first romance. Linking these two in noble comradeship ties them both into a possible adventurous past, while offering protection for Jason. Hercules was already associated with the Argonautic voyage, which he deserted at the point at which the young Hylas was drowned by the water nymphs. Hercules is also linked to a prior destruction of Troy, which Lefèvre was to expand in his *Recueil*, a text in which he refers back to his *Jason*. The web of textual cross-reference is part of Lefèvre's comprehensiveness, which attaches this story to others.

But it must not be thought that this narrative concentrates on the Argonautic adventures. They would be little enough defence of Jason. Lefèvre's 'enfance Jason' exploits well-known romance motifs (a giant, a besieged lady). The eighteen-year-old Jason sets off to begin his career at a joust to celebrate the knighting of another young hero, Hercules, where he maintains himself so well that they become friends and comrades. It is Hercules who knights him in turn, at the wedding of Pirithous and Ypodame (128ff) in Thessaille (Caxton's Thessalonycque), where the two heroes defeat the drunken centaurs and rescue the bride. This is not an adventure normally associated with Jason, but that it is a marriage where Jason is a protector of woman may have attracted Lefèvre to it.[38] He is an intrusive narrator, who glosses motive throughout, and who here emphasizes Pelias's envy of his nephew.[39] He also give Pelias one of many interior monologues in which one emotion wars allegorically against another.

---

[38] Lefèvre is not always secure with his classical references: he makes Yxione Pirithous' mother, which Caxton corrects to father.

[39] Having set Jason up as a paragon of virtue he at one point asks how many modern Jasons now exist, who respect old age, and remembers the disgraceful behaviour of Noah's sons (Lefèvre 157, Caxton 54).

Pelias knows from the outset that he is at fault, and 'knows' in the language of courtly debate, a stylization which constantly calls attention to abstract qualities. This is a linguistic move which has, among its other effects, the tendency to introduce allegorical resonances. Pelias's internal monologue, in which thoughts of murder are immediately inhibited by realization of its impracticality, indicate how low he has already sunk. His hypocrisy is shown in his overt encouragement of Jason's desire for glory while his covert prayers are for Jason's destruction.

> Et Peleus s'en retourna en Mirmidoine, priant pour Jason qu'il poeut estre fourdroyé de tonnoirre, trespercié de mille glaives, ou ensepvely en la mer, ou emporté en enfer en corps et en ame. (133)

> & Peleus returned vnto Mirmydone praying the goddes that Iason might be smyten with tonder or thurgh persyd with VC [sic] speris or to be buried in the see to thende that ther were neuer moo tidinges of him.
>
> (14)

Although Pelias's ill will is obvious to others, Jason is blind to it and impervious to other character's attempts to make him aware of it. As Roland was 'preux' and Olivier 'sage', so Jason is trusting and loyal. Still capable of giving Jason good advice, if for the wrong reasons, Pelias encourages his nephew to seek further adventure defending a young queen who is besieged by an unwelcome suitor.

Jason moves about the Greek world, but the world in which he moves is a familiar one in which knights travel from court to court, in which they are rewarded with gifts of fine horses, and find lodging with aged townspeople where they speak to the other guests. Jason may fight for glory, but other soldiers are recruited for money payments, and behave like fifteenth-century foot soldiers who pillaged the lands through which they fought. There is travel by sea where pirates are a risk. Women can travel, too, pretending to be pilgrims, and some even suffer seasickness. Characters have a mixture of Greek and Biblical names, and refer to Biblical events (such as Noah's ark and his nakedness).

As with so many medieval works, this one is built of permutations and combinations upon certain situations. There are good and bad rulers, who illustrate the importance of stern moderation and good judgement, both men and women: Aeson, Pelias, Laomedon, Appollo, Oeetes, Hypsipyle and Mirro. There are women who behave well, with modesty, and more who do not. Odd as it must seem to *multiply* Jason's beloveds, the addition of Mirro gives Lefèvre the opportunity to show one more variation. Mirro is the ruler of Olyferne, although she is only sixteen. Her rejection of the besieging suitor, the king of Sclavonie who makes war upon her to compel her to marry him, recalls the virtuous version of Dido, and imitates a familiar motif from the Alexander romances, in which the king disguises himself as an ambassador in order to see his unknown beloved. Mirro's name offers a puzzle. Lefèvre may have thought it sounded Greek, resembling, perhaps, a name like Myrrha (who was, however, scarcely virtuous). Caxton glossed it as straightforwardly allegorical, hearing 'miroir'.[40] One of Jason's triumphs comes straight from the pattern book of medieval romance: the fight with the churlish giant. 'Corfus' the Giant is one of the cynics who denies love (thought it must be added that the Mopsus, old man, and seer, whom Jason meets as he has left Mirro, shares, in a courtlier mode, some of Corfus's views).[41] The style throughout this section mixes allegorical personifications with colloquial expressions, high emotions with men who sweat because they are nervous in the presence of their beloved, deeds of arms and cynical appraisals of the value of woman's love.[42] If Lefèvre meant his book to be matter for debate, in the tradition of Machaut's poised problems of love, he has given his audience plentiful material, voiced by a succession of characters who describe what they think the characteristics of women are. There is a worldliness about the

[40] Lefèvre's original 'Ceste royne avoit a nom Mirro' (133) expands to 'This quene was callid Mirro, which is asmoch to saye as mirrour in beaute' (15). The old French sounds like the words for looking and admiring, whether in a mirror or not. Caxton emphasizes beauty rather than moral qualities.

[41] Mopsus, who is travelling incognito, is Appollo's son, king of 'Cilice', conqueror of 'Pamphile' (Lefèvre 161, Caxton 60), two areas of southern Asia Minor. See *Atlas of the Greek and Roman World*, ed. N. G. L. Hammond (Park Ridge, N.J., 1981), Maps 11a, 11b. When they first find themselves sharing a room Mopsus, who has been kept awake by Jason's lovesick complaints, Mopsus, who is not without his own cynicism, tries to convince Jason that any man should have two strings to his bow. Jason insists that women are the height of virtue, and that doubleness must be dishonour (Lefèvre 159, Caxton 56f). In Lemnos Mopsus notices that Ysiphile has fallen in love with Jason, and tries to urge him to take advantage of her love, because they will all benefit from it.

[42] Under the influence of the fire of Love, Jason begins his speech to Mirro: 'Ma dame, je vous ay servy le moins mal que j'ay peu pour deux raisons: l'une pour l'acquit de chevalerie, l'autre pour desservir, non pas vos richesses que tenez soubz le pouoir de Fortune, mais celles singulieres dont Nature vous a fait dame et sus quoy Fortune n'a poissance' but he ends by swearing that when he ceases to love her 'les poissons voleront en l'aer et les oyseaulx nageront en l'eaue' (150, 151). Caxton translates, 'Madame I haue seruid yow as well as to me is possible for two causes, principally that one for thacquite of cheualerye and that other not for to disserue the richesses that ye haue vnder the power of fortune but allonly that singuler thing that nature hath made yow lady of and vpon whiche fortune hath [?no] puissaunce' (43). Then, 'Certes that shal not be vunto the tyme that the fysshes flee in the ayer and the byrdes swymme in the water' (44). When the time comes nothing in nature is reversed.

Plate 1. BNf. MS f.fr. 331, fol. 78v, showing the news of Zecchius's
rebellious attempt to conquer the fleece being brought to King
Appollo, shown under his canopy on the left.

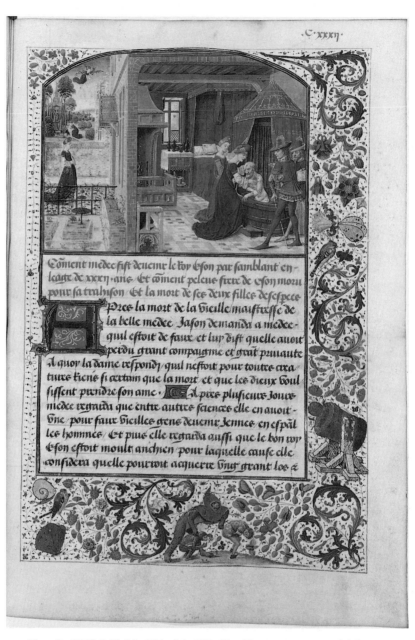

Coment medee fist deuenir le roy eson par samblant en-
leaige de .xxvij. ans. Et coment peleus frere de eson mort
pour sa trahyson. Et la mort de ses deux filles desespere-
es. Pres la mort de la vieille maistresse de
la belle medee. Jason demanda a medee
quil estoit de faux. et luy dist quelle auoit
perdu grant compaignie et grant priuaute.
A quoy la dame respondy/ quil nestoit pour toutes cra-
tures riens si certain que la mort. et que les dieux voul-
sissent prendre son ame. Apres plusieurs iours
medee regarda que entre autres sciences elle en auoit
vne pour faire vieilles gens deuenir iennes en espal
les hommes/ Et puis elle regarda aussi que le bon roy
eson estoit moult anchien pour laquelle cause elle
considera quelle pourroit acquerre vng grant los et

Plate 2. BNf. MS f.fr. 331, fol. 132. The illustrator uses multiple
representation to narrate Medea's rejuvenation of Aeson: Medea's
flight to collect herbs (her wings are the period accoutrements for
such figures, including angels), her sacrifice before the image of the
gods, then her return to Aeson's palace, whose brick facade she enters
past a formal garden.

Comment medee fist Iaſo le Roy eſon de
uem: Iennc Et comment elle fiſt pel
leus mouir par ſes propies filles qui
ſe deſeſperent a ceſte cauſe

Pres la mort de la vielle . Medee
regarda quelle auoit la ſcience de
faire vielles gens deuenir Iennes en eſpe
cial les hōmes et puis regarda oſſy que le
roy eſon eſtoit viel et lors elle conſidera
quelle pouoroit acquerre vn grant nom ſelle
lui ralongoit la vie · Si appelle Iaſon vn
Iour et lui diſt quelle feroit bien par ſon art
que ſon pere recouureroit nouuelle Ienneſſe
ainſy que ſil fuſt en laage de trente ans
Quant Iaſon or ce Il fu tout eſbahy et

Plate 3. Taken from Lefèvre's autograph, presented to Philippe le Bon
(Arsenal MS 5067, fol. 130), showing Aeson flanked by Medea, on his
left, holding the instrument with which she is bleeding him (removing
his 'aged' blood through a hole already made in his skull), and, on the
right, the rejuvenated Aeson.

Plate 4. BNf. MS f.fr. 12570, fol. 154v, illustrating the escape of the
Argo from Colchis. Medea confronts her father (the crowned figure on
the left, his hands raised in a gesture of horror) with her brother's
severed head, while her nurse holds a cloth full of body parts which
match those already in the sea between the two ships.

Comment medee jetta en la mer les mē
bres de son frere pour faire arrester son pere
qui le siculoit Et comment la royne
rsiphile se jetta en la mer du plus hault
dune montaigne

On demanderoit de ces quatre
petites galees pour quelle cau
elles mouuoient du port et quelz gens
estoient dedens Respond listoire que .
leur intencion estoit de venir apres les
gregois et que le roy oethes estoit en
lune acompaignie de quatre cens des
bourgois de la cite quil auoit fait ar
mer hastinement pour ce quil estoit ad

Plate 5. Arsenal MS 5067, fol. 117v, Lefèvre's presentation copy. The
escape scene appears to take place before the lovers have left the shores
of the city of Colchis.

Plate 6. BNf. MS f.fr. 331, fol. 139v. Here we see the moment after Medea's fire-breathing dragons have immolated the wedding guests.

Plate 7. City of Angers, Apocalypse Tapestry. St John looks on as the angels reach out to save the woman's baby.

narrative which makes one wonder if the narrator's tongue is not, from time to time, at least, firmly in his cheek.

The first six of the book's twenty-one chapters are chronologically prior to the legends as we have become accustomed to them. In this long first section Lefèvre establishes Jason as knight, friend of Hercules and (after he has freed Athens of the pirates ruled by the wicked – and otherwise un-known – Diomedes) Theseus, and lover of Mirro. Chapters 9–13 are the long intercalation on the history (or perhaps the 'history') of Colchis. Appollo, here a son of King Jupiter of Athens, receives a vision in which he is told to build an ark and take settlers from Salathie (founded by the Hebrew line of Salathiel) to Jacointe in the island of Colcos, where he is supported in government by Loth, Zechius, and Zethephius. If there is a contemporary key to this narrative of loyalty, betrayal, and bourgeois satis-faction, it is long lost, but there is no reason to think that Lefèvre had specific historical personnages in mind for his hypothetical happy city. Rather, he posits a settlement which illustrates the ways in which obedi-ence to a benign ruler brings harmony, and disobedience creates civil strife. Characters have moved by sea throughout the narrative, and Ap-pollo's 'ark' is parallel to Jason's Argo only because the way to reach an island is by ship. The new city is to live, agree the people, under Appollo's guidance, 'paix et amour s'enrachineront entre vous, et n'y aura homme qui rumeur, rancune ne noise machiner ou conspirer y oze' (180, Caxton: Pees and loue shall be roted in yow, and ther shall be no man that shall be so hardy to conspire ony Rumour, Rancour, Rebellion, ne machine ony troble in no maner of the worlde' [95]). When rebellion comes it comes from envy, as envy was the source of Pelias's disruption in the main narra-tive. There is a completely fictional description here of civic harmony and its betrayal which might well have appealed to any medieval ruler. The establishment of the fire-breathing bulls on a small neighbouring island is part of the mystery, in which Jason's coming is predicted, and instructions for him preserved in a letter passed from Appollo's daughter, Phanoles, through her daughter, Ortis (who married Oetes) to Medea. It is, therefore, in fulfilment of a prophecy that Jason takes the fleece; he is a thief only because Oetes begrudges his success and refuses him permission to marry Medea.

Lefèvre ties his insertion to the main narrative through that prophecy, and we should return to the part of the book which resembles the tradi-tional stories of Jason. Having rescued Mirro, then having had his love rejected by her because she does not yet know that he is her equal in rank, Jason leaves Olyferne, only for Mirro to follow him in order to confess that she does, indeed, love him. Their troth having been plighted, he returns to

Mirmidoine with Hercules and Theseus. Jason is the one-sandalled man, but almost arbitrarily, since he is exercising in a meadow with Theseus and Hercules when Pelias, returning from the Oracle, comes upon them all and decides to underwrite the Argonautic voyage. Lefèvre then takes them to Troy, where Laomedon rebuffs them and thus prepares the first destruction of his city. From Troy they proceed to Lemnos, where the women recite the story of their murder of their husbands and sons to frighten away the invaders, but then, convinced of the Greeks' good intentions, offer themselves to the Argonauts.[43] Jason rebuffs Queen Ysiphyle's amorous advances, only to have her climb into bed with him and insist (despite her shame at her own behaviour) that they become lovers. That is, Lefèvre makes it quite clear that he never deceives her, that she knows that what she is doing is dishonourable. Although Jason promises – swearing upon the image of Pallas – to return if he can, he gains his lover's acceptance that marriage is impossible. We may ask if we are meant to think of this as an anti-Dido, but the narrative is tacit. What we can say is that in structural repetitions, Jason's first love behaved honourably, and returned to her country to do her duty there and await him; his second foisted herself upon him. The third is Medea.

No goddess comes to Jason's aid, or betrays Medea: she loves Jason at first sight, and realizes that he is the long-foretold conqueror of the Golden Fleece. Her night-time monologues acknowledge that if she betrays herself and her father to Jason she will be forever shamed, but, faced with the certainty that if she does not help him he will die, she proceeds. Jason sadly rejects her love, because of Mirro, but Medea has better help than Ysisphile had, and her nurse enchants Jason's bed. *This* is the reason he swears his allegiance and love to her; even Mopsus is taken aback, but assumes that Jason is merely as fickle as the next knight, and not that he has been enchanted. Not until he meets Mirro again will the eyes of love perceive that only magic could have robbed him of his good faith.

Lefèvre does the best he can with the matter he has inherited, but he is in a difficult position, because he intends to follow the story (first seen in Trogus Pompeius) that Jason and Medea will be reconciled at the end. One technique is to make her nurse the guilty party. Jason performs his tasks, then flees with Medea, who has bundled up her jewels in order to escape with him. But it is she and the nurse together who cut her brother's throat in preparation for the chase (Lefèvre 211, Caxton 144). Jason is horrified

---

[43] Hercules leaves the Argonauts to seek adventure, as Lefèvre tells us is recounted in his own adventures; this is one of the moments when he may be referring to another of his own compositions (Lefèvre 172, Caxton 81). There is another instance at the punitive expedition against Laomedon (Lefèvre 235, Caxton 187).

when he sees what she has done, but the enchantment keeps his love secure.

> Dame, puis que açavoir le voulez, je vous dis que je pense a vostre cruel corage et que, se ne fust l'amour que j'ay en vous et que promis vous ay vous espouser et mener en Grece avec moy, he vous renvoyasse vers vostre pere. Et vous garder de faire plus, si chier que vous avez a moy courroucer! (215)

> Lady, syn that ye desire to knowe wheron I thinke, knowe ye for trouth that if it were not for the grete loue that I haue in you and for that I haue promised to wed you and bryng you into Grece, I wolde not do it. Wherfore kepe from hensforward that ye do no suche thing as dere as ye will haue peese bytwene you & me. (151)

It is the Nurse who stops the Argo from returning to Lemnos, in concert with Medea. When the Queen realizes that the ship will not return, she throws herself off a cliff. Ysiphile's death is thus the Nurse's doing, and when her corpse is hauled up on the Argo, it bleeds in the Nurse's presence, accusing her of murder. Lefèvre does not signal that he has chosen this version over the one in Statius, nor give the slightest explanation or comment, although he has been expansive in castigating male characters such as Pelias.

The direct speech which Lefèvre gives Medea blackens her character: she had persuaded herself that loving Jason was not dishonourable; she accounts her brother fortunate to save so many lives with his death; and blames Jason for grieving over Ysiphile. Once married to Jason she offers to rejuvenate his father. This gives her an important ally, for Eson supports her henceforth, even when Jason can bear her crimes no longer and deserts her. Once again Jason is followed by the woman he has left, who finally overtakes him in Corinth, where the king has persuaded him that the only way to forget Medea is to marry his daughter, young Creusa. Medea attempts to reason with him, but ends by attacking the wedding party with a fire-breathing dragon, and murdering first her younger son by Jason, then the king and the princess. Jason, still protected by Medea's unguents, is fire-proof; he is also still in love with Medea because of the first spell. After this both husband and wife flee separately into the woods.

Although Jason is horrified by Medea, he cannot put her out of his mind, and, when, by accident, he meets Mirro once more, it is she who recognizes why not and breaks the enchantment. Their love reestablished, they live secretly together, with Jason disguised as her usher, Sambor (an obvious anagram for Ambrose, although I have been able to find no significance to this Tantris-like reversal), so that no one will know who Jason is and he will be safe from Medea. He is not, however, safe from the jealous suspicions of one of Mirro's courtiers, who waylays Jason and injures him badly enough to keep him from Hercules' expedition to punish Laomedon. (There is an obvious parallel here to Lancelot.)

But Lefèvre is now reaching the end, and needs to find a way to rid himself of Mirro. He invents a punitive expedition against Jason by Aeson, who is loyal to Medea for all she has done for him, which results in a second siege of Olyferne. Medea uses her magic to confront the lovers (but not to kill Mirro), and Jason has the opportunity to repudiate her for her wickedness. Once more Medea's speech is that of a wicked sorceress, and when she returns to her camp and sees her remaining son, his resemblance to his father provokes her to another murder. She then disappears into the forest where she repents her misdeeds and lives a life of renunciation and mortification. But the siege continues until one of Eson's archers shoots Mirro. Jason, disconsolate, also wanders into the forest once more where, in the fullness of time, he rediscovers Medea, forgives her, and remarries her. The couple return to Mirmidoine to be reconciled with Jason's father, who forgives them both and relinquishes his kingdom into their hands. There is, as Chaucer might have put it, 'namoore to say'.

Lefèvre refers only to an old book as a source, although it is clear that he has depended upon many of the texts described in the last two chapters. Sometimes his text is very close to the *Ovide moralisé*, and at one point it seems possible that he is quoting the *Metamorphoses*. He has given himself an almost impossible task; by opening the book out away from Jason altogether, then stressing Jason's innocence and suppressing Medea's point of view, he has done what he could. The question which remains (how seriously his readers took his inventions) is not one that can be answered. The evidence of printing history and translation suggests that his books enjoyed considerable success, but whether they enjoyed *belief* is another question. It may be that readers treated his romanced history with a mixture of pleasure and scepticism. Caxton, at least, was aware of different versions of the history, reminding us once more that no one version superseded all the others.

It is conventional to remark that with the important exception of Malory's *Morte D'Arthur*, the fashion for Burgundian-style romances which William Caxton supported through imports, printing, and translation was a short-lived phenomenon.[44] In fact, it might be argued not

---

44 Like all students of Caxton, I am indebted to the research of Prof. N. F. Blake, especially to *Caxton and his World* (London, André Deutsch, 1969). He has recently collected his long series of articles on Caxton: *William Caxton and English Literary Culture* (London,

only that it was less short-lived than now appears, but also that the resurgence of Malory's popularity came later than has always been remembered. Mary, Queen of Scots, had a copy of *Jason* in her library at Holyrood House and *Jason* is named in *The Complaint of Scotland*. Several continental printers prepared English as well as French editions of it, and there survive two hand-copied manuscripts.[45] Antiquarians compared it to Malory, not always to its own detriment.[46]

Jason helps to flesh out a picture of print culture at the end of the Middle Ages. Caxton had already printed Raoul Lefèvre's huge compendium of Troy-stories, *The Recuyell of the Histories of Troy*, which was to become a source-book for history, myth, and attitudes to that Fall.[47] His new translation attached itself to that earlier work in the way that prefatory histories (for example in the cycles now called the Epics of Revolt) offered to expand upon already-known events, but tacitly. Rather than emphasizing the historical importance of the events recounted, Caxton emphasizes the book's connection to the Burgundian court. That is, there is a cultural, and contemporary, contextualization which suggests that Caxton may already have had reservations about Lefèvre's inventions. Edward IV had been made a member of the Duke's Order of the Golden Fleece in 1468. In addition, of course, the appeal to the prestige of the Burgundian court, then the most sumptuous in Europe, as the ally (in marriage as well as – perhaps, in effect, even more than – in politics) of Edward IV, conferred a certain reflected glory.[48] Caxton's dedication of his

---

Hambledon Press, 1991). The fifteenth century is still the step-child of medieval studies. For an updated descriptive bibliography, see *Middle English Prose: a critical guide to major authors and genres*, ed. A. S. G. Edwards (New Brunswick, Rutgers University Press, 1984).

[45] Listed as one of the Edinburgh Castle Books in 1578 by Julian Sharman, *The Library of Mary Queen of Scots* (London, 1879); see further Janet M. Smith, *The French Background of Middle Scots Literature* (Edinburgh, Oliver and Boyd, 1934), Introduction and chapt. 1. A list of books known in mid-sixteenth-century Scotland is recited by a shepherd who mentions 'The tail quhon that iason van the goldin fleice' in *The Complaynt of Scotlande*, ed. J. A. H. Murray, EETS e.s. 17–18 (London, 1872–3), pp. lxxii, lxxxi, 64. For the manuscripts, see Curt Buhler, *The Fifteenth-Century Book: the scribes, the printers, the decorators* (Philadelphia, University of Pennsylvania, 1960), pp. 15–40 and his 'The *Fasciculus Temporum* and Morgan Manuscript 801' *Speculum* 27 (1952), pp. 182–3 n. 29.

[46] For example, Th. F. Dibdin, 'Comparatively with the *Morte d'Arthur*, there are few digressions and few wearisome episodes . . . Upon the whole, there is much natural and beautiful colouring in this performance'. *Bibliotheca Spenceriana* (London, 1815), vol. IV, p. 196.

[47] Ed. H. Oskar Sommer (London, David Nutt, 1894). Both versions are discussed in Aeschbach, *Le Recoeil des Histoires de Troyes*.

[48] The complexities of Anglo-Burgundian relations are well described in M. R.

Jason to the Prince of Wales makes some play with the idea that the child might find the book useful in learning to read English. There is no mention of the benefits of the book, nor of Caxton's ideas about its claim to exculpate Jason from accusations against him.[49] Neither does Caxton mention the number of redactions of Lefèvre's text, nor how he acquired his own copy. Caxton shows the fifteenth-century translator's characteristic concerns with clarity (especially in the matter of English's lack of vocabulary, which encouraged 'doublets'), the effort to make a work available and comprehensible to an audience which would otherwise be unable to read it, expectation of correction from learned colleagues who were able to compare translation and original, but also appreciation of his efforts to amplify references in order to comprehend other versions, while nevertheless sustaining the version under translation. Caxton fashions himself as a participant in the new literary world: he consulted other authoritative texts for some references to the mythographical material, mainly Boccaccio and Statius. That Caxton knew of other English versions of the Jason and Medea legends he tells us in his translation of the *Recuyell,* where he refers to Lydgate's metrical interpretation of Guido delle Colonne. His prologue is as much as a publisher's blurb as anything else, and contains no more information on the book's author than Lefèvre himself gives us. Given Caxton's later practice, this may suggest that he considered Lefèvre's rank or status, if not a handicap, at least not an advantage.

His substantive additions juxtapose different accounts of Jason's genealogy and deeds, opening possibilities of additional, even contradictory, interpretation. The first comes at the end of the Author's Prologue:

Thielemans, *Bourgogne et Angleterre* (Brussels, 1966) and M. M. Postan and E. Power, *Studies in English Trade in the Fifteenth Century* (London, G. Routledge and Sons, 1933). On Caxton in particular, see M. Kekewich, 'Edward IV, William Caxton, and Literary Patronage in England' *The Modern Language Review* 66 (1971), pp. 481–7. Charles le Téméraire, who succeeded his father, Philippe le Bon, in 1467, was married to Margaret of York, King Edward's sister, a fact which did not impinge overmuch on his economic policies. See Charles Ross, *Edward IV* (London, 1974), pp. 260–9. Caxton's expansion into printing as part of his import/export business cannot be satisfactorily 'explained' as the economically rational calculation of a merchant ambitious to extend his trade and maximize his profits. Printing was capital-intensive, because of the investment in machines and materials (especially paper stocks). Most early printers, in fact, went broke. But there were intangible benefits. Caxton's self-presentation as a man interested in books and history among his social superiors (as well as equals) suggests serious participation in an area of life in which dedication to learning was the entrée.

49 Curt Bühler analyzes the variations in the surviving copies of the English version in 'Caxton's "History of Jason" ', *Papers of the Bibliographical Society of America* 24 (1940), pp. 254–61.

Thus endeth myn Auctor his prologe/ And how wel that his is sayd afore this prologe that Eson was sone to Cacus. Yet Bochace saith in the Genelagye of Goddes that he was sone to Erictheus the .xxix. sone of Iupiter/ As ye may see more playnly in the .xiij. book of the Genelagye of Goddes the .xxiiij. Chapytre. (p. 3)

The second comes at the end of the book and supplements Lefèvre's text with carefully cited authorities: the final sections of Boccaccio's account in the *Genealogia Deorum* to the effect that Jason restored Aeetes to his throne, as well as with Statius's account of Hypsipyle's *two* sons. It is easy to remark the public morality ready to emphasize, in a period of political disruption, the maintenance of legitimate authority; it is just as striking that Caxton's final comments interpret against the grain of Lefèvre's intentions, in a conclusion which would warm the heart of any Deconstructionist:

... and more haue I not red of the noble Iason/ but this haue I founden more then myn auctor rercheth in his boke/ & therefore I make here an ende of this storie of Iason. whom diuerce men blame because that he left & repudied Medea/ but in this present boke ye may see the euydent causes/ why he so did. (p. 199)

Caxton made changes which clarified his original, specifying characters names and positions, times and places of action, where the French allows ambiguity. Stylistic heightening turns Jason into 'the preu Jason' or 'the vaillyant knight Jason', so that his name seldom appears unadorned. In fact, Caxton is closer to his copy-text than Lefèvre's own French redactors.[50] At the same time, as we know from the previous chapter, Caxton appeared to be willing to allow this book to stand beside his mythographical works without any necessity to choose.

That degree of narrative toleration may raise impatience in a modern reader; and that impatience with inventions as apparently preposterous as Lefèvre's, in the *Jason* as well as the *Troy Book*, should alert us to our own attitudes to the way certain kinds of historical or pseudo-historical narratives can become 'set'. 'Inaccuracy' is an easy accusation in these circumstances, but we need to remember how broad the latitude of invention could be for Lefèvre and writers like him. Discomfort with a work like *Jason* arises from many sources, not least of them the degree of magic

---

50 Who may, of course, have been Lefèvre himself: he was a constant reviser. Whoever the reviser was, the copy he executed for Louis de Bruges (now BNf. f.fr. 331) shows how speeches were a particular temptation to him. See Pinkernell for details of the redactions.

which both Jason's and Medea's acts entail. The legendary world which contains fire-breathing bulls and dragons asks us to suspend our disbelief in the natural world of historical time. In rationalizing Jason's actions Lefèvre tried to pluck out the heart of the mystery – but his inventions, from the unknown 'Mirro' to the politics of Appollo's kingdom, achieved no adequate substitute. Perhaps there is none for a story so dependent upon the ability of an author to embody emotions, to describe both the ambitions which make men ready to sacrifice anything to their fulfilment, and the power of love's hatred to destroy.

FIVE

Some Medieval Medeas

When we consider the available source material which awaited any medieval writer interested in Ovid, or the Fall of Troy, or the legends of Jason and Medea, there is in some ways a range of choices more apparent than real. Even the categories of poetry, history, mythography come to seem divisions of convenience rather than acute distinctions. What appeared to be Ovid might be a commented Latin text, a translation which purported to represent that text, or an adaptation. But, as we have seen, not only were the medieval texts of 'Ovid' often far from representative of Ovid, even a reader whose Latin was good enough to study the *Heroïdes* or *Metamorphoses* would necessarily come to the texts with supplementary or explanatory references likely to modify Ovid out of recognition. Culturally, too, the story (or stories) 'known to all' is known as it comes embedded in views about, or arguments over, the status of classical antiquity, war, women, religion, fate, or providence, not to mention the inheritance of literary expressions of these great subjects. If history is known, or allegories become habitual, readers and writers are only the more likely to expect to recognize what they have come to believe in as familiar and as true. As the 'historical' texts wove their way into the mythographical ones, as the legendary texts were decoded to supply the matter for histories of the secular past, as the Argonautic voyage attached itself to the Fall of Troy, Jason and Medea became part of much larger constructions articulated in terms of the cultures which made use of them. Because they precede the main events, because they thereby acquire precedence, they introduce themes which are continued later. Mythographers supplied methods and materials which encouraged interpretations which expanded and complicated the Latin poetry. Their additions came from historical sources which themselves depended upon poetry and mythography, and which can be traced back to the same important innovations and inventions. So far from being the impeccable, independent, and authorized accounts of the past that they claimed to be, they were often based upon the very poetry over whose rhymed inventions they asserted their superior veracity. Medieval readers and writers could not see, as we can, how far their disparate sources agreed because they stemmed from the same source. When they contested what they found in those sources, with reservations about or deferrals to apparent authorities, they were able to make spaces for their own interpretations, to appropriate what they found to their own purposes. Although to describe their 'scruples' about their sources risks projecting anachronistic categories on them, their attitudes to authority were bound up with the vexed issues of the transmission and translation of ancient materials. The distinction between the poetic fables of the mythographers and the historians' strict adherence to truth now seems one of those arguments based upon deceptively similar terminology in a different conceptual space which so complicates the study of the Middle Ages. Yet we must not overemphasize conformity or similarity to claim that what existed in medieval interpretations was the only thing that could have existed. If the same materials were available to many medieval writers on mythological themes that were available to Raoul Lefèvre, no one else tried to create such a comprehensive revivification of a 'whole' narrative. Nevertheless, and despite the similarities of the sources, considerable variety in the depiction of the legends remained possible: the polemical variation of 'Medea' is more real than apparent.

There is, in the end, an irresolvable conflict in the legends as they came together in comprehensive attempts to create a 'whole' story, whether in the verses of Apollonius in third-century BC Alexandria or the pages of the fifteenth-century Burgundian, Raoul Lefèvre. What makes the legends of Jason and Medea unique in western literature is the broken-backed necessity of that complete history: the young hero who becomes a defeated and humiliated outcast, the ingenue who is also a serial killer. Those versions which bring the lovers together at the ends of their lives, and even claim that they restored Aeetes to his throne, insist upon a plot which outrages the decorum called poetic justice, by overturning the trajectory of traditional tales. It is that scandal which is the stories' claim upon us. The particularities of apparent history, and the status, the inalienable importance, of the history of Troy, outweighs the – perhaps naive – expectation that ancient and medieval writing took predictable shapes in which, if the good do not always end happily, at least the bad are punished.

This chapter considers different Argonautic voyages, incidental Jasons, and different kinds of Medeas, as they were created by some Italian, French, and English authors in the fourteenth and fifteenth centuries. Certain broad distinctions will be useful, but each text requires its own context; each retelling its own sense of purpose; each invention its idea of coherence. The medieval idea of the cycle of human ambition as first a rise then a fall from prosperity under the buffets of fortune is very different from classical ideas about tragedy, or falls, or fortune. Medieval ideas about, for example, kingship, legitimacy, and inheritance change the context of the legends, just as Christian ideas about the place of the irrational in human experience change the characters within those legends. Emotions may be reified as apparently allegorical personifications, but they are not persons, not gods, but methods of objectifying human internal experience, as well as interpreting female subjectivity. How those interpretations were to be interpreted, what the characters, their deeds, and their emotions were taken to illustrate, were always contestable. Above all, the medieval Medeas remained complex characters for their sometimes horrified authors.

In what follows I shall use a number of different organizing categories, authorial and formal; I shall largely discriminate narratives inset in larger histories from shorter, 'biographical' mirrors in which the characters appear as examples of behaviour to emulate or escape in narratives of Fortune's attack upon their elevated states. The narrative argument of a large-scale historical text is likely to differ from a small-scale *exemplum*. Throughout the middle ages authors of many kinds made numerous brief references to Jason and Medea as lovers – but their references contradicted each other. We now have some sense of how that came to be. There is an intersecting story to be told about medieval emulation of Ovid, in which the ostensibly Ovidian heroine herself takes on powerful life; and the Medea who inspired Dido who inspired Medea and so many other heroines reappears as a character-type upon whom medieval writers could project their own concepts of the powerful and dangerous woman. And *this* story inspires its opposite: as the extraordinary success and diffusion of the *Tristan* provoked the anti-*Tristan* emphasis on conjugal fidelity in Chrétien, so the female stereotype created by the many-times-multiplied figure of Medea inspired the anti-Medea narratives and character of the heroine of, among other tales, the Griselda. For medieval writers could appeal to their own kinds of Christian heroism (and heroinism), a passive endurance in the face of overwhelming odds which was elevated in status through the martyrs' emulation of God's own suffering. The renunciation of revenge and the forgiveness of one's enemies mark a dramatic divide between antique and Christian reactions to harm.[1] Jason's repudiation of a

---

[1] One might add a reminder here, already glanced at in the previous chapter, that the *Eclogua Theoduli* associates Medea with the Old Testament heroine, Judith, who, in effect, seduced the enemy king Holofernes in order to be able to decapitate him as he slept in the bed in which they had just made love.

dangerous wife has never appeared an exceptionally criminal act; it is in part made so because of Medea's revenge. Medea's betrayal of her father and country, her later vengeance, the evil of her murders (which antique societies understood as part of the impulse of helping one's friends and harming enemies), becomes equally – if differently – problematic, under the Christian dispensation (which emphasizes the power of repentance to redeem and regenerate a sinner through the grace of a merciful and forgiving god), because *women* normally demonstrate the genuineness of their remorse by dying, thereby conveniently removing themselves from the earthly arena and questions of human justice. Because she is not simply a myth, a legend, or a fable, but in some sense historical, Medea's success is an affront to so many aspects of medieval culture and belief that she could not fail to inspire impassioned controversy.

Precisely because of the kinds of interpenetrations which have been the subject of the previous chapters, no strict division by genre or form will suffice; there must be constant cross-reference, in criticism as in creation, and an awareness of innovation. In a period anxious about authority, writers posing as translators insisted that they interpreted a work or an author, and famously not that they were inventing an original contribution. One of the 'strong' works which was much translated and interpreted is the moralised history of Troy by the much-maligned Guido delle Colonne, and I shall begin with this main 'historical' text and some of his vernacular imitators. I shall then consider the striking and innovatory compendia of Giovanni Boccaccio, including his vernacular story-collection (and *his* vernacular 'translators'), before looking at interpretations we may wish to categorize as on the way to being (or, perhaps, on the way back to being) 'literature', or at least 'Ovidianism', of four important medieval writers: Chaucer and Gower in the fourteenth century, and John Lydgate and Christine de Pizan in the fifteenth.

Throughout we shall see familiar arguments over history becoming arguments about the exemplary status of historical characters, and, in particular, part of the quarrel over the nature of woman and her place in history.

Guido delle Colonne and the History of Troy

The success of Benoît de Ste-Maure, and the long survival of his version of the prelude to the Fall of Troy, was assured not only through the copying and imitation of his text, but because of the long life and authority enjoyed by the most important prose adaptation of his inventions, the *Historia Destructionis Troiae* (completed in 1287) of Guido delle Colonne, probably to be identified with a Sicilian judge and court poet.[2] All over Europe this book became one of the central texts for that history, and it was, in turn, the source of numerous translations, epitomes, and retellings in the vernaculars.[3] The story of Guido's work is partly a demonstration of the ways poets contested the moral condemnations which frame his version. Guido's narrative voice is loud, as is his claim to interpretative authority.

Guido's work is largely based upon a prose epitome of Benoît's poem, which he treats as a window on Dares and Dictys, whom he cites as his sources; he knows Virgil's *Aeneid* and Ovid's *Heroïdes* and *Metamorphoses*. He approaches the old French prose as an amplification which he can strip down by rationalization, and then expand in turn with moral commentary upon the events. He has a considerable and consistent critical vocabulary, distinguishes fables and histories, and carefully assesses, on his own authority, his various *auctores*. One of his over-arching purposes is to consider certain basic problems of history itself: how is it that great consequences grow from contingencies which appear trivial, and how are we to

---

[2] Ed. N. E. Griffin (Cambridge, Mass., The Medieval Academy of America, 1936) and Guido delle Colonne, *Historia Destructionis Troiae*, trans. Mary Elizabeth Meek (Bloomington, Indiana, Indiana University Press, 1974). Guido's reputation suffered for many years from anachronistic charges of plagiarism; for biographical information Robert Barth, *Guido de Columna* (Leipzig, Ferber and Seydel, 1877) is still useful; see also Raffaele Chiantera, *Guido delle Colonne: poeta e storico latino de sec. XIII e il problema della lingua della nostra primitiva lirica d'arte* (Naples, 1956), pp. 164–80.

[3] These range from Bulgarian, Serbian, and Russian, Old Norse and Old Irish, to the vernaculars of western Europe. For German, see H. Brunner, ed., *Die deutsche Trojaliteratur des Mittelalters und der Frühen Neuzeit* (Wiesbaden, Reichert, 1990). A selective survey would include, in Old Bulgarian, *Trojanska Prica*, in *Starine* (Jugoslavenska Akademija Znanosti i Umjetnosti) III (1871), pp. 156–187 (with accompanying Latin translation); in Old Norse, *Trójumanna Saga*, ed. J. Sigurdsson, in *Annaler for Nordisk Oldkyndighed og Historie* (Kongelige Nordiske Oldskrift-Selskab) IV (1848), pp. 4–100 and Randi Claire Eldevik, *The Dares Phrygius Version of Trojumanna Saga: a case study in the cross-cultural mutation of narrative* (Ann Arbor, University Microfilms, 1988); in German, Konrad von Würzburg, *Der Trojanische Krieg*, ed. A. von Keller, *Bibliothek des Litterarischen Vereins* XLIV (Stuttgart, 1858); in Irish Gaelic, *Togail Troi*, ed. R. I. Best and M. A. O'Brien (Dublin, Dublin Institute for Advanced Studies, 1966) as well as *The Irish Aeneid*, ed. G. Calder (London, 1907); in Spanish, *Sumas de Historia Trojana*, ed. R. Menedez Pidal (Madrid, 1934); in Czech, *Le topisowé Trojansstj. To gest: Wypsanj desytilete walky Reku s Kralem Pryamem* (Prague, 1812); in Polish, *Historya Trojanska, 1563*, ed. Wydal Samuel Adalberg (Crakow, Nakl. A. K. Umiejetnosci, 1896); in Serbo-Croat, *Eine altserbische Trojasage*, ed. A. Ringheim (Prague, Imprimerie de l'Etat, 1951); in Rumanian *Die Rumanische Version der Historia Destructionis Troiae des Guido delle Colonne*, ed. Radu Constantinescu (Tubingen, TBC Verlag, 1977). M. E. Barnicle treats some of these in her introduction to *The Seege or Batayle of Troy: a Middle Metrical English Romance*, EETS o.s. no. 172 (London, 1927).

understand the moral purpose of these events? For example, he has a large vision of the apparent cycles of the past as contributing to God's will in history: he gives the 'cause' of the Trojan War as Laomedon's discourtesy – an interpretation which has become familiar to us – but wonders if the suffering caused by the fall of the city (to victors as well as to vanquished) is justified because it led to the foundation of Rome, which in turn paved the way for Christianity, as well as for the foundation of other European nations. He argues that history moves cyclically towards eschatology, and cannot claim that present Europe represents an acme of peace and justice (Book II). To make his work conform to the pattern of other historical works he opens his preliminary section (Books I to IV) with a carefully arranged discussion of the geographical location of the kingdom Pelias ruled, balancing one authority against another before deferring to St Matthew, who knew beyond doubt the name of the people who inhabited Thessaly. He is concerned with *why* things happen, and how one event leads to another; the themes of the opening section are the themes of his book as a whole, and each instance is part of an implicit argument that the cycles of human behaviour do indeed repeat themselves, and that, therefore, what is true of rulers (or women) in one society will be true again in another. Even within one source he weighs the parts of the narrative which are fable, or fabulous, against those which he perceives as historical. Guido's rationalizing means that verisimilitude (of a sort) has disproportionate effect; the magical golden fleece becomes a misreported story of great wealth (since it was also true that King Aeetes possessed great treasure), but preserves Benoît's love stories which, after all, might have happened.

He is quite clear what might not have happened, and takes Ovid to task for saying that Medea had control over the sun and stars, when only God himself could have that, and he has declined to interfere with their movements except at the death of Christ. Although Guido preserves the legends of Medea, then, he labels them *as* legends: his history is at least in part the report of a report. This narratorial intervention in the history makes Guido the commentator on the events he reveals, and he moves quickly to address Aeetes, whose courtesy in sending for his daughter to compliment the visiting Greeks, eventuated in his ruin. About women Guido is an essentialist: he tells the reader (what he will endlessly repeat) that women are always in flux, always seeking a man, never contented, full of desire, and ready with cunning to achieve it. Even Medea's first speech to Jason builds in the fear of female voluptuousness and immorality, as well as the knowledge that to aid Jason she must betray her father, robbing him of his child and his treasure. Above all, Guido points out her failure to foresee that Jason would deceive her. This has been interpreted as a reflex of Guido's misogyny, but it has an important introductory function in the history as a whole – a history, after all, well-endowed with seers and prophets. The human belief in an ability to control events by foresight is constantly gainsaid by history. This is one of Guido's themes, and Medea's failure is an early example.

Not that Guido spares Jason, whom he condemns for betraying Medea, but fault is often attached to his female actors. If Jason and the Argonauts remain in Colchis for a month before returning to Thessaly, rewarded with gold and a bride, soon afterwards Jason, Hercules, and King Pelias himself will make a parallel journey back to Troy where, having defeated King Laomedon, they will spend a month looting Troy, before returning with gold and that bride, Hesione, from whom sprang the great destruction of the city. Guido's emphasis on the unforeseeable results of men's actions punctuates his story of the city's fall and, at the beginning of his book five, at the junction between the first destruction of the city and the greater war, he adjures his readers to avoid giving even the slightest injury or offence, including reminding kings of the duty of hospitality to the well meaning. Guido's theory of history, if one can use such a term, permeates his interpretation, and leaves room for other medieval writers to carry on with his – or their own – ideas of how a city comes to fall, of the place of women in the sequence of events, of competition, of the threat of foreigners, and even of the legitimacy of kings.

Some Vernacular English Histories of Troy

We have already seen how a historical version of the fall of Troy became a preliminary to histories of the European nations, and how it re-inserted itself in the mythographic tradition, in the course of the fourteenth century in the *Ovide moralisé*. Those works, with Guido's, radiated out through the European vernaculars. In England a historical version appeared in the retellings of the Fall of Troy.[4] We might expect to find the narrative material treated in similar fashion, but there are divergent patterns according to the context in which the material appears.

The Seege of Troy, a 2,000 line epitome of the history of the fall of Troy, was written probably during the first quarter of the fourteenth century, and the four extant texts appear to be independent copies of a single

---

4 Treated in detail by C. David Benson, *The History of Troy in Middle English Literature* (Cambridge, D. S. Brewer, 1980).

original.[5] The best of the four surviving manuscripts, Lincoln's Inn 150, also contains copies of *Libeau Desconnu*, *Merlin*, *King Alexander*, and *Piers Plowman*, which suggests a miscellany of historical and improving texts. Jason's voyage is dispensed with in 212 lines, and the destruction of the city appears to have been abridged into inaccuracy, since Pelyas apparently sends Jason to *Troy* in search of the 'schepis skyn of golde' (line 38), where Laomedon offends against hospitality and threatens them with immediate death if they do not re-embark immediately. There is no Colchis, no fleece, no Medea. The compression may be deliberate, for public and popular recital. This text, copied and rewritten in the fifteenth century, shows the possible influence of the Alexander romances and, in the last version, Harley 525, suggests that backward-looking nostalgia which adds rhetorical set pieces such as a single combat between Jason and Laomedon during the punitive expedition which resulted in the first destruction of the city – a combat otherwise unrecorded (lines 162a–162t). More than in many of the histories, certain of the six episodes have been assimilated to immediately-recognizable romance motifs (such as falling asleep under a tree), which suggests a simplified and popular text.

The so-called *Rawlinson Prose Troy Piece*, written in southern English prose of the fifteenth century, is a short translation which occurs in the context of ancient histories; the author/compiler names Dares and Guido as its sources, but it may descend from a French intermediary.[6] Some of the interpreters of the Troy legends used their sources with great care; this author makes a number of simple mistakes (calling Aeson's wife 'Medea', for example, Brie, p. 273) which suggest little learning. He seldom makes his presence felt, as this extract shows

> But for that worthi conquest, Jason was renowned and named as for þe worthiest conquerour in eny londe, by cause thereof specially: vppon

---

5   *The Seege or Bataille of Troy*, ed. M. E. Barnicle EETS o.s. no. 172 (London, 1927). On its date and provenance, see p. xxx. It may derive from Joseph of Exeter's Latin poem, 'Excidium Troiae', ed. E. Bagby Atwood and V. K. Whitaker (Cambridge, Mass., Medieval Academy of America, 1944). Four texts survive, which are all printed. In two of the MSS it is surrounded by histories (in the extended sense which I have developed here) and serves as a preface in one to Geoffrey of Monmouth, or is found in conjunction with historical romances (e.g. a King Alexander); if other texts which we would categorize as romances occur, so does *Piers Plowman*. This may suggest that in a pinch an oral-performative 'text' would suffice. See Benson, pp. 133–4.

6   Contained in Rawlinson D 28, in the Bodleian, it has been printed twice, first by N. E. Griffin, 'The Sege of Troy', *PMLA* 22 (1907), pp. 157–200, then by F. Brie, 'Zwei mittelenglische Prosoromane: The Sege of Thebes und The Sege of Troy (1422 bis ca. 1450)', *Archiv für das studium des neueren sprachen und literaturen* 130 (1913), pp. 40–52, 269–85, from which I quote.

which gilden flece, al þe courte and peple come reunyng fore to mervaile and wonder there vppon, euery man seying his avice þere vppon; the night folowing after his commyng ayen; Medea being in hir chambre alone, sent priuely after Jason, which with ful hert and will, come to hir vnware of eny persone, telling hir euery dele of his iourney. Of which, she was right glad and ioyfull, so þat he last with in hir chambre al þat night, where, betwen hem two, they founde a tyme and leysour, for to stele awey be night into Grece with the flece of golde and al þe tresour of þe king hir ffader, which was to þe confusioun of Medea, ffor afterward, he left hir in grete myschef, And toke anoþer lady; And he hadde by Medea ij sones, And by cause they were so like Jason, Medea slewe hem bothe. But of hir I speke no more at this tyme. (p. 276)

But this is not to say that the narrator has not assimilated the story to his own views of the world: he emphasizes contract and draws a series of parallels: Aeson/ Pyllios, Medea/Sithes (Aeetes), Medea/Jason, and Sithes/Jason. The habit of seeing things in terms of reputation is clear even in such a short text, with its emphasis upon the opinion and advice of nameless witnesses. There is, of course, tacit condemnation here, partly by the indication that the theft of the king's treasure did Medea no good, but partly also by the shift from Jason's adventure and renown to the implication by juxtaposition that their theft became her 'confusion'. He is above all concerned with legitimacy.

But not all of Guido's translators had their own theories of history, or even much by way of moralized reflections upon the past, and it is worth a brief reminder of the ways translations sometimes updated their originals for their new audiences. While some translations of Guido show more concern to interpret their material, even to recast its emphasis, others are vernacular renderings for audiences fond of romances. A translator who excised Guido's reflections could make a story of Troy which was precisely that, a story like other stories. There is not always anxiety about the place of the secular past.

Two which date from around 1400 show contrasting aspects of these treatments of the history. The *Laud Troy Book* is in loose four-stress couplets which follow Guido's main outline, while excising many of his learned digressions.[7] The *Laud*-author affects to see the narrative as the

---

7 *The Laud Troy Book*, ed. J. E. Wulfing, EETS o.s. 121, 122 (London, 1902–3); only the volumes of text appeared. Dorothy Kempe's 'A Middle English Tale of Troy', *Englische Studien* 29 (1901), pp. 1–26 was so critical of the poem's lack of literary quality that it provoked three long ripostes from the editor in which he listed the vast number of 'poetic' features which he found in the text. These appeared as 'Das Laud-Troybook', *Englische Studien* 29 (1901), pp. 374–96 and then 'Das Bild und die bildlliche

romance of Hector, one among the many heroes of Romance whose stories are told and retold at feasts; that is, he is pulling the history of a city towards the story of a knight. The Argonautic prelude introduces the concentration on the heroes, or knights, but he keeps referring to the destruction of Troy to come, at the expense of a complete recital of the end of Jason's adventure; suppressions avoid political or social implications. The following is a representative passage, but the clumsiness of the verse should not distract us from the advertisement for *all* romances, here reduced to public entertainments:

> Off Bevis, Gy, and of Gauwayn,
> Off kyng Richard, & of Owayn,
> Off Tristram, and of Percyuale,
> Off Rouland Ris, and Aglauale,
> Off Archeroun, and of Octouian,
> Off Charles, & of Cassibaldan,
> Off Hauelok, Horne, & of Wade; –
> In Romaunces that of hem ben made
> That gestoures often does of hem gestes
> At Mangeres and at grete ffestes.   (lines 15–24)

It is worth remembering that the affectation of oral performance can itself be a strategic self-reflection, but we cannot know what the *Laud*-author intended. Situating his romance in this context of French and British 'matters' certainly does not suggest an emphasis on learned sources.

By contrast, the *Alliterative Troy Book* is a serious and close translation of over 14,000 long lines, which also gives the impression of oral performance.[8] Given its length, however, it is likely to have been composed for readers, although they may have subvocalized the text. This history reflects

verneinung im Laud-Troy-Book', *Anglia* 27 (1904), pp. 555–80, 28 (1905), pp. 29–80. Quaintly dated as such controversies may now appear, lists such as Wulfing's are now, of course, regularly used to analyze the unconscious interests of authors. Benson notes the association with rural life (pp. 70f and nn.), which we may consider to be the development of a register at some remove from idealized French romances. Elizabeth C. Sklar suggests the possibility of a lost medieval English intermediary between the *Laud Troy Book*, the *Gest Historiale*, and Chaucer in 'Guido, the Middle English Troy Books, and Chaucer: the English Connection', *Neophilologus* 76 (1992), pp. 616–28. See Benson, chapt. 3.

8 The 'Gest Hystoriale' of the Destruction of Troy: an alliterative romance translated from Guido delle Colonne's 'Hystoria Troiana', ed. G. A. Panton and D. Donaldson, EETS o.s. 39, 56 (London, 1869, 1874). Early articles on this text were concerned with questions of authorship and literary value, such as S. O. Andrew's demonstration that the author of the alliterative Alexander could not also have written the *Gest*, 'The *Wars of Alexander* and the *Destruction of Troy*', *RES* 5 (1929), pp. 267–72. Benson, chapt. 4.

the concerns of the medieval Englishman who wrote it, who surveys his sources and the problems of poetry and history, and whose anachronisms and departures from Guido fulfill our expectations of what might be expected of a late-medieval vernacular and verse historian. We may guess that the translator was attached to one of the provincial courts which still encouraged composition in the old metres, but we know little more than that implies. His rhetorical expansions celebrate the *topoi* of history, from descriptions to catalogues to arguments and defences, even speeches before battles. But he is also constrained by his verse-form, and one notices that whatever he thinks of gentle Jason's behaviour, Jason's name is also associated with words such as 'joyful' and 'jolly' because of alliteration. The first three passus are devoted to the Argonautic prelude. We may look for the French emphasis on disunity and competition with a central monarch: we find that the history begins with a usurpation. This author *is* learned, and cites other authorities than Guido, including Ovid. He is concerned with issues of inheritance, and stresses that Pelias was right to fear Jason. By his anticipation of the deeds of the Myrmidons he makes one feel that the story he tells has wider ramifications.

He uses dialogue – like a good rhetorical historian – to create his own interpretation, as in Pelias's disingenuous speech to Jason: 'Cosyn, it is knowen þat I am Kyng here, And mekyll comfordes me the crowne of this kyde realme' (212–3), and Pelias offers Jason *half* his kingdom. This kind of unremarked change in the narrative to illustrate untrustworthiness is typical of his skill. The Argonauts set off, and no doubt make their stop at Troy (there is a lacuna in the manuscript which corresponds to that misadventure) before arriving at Colchis. The author translates Guido's text, and includes a rebuke to Jason for betraying Medea, as well as a rebuke to her (III.714–47); there is nothing particularly anti-feminist about his narrative. As David Benson has pointed out, he has omitted a number of Guido's moralizations to concentrate upon the material of the history, in that rationalizing movement of extraction which we have seen elsewhere. Had the native manner of poetry survived this text might have been influential; it remains an important text of the alliterative revival.

The most important English translation of Guido – in terms of subsequent influence – is John Lydgate's. More is known of its genesis and composition than of many such texts. It was commissioned by (or on behalf of) Henry V when he was still Prince of Wales, and written between 1412–20 in the loose five-stress couplet marked by aureation which C. S. Lewis dubbed 'the fifteenth-century heroic line'.[9] It might be less

---

[9] *Lydgate's Troy Book*, ed. Henry Bergen, EETS e.s. 97, 103, 106, 126 (London, 1906–33).

condemnatory to think of the line as narrative-historical, and to try to forget the implicit insistence upon the kinds of 'epic' writing which were to come later. There is nothing 'epic' in Lydgate's conception of his text, which is neither the foundation poem of a people nor the story of the fall of one man. If the conjectures about Lydgate's dates are more or less correct, the *Troy Book* is his earliest extended project, but the work of a man in his forties whose life has already encompassed the upheaval of the so-called Lancastrian revolution, the usurpation through which Henry Bolingbroke became Henry IV. That is, Lydgate may have entered the cloister as a child, but his young manhood could not be untouched by the knowledge of spectacular political falls.

Lydgate consistently denies himself the status of an auctor, yet that apparent self-denial is modesty appropriating other authors' authority. If Lydgate describes himself as merely a translator, he turns attention from the degree of his own amplification of Guido, supplemented by numerous other works, from the usual medieval Ovids to Christine de Pisan's *Epistre d'Othéa* (which I shall discuss below). As modern readers, although we can reorient our views about epic, romance, or history, we cannot forget that Lydgate is a reader, indeed, a memorizer, of Chaucer, and one sometimes hears the murmur of Chaucer's poetry underneath Lydgate's amplifications, as, for example, Troilus's pledge to Criseyde through Jason's long speech of devotion to Medea (lines 2374–2416).[10] The assimilation of Chaucer is purposive, a way of saving poetry for exemplifying history; Lydgate appropriates Chaucer to his own serious purposes, and we believe his deference to his master at our peril.

Although he retains Guido's observation on Medea's folly in following Jason, Lydgate always keeps her as an ingenue, her father's sole heir, and blames Jason for betraying the woman who gave herself to him so

---

'The fifteenth-century Heroic Line', *Essays and Studies* 24 (1938), pp. 28–41. Benson's discussion of Lydgate is particularly good. He was the first to identify Christine as one of Lydgate's sources (chapt. 5).

[10] As an example of the way that Chaucer's language has permeated Lydgate's:

> What þat þe cok, comoun astrologer,
> þe mydnyȝt hour with his vois ful clere
> Be-gan to sowne, and did his besy peyne
> To bete his brest with his wyngys tweyne,
> And of þe tyme a mynute wil not passe
> To warnen hem þat weren in þe place
> Of þe tydes and sesoun of þe nyȝt,
> Medea to awayte vp-pon hir knyȝt
> Ful redy was . . . (lines 2813–2821)

Chaucer's romantic vision is here transformed into a furtive and hasty escape.

completely, thinking no wrong. It is clear in Lydgate's version that it is Jason who swears devotion to Medea, spontaneously, unreservedly, and apparently unfeignedly. The fluidity of possible interpretation made possible by interlocking historical material manifests itself elsewhere and in Lydgate's other works he was to give a different picture.[11] What is striking about Lydgate's morality is his insistence that God's Providence works within a human lifetime, that men and women are rewarded and punished according to their deserts. Medea suffered because she began badly, and 'For her gynnyng was nat vertuous,/ An ende folweth ful contagious' (3619–20); where lust enters in, trouble follows.

Lydgate's amalgamations suggest that he has read his Ovid with a detailed commentary (he mentions the *Metamorphoses* and refers to the *Heroïdes*); here we see once again the compounding of poetry and history, which once more legitimates the narrative we have come to recognize. For Lydgate Jason and Medea are *both* culpable.

> Of hir Guydo writ no wordis mo,
> Ne maketh of hir non other mencioun,
> By-cause, I trow in myn opinioun,
> Þat hir sorwes, ende and euerydel,
> Rehersed ben ful openly and wel
> Methamorphoseos, & wryte þer ful pleyn:
> Wher as Naso recordeth in certeyn
> Hir deth nat only, nor hir heuynes,
> But parcel eke of þe vnkyndenes
> Of þis Iason, and telleth pleynli how
> Medea hir bothe sonys slowe,
> For þei wer like her fader of visage;
> And telleth eke, þat put hir moste in rage,
> How falsely he, I can hym not excuse,
> Loued another þat called was Ceruse;
> Eke in his pistles, who so taketh hede,
> Hir dedly sorwe he may beholde & rede,

---

11 Lydgate has traditionally been castigated for his inability to resist *amplificatio*, but his control of the complexities of the past appears in the course of the Hypsipyle section of his *Siege of Thebes* (lines 3019–3519), where Jason receives only a passing mention (lines 3188ff), and Lygate refers the interested reader to Boccaccio's *De Claris Mulieribus* and, in passing, to the *Genealogia*, as well as mentioning Petrarch. *Siege of Thebes*, ed. Axel Erdmann (London, Oxford University Press for the Chaucer Society, 1911). If an *amplificatio* of my own may be permitted here, it is precisely in this section of the *Siege* that Lydgate's ability to imitate Chaucer is at its most eloquent: the speech on the necessity of death which Adrastus makes to Lycurgus and his wife, on the model of Aegeus to Theseus in the *Knight's Tale*, becomes an implicit appropriation of Chaucer's Theban poem to Lydgate's own poetical history.

And how þat sche hir trouþ abou3te sore.
Of Medea 3e gete of me no more
In al þis boke, nor of hir auenture. (3696–3715)

There is always a reason behind Lydgate's imitations: in this first section, of course, there is the anticipation of betrayal – by kin, by sovereigns, by lovers – which will come later in the poem, and is a theme of the Troy-history which I have already pointed out in my discussion of Benoît. But there is also, throughout, Lydgate's ambition to write seriously, in poetry which, as moral *exempla* or as history, will create for the English language what Chaucer left to be done. And Chaucer indeed left a space in historical narrative, both of the classical and of the English past. Lydgate is concerned with public order, with legitimacy, with the place of fortune and the responsibility of men for their actions. He is a thinker – as well as a writer – of the second order, from whom we can extract society's straightforward concerns in ways that are, even when internally contradictory, straightforward.

Giovanni Boccaccio's Exemplary Compendia

By contrast to the translators and interpreters of Guido, we may consider a far more original – and a far greater – author, who also returned repeatedly to Medea, sometimes where she is least expected. For Boccaccio, the orientation between 'fable' and 'history' was sometimes not only explicit, but the source of irony. In his hands the story of 'Medea' ramified away from a character into stories of the state or the city: not 'Medea' only, but Aeetes and, remarkably, one extended anti-Medea. Rarely, we are in the advantageous position of hearing authors allude to questions of authority. In the fourteenth century, when Petrarch adapted Boccaccio's vernacular tale of Griselda for his own Latin narrative, he deliberately made a story in the 'historical' style into a moral fable. The letter which accompanies the text includes

> Quisquis ex me queret an hec vera sint, hoc est an historiam scripsim an fabulam, respondebo illud Crispi: 'Fides penes auctorem (meum scilicet Johannem) sit.'

> [If anyone asks me whether these things are true, whether I have written a history or a fable, I shall reply with this statement of Crispus, 'The truth lies in the author, that is, John [Boccaccio].']12

12 Petrarch, *Letteres Seniles* XVII.3, quoted from *The Literary Relationships of Chaucer's*

The truth might lie in the author when the author was known and the narrative the kind of invented (and clearly invented) fiction upon which nothing depended, but the narratives of pagan antiquity posed more difficult problems. Boccaccio's own practice was a kind of morphology of mythology, an extended rationalization of as many texts as he could collate, in three important Latin works, the *Genealogia Deorum Gentilium*, the *De Casibus Virorum Illustrium*, and the *De Mulieribus Claris*[13] No morphology is neutral, and Boccaccio was not simply solving an intellectual puzzle, or preserving a past from oblivion. Particularly in the works meant for circulation as *exempla*, Boccaccio pressed the past into use as a meditation on vice and virtue, the discontents of civilization and citizenly values.

The *Genealogia*, traditionally reputed to have been copied and circulated before it was finished, and apparently without Boccaccio's permission, became a standard reference text for readers who wished to disentangle the complexities of Graeco-Roman mythology. Boccaccio's approach was to create an Almanach de Gotha of inter-related families, with its implication of competing noble houses, and he 'solved' the problem of contradictory accounts by positing the existence of a series of 'gods' with the same name, Jupiter I, Jupiter II, and so forth.[14] This organization by lines of descent implied the division of the narratives by family group, and, although this is not the place to discuss the book in detail, an alert reader can see the development of competitiveness, and the relative success of different filiations. Medea appears in Book IV with the Titans, Hypsipyle in Book V, chapter 29, among the progeny of 'Jupiter II', and Jason in Book XIII in the family of Jupiter III. The first dismemberment is of the 'complete' narrative itself, which introduces the theme of fission, the strategy

Clerk's Tale, ed. J. Burke Severs (New Haven and New York, Yale University Press, 1942), pp. 291–2. My translation. Petrarch himself exploits the familiar list of heroines in his *Trionfi*, 'Trionfo d'amore' I.115ff. Ariadne, Medea, and Hypsipyle appear in a Heroidean list.

13   *Genealogia Deorum Gentilium Libri*, ed. V. Romano, 2 vols (Bari, G. Laterza, 1951). *For an English translation, see Boccaccio on Poetry*, ed. and trans. Charles Osgood (New York, 1930). *De Casibus Virorum Illustrium Libri novem*, ed. Pier Giorgio Ricci and Vittorio Zaccaria (Milan, Mondadori, 1983) and (Vienna, H. Ziegler, 1544), as well as by Henry Bergen in his text of both Lydgate's translation (see below). *De Mulieribus Claris* (Ulm, 1473), and ed. and trans. Vittorio Zaccaria in *Tutte le opere de Giovanni Boccaccio*, X (Rome, Mondadori, 1967). English translation: *Concerning Famous Women*, ed. and trans. G. A. Guarino (London, 1964).

14   Romano provides an index to passages referred to (II, pp. 867–93), which indicates that Boccaccio collated the chief classical poems of Virgil, Ovid, and Statius with their commentaries, including recent ones (e.g. Pierre Bersuire), and late-classical histories such as those by Dares, Dictys, and Justin. This euhemerist approach to the pagan gods is discussed by E. Gilson, 'Poésie et verité dans la "Genealogia" de Boccace', *Studi sul Boccaccio* 2 (1964), pp. 253–82.

which emphasizes one aspect of the legends by occluding others, often by attributing confusion or disagreement to authorities who may or may not be cited.

While the *Genealogia* rationalizes the pagan accounts, it both complicates the problem of their status as representations as well as the authority of pagan authors, while – as Boccaccio's habit is elsewhere – rehearsing of 'gods' what is true of the behaviour of men. Boccaccio treats a vast range of texts as material from which he could, by dint of his own efforts, extract 'information'. In so doing, of course, he reduces those authorities to a sameness of reliability and he elevates his own authority as the arbiter of their relationships. His euhemeristic approach further presupposes the assimilation of mythological stories to historical time, although he avoids locating them specifically. Boccaccio's rationalizing organization extends to his judgements of possibility, including the limits of magic. In this sense, he sets himself up as a model reader, capable of distinguishing literal from metaphoric descriptions. His Jason and Medea entries overlap, but are consistent. If in both cases he distinguishes history from fable, in neither case does he intervene with moral judgement. We might, however, consider that his apparent inclusiveness, as well as his apparent objectivity, suppresses aspects of the relationship between Jason and Medea (the oath, the second marriage) which might lead to reservations about the hero.

In Book IV Boccaccio follows Ovid (especially the *Heroïdes*) and Apollonius Rhodius for Medea, warning us that 'huius Medee grandis recitatur historia quandoque fabulis mixta'.[15] Nevertheless, Boccaccio gives a complete narrative. Inspired by Venus, Medea fell in love with Jason, who had been sent by his uncle, Pelias (whom Boccaccio has not confused with the father of Achilles, Peleus). Medea aids Jason to win the fleece, they marry, and flee, taking her younger brother, Absurthus (or Egealeus) with them. This double naming suggests that Boccaccio has compared Ovid to Justin's version of Trogus Pompeius, and 'corrected' accordingly, without acknowledging his preferences. Oetes, Medea's father, pursued the fugitives, who cut Absyrthus into pieces which they threw overboard to distract him. They escaped and returned to Thessaly, where Aeson, Jason's father, was so happy that, insists Boccaccio, he *seemed* to shed years of his life ('Ubi precibus Iasonis Esonem patrem annositate decrepitum in robustiorem retraxit etatem.'). So the magic to protect Jason is acceptable, but not the magic which rejuvenated Aeson. Similarly, Boccaccio tells us that Medea

---

15 It is not clear how well Boccaccio could read Greek, nor whether or not he read Apollonius for himself, with help, or from a commentary. He refers to Greek forms, but many medieval writers did that. Chaucer probably used his references to Apollonius, and not his own reading of either the Greek or the Roman epics.

turned the daughters of Pelias against their father to ensure his death, which led Jason to repudiate her and marry Creusa, daughter of King Creon of Corinth. Medea's present to the bride devoured Creusa in flames, she killed her and Jason's children, and fled to Athens where she married King Aegeus, and bore him a son, Medus. She tried to poison Theseus, Aegeus's son, when he returned from an expedition, but failed, and had once more to flee. Then Boccaccio follows Justin, turning authority with an expression of his own ignorance: 'Et tandem nescio quo pacto Iasoni reconciliata una secum in Colchos rediit.' This reconciliation is followed by *Jason's* last expedition to restore Oetes to his throne. Once more a 'complete' narrative appears merely to present a historical sequence.

In Book XIII, chapters 14–28, Boccaccio appeals to the authority of Homer to trace Jason's family back to Aeolus, god of the winds, through his son Erictheus, and his grandson, Aeson. This patrilineal emphasis causes some disconnection in the narrative, but as a compilation of commentary-inspired information, it is impressive. Boccaccio appeals to Ovid for Jason's journey to Colchos at the behest of his uncle, Pelias, where he won both the fleece and Medea. Returning to Aeson, Boccaccio repeats his interpretation that joy made Aeson appear to shed years of his life. Only then does Boccaccio begin from the prophecy of the one-sandalled man, which he attributes to Lactantius's commentary on Statius. He uses Statius for the heroes gathered for the expedition on the Argo, for the sojourn at Lemnos (including Hypsipyle's liaison with Jason and her pregnancy), and Jason's success at Colchis.[16] He follows Apollonius for the route of the homeward journey, gives Lactantius as authority for naming Creon's daughter Glauce while citing Seneca's authority for her as Creusa. He cites Seneca here for Medea's murder of her children, then mentions her escape to Athens and her reconciliation with Jason, who restores Oetes to his kingdom. Here, too, Boccaccio emphasizes the admixture of poetic invention in their history; the tacit message combines regal legitimacy and reconciliation.

There remains something of a puzzle, nevertheless, which is the project of the *Genealogia* itself. Did Boccaccio have what we now call a hidden agenda? Was it, were they, perhaps not so hidden? Had he more than one, given that the poet as acknowledged legislator is such an important part of

---

[16] Fulgentius, the early sixth-century mythographer, retold and analyzed fifty myths in his *Mitologiarum libri tres*. His reading of Statius makes Hypsipyle a distraction – the familiar female snare and delay – on the way to Thebes (the soldiers are the soul going to fight Creon). See Fulgentius, *Opera*, ed. Rudolf Helm (Leipzig, Teubner, 1898), and Leslie George Whitbread, ed. *Fulgentius the Mythographer* (Ohio, Ohio State University Press, 1971).

his final sections? There is a kind of balance to this carefully-referenced sequence of events which appears to read them as historical, i.e. to interpret literally (including emphasizing the metaphorical) wherever possible. It insists that under the fables of poets, as Caxton has it, we may read – if we know how to interpret – accounts of the past. The whole last section is a defence of poetry which stresses not its guidance to the past, but its moral utility. This is part of a two-pronged defence of pagan writing, the effects of which are not only to legitimate the reading of pagan texts, but contingently to reemphasize their status, and the status of secular concerns with such this-worldly matters as ambition, kingship, and the full panoply of heroic adventure.

Some of the force of Boccaccio's civic concerns reappears in his other Latin works. The medieval tendency to see history as a tragic pattern of individual falls combines a view of the necessary failures which accompany ambition and a deeply contradictory assertion that Fortune is fickle and arbitrary, but can at least be depended upon to abandon one at the end. The idea that such stories are mirrors for princes, who can learn from them what to emulate and what to avoid, continued long beyond the end of the Middle Ages. It is the kind of legitimation which also, by appealing to non-princely *schadenfreude*, preaches a kind of political quietism. Petrarch had already written such a collection, in his *De Viris Illustribus*. To find a precedent for the use of biography as moral exemplum one might go back as far as Plutarch's paired lives of famous Greeks and Romans. Those, however, were extended essays. Boccaccio's historical demonstration of tragic falls began with his *De Casibus Virorum Illustrium*, which was to have a long afterlife in translation, in Laurent de Premierfait's French as well as Lydgate's English, and as an inspiration as late as Sackville and Norton's *Mirror for Magistrates*.[17] Chaucer's Monk takes his place in this procession of drawers of lessons from the public facts of history. Before considering those male falls, let us consider the fortunes of some female protagonists.

Boccaccio also turned his attention to famous, or notorious, women, who took their place, exceptionally, in public affairs, in his *De Claris Mulieribus*. And here, too, there are curious contradictions in the project, which collects outstanding women known for good – and for evil. This was an important text for him, which he began as early as 1359 and continued to revise for fifteen years. It is hard to imagine the extension of

---

17 From about the period 1534–47 there is another translation, with a transcription of the relevant portions of the original, Henry Parker, Lord Morley, *Forty-Six Lives Translated from Boccaccio's De Claris Mulieribus*, ed. H. G. Wright, EETS o.s. 214 (London, 1943).

biographical exempla without the influence of Ovid's *Heroïdes* in addition to the historical 'falls'. Boccaccio himself notes the eccentricity of his book in its preface:

> Nor do I want the reader to think it out of place if together with Penelope, Lucretia, and Sulpicia, who were very chaste matrons, they find Medea, Flora, and Sempronia, who happened to have very strong but destructive characters. For it is not my intention to give the word 'famous' so strict a meaning that it will always seem to signify 'virtuous', but rather to give it a wider sense, if the reader will forgive me, and to consider as famous those women whom I know to have become renowned to the world through any sort of deed. But since I have extolled with praise the deeds deserving of commendation and have condemned with reproach the crimes, there will sometimes be not only glory for the noble, but opprobrium for the wicked.[18]

This disingenuous preface leads in a number of directions. It is not surprising to see Boccaccio's emphasis on chastity as women's (especially Christian women's) supreme virtue, or as the focus of their lives. The range of women's actions is constricted by the necessities of their gender, but not restricted to the focus of desire, or to their assistance to men. Boccaccio is, however, through the repetitions of his examples, once again suggesting a morphology which is also a moral categorization of the nature of women. What makes exceptional women is 'ingenium', cunning intelligence, and that 'ingenium' may be used for good or ill. The outcome of their superior gifts of intelligence is an almost arbitrary matter, depending more on fortune than good judgement. Boccaccio's outstanding woman is a dangerous being. By organising the examples in chronological order Boccaccio makes a tacit demonstration of the nature of woman in all times and places; the modern instances are culminations which show that nothing has changed. In addition, by placing the women in chronological order, Boccaccio can, contingently, refer to the loss of innocence, the end

---

[18] *De Mulieribus Claris*, ed. and trans. Vittorio Zaccaria in *Tutte le opere di Giovanni Boccaccio*, X (Rome, Mondadori, 1967), pp. 24, 26. Trans. G. A. Guarino, *Concerning Famous Women* (London, 1964), pp. xxxvii–xxxviii. Nec volo legenti videatur incongruum si Penelopi Lucretie Sulpitieve, pudicissimis matronis immixtas Medeam, Floram Semproniamque compererint, vel conformes eisdem, quibus pregrande sed pernitiosum forte fuit ingenium. Non enim est animus michi hoc claritatis nomen adeo strictim summere, ut semper in virtutem videatur exire; quin imo in ampliorem sensum – bona cum pace legentium – trahere et illas intelligere claras quas quocunque ex facinore orbi vulgato sermone notissimas novero. . . . Verum, quoniam extulisse laudibus memoratu digna et depressisse increpationibus infanda non nunquam, non solum erit hinc egisse generosos in gloriam et inde ignavos haberus ab infaustis paululum retraxisse. . . .

of the simplicity of life which was brought about by the introduction of husbandry, then the arts of women in the production of cloth and clothes, and so forth. There are tell-tale moments, such as the reference to Eve as a *citizen* of Eden, with the *laws* of marriage and inheritance, which reveal Boccaccio's concern with civil society as a whole.[19]

Law and the Father are tacitly linked: Medea and Hypsipyle appear in contiguous chapters further related by cross reference, as in Ovid, and comparative contrast: the passive sufferer (who yet saved her father); the active and intelligent virago (who betrayed Aeetes). Both are connected by their actions to their kingly fathers and to their exiles from their father-lands as much as to Jason. Boccaccio's main source for Hypsipyle is Statius, for Medea, Ovid. But the events in Colchis are not what we expect. He refers to Medea sowing discord in the state (and similarly once she arrives in Thessaly), and to Aeetes' fall: 'What sensible man can imagine that the destruction of a wealthy king could occur in the twinkling of an eye?'[20] Yet Boccaccio knows Justin's story of her restoration of her father to his throne, and includes it, along with her reconciliation to Jason. He ends with some moral reflections on this history as an example of the lust of the eyes: had Medea not seen Jason, nothing would have followed. She would not have mis-used her power; here Boccaccio's word-play connects her to the power of the father: 'Certainly, if powerful Medea had closed her eyes or turned them elsewhere when she fixed them longingly on Jason, her father's power would have been preserved longer, as would her brother's life, and the honor of her virginity would have remained unblemished'.[21] Boccaccio's mini-sermon becomes one of the dangers of appearances, which lead us to value falsely those things which stain the soul. It is an odd disquisition, unless we see the connection between the woman's power and the threat to the father. This insistence upon the men in the story is important, also, in Boccaccio's other treatment of it in his collection of falls.

Boccaccio alone makes of Medea's father a potential tragic figure. To use the word 'tragedy' in the medieval context is to run a series of risks, since it is not clear that Boccaccio and his contemporaries meant by it

---

[19] Thus his omissions are also significant: the Ovidian list of dangerous women, including Ariadne and Ino, are significant by their absence, and Dido's story follows the version of the chaste widow, not the love-story familiar from Virgil.

[20] Guarino, p. 35. 'Quis hoc etiam sensatus arbitraretur homo quod ex uno oculorum intuitu opulentissimi regis exterminium sequeretur?' (pp. 84, 86).

[21] Guarino, p. 37. 'Eos quippe si potens clausisset Medea, aut aliorsum flexisset, dum erexit avida in Iasonem, stetisset diutius potentia patris, vita fratris et sue virginitatis decus infractum: que omnia horum impudicitia periere' (p. 88).

more than the story of a great man who moves from prosperity to misery because of the blows of Fortune.[22] In Boccaccio's collection of tragic falls, *Des Casibus Virorum*, among the princes he chose as *exempla* is Aeetes, an unusual way into the legends. Aeetes' appearance in Boccaccio's procession of fortune's victims is a brief emblem:

> There before the others stands King Aeëtes of Colchis. Because of his magnificent regalia and unprecedentedly splendid riches the barbarians thought him the son of the sun. He curses with a querulous voice that Jason of Thessaly should have come to Colchis, he by whose perfidy the Golden Fleece was stolen, Aegialeus his son mournfully cast down to die, Medea led into unclean desires and flight. And in his old age he has fallen down from the brightness he anticipated into an execrable darkness.[23]

Fortune's instrument as Aeëtes' enemy is Jason, and here Medea is referred to as one of among her father's losses. The attack is by one man upon another, including the ruin of his house and all its treasures. There is no sense of Aeetes having had a choice, or even of his responsibility for what happened to him. The sins of pride and ambition are displaced onto Medea, and the light imagery is an ironic evocation of other falls. This is an original reorientation of interest, due apparently to Boccaccio alone. These collections had immense circulation throughout Europe; they were popularized by a series of translators who expanded them (or who, like Christine, adapted them for her own purposes), and whose work will concern us below.

I have spoken of Boccaccio's fascination with Medea, and of his 'anti-Medea'. There is one further place in Boccaccio's work where the motifs of Medea's story reappear, although in a form so distant as to be almost invisible. If I am right that the character of Medea ramified into a variety of other women, who, because they were so many and so consistent,

---

[22] In his excellent study, Willard Farnham emphasizes the continuities in thought about tragedy from Boccaccio onwards, but it might be said that the continuities lie in the potential of the plots rather than in the commentary on them. See his *The Medieval Heritage of Elizabethan Tragedy* (Oxford, Blackwell, 1956), chapts. three to five. In stressing that there are patterns of retribution the medieval authors assume what tragedy often asks. See H. A. Kelly, *Ideas and Forms of Tragedy from Aristotle to the Middle Ages* (Cambridge, Cambridge University Press, 1993).

[23] Stabat enim ante alios aeta colchorum rex ob insignem magnificentiam/ & diuitiarum nondum visum splendorem/ a barbaris solis creditus filius: & querula voce execrabatur/ in colchos thessali Iasonis aduentum: eo quod eius perfidia aureum raptum sit vellus. aegialeus filius nece flebili oppressus: & in insanam libidinem adque fugam medea deducta: & suum senium ex fulgore praecipuo in detestabiles tenebras deuolutum. Quoted from the Appendix to Bergen's edition of Lydgate, IV, p. 146.

helped create a sense of women's capacities for destruction, a stereotype or *topos* of the dangerous and powerful woman, then the continued existence of that stereotype was as likely to inspire new compositions which explored or modified its main features, including reversing them. Boccaccio had returned so many times to Medea, and to 'Medean' women, in the course of his work, that there is no question that he had her firmly in mind. Perhaps we may see her story behind the last story of the last day of the *Decameron*, which is Boccaccio's own inspiration.[24] There is no question but that the story of Griselda is his story, his invention, nor that it combines – as 'new' stories usually do – recognizable aspects of traditional tales. It also invites complex ways of reading, for the literal tale invited, from the outset, allegorical interpretation. Griselda's fortitude can be a model of the soul's willing martyrdom, of that aspect of patience and *refusal* to respond with anger or revenge which is open to both women and men. Socially, of course, the refusal to act, housed in a female character, is socially persuasive: the audience do not expect action, as they might well expect action from a man. The gendering of patience, on this description, is contingent. We might contextualize Griselda's cheerful stoicism in classical terms (although they would then have to appear to be 'natural' in an untutored woman), or in the tradition of Christian fortitude, or as a response to those aspects of powerful woman to which Boccaccio created a riposte. We might then read his story as an anti-Medea.

We are used to the idea of reading twelfth-century rebuttals of the *Tristan* story, or responses to the moral questions to which Tristan and other love-stories give rise. The skeptical will immediately point out that most such anti-Tristans mention one or other of the characters in his tale, and that such mentions are distinctly lacking in Boccaccio's tale or its imitations and derivatives. That is quite right, but analogues are not sources, and I am not trying to say that Boccaccio thought out a rhetorical refutation point by point, only that the congeries of motifs is so striking as to be unlikely to be accidental. Later, in numerous Renaissance texts, certain female characters do indeed compare themselves to Medea, either in horror or in emulation. Griselda, however, cannot do that: she is not

---

24 *Decameron* quoted from the popular edition of V. Branca (Florence, Felice le Monnier, 1960), pp. 643–59. Although its sources have supposedly been traced to such folktale motifs as Cupid and Psyche, patient wives in the hands of Otherworldly magical husbands, and even the *Mahabharata*, the suggestions are, in fact, a tissue of unproven speculations which were part of the German fashion for comparative-philological source hunting at the end of the last century. See Severs, *Relationships of Chaucer's Clerkes Tale*, pp. 3–6.

educated.[25] Dioneo, however, who tells the tale, is, and has a special status among the narrators. It will be recalled that it is Dioneo who has permission to tell a tale each day outside the theme, Dioneo whose special status has made critics see him as a Boccaccio-like commentator upon the project of the story-collection as a whole.[26] That Griselda is the last word gives it, of course, the strongest position. But to what end?

Gualtieri is urged to marry by his people (the 'people' provide a chorus throughout the tale), but marries out of his rank (here, too, what we might call social mobility is gendered in obvious ways); he asks for the peasant woman's hand from her father and marries her publicly; he takes her naked ('la fece spogliare ignuda') and powerless to his kingdom; she transforms herself into an acceptable consort (her high worth had been hidden under her poor clothes – clothes are the crucial important image throughout); she is entirely without pride; two children appear to be murdered (the chorus of ladies are sympathetic to their mistress, but Griselda never complains; the male chorus call Gualtieri a barbarian); Gualtieri pretends to repudiate Griselda in order to marry better; Griselda is calm (against the nature of woman); she asks for a shift in return for her maidenhead and goes back to her father (who has kept her old clothes); Gualtieri sends for Griselda to prepare his wedding; Griselda greets the bride (her daughter), and her only reaction to Gualtieri is to ask him not to treat his new wife as harshly as he treated the old; Gualtieri, who has been much moved with sympathy for his obedient and loving wife, now reveals what he has done, and they are reconciled to each other, and rejoice in their children. Griselda is taken by the court ladies and reclothed in her own magnificent gown ('nobile robe').

The removal is class rather than country; the infanticide apparent rather than real, the husband's test rather than the wife's revenge; the important garment already her own and not magical; and the second marriage a sham. Griselda is the Christian redemption of themes adumbrated in the pagan story. One can see so many of the motifs repeated that it is not impossible to speculate that their association in Boccaccio's mind may have come from other than folklore sources. I have already referred to Petrarch's reaction to this story, and it is well-known that it was also translated into French more than once, by Philippe de Mézières and by an

[25] See, among other examples, the discussion of Thomas Achelley in Götz Schmitz, *The Fall of Woman in Early English Narrative Verse* (Cambridge, Cambridge University Press, 1990), pp. 205ff.

[26] See A. Duranti, 'Le novelle di Dioneo', which argues for this final tale as a resolution to Dioneo's apparent reservations as he reacted each day to the theme, in *Studi di filologia e critica offerti dagli allievi a Lanfranco Caretti*, I (Rome, Salerno Editrice, 1985), pp. 1–38.

anonymous translator, through whom it came to Chaucer.[27] Laurent de Premierfait must be recalled in evidence as well, since he translated the *Decameron*, where readers might have found the tale in its original context.

Critics, especially Chaucerians, have emphasized the centrality of patience in the tale, and, indeed 'patient Grisel' became a byeword.[28] That afterlife of interpretation does not restore an obvious centrality to Boccaccio's conception; it is right, for Christian patience and fortitude in the face of injustice is undeniably a virtue, but it is also a *lectio facilior*. Whatever Gualtieri praised Griselda for, other literary reminiscences are at work. We emphasize patience at our peril, as Boccaccio warns us early in the tale, when Dioneo criticizes Gualtieri's foolishness. Perhaps Boccaccio ended the *Decameron* with a tale in which readers would find reconciled some of the most profound questions about the conflict between male and female power. Griselda always has the word at her command. She never uses it. In transcending revenge, the tale redeems love. In refusing tragedy, although Dioneo warns us that Gualtieri's behaviour was worse than foolish, Boccaccio reminds us of that other option, in which, with great good fortune, fortitude saves us all.

Mirrors before Magistrates

Boccaccio's exemplary collections were multiplied both through copying and through translation. He does not seem to have meant them as focussed particularly on rulers, but that was how they came to be presented; political example was a useful legitimation. As speaking pictures of fatality, they prepare the ground for ideas of tragedy, but they were always textual, in the sense of readerly historical lives. In France, in the translations of Laurent de Premierfait, Boccaccio's Latin works became widely known, as luxurious French manuscripts attest. Laurent's collection, *Des Cas des Nobles Hommes et Femmes*, amplified the individual entries, and added new examples, including a selection of women. He inserted

---

[27] See E. Golenistcheff-Koutouzoff, *L'Histoire de Griseldis en France du XIVe au XVe siècle* (Paris, 1933; repr. Geneva, Droz, 1975) and Mario Roques, *L'Estoire de Griseldis* (Geneva, Droz, 1957). *Letteratura italiana: Le Opere*, I. *Dalle Origini al Cinquecento*, ed. A. Rosa (Turin, Einaudi, 1992), pp. 473–592. A. Morabito, 'La Diffusione della storia di Griselda dal XIV al XX secolo', *Studi sul Boccaccio* 17 (1988), pp. 237–85.

[28] Not only in English. Anna Baldwin, 'From the *Clerk's Tale* to *The Winter's Tale*', in *Chaucer Traditions*, ed. Ruth Morse and Barry Windeatt (Cambridge, Cambridge University Press, 1990), pp. 199–212, which supplies an overview of recent scholarship.

descriptions of the murders of Aegialius and Creusa, of Medea's marriage to Aegeus, her reconciliation to Jason, and of Jason's final restoration of Aeetes to his throne. Laurent first translates Boccaccio and then adds his own expansions, almost as if they were lemmata in a commentary.[29] And they continued to be adapted, and printed, e.g. by Colard Mansion, Caxton's collaborator.[30]

Like Boccaccio's other collection of famous historical characters, this gathering of unfortunates was translated and expanded, first by Laurent de Premierfait, and then by John Lydgate, in his *The Fall of Princes*.[31] For English readers, Boccaccio *was* John Lydgate, whose amplified translations were read by generations, and who is so careful to authorize his own work through Boccaccio's. The story of their interpretations is a fascinating one, but here we shall be concerned only with Jason and Aeetes, Medea and Hypsipyle. Neither Laurent nor Lydgate seems to have assumed that his readers would understand all of Boccaccio's allusions. Or, perhaps, and as so often, Boccaccio's verbal illustration invited amplification for vernacular audiences.[32] Boccaccio's original disappears under the weight of their learning, and this is a cue to the uses to which his books, as sources, were put. But there are innovations: above all, Lydgate's view of Fortune is that men contribute to her power by their own choices and decisions; men are responsible for what they do, and God recognizes this in punishment and reward. Lydgate has the not-uncommon anxiety about ordinary people, whom he often sees as a threat, because the rise of a churl encourages him

---

29 For an extended discussion of the influence of these books in the Renaissance, see Pamela Benson, *The Invention of the Renaissance Woman* (University Park, Pennsylvania, Pennsylvania State University Press, 1993).

30 See, for example, D. Laing, *Facsimiles of Designs from Engraved Copperplates Illustrating Le Liure de la Ruyne des Nobles Hommes et Femmes par Jehan Bocace de Certald: Imprimé à Bruges par Colard Mansion, Annon M.cccc.lxxvi* (Edinburgh, 1878).

31 *Lydgate's Fall of Princes*, ed. Henry Bergen, EETS e.s. 121–4 (London, 1924–7). *Des Cas des Nobles Hommes et Femmes*, ed. P. M. Gathercole, Studies in Romance Language and Literature, 74 (Chapel Hill, University of North Carolina Press, 1968). See also her 'The Manuscripts of Laurent de Premierfait's Works', *Modern Language Quarterly* 20 (1958), pp. 262–70 and 'Lydgate's "Fall of Princes" and the French Version of Boccaccio's "De Casibus" ', in *Miscellanea di Studi e ricerche sul quattrocento francese*, ed. Franco Simone (Turin, Giappichelli Editore, 1966), pp. 167–78; Ricarde Müller, *Ein Frauenbuch des frühen Humanismus* (Stuttgart, Steiner, 1992). There is a further transcript of the Latin which accompanies an edition of an anonymous translation of the *De Mulieribus Claris*, *Die Mittelenglische Umdichtung von Boccaccios De Claris Mulieribus nebst der lateinischen Vorlage zum ersten Male vollständig herausgegeben*, ed. Gustav Schleich (Leipzig, Mayer und Muller, 1924), Palaestra, 144. This text does not seem to have circulated; it is a compressed translation into rhyme royal stanzas which moves the women about.

32 H. G. Wright thought the translations of the Latin texts likely to be aimed at women; see *Boccaccio in England from Chaucer to Tennyson* (London, Athlone Press, 1957), chapt. one.

to act out his viciouness.[33] This double fatality was rehearsed by earlier authors, including his master, Chaucer, whose comedies and tragedies he mentions in a context in which he also lists other writers' dual creations (and which is well-known because it contains the titles of many of Chaucer's works).[34]

Lydgate's message is a public one which defends poetry as exemplary and beneficial to society *because* it tells both kinds of tale (and Lydgate's list here is important, because he assimilates himself and Chaucer to classical authors such as Ovid and Seneca), and, at the same time, assimilates his own readers to a proud tradition of study amongst classical rulers, including Caesar.[35]

> Bi smale whelpis, as summe clerkis write,
> Chastised is the myhti fers leoun,
> And whan the suerd off vengaunce eek doth bite
> Vpon pryncis for ther transgressioun,
> The comon peeple in ther opynyoun,
> For verray dreede tremble don & quake,
> And bi such mene ther vices thei forsake.
>
> And such also as ha be defoulid
> In ther vicis bi long contynuaunce,
> Or in ther synnys rustid and Imowlid,
> Bi good example may come to repentaunce:
> Who hym repentith, the Lord will hym auaunce,
> And hym accepte, in hih and louh estat, –
> The meek preserue, punyshe the obstynat.
>
> (Prologue, lines 211–24)

If Lydgate continues to amplify what he found in Laurent, he expands in ways familiar from his other works. Lydgate's ambition to instruct is

---

[33] Lois A. Ebin argues for this aristocratic point of view in her excellent short study, *John Lydgate* (Boston, Twayne, 1985), connecting Lydgate's views to his underlying opinion in the longer historical poems.

[34] A. C. Spearing suggests that Lydgate is 'completing' Chaucer, in his *Medieval to Renaissance in English Poetry* (Cambridge, Cambridge University Press, 1985), 66–88. Like Larry Scanlon, whose stimulating identification of the exemplary tradition in medieval literature opens new ways of thinking about medieval genres, I find Lydgate's apparent deference more aggressive than self-effacing. See his *Narrative, Authority, and Power: the medieval exemplum and the Chaucerian Tradition* (Cambridge, Cambridge University Pres, 1994), chapt. 9.

[35] That this invitation, or instruction, to secular men to read, was part of a familar defence is one of the points of Helen Cooper's essay, 'Romance After 1400', in *The Cambridge History of Medieval Literature*, ed. David Wallace (Cambridge, Cambridge University Press, 1996).

embedded in a world of books, classical, continental, and English. The place – or space – Lydgate created for himself appeared for many years to be a ham-fisted imitation of literary Chaucer. But Lydgate, too, is capable of putting his predecessor to use, to recruiting Chaucer to his own purposive rereading of vernacular poetry. Larry Scanlon's identification of the *exemplum*-tradition in late-medieval writing helps us to see the ways that writers like Lydgate interpreted the past as a sequence of moments for moral interpretation:

> In canonizing Chaucer, Lydgate also helps institutionalize the peculiarly appropriative form of textual authority Chaucer embodies: vernacular, lay, yet claiming a spiritual prestige and ideological efficacy analogous to the Latin traditions of the Church. This quasi-sacral secular authority belongs to precisely that set of textual traditions modernity will come to call literary. (322)

The literal episode is not an *allegorical* lesson so much as a historical illustration, conveyed for reinterpretation in the style established by his masters (who include more authors than Chaucer alone). We may not wish to read Chaucer Lydgate's way, but we can understand Lydgate's rewriting. His Aeëtes is thirty-four stanzas long, and no longer Aeetes, but the history of Jason and Medea, including her flight to Athens, reconciliation to Jason, and restoration of her father to his throne. His political question asks how a woman could betray her father for a stranger, and then kill her brother; his religious question asks how she and Jason could eventually be reconciled.

> She took hir brothir & slouh hym cruely,
> And hym dismembrid, as bookis make mynde,
> And pecemeel in a feeld behynde
>
> She gan hym caste, al bespreynt with blood,
> Wheroff his fader, whan he hadde a siht,
> Ful pale off cheer, stille in the feeld he stood
> Whil she and Iason took hem onto fliht.
> I trowe that tyme the moste woful wiht
> That was a-lyue, whan he dede knowe
> His child dismembrid and abrood Isowe
>
> Which cause was, allas and wellaway,
> That he so stynte, as man disconsolat
> Whil that Iason fro Colchos went a-way,
> And Medea, most infortunat,
> Was ground and roote off this mortal debat.

> For who sauh euer or radde off such a-nothir,
> To saue a straunger list to slen hir brothir?
>
> Forsook hir fader, hir contre & kynreede,
> The lond enporished thoruh hir robberie.
> Off hir worshep she took noon othir heed:
> Loue had hir brouht in such a fantasie.
> (2117–2237, my punctuation)

Then he gives Ovid's metamorphoses of Aeson and the murder of Pelias, which he attributes to 'envie and venymous hatreede'. Lydgate's essentialism, here, is to praise women, for Medea offends against their nature:

> For she it wrouhte onli off vengaunce,
> As roote & ground off this cruel deede,
> A-geyn the nature off al womanheede,
>
> Supposyng in hir opynyoun,
> How that the deth gretli sholde plese
> Off Pelleus onto hir lord Iasoun,
> Thoruh gret encres sette his herte at ese –
> But it rebounded into his disese,
> That fynali Iason hir forsook
> For hir offence.... (lines 2308–2317)

Medea's malice, envy, and desire for vengeance lead her to kill Creusa, and her murder of her children is also 'withoute routhe or womanli pite' and 'a-geyn nature' (lines 2346, 2349). Lydgate recasts Boccaccio's (and Laurent's) whole passage, and amalgates sources which he claims to have used, for a character who is consistent in her evil intent.

> Hir herte off malis, cruel & horrible,
> As she that was with tresoun euer allied,
> Whan that she sauh hir purpos most odible
> Be kyng Egeus fulli was espied,
> She hath hir herte & wittis newe applied,
> As in ther bookis poetis han compiled,
> A-geyn to Iason to be reconsiled.
>
> She fledde away for dreed of Theseus,
> List he hadde doon on hir vengaunce,
> And fynali, as writ Ouidius,
> And moral Senec concludith in substaunce,
> In his tragedies makyng remembraunce,
> How Medea, lik as poetis seyn,
> Onto Iason restored was a-geyn.

> Touchyng the eende off ther furious discord,
> Poetis make theroff no mencioun
> Nor telle no mene how thei fill at accord,
> But yiff it were bi incantacioun,
> Which so weel koude turne up-so-doun
> Sundry thyngis off loue & off hatreede.
> And in Bochas off hir no mor I reede,
>
> Sauff whan she hadde fulfillid hir purpos,
> Myn auctor tellith, that Iason and Mede
> Resorted han a-geyn onto Colchos
> Hir fadir Oetes, & from his pouerte
> Brouht hym a-geyn into his roial see,
> And to his crowne bi force thei hym restore:
> Touchyng his eende, off hym I find no more.
>
> (I.2374–2400)

If he gives a relatively complete narrative, his references to his source poets are *more* than complete – as must be clear to readers of this book – since they do not supply what he tells. Perhaps his insistence upon a chorus of classical writers as authorities for the reconciliation of Jason and Medea and their restoration of Aeetes reinforces that part of the tale (against what his master, Chaucer, told), that final, if obscure, rescue of Aeetes from his own Fall. The reversal of love or hatred which is the result of 'incantacioun' may appear a rather desperate expedient, yet it is consistent with other interpretations.

The conclusion draws on the variableness of Fortune:

> Thus his fortune hath turnyd to and fro,
> First like a kyng hauyng ful gret richesse,
> Afftir lyuyng in pouert and in wo,
> Sithen restorid to his worthynesse:
> Thus ay is sorwe medlid with gladnesse   (I.2404–6)

The echoes of Chaucer's Knight and Monk are apparent, and it is clear that Lydgate sees his relation to Chaucer as in some sense parallel with Boccaccio's to Petrarch. For all his protestations of modesty, as Larry Scanlon has also argued, Lydgate has his own views about his *exempla*. Not only does he supplement his sources with his own researches, he has his own theories of what contributes to a fall.[36] One of the effects of the Boccaccian

---

36 In the older view, even Lydgate's best defenders are not always his best friends: as Derek Pearsall put it, 'The trouble with Lydgate is his incredible facility; he never struggles', *John Lydgate* (London, Routledge and Kegan Paul, 1970), p. 133. Alain Renoir searches for signs of the renaissance to come in his *The Poetry of John Lydgate* (London,

tradition of 'falls' was to bring history back towards tragedy. Boccaccio's own combination was one which emphasized the danger of women who were powerful because of their exceptional intelligence, as well as drawing pictures of women whose energy included sexual energy, and a willing ability to get what they wanted from and through men.

To translate and amplify Boccaccio was one kind of interpretation. But not all those who imitated his compendia were straightforward admirers. His views could also be contested. Christine de Pizan, who opposed the misogyny of Jean de Meun in reopening the Quarrel of the Rose, also took issue with Boccaccio's views of the place of women in history. Here I am concerned with her mythographic-historical allegory, the *Epistre d'Othea*, a text of about 1400 which, although apparently designed to be used as a primer for a child reader to teach morality, is a thinly-disguised Mirror for Princes.[37] In it 'Othea', an otherwise unknown Greek goddess, narrates and interprets one hundred brief classical tales, most frequently from the story of Troy. The little verses which appear under each picture allude to larger sequences, since they are too short to tell the whole tale. There is a degree of narrative dismemberment which we have seen from time to time in the telling of such tales, from the verses of Pindar, which not only helps to control the ways the episodes will be read, but which has implications for the *Epistre* as a whole. Contingently, while attending to the interpretative act which teaches what is to be emulated or avoided, Othea inscribes the importance of the secular history which supports the fables: making them safe for interpretation is a way of making them important, and assuming knowledge of the history of Troy makes it a story 'known to all'. As she did throughout her career, Christine also enlarged the usual scope of such interpretations by including an unusual number of women in the course of them. She habitually reoriented the traditional view of history as a masculine narrative by making women present and positive.

Let us first consider the episodes which deal directly with the legendary material of Jason and Medea. For Christine, like Gower (and, it might be said, like Seneca), it is envy and ingratitude which are the subjects. These failings, like so many of the private vices, could be removed from their

---

Routledge and Kegan Paul, 1967), which discusses Jason and Medea as a relatively faithful translation of Laurent, pp. 64–6.

[37] See the excellent discussion of Christine's political intentions, analyzed through both text and illustrations (she supervised the production of several manuscripts, each of which shows her thinking of the particular requirements of the recipient), *Christine de Pizan's 'Epistre Othéa': Painting and Politics at the Court of Charles VI* (Toronto, Pontifical Institute of Mediaeval Studies, 1986).

particular context and treated as universal human problems, but in the work as a whole, they become motifs of the major errors made by rulers.

LIV Texte

Ne ressembles mie Jason
Qui par Medee la toyson
D'or conquist, dont puis lui rendy
Tres mauvais guerredon & rendy

Glose: Jason fu un chevalier de Grece, qui ala en estrange contree, c'est a savoir, en l'isle de Colcos, par l'enditement Peleus, son oncle, qui par envie sa mort desiroit. La avoit un mouton qui la toison avoit doree et par enchantement estoit gardé, mais comme si fort en fust la conqueste que nul n'y venist qui la vie n'y perdit. Medee, qui fille fu au roy de celle contree, tant prist grand amour en Jason que par les enchantemens que elle savoit, dont souveraine maistresse estoit, donna charmes et apprist enchantemens a Jason, par quoy il conquist la toison d'or; dont il ot honneur sur tous chevaliers vivans, et fu restoré de mort par Medee, a qui il ot promis a tous jours estre loyaulx amis. Mais apres foy lui menty, et autre ama, et du tout la laissa et relenqui, non obstant fust elle de souveraine beaute. Pour ce dit au bon chevalier que Jason ne doit ressembler, qui trop descongnoissant et desloyaulx a celle qui trop lui ot fait. Comme ce soit villaine chose et a tout noble de estre ingrat et maucongnoissant d'aucun bien, s'il l'a receu soit de dame, damoiselle ou autre personne; ains a tous jours lui en doit souvenir et le guerredonner a son povoir. A ce propos dit Hermes: "Ne vueilles point attendre a remunerer a cellui qui t'a bien fait, car souvenir t'en doit a tous jours.

Allegorie: Jason, qui fu ingrat, ne doit le bon esperit ressembler, qui des benefices receus de son createur ne doit estre ingrat. Et dit saint Bernard sur Chantiques que ingratitude est ennemie de l'ame, amenrissement de vertus, dispercion de merites, perdicion de benefices. Ingratitude est aussie comme un vent sec, qui seche la fontaine de pitie, la rosee de grace et le ruissel de misericorde. A ce propos dit le sage: 'Ingrati enim estis spes tanquam hibernalis glacies tabescet, et dispariet tanquam aqua supervacua.' Sapience .xvj.+ capitulo.[38]

---

[38] Quoted from the edition contained in H. D. Loukopoulos, *Classical Mythology in the Works of Christine de Pisan, with an Edition of* L'Espistre d'Othea *from the Manuscript Harley 4431* (Microfilm copy of her unpubl. Ph.D., Wayne State University, 1977), pp. 227–28. I have compared her readings to a photographic reproduction of *Les Cent Histoires de Troye* (Paris, Philippe Pigouchet, 1490) in the Warburg Library (which reads rendist/tendist for the two rhymes here given as 'rendy') and to the text in British Library Royal 17.E.iv. The 'translation' is by Stephen Scrope, *The Epistle of Othea: translated from the French Text of Christine de Pisan*, ed. C. F. Buhler, EETS o.s. 264 (London, 1970).

LIV Texte

Resemble nat Jason, that man
The which thorugh Meede þe flees wan
Of goolde, for þe which soone aftirward
He yaf hir right yvil guerdon & harde.

Glose: Jason was a knyght of Grece, the which went in-to straunge
contreis, þat is to seie, in-to þe ile of Colcos, be þe enorting [urging] of
his vncle Pelleus, þe which of envie desired his deth. There was a scheep
þat hadde a flees of goold and it was kepte be enchauntement, but the
conquest was soo stronge þat [noon] com þider but that loste þe lijf.
Meede, the which was þe kingis doughtir of þat contre, took so greete
loue to Jason that be þe enchauntementis þat sche couthe, of þe which
she was a souereyne maistres, made charmes & lerned Jason to en-
chaunte, be þe which he wanne the flees of goold; wherbi he had worschip aboue alle knyghtis lyuynge, and be Meede was reserued from
deth, to whom he had promissed euer to be trewe frende. But aftir he
fayled of his feiþ [& loued anothir], and left hir hooly & forsooke hir,
nat-wiþstandinge sche was [of] souereyne beaute. Therfore it is seide to
þe good knyght that he schold nat be like to Jason, þe which was to
vnknowing and to vntrewe to that the which had schewid [him] myche
goodnes. Wherfore it is to vileynose a thing for a knyghte or any noble
persoone to be rekeles or yvilknowing of goodnessis, if any he haue
receyved, be it of lady, of gentilwomman or of any othir persoone; for he
scholde evir þinke þeron and guerdon it to his powere. To this purpos
Hermes seiþ: Be not slowe ne delaiynge to remembre of him that hath
doon the good for þou scholdist euere þinke þeruppon.

Allegorie: The good spirit scholde nat be like to Jason, the which was
rekeles, þat is to seie, he schold nat be rekeles ne vnknowing of the
beneficis receyved of his maker. And Seint Bernarde seith vppon the
Canticles that vnknowing is enemye to þe soule and leser of vertuis, a
dispreising of meritis and a lesing of beneficis, and also ingratitude
farith as nought, þe which drieth þe welle of pite, þe dewe of grace and
þe ryuer of merci. And to this purpos þe wise man seith: Ingrati enim
spes tanquam [ibernalis] glacies tabescet, & disperiet tanquam aqua
supervacua. Sapientie xvjmo capitulo.

Christine often works by indirection and by the use of negatives: here, by
emphasizing a model of behaviour-to-be-avoided, she concentrates on an
episode in which the male character is at fault. Unlike the more expanded
historical treatments of the stories (including her own), this partial account focusses attention on its moral, more than allowing the reader to
consider the literal narrative for himself. Medea has become the object of

Jason's failure to honour his promise. Christine's suppressions here are a way of making a character an icon of a vice; there is no argument about the rights (or wrongs) of the case. The particular kind of ingratitude stressed here is to the powerless. Arguments might be extended to tease out the implications (since women are so often precisely without power), but all Othea says is that ingratitude is vicious.

Christine's method throughout is to place the classical reference in an acceptably Christian frame. Here she follows her frame and cites one pagan and one Biblical moralist, as well as a famous exegete on Song of Songs.

LVIII Texte

Ne laisses ton sens avorter
A fol delit, ne emporter
Ta chevance, se demandee
T'est, et te mires en Medee

Glose: Medee fu une des plus savans femmes de sors qui oncques fust et qui plus ot de science selon que dient les histoires. Et non obstant ce elle laissa son sens avorter a sa propre voulente pour son delit accomplir, quant a fole amour se laissa maistriser, si que en Jason mist son cuer et lui donna honneur, corps et chevance; dont puis lui rendi mauvais guerredon. Pour ce dit que le bon chevalier ne doit en soy laissier vaincre raison a fol delit en quelconques cas, se il veult user de la vertue de force. Et dit Platon: 'Un homme de leger courage s'enuie tost de ce qu'il ayme.'

Allegorie: Que son sens ne laisse avorter a fol delit peut estre entendu que le bon esperit ne doit laissier seignourir sa propre voulente; car se la seignourie de propre voulente ne cessoit, il ne seroit point d'enfer, ne le feu d'enfer n'aroit point de seignourie mais que sus la personne qui laisse seignourir sa propre voulente, car propre voulente se combat contre Dieu et s'orgueillest; c'est ce qui despoulle paradis et revest enfer et vuide la value du sanc de Jhesucrist et soubzmet le monde a la servitude de l'ennemi. A ce propos dit le sage: 'Virga atque correccio tribuent sapienciam; puer autme qui dimitum [Vulgate: dimittitur] proprie voluntati confundet matrem suam.' Proverbiorum .xxix.+ capitulo.[39]

LVIII Texte

Thi witte to be enortid suffre noughte
To foli delites, ne ther-to broughte
Thi worschip; if it the askid be,
Anoon beholde þe wele in Mede.

[39] *Epistre*, pp. 233–4.

Glose: Mede was oon of þe connyngist wommen of sorcerye þat euere was and had moost connynge as that stories seiþ. Not-withstanding sche suffrid hir witte to be enortid atte þe owne wille for to fulfille hir delite, as in lewde loue sche suffrid hir to be maistried, so þat sche sette hir herte uppon Jason and yaf him worschip, bodi and goodes; for þe which aftirward he yaf hir a ful yvil reward. Wherfore Othea seiþ þat þe good kny3te scholde not suffre reson to be ouercomen with lewde delite in no maner caas, if he wil vse of þe vertu of strengthe. And Platon seiþ þat a man of li3t corage is soon meved wiþ þat þe which he loueth.

Allegorie: That a man schulde not suffre his witte to be enortid to lewde delite may be vnderstanden that þe good spirit schulde not suffre his propir wille to haue dominacion; for, if dominacion of propre wille ceced not, þer schold be noon helle ne þe fire of helle schulde haue no dominacion but uppon þe personne þat suffriþ his propre wille to be lord of him, for propre wil feightith ayens God and emprideth þe silf; that is þe which despisith paradijs and clotheth helle and voidith þe valew of þe blood of Crist Jhesu and submittith þe worlde to þe þraldom of þe fende. [To this purpos the wise man seyeth]: Virga atque correccio tribuent sapientiam; puer autem qui dimittitur proprie voluntati confundet matrem suam. Prouerbiorum xxixe capitulo.

Once again Christine emphasizes the negative (Do not succumb to temptation), and makes the vice gender-neutral. She has in effected elevated the female *exemplum* to the high status of a Fall due to a sin which could be exhibited by either gender. The castigation of loss of self-control which stems from Medea's foolish desire for Jason, who deceived her, becomes a castigation of anyone who allows his reason to be overcome by desire, not simply because the desire itself is wrong, but because desire leads to misjudgements in which one can be betrayed. If one subtext in these two extracts is the way Medea opened herself to deception by Jason (by assuming he would keep his word out of princely gratitude), another is the history of Troy, a larger historical lesson for princes who might be aware of the cycles of the past. So the reader can construct interpretations which have to do with abstract vices and virtues illustrated by ancient history if he re-members the whole.

If one steps back from the individual lessons and looks at the structure of the whole, the repetition of certain vices, and the use of characters of both genders, further emphasizes the way the literal stories illustrate the allegorical morals. For example, the first destruction of Troy, part of the Argonautic prelude to the main history, which results from the negative behaviour of Laomedon (e.g. section XXXIII), is repeated at the end of the sequence in Circe's rather different of Ulysses' sailors after the city has fallen, as it were beyond the finish of the central history (Section XCVIII). Only if one puts the whole history together again in chronological order does this become clear, only then does one see that the thirty-third section is balanced by the ninety-ninth. Unsurprisingly, Section LXVI also concerns the Destruction of Troy, Laomedon, and Hercules. The reference frame, which is consistent throughout the text, continually shifts attention away from her own contribution (or, more precisely, Othea's). That chronological history exists as a dismembered subtext for anyone who knows the whole history, and helps to explain the curious way that the *Epistre* ends. In a way similar to the two extracts I have considered, Christine also exploits the story of Ino (XVII, XCIX). Its first appearance is unusual, because Christine attributes both the mad fury and the murder of the children to Athamas, not to Ino. But the second, which appears in the strong position of the last allegory, recounts the opening of the history of Troy from the morphological unit I described at the outset of this book as *before* the legends of Jason and Medea: Christine ends with the beginning, the story of Phrixus, Helle, and the Golden Fleece.

Ovidian Heroinism

In Chapter One I showed how depictions of Medea came to be used as models for other female characters, and in Chapter Three I discussed the Ovidian associations of this group of vengeance-hungry mothers. Among the many striking differences between Ovid's letter-collection, with its vibrant moments, and the frame-tale narratives which used them, is precisely the addition of the frame. The voice or voices which tell or comment upon the tales, the development of cross-reference and parallelism, and the sense of interpretable structure, all create models of reading. Boccaccio's insistence upon daily themes in his *Decameron* is an invitation to more apparently literary reading, as it were, ringing changes on structure and point of view which include the idea that the themes can be secular, about plotting, and comment upon velleities hitherto restricted to *fabliaux*. The *Decameron* contrasts both with his own Latin collections and with the morally exemplary compendia of Gower and Lydgate. It insists upon the equality of women's points of view. But Chaucer's interpretation of the use of frames suggests a more profound and more radical instability.

Where the *Heroïdes* is used as one source among many, the women who write its letters may find themselves re-associated with other characters from Latin poetry and mythology. They may equally well be selected or redistributed according to the needs and inclinations of the classicizing writer. Nor need the Ovidian list come from Ovid: it might come indirectly through a similar list with or without explicit recognition of the women's similarities. The place of a poem such as *Le Livre de Leesce* of Jean Le Fèvre de Ressons suggests a fourteenth-century example of a classicizing reaction to earlier texts. Le Fèvre is best known as the translator of the *Lamentations* of Matheolus, a Latin misogynistic tract which it, to all intents and purposes, superseded.[40] On the Woman Question Le Fèvre was equally influenced by Jean de Meun, although his own poetic gifts were more humdrum. Nevertheless, in his own original poem, which affects to be a defence of women, he cites Medea twice, both as learned (lines 3636–39 on her great 'science', but not the uses to which it was put) and as betrayed. This defence comes in the course of a castigation of men, whom he blames as the root of women's going astray, either because they have failed to protect or control the weaker sex, or because they have offended them (lines 2370–2412, pp. 74–6). That such explanations were available, and might arise at any time, even in the hands of someone like Le Fèvre de Ressons, is an important reminder of the breadth of reading and interpretation which complicate the story I have been telling.

These women make their appearance at length in Gower's well-known story-collection of the late fourteenth century, *Confessio Amantis*, which updates and rewrites its more famous French predecessor, *Le Roman de la Rose*.[41] The large-scale moral education which is the thrust of the frame places the tales by rereading them in unfamiliar interpretative contexts. Gower invites his alert audience to rethink the virtues and vices illustrated in the tales. Ovid's correspondents are material to be redistributed: Thisbe appears in Book III; in the course of Book IV, Dido and Penelope reproach their loves with sloth, and beg them to return, while Phyllis refines her accusation with further charges of forgetfulness. The idea of desire as a function of Sloth is an original one; lying is much more energetic.

Book V moves through more serious mortal sins, from Avarice to False Witness and Perjury, from Ingratitude and Ravine to Sacrilege. As things

---

[40] Jean Le Fèvre de Ressons, *Les Lamentations de Matheolus et le Livre de Leesce (poèmes français du XIVe siècle)*, ed. A. G. Van Hamel (Paris, Bibliothèque de l'Ec, 1905). I owe this reference to Ms Helen Phillips.

[41] *Confessio Amantis*, ed. G. C. Macaulay, EETS e.s. 81, 82 (London, 1900–1). Recent defences of Gower include R. F. Yeager, *John Gower's Poetic: the search for a new Arion* (Cambridge, D. S. Brewer, 1990). There is always a problem in writing about Gower that one is irresistibly drawn to writing about Chaucer's treatments of the same stories. So Jason-the-betrayer is attracted to the Falcon of *The Squire's Tale*, who complains of the Tercelet's betrayal (*ST* 538–57). Jean de Meun makes a similar allusion in the *Roman de la Rose* at 13,199ff, 232.

get worse we find the women central to the dangerous nexus: Jason and
Medea, Ino (the editor calls the tale 'Phrixus and Helle', but the important
figure is the step-mother), Ariadne and Theseus, the terrors of Procne and
her sister, and finally Paris's kidnapping of Helen from the Temple.
Throughout this section the Latin marginal commentary connects the
avarice, false witness or perjury of lovers to the political world in which
servants fail their lords, and section four is headed with Latin verses which
preach against this most frightening of medieval betrayals: breaking one's
word. Confessor preaches against the decadence of the Age: False Witness
and Perjury are now common sins. Gower has used structures of variations on his themes to bind the stories together and to ask us to think
about their permutations and combinations. It is not only Chaucer whose
structures reveal his ideas.

As so often with Gower, the full meaning of the tales only becomes clear
when one looks not only at the tale, but its place in the sequence, and its
associations. Here, of course, Troy is not far to seek. If, in the local context
of the story of Jason's betrayal, Genius's moral is:

> Thus miht thou se what sorwe it doth
> To swere on oth which is noght soth,
> In loves cause namely.
> Mi Sone, be wel war forthi,
> And kep that thou be noght forswore:
> For this, which I have told tofore,
> Ovide telleth everydel   (V. 4223–9)

one might, nevertheless, argue that the thrust of the example is not 'love's
cause', but male adventure, and, behind the narrative actually being told, a
political, public concern with the causes of war. In addition, this intertextual recuperation insists upon Gower as a reader of Ovid. 'For this' appears
to refer to the story just told, yet it encompasses the story *and* its moral.
Gower solves the problem of contradictions inherent in a totalizing narrative by careful selection: refusing to allow them to arise. By contextualizing
this narrative within the heading 'avarice' (subheading, 'perjury'), Gower
concentrates our expectations upon loyalty and betrayal rather than a
more general political analysis, and leaves the reader to apply the Mirror
for Princes implications of private morality.[42]

The Jason and Medea story is one of the longest in the *Confessio*

---

[42] But see A. J. Minnis, 'John Gower *Sapiens* in Ethics and Politics', in *John Gower's Confessio Amantis: a critical anthology*, ed. Peter Nicholson (Cambridge, D. S. Brewer, 1991), pp. 158–80.

Amantis. If we then add the tale of Phrixus and Helle which follows, and which grounds the story of Jason and Medea by giving its prelude, and then further realize that slightly later in the same book we have another part of the longer sequence, Paris's 'rape' of Helen, we can see Gower circling around a history of Troy which he does not tell. That is, he has dismembered the larger history for the sake of the sins, but the sins exist in the context of another tale which can be reassembled by the learned – or by a reader who takes the stories in a slightly different order. The connection through the women introduces a slippery accusation: the betrayals come from men, but it is the temptation posed by the women, as well as their revenges (and not male refusal to resist temptation), which ultimately injures the state.

Because of the Chaucerian and 'Romance' associations of the *Confessio Amantis*, scholars have often concentrated on 'courtly' aspects of the narrative. This is certainly a possible way to read the text, but the style sends a mixed message. One might argue that Gower recounts his courtly tale largely from Medea's point of view, with neither any particular emphasis on the character of the hero, nor authorial interpretative directions in the course of the narrative of the kind which both Benoît and Guido have made familiar. But Gower is not impervious to the temptations to ramify, and he expects us to think about his juxtapositions. Ino's destructive behaviour invites the recognition of families as states in little. Gower's celebrated interest in incest also comes into play here, because one association lies in kinship patterns and the destruction of siblings. Betrayal within the family is treason to the state.

If Gower's focus is upon private morality, it is in the extended sense just described. Anything which ties the characters to public roles, any discussion of kingship, is eloquent by its inexplicitness. To those familiar with possible versions of the legends, Gower's omissions point his moral. The air of gentle romance prepares the startling climax.[43] During the early part of the narrative, he leaves Jason much as he found him in Benoît.[44] There is no aged Aeson abdicating to his treacherous brother. It is Jason himself who aspires to adventure, as part of his constant desire for glory, although Gower warns us that Jason's quest was 'ful dere . . . boghte'. This shift towards Medea has several consequences. In the historical versions Jason's quest was tied to Troy because it was the first cause of the Trojan War.

---

[43] In this context it is relevant to note that the edition in J. A. W. Bennett's *Selections from John Gower* (Oxford, 1960) suppresses the ending without acknowledgement.

[44] Derek Pearsall argues for 'warm, imaginative sympathy' (p. 77) with Medea and Jason, in 'Gower's Narrative Art', in Nicholson, pp. 62–80.

Here, although Hercules is Jason's companion, and important as a confidant, neither Lemnos nor Troy figures in their adventures, except as that kind of *occupatio* which adds depth to this tale by suggesting the shadowy companion-narrative to which Gower can refer.

> ... bot on the weie
> What hem befell is long to seie;
> Hou Lamedon the king of Troie,
> Which oghte wel have mad hem joie,
> Whan thei to reste a while him preide
> Out of his lond he hem congeide;
> And so fell the dissencion,
> Which after was destruccion
> Of that Cite, as men mai hiere:
> Bot that is noght to mi matere. (V.3301–3310)

Gower's lovers pass from preliminaries to bed with scarcely a pause for breath; once there Medea gives Jason an admirably succinct account of the trials to come, then swoons back into the arms of her maid like the most timid of romance heroines. This disjunction between what Medea appears to be and what she does both helps to control the reader's reaction, and also keeps her apparently disempowered despite her magic. Her response to Jason's success, standing, as it does, as uncommented dialogue, suggests the interpretation of her as an ingenue:

> 'Ha, lord, now al is wonne,
> Mi kniht the field hath overcome:
> Nou wolde god he were come;
> Ha lord, that he ne were alonde'. (V.3744–7)

These may look like the clichés of romance, and, indeed, that is what they are, but they are here in order to push Medea towards a certain kind of heroine. The lovers are joyful; there is scarcely any mention of Aeëtes, Apsyrtus is not mentioned at all. The Greeks simply flee within a day, carrying off their double prize. Jason and Medea settle in Greece, have two sons, and appear to be on the verge of happily ever after.

There is still no sense that Medea is powerful in and of herself. She accedes to Jason's request and rejuvenates his father, but, consistent with Gower's playing down of Medea's own decisiveness, her magic is merely marvellous, described 'for the novellerie' (V.3955).[45] It is only when we

---

[45] On the language of these metamorphoses, see Christopher Ricks, 'Metamorphosis in other words', in *Gower's Confessio Amantis: Responses and Reassessments*, ed. A. J.

read back from the end of the story and back from the end of the whole section, that we see that Gower has built a sequence of revenges for women who put themselves into the hands of men who were not trustworthy, and repeated structures of betrayal between children and parents. When he finally reaches the betrayal, it is almost as if it is himself he is bringing up short: Jason betrayed Medea and took another wife, then

> And whan that yonge freisshe queene
> That mantel lappeth hire aboute,
> Anon thereof the fyr sprong oute
> And brente hir bothe fleissh and bon.   (V.4206–9)

There was almost no warning: Gower has shifted Medeas as dramatically as we have seen. So quickly comes *peripeteia*, so suddenly revenge. The apparent safety of 'romance' was a mirage. Here Gower controls the narrative by reference to Ovid. In the context of the whole of Book V, however, this tale is matched by the tale of Theseus and Ariadne, which contains its own cross-references to the fall of Troy, as well as the narrator's desire for revenge on Ariadne's behalf. But the matching tale which acts out that revenge is the third long tale in this section, that of Tereus and Procne, in which, of course, the destruction of a child by his mother is the climax of the revenge. A detailed examination of Gower's Book V would examine the verbal reminiscences from story to story. It would also accent the public declarations of the private tragedies, by women as women, or by women as birds, interpreted by Genius. In this kind of reading Gower's 'plain style' becomes the means to complex interpretation. It is far from an innocent or naive representation of a sequence of tales.

Chaucerian Heroinism

Chaucer referred several times to Medea in the course of his poetry, and wrote about Jason's victims in his *Legend of Good Women*.[46] She appears as part of a Heroïdean list when the narrator of *The Book of the Duchess* is

Minnis (Cambridge, D. S. Brewer, 1983), pp. 25–49. Gower had the option of putting this tale together with his section on witchcraft and sorcery; that he did not is further evidence that it is not *this* aspect of the story which is his primary interest. Gower's language of families and exchange merits analysis: perjury offends the system of exchange, and betrayal is often 'bought' and repaid by revenge.

[46] There are interesting questions to be asked about Chaucer's sources here, but also about his technique of suppression. Two of his French contemporaries used not dissimilar approaches. Oton de Grandson makes Medea apparently innocent of wrongdoing by

trying to dissuade the man in Black from despair by threatening him with the damnation which rewarded Dido, Phyllis, and Medea (but he adds Echo and Samson); in a similarly Ovidian list in *The House of Fame* (lines 400–1) where the narrator enumerates the classical heroes who betrayed their beloveds; she also appears later in the same poem in the company of Circe and Calypso in the list of magicians. These occurrences are already unusual, since Chaucer refers to her as slaying her children 'for' Jason (an obvious ambiguity, which ought to mean 'on account of' in context, but only if one knows the story, line 727) in the first list, and as someone who knew the art of healing or poisoning in the second (that is, natural magic, lines 1265–71). This is Medea neither as evil sorceress nor as betrayed by love.

It is in *The Legend of Good Women* that we find Chaucer exploring, under the cover of a 'legendary' (a type of collection usually dedicated to saints' lives for the use of pious readers), the problem of 'faithful' women. Chaucer's *Legend of Good Women* poses many problems, some of which appear to be the point of its composition.[47] Certain of its features coincide with the concerns of this book, and it is those, and only those, which I shall single out. Chaucer opens with a few lines on heaven and hell, about which he makes the joke that although we know their existence to be true, none of us have been there. Experience, in this case, yields to authority, the authority of old books, or perhaps one should more accurately say the question of the authority of old books. This is not a new subject for Chaucer, nor is the question of the status of those old books, or the truth

suppressing any mention of Apsyrtus or Pelias in Balades LXXIV and LXXVII in A. Piaget, ed. *Oton de Grandson sa vie et ses poésies* (Lausanne, 1941), I, pp. 373, 379–80. Guillaume de Machaut introduces Medea in the section of the *Jugement du Roy de Navarre* in which Franchise argues that 'on ne porroit trouver en homme/si grant loyalté comme en femme'. In his thirty-four-line summary Jason is blamed for ingratitude as well as disloyalty, in words that are partly borrowed from the *Ovide moralisé*. The result of this skilfully condensed summary may be thought to be a rather dubious defence, since Machaut does not entirely suppress Medea's murders, nor her later deception of Aegeus in Athens. E. Hoepffner, ed. Guillaume de Machaut, *Oeuvres* (Paris, Firmin-Didot et Cie., 1908), lines 2770–2804. All quotations from Chaucer are from the Riverside edition, ed. L. D. Benson (Cambridge, Mass. and Oxford, 1987).

47 The bibliography on this work is expanding; to Robert Worth Frank, Jr.'s pioneering study, *Chaucer and the Legend of Good Women* (Cambridge, Mass., Harvard University Press, 1972), where a composition date of 1386 is suggested, may be added Lisa Kiser, *Telling Classical Tales: Chaucer and the Legend of Good Women* (Ithaca and London, Cornell University Press, 1983) and Sheila Delany, *The Naked Text: Chaucer and the Legend of Good Women* (Berkeley, University of California Press, 1994). For an important comparison between Chaucer and other users of the legends, see Carol Meale, 'Legends of Good Women in the European Middle Ages', *Archiv für das Studium der Neuren Sprache und Literaturen* 144 (1992), pp. 55–70.

of their contents. Because it is familiar to readers of Chaucer, it is easy to recognize and then disregard. Yet, stitched into the dream vision are a series of questions to which Chaucer returns: the questions of the truth of old stories. Just as the prologues to the three early dream visions set the context of the stories which follow them, so the Prologue to the *Legend* refers to issues which set the scene for the old stories which are to come. Both 'truth' and 'credence' are repeated in the course of the Prologue, and he sets the problem as follows:

> Than mote we to bokes that we fynde,
> Thurgh whiche that olde thinges ben in mynde,
> And to the doctrine of these olde wyse,
> Yeve credence, in every skylful wise,
> That tellen of these olde appreved stories
> Of holynesse, of regnes, of victories,
> Of love, of hate, of other sondry thynges,
> Of whiche I may not maken rehersynges.
> And yf that olde bokes were aweye,
> Yloren were of remembraunce the keye.
> Wel ought us thanne honouren and beleve
> These bokes, there we han noon other preve.   (F 17–28)

The G-version has a slightly expanded return to this subject (I follow the consensus that G is perhaps a decade later than F):

> But wherfore that I spak, to yeve credence
> To bokes olde and don hem reverence,
> Is for men shulde autoritees beleve,
> There as there lyth non other assay by preve.
> For myn entent is, or I fro yow fare,
> The naked text in English to declare
> Of many a story, or elles of many a geste,
> As autours seyn; leveth hem if yow leste.   (G 81–8)

Chaucer's own authority in this is nothing from experience; as in his other poems, he insists upon his own innocence of Love, although he serves the Daisy. This modest denial becomes the proudest kind of assertion.

First, the question of Love-service, and courtly games about taking sides, allow him to return to the competition between the Flower and the Leaf as itself an old story (F 194–6). Then, when Alceste comes to the Dreamer's rescue, she questions the kinds of evidence which might create the impression that the dreamer was really guilty in his compositions of offending the God of Love. We may consider that the Dreamer's defence (that in translating works which represent false lovers he encourages his readers to avoid their behaviour) is no different from defences of historical or other kinds of representation which medieval writers used. It is Alceste's dismissal of that defence which tell its own tale:

> Lat be thyn arguyng,
> For Love ne wol nat countrepleted be
> In ryght ne wrong; and lerne that at me!
>
> (F 475–7, similarly in G 465–7)

If Love tolerates no argument, no contradiction, what becomes of the idea that lovers can discuss the truth? The God of Love makes Alceste the model of a true tale (F 507, G 495), but Alceste's story is itself another return to the subject, the truth of old books – for it is in an old book in the Dreamer's chest that he has read about her. And what, in the end, does this make of the God of Love's claim that no true lover shall go to hell? His final instruction is that the Dreamer write the stories of true lovers he has read in old books. This resolves nothing.

Nor does context help: the legends come from Ovid, but where does the idea of the legendary come from? Unlike many of the legends, the setting of the double story of Medea and Hypsipyle is the history of Jason's Argonautic voyage, as it is familiar from historical texts such as Guido, to whom Chaucer refers.

No one has yet achieved a comprehensive interpretation of this odd collection, and, once again, I have no complete reading to offer, but some further suggestions may help illuminate what Chaucer did, or might have intended. To the question of who the lady at the centre of the prologues is, we attend to the literal reading, and take Alceste to be Alceste (whether or not she is also allegorically the daisy, the virgin, or a particular noble lady): she thus reassumes her place as that most loving of wives, who gave life itself to her beloved, and received life, and faithful loving, in return.[48] Although she is not an Ovidian heroine, she is famous for her willing self-sacrifice, as Thisbe (who does appear in the *Metamorphoses*) was renowned for the pathos and misfortune which came from her devotion. There is, thus, second, the very idea of faithfulness (of women) and betrayal (by men), a typically Chaucerian double inversion of an inherited theme.

The question of Chaucer's selection of heroines, here as elsewhere, is, if not easily predictable, not surprising, either. Insofar as a 'legend' is a

---

[48] The problem here, as Adrian Poole points out, is the disappearance of Admetus, in his *Tragedy: Shakespeare and the Greek Example* (Oxford, Blackwell, 1987), pp. 127–8.

'martyrology', one expects martyrs. We have often seen the nexus of women interconnected by their literary descent from Medea, their power, and their association with Jason, Theseus, and Hercules; these account for five more of the remaining ten heroines (Dido, Hysipyle, Medea, Ariadne, Philomela).[49] Phyllis and Hypermnestra come from the *Heroïdes*. The odd two heroines, Cleopatra and Lucrece, are historical examples. If Lisa Kiser is right that this collection is a parody of the kind of representation normally found in saints' lives, then there is a strong argument that the work is deliberately cut off (through its suppression of parts of the stories which would contradict Chaucer's ostensible representation of the women as love's martyrs). Love *is* more complicated than a calendar allows; misinterpretation *is* the unavoidable result of partial translation, the only available corrective is the reader's knowledge, and that, too, is far from easy or even dependable.[50] There are not nine (or fifteen) missing heroines at all – but this can only be speculation.

When Gower wrote of Jason's perjury he spent most of the tale writing about Medea; Chaucer, ostensibly writing of Medea and Hypsipyle in *The Legend of Good Women*, concentrated on Jason.[51] He does this several times, following, perhaps, the narratives of the *Ovide moralisé*, which began with the men rather than the women. Jason's double betrayal has the

---

[49] We can test this, as before, by asking who is missing, and why. Ino, Agave, and Althaea have no place in this list because they are not lovers, but murdering mothers. H. A. Kelly's view that Chaucer might have added Penelope, Laodamia, Deianira, Hermione, Helen, and Polyxena seems to me to emphasize the Trojan War aspect of Ovid's collection (although one would expect not Polyxena but Briseis) but, with the expansions, to lose the associations I have been teasing out. See his *Love and Marriage in the Age of Chaucer* (Ithaca and London, Cornell University Press, 1975), pp. 113–18. Chaucer's 'Ovid' is certainly partly the *Ovide moralisé*; the 'Philomena' translates Chrétien's story.

[50] Lisa Kiser, *Telling Classical Tales*, chaps. 3 and 4. Lee Patterson writes with his usual illuminating scope, mainly on *Anelida and Arcite* as a memorial poem (one might add a memorial poem written in the light of Ovidian letters) in 'Thirled with the Poynt of Remembrance: Memory and Modernity in Chaucer's Poetry', *Modernité au Moyen Age: le défi du passé*, ed. Brigitte Cazelles and Charles Méla (Geneva, Droz, 1990), pp. 113–51. He shows Chaucer thinking both of Dido in the *Heroïdes* (133 n. 45) and of Jason and Medea in *The Legend of Good Women* (135 n. 49). Patterson's reminder that Chaucer associates Boethianism, Thebes, and Ovidian love (140) is important for implications of tragedy. I have dealt with a similar association in 'Absolute Tragedy: Allusions and Avoidances' *Poetica* 38 (1993), pp. 1–17.

[51] '. . . What is most significant about the false lover, Chaucer perceived, is not that he is false, but that he is successful', writes R. W. Frank, Jr. In *Chaucer and Medieval Estates Satire*, Jill Mann suggested three techniques for the successful disjunction which keeps Chaucer's villains amusing: the omission of the victim, the creation of tension between our moral judgements and emotional reactions, and the distancing of the narrative from moral judgement. Frank's argument agrees with this analysis. It is important, I think, that the victims should not only be private individuals, but women, who must, in the end, bear blame for allowing themselves to give up their honour.

same effect I noted earlier in the multiplication of seduced and abandoned women: in this context of loss of dignity, two threatens to become ridiculous. This use of gender is visible in the feminization of Jason himself, who uses what appear to be maiden's wiles to win Medea's heart:

> And Jason is as coy as is a mayde;
> He loketh pitously, but nought he sayde,
> But frely yaf he to hire conseyleres
> Yiftes grete, and to hire officeres.
> As wolde God I leyser hadde and tyme
> By proces al his wowyng for to ryme!
> But in this hous if any fals lovere be
> Ryght as hymself now doth, ryght so dide he,
> With feynynge, and with every subtil dede.
> Ye gete namore of me, but ye wole rede
> Th'origynal, that telleth al the cas. (*LGW* lines 1548 58)

This points in several directions. First, this is a 'court' work, which fans out towards the hypocrisy traditionally situated in courts in order to criticize their workings, and in particular the ways that counsellors can be (perhaps must be) bribed. The collusion which appeals to what everybody knows, and which includes a kind of love-paranoia with the references to the behaviour of the audience, direct attention away from the potential tragedy either of the tale or of everyday seduction towards the double authority of 'what everyone knows' and Ovid. For that throw-away reference to the original is another of those reminders that truth exists, and resides elsewhere, in someone else's text.[52] Chaucer's suppressions are too easy; they demand another story. That the court of Alceste itself was built upon a kind of betrayal is one of the truths which Chaucer suppresses throughout the poems.

There is testimony to the popularity of the *Heroïdes* in the number of French translations in beautiful (and beautifully illustrated) manuscripts, including manuscripts of the *Histoire ancienne jusqu'à César*.[53] As we saw in Chapter Two, Ovid's *Heroïdes* set the model and were for centuries

---

52 John Fyler is severe about the restraints imposed by Chaucer's sources in his *Chaucer and Ovid* (New Haven and London, Yale University Press, 1979), chapt. 4. He finds hilarity in this section, and the following one, on Philomena. This is surprising. Certainly there are insoluble problems about tone throughout this work, but Chaucer never treats rape with levity. For a view of the legal arrangements between Jason and his lovers, see H. A. Kelly, *Love and Marriage*, esp. chapt. 4.

53 Hypsipyle, with her twins, and Medea, with her sons, are illustrated in BNf. f.fr. 874 (f. 50, f. 59v) and 875 Hypsipyle at f. 30 and Medea at f. 71v. The letters which the women are writing are in something more or less like Greek characters, e.g. BNf. f.fr. 254 and

celebrated as truthful depictions of women in the throes of passion. And far beyond the end of the Middle Ages. 'Heroides' as a genre come to be written in France, combining the titillation of the apparently autobiographical with all the skill of rhetoric, and they lie behind *The Portuguese Letters* and, ultimately, Richardson's epistolary fiction.[54] In England, Turberville and Lyly, Drayton and Dryden translated them and imitated them. All these new 'heroides' assume male readerships; all raise questions of female subjectivity.[55] Where, in the medieval *exemplum*, the emotion of women might come to stand for, to figure, the soul's capitulation to irrational passion, in later portrayals their erotic potential overcame the Christian focus (through allegory) on the need for human mastery of the Will. Under both descriptions women were ideal literary laboratories for study, since their weaker minds made them more susceptible to seduction, and to the errors of judgement which stem from a mind clouded by strong feeling. That 'heroic' women such as Medea did not seem entirely 'weak' either in thought or action remained a central contradiction.

The City of Women

Christine de Pizan came repeatedly to the legends of Jason and Medea, and found in them a variety of interpretations, and a steady refusal to essentialize Medea – as she did any other of her female characters.[56] I have

301 and Grenoble 860, described by Léopold Constans, 'Une Traduction française des *Héroïdes* d'Ovide au XIIIe siècle', *Romania* 43 (1914), pp. 177–98.

54 See *Ovide en France dans la Renaissance* (Toulouse, Publications de l'Université de Toulouse, 1981). For the revival of the genre, see Renata Carocci, *Les heroïdes dans la seconde moitié du XVIIIe siècle 1758–1788* (Paris, Nizet, 1988); Joan DeJean, *Tender Geographies* (New York, Oxford and Columbia University Presses, 1991); Pamela Benson, *The Invention of the Renaissance Woman: The Challenge of Female Independence in the Literature and Thought of Italy and England* (University Park, Pennsylvania State University Press, 1992); Götz Schmitz, *The Fall of Woman in Early English Narrative Verse* (Cambridge, Cambridge University Press, 1990).

55 Discussed in the introduction to Robert Adams Day, *Told in Letters: Epistolary Fiction Before Richardson* (Ann Arbor, University of Michigan Press, 1966, esp. 10–26. Turberville and Drayton are the subject of Deborah Greenhut, *Feminine Rhetorical Culture: Tudor Adaptations of Ovid's* Heroïdes (New York, Peter Lang Verlag, 1988). Florence Verducci extends the discussion of Ovid's influence in *Ovid's Toyshop of the Heart*, chapt. 1. In her ground-breaking study, *Literary Women* (London, L. H. Allen and Co., 1977), Ellen Moers discusses the importance of letters, and especially the derivatives of Ovid, for the expression of feminine points of view, pp. 160–72.

56 Christine referred to these legends often in the course of her writing, e.g. 'Le chemin de long estude', *Oeuvres Poétique de Christine de Pisan*, ed. M. Roy (Paris, 1891) vol. II, pp. 92–3, lines 1455–68. For her use of Machaut in the 'Chemin' see P. G. C. Campbell,

already discussed her own work of secular history, the *Mutacion de Fortune*, in Chapter Two, and her historical allegory, *L'Epistre d'Othea*, above. In Christine's other extended allegory, the *Livre de la Cité des Dames*, written in 1404–1405, she set about explicitly defending women from centuries of male castigations and distortions. The book is a dream vision in several parts, and has only recently begun to attract serious study.[57] It deploys allegory for a reinterpretation of history, and women's place in it; it assumes the authority to recontextualize and redescribe the gifts, talents, and deeds of women; in its ambitious intertextuality it appropriates and re-turns the examples of Boccaccio, adding copious 'modern examples' to demonstrate women's contribution to the most public aspects of life.

Christine always asserted her status as a mother, a head of a household, the support of her family, and a woman learned beyond her gender. We have already seen this in her autobiographical introduction in the *Mutacion de Fortune*, where the performance of gender was initially masculine. Here she generalizes out from her own motherhood to the essential role played by women in the support of civilization, the building of a just and righteous city through the raising of children as well as the governing of cities and the writing of books. She appropriates the learned voice and makes of it an active role. The wording of her questions to the allegorical Ladies allows her to exemplify women as rulers, as creators, as discoverers of areas of learning, as persons capable of sound judgement, and even of great faithfulness as lovers. Above all, the way the answers come responds only to the questions as she has asked them; by resisting amplification the author cites only those aspects which are useful to her of the stories which she selects.

Of the many advantages of the dream vision, one is that it avoids explictly claiming authority for writing. The pose is that Christine merely records what she witnessed, and she witnessed from ignorance. There is none of Laurent's or Lydgate's pressure to tell a whole story. When the

L'Epitre d'Othéa: études sur les sources de Christine de Pisan (Paris, Champion, 1924), p. 100. In the *Epistre au dieu d'Amours* Christine uses Medea and Dido as a contrast of fidelity to Jason and Aeneas; in *Le Debat des Deux Amans* she associates (taken from Machaut) Medea, Dido, Ariadne as women who aided heroes.

57 Maureen Quilligan, *The Allegory of Female Authority: Christine de Pizan's Livre de la Cité des Dames* (Ithaca and London, Cornell University Press, 1991); Christine de Pizan, *The Book of the City of Ladies*, trans. Earl Jeffrey Richards (New York, Persea, 1982), from which I have taken my quotations; and, on its reception, *The Reception of Christine de Pizan from the Fifteenth through the Nineteenth Centuries: Visitors to the City*, ed. Glenda K. McLeod (Lewiston, Edwin Mellen, 1991). There is an important essay by Patricia A. Phillippy, 'Establishing Authority: Boccaccio's *De claris mulieribus* and Christine de Pizan's *Le Livre de la Cité des Dames*', *Romanic Review* 77 (1986), pp. 167–94.

allegorical ladies appear, Christine does not know who they are, but is impressed by the majesty and authority of their looks – establishing the moral authority of the allegorical figures I.3.1 (p. 8). They explain that they are daughters of God born to help men stick to the right paths. The ladies have been moved by pity at women's passive endurance and suffering to come and instruct Christine to edify the City of protection for them. They are Reason, Rectitude (Droitture) and Justice. They are interconnected (both like a trinity – as V. A. Kolve has also shown – and like three fates, though they do not say so).

Among the male authorities Christine emulates, but sometimes corrects, the most obvious, perhaps, is Boccaccio, whom she has reinterpreted before; but the essential shape of the 'city' derives, of course, from Augustine, whose City of God lies behind her allegory. She is strict with Ovid, too, in a traditional rebuttal, imputing his misogyny to a punished old age in which he could no longer exercise his own voluptuousness.[58] If the *Mutacion* was a reinterpreted, but traditional, history, and the *Epistre* was an interpretable historical allegory, the *Cité* presents another alternative. The examples of the ladies rewrite history, with an awareness that the past is a foreign country unusual in Christine's time and place. The early cases are all reigning queens who had to substitute for male kings: the first example, of Semiramis, shows Christine aware that in the past actors were not subject to 'written law', and speculates upon the guilt of, first, Semiramis (her opening example, who committed incest with her son). That is, even where she acknowledges that her female figures did what men accuse them of, she has explanations for why that might have been. She did not need to read Boccaccio to learn how to offer multiple motives for what their characters do, but she is like him in her ability to see history from the characters' points of view.

Throughout she questions the authority of poets (e.g. Homer and Virgil) and allows that they can make mistakes. She sometimes turns accusations around to defend where it seems inevitable that she must condemn; for instance, to the accusation that women are greedy she replies that women are not naturally gluttonous, and if they were their desire to control it would be praiseworthy. The old adage that women are made to weep becomes a praise of the gift of tears, of speaking, of sewing. To the accusation that women are failed men, incapable of performing men's tasks, she replies with examples of women doing exactly that, but also asserts that men's and women's gifts are different, and that it is appropriate to ask one man to do something which would require several women.

[58] See also Quilligan, *Allegory of Female Authority*, p. 63.

To the accusation that women have weak bodies she replies that this takes account only of one feature, and ignores women's daring and boldness. To the view that women are ignorant she counters that only because they are kept at home untaught do they appear simple – this is due to a failure to teach, not an inability to be taught. It is in the context of learnedness that Medea first appears. In I.32 Medea and Circe appear (and there are references to Boccaccio); Medea is described only as a king's daughter who knew herbs, spells:

Cy dit de Medee et d'une autre royne nommee Circés:

Medee, de laquelle assez d'istoires font mencion, ne sceut pas moins d'art et de science que celle devant ditte. Elle fu fille de Othés, roy de Colcos, et de Perse, moult belle, de corsaige haulte et droitte et assez plaisant de viaire. Mais de sçavoir elle passa et exceda toute femmes; elle savoit de toute herbes les vertus et tous les enchantems que faire se pevent; et de nulle art qui est[re] puis[t] sceu, elle n'estoit ignorente. Elle faisoit, part vertu d'une chançon qu'elle savoit, troubler et obscurcir l'air, mouvoir les vens des fosses et cavernes de la terre, commouvoir les tempestes en l'air, arrester les fleuves, confire poysons, composer feux sans labour pour ardoir quelconques chose qu'elle vouloit, et toutes semblablees choses savoit faire. Ceste fu celle qui par l'art de son enchantement fist conquerre a Jason la toyson d'or.   (pp. 732–3)

[Medea, whom many historical works mention, was no less familiar with science and art than Manto. She was the daughter of Aetes, king of Colchis, and of Persa, and was very beautiful, with a noble and upright heart and a pleasant face. In learning, however, she surpassed and exceeded all women; she knew the powers of every herb and all the potions which could be concocted, and she was ignorant of no art which can be known. With her spells she knew how to make the air become cloudy or dark, how to move winds from the grottoes and caverns of the earth, and how to provoke other storms in the air, as well as how to stop the flow of rivers, confect poisons, create fire to burn up effortlessly whatever object she chose, and all such similar arts. It was thanks to the art of her enchantment that Jason won the Golden Fleece.]   (p. 69)[59]

The shape of the dialogue between the enquiring Christine and the Allegorical Ladies controls the examples throughout. In Book II she deals with the accusation that women are fickle, and is given many examples to show that they are no more fickle than men are. Indeed, some women have been

59 Christine de Pizan, *Le Livre de la Cité des Dames*, ed. Maureen Cheney Curnow (Ann Arbor, Michigan, University Microfilms, 1978). English translation from *The Book of the City of Ladies*, trans. Earl Jeffrey Richards (New York, Persea, 1982).

much too constant, as can be seen in the loves of Dido (II.55), then Medea (II.56). Here, once more, by supplying such an example limited to the illustration of faithfulness in love, Christine evades the problems that a complete narrative would reveal.

De Medee amoureuse.

Medee, fille du roy de Colcos qui tant avoit de savoir, ama de trop grant et de trop ferme amour Jason. . . . Medee, la fille du roy, qui vid Jason de tel biauté, de lignee royal et de si grant renommee que il luy sembla que bon mariage seroit pour elle et que mieulx ne pourroit employer s'amour, le voulst garder de mort, car trop grant pitié luy prist que tel chevalier deust ainsi périr. Sy parla a luy longuement et a loisir. Et a brief dire, elle luy bailla charmes et enchantemens, comme celle qui tous les savoit, et luy aprist toute la maniere comment et part quel voye il conquerroit la toyson d'or, par sy que Jason luy promist la prendre a femme sans jamais autre avoir et que loyal foy et amour a tousjours luy porteroyt. Mais de ceste promesse luy menti Jason, car aprés ce qu'il fu du tout advenu a son entente, il la laissa pour une autre. Dont elle, qui plus tost se laissast detraire que luy avoir fait ce tour , fu comme desespere[e], ne oncques puis bien ne joye son cuer n'ot. (pp. 931–2)

[Medea, daughter of the king of Colchis, and who possessed such great knowledge, loved Jason with a too great and too constant love. . . . Medea, the king's daughter, noting Jason's beauty, royal lineage, and fame, and seeing that he would make a good husband for her and that she could not make better use of her love elsewhere, resolved to protect him from death, for too much pity overwhelmed her at the thought that this knight would have to die in such a way, and so she spoke to him for along time at leisure. Put briefly, she gave him charms and enchantments, and, in her expertise, she taught him how to win the Golden Fleece on the condition that Jason promised to take her as his wife and no other woman and to show her forever loyal faith and love. However, Jason lied about his promise, for after everything went just as he wanted, he left Medea for another woman. For this reason, Medea, who would rather have destroyed herself than do anything of this kind to him, turned despondent, nor did her heart ever again feel goodness or joy.]
(pp. 189–90)

Medea's vices, such as they are, seem to stem from an excess of virtue: too much knowledge put to the service of an unworthy object, too much love for that object. Christine turned the stories to the study of the emotions and actions they concerned.

It can be difficult to avoid taking that rare creature, a woman writer, as an allegory of a different kind, a representative of an alternative view, a proto-feminist, a dissenting, subversive voice. Christine de Pizan is that solitary and out-standing figure, a woman living by her writing, dependent upon patrons, and defending women as a woman capable of playing male writers at their own game of reference and redaction, ready to cite authorities when necessary from the breadth of her own unusual learning.[60] No one was more aware of her anomalous – and lonely – position than she was herself; no one was more alert to the reactionary temptation to counter mysogyny with undifferentiated gynophilia. Christine resisted essentialisms of both kinds: as she resisted the accusation that all women were wicked, so she refused to claim that they were, on the contrary, outstandingly good, victimized, or even in the right. Neither men nor women were always anything. If her women are heroines, they are heroines in a new key, but the door they unlock remains deeply Christian and traditional: for the Queen of the city is the Queen of Heaven, and her closest companions are the martyrs whose fortitude maintained their virtues. The end of history remains the Christian telos.

For medieval readers and writers, the beginning of secular history, the preface to the Trojan War, was always the origin of the legends of Jason and Medea. Depending upon the authority of the source, or sources, they consulted, they could interpret those legends in different ways. To the actions of historical figures certain kinds of decorum did not apply: historical actors *could* be both heroic and despicable. The narrative could be contained in parts, or in outline. Where their actions could be pressed into allegorical examples, either *in bono* or *in malum*, those parts required no consistency or coherence. To the characters of historical figures, speculation could always apply, but character was almost always subordinate to other concerns, and it is the rare author who concentrates on motive. Indeed, the kind of author who concentrated on motive was likely to be innovatory, and most unusual. For most authors, Jason could be the hero who successfully sought the Gold Fleece, Medea could be one of the women seduced and abandoned by their lovers. It is only when authors

---

[60] In a series of important articles Joël Blanchard has argued for her place as a political writer, capable of advising rulers on a variety of issues. See, for example, 'L'Entrée du poète dans le champ politique au XVe siècle', *Annales ESC* 41 (1986), pp. 43–61. Her assumption of authority has been further demonstrated by Kevin Brownlee, in 'Discourses of the Self: Christine de Pizan and the *Rose' Romanic Review* 79 (1988) pp. 222–48 and his 'Structures of Authority in Christine de Pizan's *Ditié de Jehanne d'Arc'* in *Discourses of Authority in Medieval and Renaissance Literature*, ed. Kevin Brownlee and W. Stephens (Hanover and London, 1989), pp. 131–50; and V. A. Kolve, who considers the iconographic evidence in 'The Annunciation to Christine: Authorial Empowerment in *The Book of the City of Ladies Iconography at the Crossroads*, ed. Brendan Cassidy (Princeton, Princeton University Press, 1993), pp. 171–196.

generalize from selected episodes that consistency and coherence begin to be problematic, only when the appeal from particular examples to known truths about human behaviour that we begin to see how much 'literary' treatments of 'historical' examples have modified ideas of gendered behaviour. Boccaccio is not alone when he implies that cunning intelligence, that superior gift, becomes an amoral force likely to be ill-used when it endows women with the ability to enforce their wills, or wilfulnesses. To have drawn the history of these legends is to have seen ideas of falls recreating a generic orgin, that of tragedy, emerging from the inevitabilities of histoy.

Only beyond the end of the Middle Ages, when ancient history and its mythographical tradition reassumed the status of fiction; when, almost paradoxically, the ancient world posed a possible alternative to Christian moralities, did heroic women who reacted to their wrongs with more than fortitude and endurance once again propose transgressive models to historians, poets, and playwrights. The variety of Jasons and Medeas created by writers who claimed to be interpreting the past suggests no master narrative, no coercive or necessary depiction of the duplicitous couple. The history of their appearance in our literature illustrates the range of possibilities, as well as the limits, of invention.

CONCLUSION

Silence, Exile, and Cunning Intelligence

Medea and Jason's sons were called Pheres and Mermeros. We have this on the authority of Apollodorus and Pausanias.[1] Like Astyanax, these children have no future, so how is it that they acquired names? There is a kind of narrative superabundance about the specificity which goes well beyond merely identifying them, and their place in the story. Euripides' dying Alcestis asks her husband to promise not to inflict a step-mother on their children (whom we never see) to protect them from the anticipated jealous ambitions of a new wife, the universal step-mother. To think about Medea's children is immediately to wonder what they knew, how they behaved when their father left them and their mother spent all her time weeping, whether they wondered why, when she gave them bridal gifts to carry to their father's new wife, she forbade them to open the caskets in which they were stored. To think about them is immediately to begin to flesh them out, to give them a point of view, perhaps two, from the range of our experience of children, of separation, of love and hatred. For Euripides their presence is a constant reminder of something more concrete than 'family' as an idea; he emphasizes the pleasure parents feel in their children's skin: their warm softness is what inhibits Medea, for a moment, and the smell and touch of his infants is what Jason pleads for before she kills his son. One reason for her murders is to anticipate the cruelty of the Corinthians, but Medea, like Alcestis, has already worried about the fate of her children once Creusa (or Glauce) begins to have

---

1 Vassiliki Gaggadis-Robin, *Jason et Médée sur les sarcophages d'époque impériale* (Rome, Ecole française de Rome, 1994), p. 38, pp. 147ff. Diodorus Siculus gives three children, twins called Thessalos and Alcimenes and Tissandros (IV.54). He preserves the ancient, pre-Euripidean tradition which made Medea heir to Corinth in her own right (which thus contradicts the tradition of Jason's repudiation, in Corinth, of his non-Greek wife), and the report that she killed her children by accident while trying to render them immortal. Pausanius (II.3.6) attributes to the poet Kinaithon the story that the children were a son, Medeios, and a daughter, Eriopie.

children of her own. To see the story from their point of view is to see it differently. Like Astyanax frightened by Hector's war-helmet, the children remind us of common experience and the universal vulnerability and ignorance of childhood. Medea's children are homeless exiles. Yet, throughout the Middle Ages, their place in the story recedes to nothing. One might have anticipated a moral to be drawn between the innocence of children before their parents' plans and the position adults might be thought to be in vis-à-vis the gods.

If we say, 'We know that Jason's sons were called Pheres and Mermeros', we succumb immediately to the kind of narrative desire which treats imaginative fictions as in some sense the equivalent of historical accounts. We align ourselves with that cool anonymous scholarship which works through research to find out what happened. Better to record that Jason's mother is variously named, sometimes Polymede (or Polymele, or Polypheme, a daughter of Autolycos), Alcimede (in a Minoan-derived tradition), or Amphinome, to say that on the late authority of Pausanias Jason's children are given names. Nonetheless, the narrative acquires authority, and there comes a point when certain of its events cannot be changed. Medea becomes, after Euripides, a foreign princess, the murderer of her children. There is no greater testimony to the strength of a strong poet than his success at making a legend what he wants it to be. The moment comes when we think we know what happened, that there are events to be known. Even the great poet is constrained by that expectation, and finds himself trying to manoeuvre around ineffaceable events which never occurred. When Statius names Jason's and Hypsipyle's sons, who march in the army towards Thebes, he, too, sets a version into a legend, and Homer's reference to Hypsipyle's trader son is effaced. It becomes almost impossible not to reject the inventions (the additions) of a writer such as Raoul Lefèvre with the patronizing shrug such gothic fantasies long appeared to deserve: he got it wrong. 'It' and 'wrong' remain with us, even after the Middle Ages, when 'it' was restored to fiction and rewritten by playwrights such as Corneille, whose inventions could not withstand the operatic dramatizations of Cherubini and Charpentier. The idea of the powerful sorceress had become too strong.

If we think of Seneca's words, 'Medea superest', we must wonder what that means. Who does Medea think that she is? Perhaps we must ask, Who does *whose* Medea think she is? Is she a witch? Certainly all the Medeas we have looked at have had access to drugs, to what appears to be non-normal strength, to the control of dragons which allow them to fly. All of them claim to be descended from the Sun. But beyond this, all of them, like heroic women throughout Greek literature, have an intelligence and courage which makes them exceptional among women as well as unusual among men; the male strength they boast of in their woman's body is a strength rare among men as well. It might even be denied that it is a strength in the straightforward physical way in which men's bodies are stronger than women's or children's: it is not 'strength' but a superior degree of courage and intelligence gendered as male because complimentary. One control over this question is to contrast Medea to her sister, Chalciope, or her brother, Apsyrtos. Neither of them appears to have superhuman powers (unlike their aunt, Circe). But we do not know what the categories or boundaries of normal/paranormal powers were in all the societies in which Medea was written about; we do not know to what extent fifth-century Greek authors projected upon their mythical bronze age heroes and heroines ideas of human possibility. As a woman knowledgeable about *pharmakon*, Medea may be unusually cunning and intelligent, but that does not make her paranormal. Categories applied to Medea tell us as much about the categorizers as they do about the legends.

Has she always been a model for what men fear? However problematic the meaning of a myth may be, it is not even clear what we ask when we ask what is the meaning of a legend. Legends change too much as they are retold for them to embody 'a' meaning. Nevertheless, there are recurring themes. Both Medea and Jason may begin by being supported by gods (Jason, for example, enjoys Hera's favour in some early versions), but there is no sense that Jason's repudiation of Medea is motivated by a god's desire or revenge any more than Medea's ability to kill results from an *atê*, a madness divinely inspired. Rather, Medea is that stranger taken into the patriarchal house who may be the traitor within the gates. Medea and the imitations of Medea raise the problem of dynastic succession, where the threat to the patriarch lies in her ability to use her cunning intelligence to destroy the house, as Medea robs Jason of progeny. It is the measure of Medea's strength that as her love made Jason's conquests possible, her ill-will destroys him: her 'strength' is cunning intelligence.

Whether or not Medea is close to the gods, she is always a human princess of Colchis. It may be that this location grew from Greek trading, and the expansion of Corinth. Modern Rion, on what was the Phasis, on the shore of the Black Sea, is certainly far from Greece, but it is neither Persia nor any obvious 'Eastern' kingdom. How much does Medea's foreignness matter, and when? Clearly for Euripides it legitimated that fawning flattery which – because Medea has the cunning to exploit it – enabled his character to pretend to be that kind of essentially weak and untrustworthy Asiatic who was both despised and feared. But for a Roman to write about a Greek afraid of a foreigner was to resituate what was self, what Other. For a Christian from Western Europe this could only become more strange. The places from which Jason and Medea are driven had all become distant; their exile is a sequence of removals. If this study were to be extended, that sense of exile would become increasingly important; and it would be fascinating to situate the legends within the specificities of neo-classical drama in the seventeenth century or the colonial dilemmas of our own.[2]

This book takes its place in a succession of studies of these legends which have been the purview of classicists and anthropologists, for none of whom have the Middle Ages been of prime interest. Nevertheless, this field is informed by inherited categories which reach back over a century. Nineteenth-century ideas about strong women sometimes came in the context of a matriarchal society only faintly depicted in such ideas as 'Amazons'. The idea of 'Mother Right', as described by scholars such as J. J. Bachofen, became important in another, modern 'scientific' context of implications far more sinister than the influence of their theories on novelists like Graves. Bachofen, i. e. as explicated by Sander Gilman, talks about Amazon society as a necessary step in the dialectic of the progress of civilisation.[3] For Hegel the Amazon was a sign of sexual degradation, but Bachofen sees her primitive quality as contributing – through the need for men to oppose her – to progress. On this kind of nineteenth-century reading Medea appears both primitive and degenerate, and she was so depicted in more than one modern European reinterpretation.[4]

---

[2] Corneille twice used the legends: his first tragedy, *Médée*, 1634, imitates Seneca's *Medea*. Later he used what I have described as the early morphological units of the legends for *La Toison d'Or*, a spectacle of 1660 written for the marriage of Louis XIV and Marie-Thérèse. This odd spectacle focusses on a wooing of Medea in Colchis, and includes the sudden arrival of the abandoned Hypsipyle, who first snubs Medea (who is not a queen and therefore of lesser rank than Hypsipyle), then solves the problem of rivalry by falling in love with an adult Apsyrtus. Although the play is said to be based on Valerius Flaccus, only the first scene has any connection with the poem. Ed. M. Rat, *Théâtre Complet de Corneille* , vol. III (Paris, n.d.). For *Médée* see *Théâtre Complet de Corneille*, ed. G. Couton, vol. I (Paris, 1971).

[3] 'This sense of the creativity inherent in the primitive underlies yet another perception of the nineteenth century concerning the close analogy between sexual deviancy and the nature of the state. The state can be undermined or revolutionized by retrogressive models of sexuality, and the state bears within its own history this potential just as the body does. The state must have the means to control or harness this force. Bachofen's assimilation of this idea can be seen in his view of the necessary progression from the Amazonian reaction against the bondage of woman in the hetaeristic state to the matriarchy: from lawlessness through lawlessness to mother law', *Difference and Pathology: Stereotypes of Race and Madness* (Ithaca, Cornell University Press, 1985), pp. 194–5.

[4] The colonial setting of Henri LeNormand's play, *Asie*, of 1938, rewrites Medea as an Indo-Chinese princess, whose children display the weakness to be expected (according

As we ask if there are constants in these legends, certain ideas, as well as events do indeed repeat themselves. Medea is always the stranger, because removed from her home, her family, her extended kinship group, her country. She begins by choosing a kind of exile, but it is different in kind from that which is then forced upon her when she offends the societies into which Jason introduces her. Her disruptions are dismemberings, of Apsyrtos, of Pelias, of her sons, after which she flees. *This* invites us to follow modern interpretations of anthropological ideas of sacrifice and scapegoating, where the victim is marked by doubleness – women as objects of desire/fear. In the hands of literary critics such as René Girard, ideas of violence and the sacred assume that normally the double characters are the victim. Medea is, especially in the Greek paintings and sculptures which the poems describe, deeply double, with her contradictory emotions. She finds herself in the ideal rhetorical situation of a figure in the throes of a difficult decision. But she is not, on the face of it, the victim of sacrifice.

Medieval treatments of the legends can be broadly categorized, as we have seen, on two focal points: a male-dominated story of Jason's position as forerunner to the Trojan War, in which Medea is, indeed, betrayed, and Medea's retaliation, her threat to male order. That everyone who treats the legends 'gets right'. That is the aspect which has authority, which remains convincing. Although compendia were compiled by mythographers which registered the many adventures of the Argonauts, and noted the connections between different stories, when poets singled Jason and Medea out, their visions were restricted to the events made famous by the historians and by Ovid. The omissions are many: the adventures which the Argonauts enjoyed on their journeys, especially the episode in Lemnos (which Lefèvre treats in some detail). Statius's Hypsipyle seldom makes much of an appearance in the narrative.

In myths which explain natural or historical phenomena the agents seldom have much by way of character, beyond, perhaps, curiosity or wrath (which might be thought to be less 'character' than characteristics fatal to women and men respectively). Even in many Greek tragedies, where the agents are constructs of dialogue, few give the impression of representing idiosyncratic persons. Euripides is different here as in so much, but even his characters have little of the specificity we associate with later styles of writing. This makes it easier to imagine his personnages as types, instances of human possibility, a kind of universality and not the

to contemporary racial theories) of mixed-race offspring. This concentration on the colonial enterprise finds a new way of adapting the legends' themes.

horror of one particular fate. This is the emphasis of both Euripides' and Seneca's choruses, who attach the Agon to human fatality and to the gods. Medieval narrators, in the position of choral commentators, are bound by the attachment of the legend to history, and thus find themselves rooted in the specificities which Benjamin distinguished as sorrow rather than tragedy.

Jason remains a hero, the hero who conquered the Golden Fleece and stole away the king's daughter, whose love he later betrayed; Medea is the ingenue smitten with love for the Greek prince for whom she committed a sequence of crimes: betrayed her father, murdered her brother, persuaded her husband's cousins to kill their father, then punished Jason for breaking his oath to her. At some point in comprehensive versions her 'character' is dramatically reversed. Jason's remains more problematic. When Dante put him in the first bolgia in hell, among the deceivers associated by their sexuality, he described him in terms which suggested that his punishment was the less because the woman he deceived was herself a deceiver – but that woman is Hypsipyle, not Medea:

> Quelli è Iasón, che per cuore e per senno
> li Colchi del monton privati féne.
> Ello passò per l'isola di Lenno
> poi che l'ardite femmine spietate
> tutti le maschi loro a morete dienno.
> Ivi con segni e con parole ornate
> Isifile ingannò, la giovinetta
> che prima avea tutte l'altre ingannate.
> Lasciolla quivi, gravida, soletta;
> tal colpa a tal martiro lui condanna;
> e anche di Medea si fa vendetta.

> [That is Jason, who by courage and by craft despoiled the Colchians of the ram. He passed by the isle of Lemnos when the bold and pitiless women had given all their males to death. There, with tokens and with fair words, he deceived the young Hypsipyle who first had deceived all the rest. He left her there pregnant and forlorn: such guilt condemns him to such torment; and Medea too is avenged.][5]

In Dante's vision Jason has preserved his regal aspect as he walks along in the crowd of the damned who are being scourged. The association of

---

[5] Quoted from the edition and translation of Charles S. Singleton (Princeton, Bollingen Series 80, 1970), XVIII.86–96, pp. 188–9.

ornate speech, deception, and broken promises is familiar, but it is at first puzzling that he is condemned for his betrayal of Hypsipyle, until we realize that tacitly Dante is agreeing that he deserved punishment as well for what he did to Medea. Courage, craft, and deception, here, can be turned in both directions, to good or ill, for Hypsipyle's crafty preservation of her father's life did not protect her against Jason's greater skill in falseness. This comparative sense is parallelled in the double vengeance. Once more Dante's compression assumes both that we know the stories, and that we will be surprised and engaged by his choice of emphasis: not the murderess, but the deceiver, not the woman's revenge, but God's.

From the first Stoic analyses of Medea's dilemma, the emphasis has been upon the problem of love, of her desire for Jason, her jealousy and revenge. For Medeas of antiquity there is more at stake than the marital home: Jason's desertion means she loses all status, all civic rights, all hope for her children; it makes her a banished exile, a non-person. What it is that she remains is a defiant assertion that her being, her identity, is greater than her status as Jason's wife. The stoics' insistence that she would have been happy in her banishment had she only been able to overcome her desire to retain Jason (that is, had she transcended human love), is itself one of those crucial strong readings of a story which sets a narrowing of interpretation for hundreds of years to come. In the different context of the Middle Ages she remains the victim of love, and even writers who argue in her defence insist upon the injury which men typically inflict upon women, desertion.

Medea and the imitations she inspired, above all through Virgil's Dido, initiated a critical model of what could be assumed to make a woman a threat. The power of her intelligence, her sexuality, her cunning, insofar as the three can be disentangled, trap the men who come into contact with her. In a sense he (the double Jason, the deceiving Aeneas, the lying rapist Tereus) becomes her victim more than she has been his; his intelligence is no match for her unscrupulousness. Only Aeneas escapes, and even he escapes only at the price of undying territorial enmity. The hatred between his country and Dido's results from the ingratitude of an exile.

Dynastic rivalry, succession, legitimacy – these became questions which attached themselves to the historical versions of the legends as they were recounted in the Middle Ages. The 'engin' which Medea demonstrates in the pages of Benoît de Ste.-Maure is an insufficient attempt to control power and inheritance; it acknowledges that the cunning will be outwitted by the yet-more-cunning; it illustrates, in the context of the history of Troy, the often-repeated disruptive effects of love (or sexual passion) upon male order. Unlike the apparently private tragedy of the Ovidian heroine, the historical hero's fall entails the destruction of a city and a people. *That* fall comprehends the cycle of history in which great kingdoms come to dust through such contingencies as the pine of Pelion or the uncontrolled passion of women.

BIBLIOGRAPHY

Aarne, A., Stith Thompson, *The Types of the Folk Tale: A Classification and Bibliography* (Helsinki, FF Communications, 184, 1961).

Ahl, F. M., 'Statius *Thebaid*: A Reconsideration', *Aufstieg und Niedergang der römischen Welt* 32.5 (1986), pp. 2803–912.

Allen, Judson Boyce, *The Friar as Critic: Literary Attitudes in the Later Middle Ages* (Nashville, Tennessee, Vanderbilt University Press, 1971).

Anderson, David, *Before the Knight's Tale: Imitation of Classical Epic in Boccaccio's 'Teseida'* (Philadelphia, University of Pennsylvania Press, 1988).

Andrew, S. O., 'The *Wars of Alexander* and the *Destruction of Troy*', *RES* 5 (1929), pp. 267–72.

The Argonautica of Apollonius Rhodius Book III, ed. M. M. Gillies (Cambridge, Cambridge University Press, 1928).

Apollonius Rhodius, *Argonautica Book III*, ed. Richard Hunter (Cambridge, Cambridge University Press, 1989).

———, *Jason and the Golden Fleece (The Argonautica)*, trans. Richard Hunter (Oxford, Clarendon Press, 1993).

Armstrong, C. A. J., 'Verses by Jean Miélot on Edward IV and Richard Earl of Warwick', *Medieum Aevum* 8 (1939), pp. 193–7.

———, *England, France, and Burgundy in the Fifteenth Century* (London, Hambledon Press, 1983).

Artaud, Antonin, *Oeuvres Completes*, III (Paris, Gallimard, 1961).

Auerbach, Eric, *Scenes from the Drama of European Literature* (New York, Meridian, 1959).

Augustine, *City of God* III.ii., ed. G. McCracken *et al.* (London, Loeb, 1957–72).

Backmann, G. A., *Trojaroman und Normanchronik: Die Identität der beiden Benoît und die Chronologie ihrer Werke* (Munich, Max Hueber Verlag, 1965).

Bacon, Janet Ruth, *The Voyage of the Argonauts* (London, Methuen, 1925).

Baldwin, Anna, 'From the *Clerk's Tale* to *The Winter's Tale*', in *Chaucer Traditions*, ed. Ruth Morse and B. A. Windeatt (Cambridge, Cambridge University Press, 1990), pp. 199–212.

Barkan, Leonard, *The Gods Made Flesh: Metamorphosis and the Pursuit of Paganism* (New Haven and London, Yale University Press, 1986).

Barth, R., *Guido de Columna* (Leipzig, Ferber and Seydel, 1877).

Bate, Jonathan, *Shakespeare and Ovid* (Oxford, Clarendon Press, 1993).

Bayer, Johannes, *Vranometria: omnium asterismorum continens schemata, nova methodo delineata, aereis laminis expresa* (Ulm, Sumptibus Iohannis Gorlini, 1661).

Benjamin, Walter, *Origins of German Tragic Drama*, trans. John Osborne (London, New Left Books, 1977).

Bennett, J. A. W., 'Caxton and Gower', *The Modern Language Review* 45 (1950), pp. 215–16.

Benoît de Ste.-Maure, ed. A. Joly, *Benoît de Sainte-More et le Roman de Troie*, in *Mémoires de la Société des antiquaires de Normandie* 27 (1869–70).

Le Roman de Troie en prose (version du Cod. Bodmer 147), ed. Vielliard, Françoise (Geneva, Fondation Martin Bodmer, 1979).

Le Roman de Troie en prose, ed. E. Faral and L. Constans (Paris, Champion, 1922).

Benson, C. David, *The History of Troy in Middle English Literature* (Cambridge, D. S. Brewer, 1980).

Benson, Pamela, *The Invention of the Renaissance Woman: The Challenge of Female Independence in the Literature and Thought of Italy and England* (University Park, Pennsylvania, Pennsylvania State University Press, 1993).

Beye, Charles Rowan, 'Jason as Love-Hero in Apollonios' *Argonautika*', *Greek, Roman, and Byzantine Studies* 10 (1969), pp. 31–55.

———, *Epic and Romance in the 'Argonautica' of Apollonius* (Carbondale, Southern Illinois University Press, 1982)

———, *The Iliad, the Odyssey, and the Epic Tradition* (London, 1968).

N. F. Blake, *Caxton and his World* (London, André Deutsch, 1969).

———, *William Caxton and English Literary Culture* (London, Hambledon Press, 1991)

Blanchard, Joël, 'Compilation et légitimation au XVe siècle', *Poétique* 74 (1988), pp. 139–157.

———, 'L'Entrée du poète dans le champ politique au XVe siècle', *Annales ESC* 41 (1986), pp. 43–61.

Bloomfield, Morton W., 'A Grammatical Approach to Personification Allegory', in *Essays and Explorations* (Cambridge, Mass., Harvard University Press, 1970), pp. 242–60.

———, *Metaphoric Worlds: Conceptions of a Romantic Nature* (New Haven and London, Yale University Press, 1988).

———, *Allegory, Myth, and Symbol* (Cambridge, Mass., Harvard University Press, 1981).

Blumenfeld-Kosinski, Renate, 'Verse and Prose in the *Histoire ancienne jusqu'à César* (in BN f. 20125)', *Zeitschrift fur Romanische Philologie* 97 (1982), pp. 41–6.

Boccaccio, Giovanni, *Genealogia Deorum Gentilium Libri*, ed. V. Romano, 2 vols (Bari, G. Laterza, 1951).

———, *De Casibus Virorum Illustrium Libri novem*, ed. Pier Giorgio Ricci and Vittorio Zaccaria (Milan, Mondadori, 1983).

———, *De Casibus Virorum Illustrium Libri novem* (Vienna, H. Ziegler, 1544).

———, *De Mulieribus Claris*, ed. J. Zainer (Ulm, 1473).

————, *De Mulieribus Claris*, ed. and trans. Vittorio Zaccaria in *Tutte le opere de Giovanni Boccaccio*, X (Rome, Mondadori, 1967).

————, *Concerning Famous Women*, ed. and trans. G. A. Guarino (London, 1964).

De Mulieribus Claris, Die Mittelenglische Umdichtung von Boccaccios De Claris Mulieribus nebst der lateinischen Vorlage zum ersten Male vollständig herausgegeben, ed. Gustav Schleich (Leipzig, Mayer und Muller, 1924), Palaestra, 144.

Forty-Six Lives Translated from Boccaccio's De Claris Mulieribus, trans. Henry Parker, Lord Morley, ed. H. G. Wright, EETS o.s. 214 (London, 1943).

————, *Boccaccio on Poetry*, ed. and trans. Charles Osgood (Princeton, Princeton University Press, 1930).

————, *Decameron*, ed. V. Branca (Florence, Felice le Monnier, 1960).

Bolgar, R. R., *The Classical Heritage and Its Beneficiaries* (Cambridge, Cambridge University Press, 1954).

Bonnard, Jean, *Les Traductions de la Bible en vers français au moyen âge* (Paris, Imprimérie Nationale, 1884).

Bossuat, A., 'Les Origines troyennes: leur rôle dans la littérature historique au XVe siècle', *Annales de Normandie* 8 (1958), pp. 187–97.

Bouvrie, Synnøve des, *Women in Greek Tragedy: an anthropological approach* (Oslo, Norwegian University Press, 1990).

Boyle, A. J., 'In Nature's Bonds: a Study of Seneca's "Phaedra" ', in *Aufstieg und Niedergang des römischen Welt* (1985), pp. 1284–1347.

————, ed. *The Imperial Muse: Flavian Epicist to Claudian* (Berwick, Victoria, Ramus Essays, 1990).

————, and J. P. Sullivan, eds, *Roman Poets of the Early Empire* (Harmondsworth, Penguin, 1991).

Brownlee, Kevin, 'The Image of History in Christine de Pizan's *Livre de la Mutacion de Fortune*' *Yale French Studies: Contexts: Style and Values in Medieval Art and Literature* (New Haven and London, Yale University Press, 1991), pp. 44–56.

Brownlee, Marina, *The Severed Word: Ovid's Heroides and the Novela Sentimental* (Philadelphia, University of Pennsylvania Press, 1994).

Brunel, J. 'Jason [monokrepis]', *Revue Archéologique*, 6e. série 4 (1934), pp. 34–43.

Brunner, H., ed., *Die deutsche Trojaliteratur des Mittelalters und der Frühen Neuzeit* (Wiesbaden, Reichert, 1990).

Bühler, Curt, 'The *Fasciculus Temporum* and Morgan Manuscript 801' *Speculum* 27 (1952), pp. 178–83.

————, 'Caxton's "History of Jason" ', *Papers of the Bibliographical Society of America* 24 (1940), pp. 254–61.

————, *The Fifteenth-Century Book: the scribes, the printers, the decorators* (Philadelphia, University of Pennsylvania 1960).

Burnett, Anne, 'Medea and the Tragedy of Revenge', *Classical Philology* 67 (1973), 1–24.

Calame, Claude, *Thesee et l'Imaginaire Athenien: légende et culte en Grèce antique* (Lausanne, Payot, 1990).

Calasso, Roberto, *The Marriage of Cadmus and Harmony*, trans. Tim Parks (New York, Knopf, 1993).

Calmette, J., *The Golden Age of Burgundy*, trans. D. Weightman (London, Weidenfeld and Nicolson, 1962; orig. *Les Grands ducs de Bourgogne*, Paris, Albin Michel, 1949).

The Cambridge History of Classical Literature, ed. P. E. Easterling and B. M. W. Knox (Cambridge, Cambridge University Press, 1985).

Campbell, Mary B., *The Witness and the Otherworld: Exotic European Travel Writing: 400–1600* (Ithaca, Cornell University Press, 1988).

Campbell, P. G. C., *L'Épitre d'Othéa: Étude sur les sources de Christine de Pisan* (Paris, Champion, 1924).

Carocci, Renata, *Les heroïdes dans la seconde moitié du XVIIIe siècle 1758–1788* (Paris, Nizet, 1988).

Castro Leiva, Luis, 'The Idea of the Fact in English Law' (Cambridge University, unpubl. Ph.D. dissertation, 1976).

Champion, Pierre, *Histoire Poétique du quinzième siècle* (Paris, Champion, 1923).

Chastellain, Georges, *Oeuvres*, ed. Kervyn de Lettenhove (Brussels, F. Heussner, 1863–6).

Chance, Jane, *Medieval Mythography: from Roman North Africa to the School of Chartres, A.D. 433–1177* (Gainesville, Florida, University of Florida Press, 1994).

Chaucer, Geoffrey, *Complete Works*, ed. L. D. Benson (Cambridge, Mass. and Oxford, 1987).

Chesney, Kathleen, 'A neglected prose version of the *Roman de Troie*', *Medium Aevum* 11 (1942), pp. 46–67.

Raffaele Chiantera, *Guido delle Colonne: poeta e storico latino de sec. XIII e il problema della lingua della nostra primitiva lirica d'arte* (Naples, Casa Editrice 'Federico & Andria' de P. Federico 1956).

Chrétien de Troyes, *Philomena: conte raconté d'après Ovide par Chrétien de Troyes*, ed. C. de Boer (Paris, Paul Geuthner, 1909).

Christine de Pizan, *Oeuvres Poétique de Christine de Pisan*, ed. M. Roy (Paris, 1891).

———, *Classical Mythology in the Works of Christine de Pisan, with an edition of* L'Epistre Othea *from the manuscript Harley 4431*, ed. H. D. Loukopoulos (unpublished Ph.D., Wayne State University, 1977).

The Epistle of Othea: translated from the French Text of Christine de Pisan, trans. Stephen Scrope, ed. C. F. Buhler, EETS o.s. 264 (London, 1970).

———, *Le Livre de la Cité des Dames*, ed. Maureen Cheney Curnow (Ann Arbor, Michigan, University Microfilms, 1978).

————, *Le Livre de la Cité des Dames* (Paris, Stock, 1986).

————, *The Book of the City of Ladies*, trans. Earl Jeffrey Richards (New York, Persea, 1982).

————, *Les Cent Histoires de Troye* (Paris, Philippe Pigouchet, 1490)

————, *Le Livre de la Mutacion de Fortune*, ed. Suzanne Solente, Société des Anciens Textes Français (Paris, Pinard, 1959–64).

Clauss, James J., *The Best of the Argonauts: The Redefinition of the Epic Hero in Book 1 of Apollonius's* Argonautica (Berkeley, University of California Press, 1993).

Clogan, P. M., 'Chaucer and the *Thebaid*' in *Studies in Philology* 61 (1964), pp. 599–615.

————, *The Medieval Achilleid of Statius* (Leiden, Brill, 1968).

Coleman, Janet, *Ancient and Medieval Memories: studies in the reconstruction of the past* (Cambridge, Cambridge University Press, 1992).

The Complaynt of Scotlande, ed. J. A. H. Murray, EETS e.s. 17–18 (London, 1872–3).

Conacher, D. J., *Euripidean Drama: Myth, Theme, and Structure* (Toronto, University of Toronto Press, 1967).

Constable, Giles, 'Forgery and Plagiarism in the Middle Ages', *Archiv für Diplomatik* 29 (1983) pp. 1–41.

————, 'Forged Letters in the Middle Ages', *Fälschungen im Mittelalter* (Hannover, 1988–90) V, pp. 11–37.

Constans, Léopold, 'Une traduction française des *Heroïdes* d'Ovide au XIIIe siècle', *Romania* 43 (1914), pp. 177–98.

Conte, Gian Biagio, *Genres and Readers: Lucretius, Love Elegy, Pliny's Encyclopedia*, trans. Glenn W. Most (Baltimore, Johns Hopkins University Press, 1994).

Cooper, Helen, 'Gender and Personification in *Piers Plowman*', *Yearbook of Langland Studies* 5 (1991), pp. 31–48.

————, 'Romance After 1400', in *The Cambridge History of Medieval Literature*, ed. David Wallace (Cambridge, Cambridge University Press, 1996).

Costa, C. D. N. ed., *Seneca* (London, Routledge and Kegan Paul, 1974).

Courtney, E., 'On Valerius Flaccus', *The Classical Review* n.s. 11 (1961), pp. 106–7.

Dares and Dictys, *De Excidio Troiae Historia*, ed. Ferdinand Meister (Leipzig, Teubner, 1873).

————, trans. R. M. Frazer, *The Trojan War* (Bloomington, Indiana, Indiana University Press, 1966).

Davis, Peter J., *Shifting Song: the Chorus in Seneca's Tragedies* (Hildesheim and New York, Olms-Weidmann, 1993).

Day, Robert Adams, *Told in Letters: Epistolary Fiction Before Richardson* (Ann Arbor, University of Michigan Press, 1966).

Débat des hérauts d'armes de France et d'Angleterre, ed. L. Pannier and P. Meyer (Paris, Firmin Didot et Cie., 1877).

DeJean, Joan, *Fictions of Sappho, 1546–1937* (Chicago, Chicago University Press, 1989).

———, *Tender Geographies* (New York, Oxford and Columbia University Presses, 1991).

Delaissé, L. M. J., *La Miniature Flamande* (Brussels, 1959).

Delany, Sheila, *The Naked Text: Chaucer and the Legend of Good Women* (Berkeley, University of California Press, 1994).

Démats, Paule, *Fabula: trois études de mythographie antique et médiévale* (Geneva, Droz, 1973).

Derrida, Jacques, 'Plato's Pharmacy', in *Dissemination*, trans. Barbara Johnson (London, Athlone Press, 1981).

Desbordes, Françoise, *Argonautica: Trois études sur l'imitation dans la littérature antique* (Brussels, Latomus, 1969).

Desmond, Marilynn, *Reading Dido: Gender, Textuality and the Medieval 'Aeneid'* (Minneapolis, University of Minnesota Press, 1995).

Detienne, Marcel and Jean-Pierre Vernant, *Les Ruses de l'intelligence* (Paris, Flammarion, 1974); translated as *Cunning Intelligence in Greek Culture and Society*, J. Lloyd (Chicago, University of Chicago Press, 1991; orig. Brighton, Harvester, 1978).

Dibdin, Thomas Frognall, *Bibliotheca Spenceriana* (London, Longman, Hurst, Rees & Co., 1815).

Dogaer, G., and M. Debae, *La Librairie de Philippe le Bon: exposition organisëe à l'occasion du 500e anniversaire de la mort du duc* (Brussels, 1967).

Donaldson, Ian, *The Rapes of Lucretia: a Myth and its Transformations* (Oxford, Clarendon Press, 1982).

Doutrepont, Georges, *Inventaire de la 'librairie' de Philippe le Bon (1420)* (Brussels, Kiessling et Cie., 1906).

———, 'Jason et Gédéon, patrons de la Toison d'Or', in *Mélanges Godefroid Kurth* (Paris and Liége, Champion, 1908).

———, *La Littérature française à la cour de Bourgogne* (Paris, Champion, 1909).

———, *Les Mises en proses des épopées et des romans chevaleresques du XIVe au XVIe siècle* (Brussels, Palais des Académies, 1939).

Drews, R., 'The Earliest Greek Settlements on the Black Sea', *The Journal of Hellenic Studies* 96 (1976), pp. 18–31.

Dronke, Peter, *Fabula: Explorations into the Uses of Myth in Medieval Platonism* (Leiden, Brill, 1974).

DuBois, Page, *Centaurs and Amazons: women and the prehistory of the great chain of being* (Ann Arbor, University of Michigan Press, 1984).

Duranti, A., 'Le novelle di Dioneo', *Studi di filologia e critica offerti dagli allieri a Lanfranco Caretti*, I (Rome, Salerno Editrice, 1985), pp. 1–38.

Durrieu, P., 'Notes sur quelques manuscrits français conservés dans des bibliothèques d'Allemagne', *BEC* 53 (1892).

Dyck, A. R., 'On the Way from Colchis to Corinth: Medea in Book 4 of the "Argonautica" ', *Hermes* 117 (1989), pp. 455–70.

Ebin, Lois A., *John Lydgate* (Boston, Twayne, 1985).

Eco, Umberto, 'Tipologia della falsificazione', *Fälschungen im Mittelalter* (Hannover, 1988–90) I, pp. 69–82.

Edwards A. S. G., ed., *Middle English Prose: a critical guide to major authors and genres* (New Brunswick, Rutgers University Press, 1984).

Ehrhart, Margaret, *The Judgment of the Trojan Prince Paris in Medieval Literature* (Philadelphia, University of Pennsylvania Press, 1987).

Engels, Joseph, *Etudes sur l'Ovide Moralisé* (Groningen, 1943).

———, 'Berchoriana: I', *Vivarium* 2 (1964), pp. 62–124.

———, 'L'Edition critique de l'*Ovidius Moralizatus* de Bersuire' *Vivarium* 9 (1971), pp. 19–24,

———, 'Les Commentaires d'Ovide au XVIe siècle', *Vivarium* 12 (1974), pp. 3–13.

Euripides, *Medea*, ed. Denys Page (Oxford, Clarendon Press, 1938).

———, *Hypsipyle*, ed. G. W. Bond (Oxford, Oxford University Press, 1969).

———, *Hypsipyle: Text and Annotation based on a Re-examination of the Papyri*, ed. W. E. H. Cockle (Rome, Anteneo, 1987).

Farnham, Willard, *The Medieval Heritage of Elizabethan Tragedy* (Oxford, Blackwell, 1956).

Fineman, Joel, *The Subjectivity Effect in Western Literary Tradition: Essays Towards the Release of Shakespeare's Will* (Cambridge, Mass., MIT Press, 1991).

Finley, M. I., 'Myth, Memory, and History', *History and Theory* 4 (1964–5), pp. 281–302.

———, *The Use and Abuse of History* (London, Hogarth Press, 1986).

Flacelière, R., *Thésée: Images et récits* (Paris, Boccard, 1958).

Fletcher, Angus, *Allegory: the Theory of a Symbolic Mode* (Ithaca, Cornell University Press, 1964).

Frank, Robert Worth, Jr., *Chaucer and the Legend of Good Women* (Cambridge, Mass., 1972).

Fowler, K., *The Age of Plantagenet and Valois: the struggle for supremacy 1328–1498* (London, Elek, 1967).

Fränkel, H., *Ovid: A Poet Between Two Worlds* (Berkely and Los Angeles, 1969).

Frappier, Jean, 'Remarques sur la peinture de la vie et des héros antiques dans la littérature française du XIIe au XIIIe siècle', in *L'Humanisme médiéval dans les littératures romanes du XIIe au XIVe siècle*, ed. A. Fourrier (Paris, Klincksieck, 1964), pp. 13–51.

Frécaut, J. M., *L'Esprit et l'humour chez Ovide* (Grenoble, 1972).

Friedman, John Block, *Orpheus in the Middle Ages* (Cambridge, Mass., Harvard University Press, 1970).

Frye, Northrop, 'Allegory', *Princeton Encyclopedia of Poetry and Poetics*, ed. Alex Preminger (Princeton, Princeton University Press, 1974), pp. 12–15.

————, *The Great Code: The Bible and Literature* (London, Routledge and Kegan Paul, 1982).

Fulgentius, *Opera*, ed. Rudolf Helm (Leipzig, Teubner, 1898).

Fulgentius the Mythographer, ed. Leslie George Whitbread (Ohio, Ohio State University Press, 1971).

Fyfe, Helen, 'An Analysis of Seneca's *Medea*', *Ramus* 12 (1983), pp. 73–93.

Fyler, John, *Chaucer and Ovid* (New Haven and London, Yale University Press, 1979).

Gaggadis-Robin, Vassiliki, *Jason et Médée sur les sarcophages d'époque impériale* (Rome, Ecole française de Rome, 1994).

Gardner, John, *Jason and Medeia* (New York, Knopf, 1973).

Garner, Richard, *From Homer to Greek Tragedy: The Art of Allusion in Greek Poetry* (London, Routledge, 1990), pp. 90–7.

Gathercole, P. M., 'The Manuscripts of Laurent de Premierfait's Works', *Modern Language Quarterly* 20 (1958), pp. 262–70.

————, 'Lydgate's "Fall of Princes" and the French Version of Boccaccio's "De Casibus" ', in *Miscellanea di Studi e ricerche sul quattrocento francese*, ed. Franco Simone (Turin, Giappichelli Editore, 1966), pp. 167–78.

Genet, J.-Ph., 'Droit et histoire en Angleterre: la préhistoire de la "revolution historique" ', in *L'Historiographie en occident du Ve au XVe siècle, Annales de Bretagne et des Pays de l'Ouest* 87 (1980), pp. 319–66.

Ghisalberti, Fausto, 'Medieval Biographies of Ovid', in *Journal of the Warburg and Courtauld Institutes* 9 (1946), 10–59.

————, 'L'"Ovidius moralizatus" de Pierre Bersuire' *Studi romanzi* 23 (1933), pp. 5–136.

Gilson, E., 'Poésie et verité dans la "Genealogia" de Boccace', *Studi sul Boccaccio* 2 (1964), pp. 253–82.

Girard, René, *La Violence et le Sacré* (Paris, Pluriel, 1972).

Goffart, Walter, *Narrators of Barbarian History* (Princeton, Princeton University Press, 1987).

Goldhill, Simon, *Reading Greek Tragedy* (Cambridge, Cambridge University Press, 1986)

————, *The Poet's Voice: Essays on Poetics and Greek Literature* (Cambridge, 1991).

————, and Robin Osborne, *Art and Text in Ancient Greek Culture* (Cambridge, Cambridge University Press, 1994).

Golenistcheff-Koutouzoff, E., *L'Histoire de Griseldis en France du XIVe au XVe siècle* (Paris, 1933; repr. Geneva, Droz, 1975).

Götting, Martin, *Hypsipyle in der Thebais des Statius* (Wiesbaden, Sändig, 1969).

Gower, John, *Confessio Amantis*, ed. G. C. Macauley, EETS. e.s. 81, 82 (London, 1900–1).

————, ed. J.A.W. Bennett, *Selections from John Gower* (Oxford, Clarendon Press, 1960).

Oton de Grandson sa vie et ses poésies, ed. A. Piaget (Lausanne, 1941).

Graves, Robert, *The Golden Fleece* (London, Cassell and Co. Ltd, 1944).

Greene, Robert, *The Tale of Troy*, in *The Dramatic and Poetical Works of Robert Greene and George Peele*, ed. A. Dyce (London, 1861).

Greenhut, Deborah, *Feminine Rhetorical Culture: Tudor Adaptations of Ovid's Heroïdes* (New York, Peter Lang Verlag, 1988).

Griffin, N. E., 'Un-Homeric Elements in the Medieval Story of Troy', *Journal of English and Germanic Philology* 7 (1907–8), pp. 32–52.

————, *Dares and Dictys: An Introduction to the Study of Medieval Versions of the History of Troy* (Baltimore, J. H. Furst, Co., 1907).

Grimal, Pierre, *The Dictionary of Classical Mythology*, trans. A. R. Maxwell-Hyslop (Oxford, Blackwell, 1987; orig. Paris, Presses Universitaires de France, 1951).

Guenée, Bernard, *Histoire et culture historique dans l'Occident médiévale* (Paris, 1980).

————, *Politique et Histoire au Moyen Age: recueil d'articles sur l'historiographie médiévale (1956–1981)* (Paris, Publications de la Sorbonne, 1981).

Guido delle Colonne, *Historia Destructionis Troiae*, ed. N. E. Griffin (Cambridge, Mass., The Medieval Academy of America, 1936).

Guido delle Colonne, *Historia Destructionis Troiae*, trans. Mary Elizabeth Meek (Bloomington, Indiana, Indiana University Press, 1974).

The Seege or Bataille of Troy, ed. M. E. Barnicle EETS o.s. no. 172 (London, 1927).

The 'Gest Hystoriale' of the Destruction of Troy: an alliterative romance translated from Guido delle Colonne's 'Hystoria Troiana', ed. G. A. Panton and D. Donaldson, EETS o.s. 39, 56 (London, 1869, 1874).

The Laud Troy Book, ed. J. E. Wulfing, EETS o.s. 121, 122 (London, 1902–3).

Hall, Edith, *Inventing the Barbarians* (Oxford, Clarendon, 1989).

N. G. L. Hammond, ed., *Atlas of the Greek and Roman World* (Park Ridge, NJ, 1981).

Hash, R. W., *The Jason Theme in Greek and Roman Literature* (Vanderbilt University unpublished Ph.D., 1969).

Hatzichronoglou, Lena, 'Euripides' *Medea*: Woman or Fiend', in *Woman's Power, Man's Game: Essays on Classical Antiquity in Honor of Joy K. King* (Waukonda, Illinois, Bolchazy-Carducci, 1993), pp. 178–93.

Henderson, John, 'Poetic Technique and Rhetorical Amplification: Seneca *Medea* 579–669', *Ramus* 12 (1983), pp. 94–113.

Herodotus, ed. and trans. A. D. Goodley (London, Loeb Classical Library, 1921).

Hesiod, *Works and Days* 992–1002, *Theogony*, ed. M. L. West (Oxford, Clarendon Press, 1966).

Hexter, Ralph, *Ovid and Medieval Schooling: Studies in Medieval School Commentaries on Ovid's 'Ars Amatoria', 'Epistuale ex Ponto', and 'Epistulae*

Heroidum' (Munich, Münchener Beiträge zur Mediävistik und Renaissance-Forschung, 38, 1986).

Homer, *Iliad*, trans. Robert Fitzgerald (New York, Doubleday, 1961).

——, *The Iliad*, trans. Martin Hammond (Harmondsworth, Penguin, 1987).

Hunter, Richard, *The Argonautica of Apollonius: literary studies* (Cambridge, CUP, 1993)

Huxley, G. L., *Greek Epic Poetry from Eumelos to Panyassis* (London, Faber and Faber, 1969)

Higden, Ralph, *The Universal Chronical of Ranulph Higden*, ed. John Taylor (Oxford, Clarendon Press, 1966).

Hindman, Sandra L., *Christine de Pizan's 'Epistre Othéa': Painting and Politics at the Court of Charles VI* (Toronto, Pontifical Institute of Mediaeval Studies, 1986).

Huchet, Jean-Charles, *Le Roman Médiéval* (Paris, Presses Universitaires de France, 1984).

Hyginus, *Fabulae*, ed. H. J. Rose (Leiden, 1934)

Itinerarium Peregrinorum et Gesta Regis Ricardi, ed. William Stubbs (London, Rolls Series, 1864).

Jacobson, Howard, *Ovid's Heroïdes* (Princeton, Princeton University Press, 1974).

Jaeger, C. Stephen, *The Origins of Courtliness: Civilizing Trends and the Formation of Courtly Ideals 939–1210* (Philadelphia, University of Pennsylvania Press, 1985).

Jean de Flixecourt, *Li Rommans de Troies: a translation by Jean de Flixecourt, 1262*, ed. G. Hall (University of London unpub. Ph.D. dissertation, 1951).

Jocelyn, H. D., *The Tragedies of Ennius* (Cambridge, Cambridge University Press, 1967).

Johnston, A. *Enchanted Ground* (London, Athlone Press, 1964).

Jones, Rosemarie, *The Theme of Love in the Romans d'Antiquité* (London, 1972).

Joseph of Exeter, *De Excidio Troiae Historia*, ed. Ferdinand Meister (Berlin, Teubner, 1873).

——, 'Excidium Troiae', ed. E. Bagby Atwood and V. K. Whitaker (Cambridge, Mass., Medieval Academy of America, 1944).

Thabridgment of the Histories of Trogus Pompeius, collected by Iustine, trans. Arthur Goldyng (London, Thomas Marshe, 1564).

Ivstini, M. Ivniani, *Epitoma Historiarvm Philippicarum Pompei Trogi*, ed. Otto Seel (Stuttgart, Teubner, 1972).

Justin, Cornelius Nepos, and Eutropius, trans. J. S. Watson (London, 1833).

Kekewich, M., 'Edward IV, William Caxton, and Literary Patronage in England' *The Modern Language Review* 66 (1971), 481–7.

Kelly, Donald, *Foundations of Modern Historical Scholarship* (New York, Columbia University Press, 1970).

Kelly, Douglas, *Medieval Imagination: Rhetoric and the Art of Courtly Love* (Madison, University of Wisconsin Press, 1978).

Kelly, H. A., *Love and Marriage in the Age of Chaucer* (Ithaca and London, Cornell University Press, 1975).

Kelly, H. A., *Ideas and Forms of Tragedy: from Aristotle to the Middle Ages* (Cambridge, Cambridge University Press, 1993).

Kempe, Dorothy, 'A Middle English Tale of Troy', *Englische Studien* 29 (1901), pp. 1–26.

Kiser, Lisa, *Telling Classical Tales: Chaucer and the Legend of Good Women* (Ithaca and London, Cornell University Press, 1983).

Knox, B. M. W., 'The Medea of Euripides' *Word and Action: Essays on the Ancient Theatre* (Baltimore and London, Johns Hopkins University Press, 1979).

Kolve, V. A., 'The Annunciation of Christine: Authorial Empowerment in *The Book of the City of Ladies*', in *Iconography at the Crossroads*, ed. Brendan Cassidy (Princeton, Princeton University Press for the Department of Art and Archaeology, 1993).

Konstan, David, 'Neoteric Epic: Catullus 64', in *Roman Epic*, ed. A. J. Boyle (London, Routledge, 1993).

Krill, Richard M., 'Allusions in Seneca's Medea' *The Classical Journal* 68 (1992–3), pp. 199–204.

Laborde, L. E. S. J. de, *Les Ducs de Bourgogne: Etudes sur les lettres, les arts et l'industrie pendant le XVe siècle et plus particulièrement dans les pays-bas et le duché de Bourgogne* (Paris, 1849–52).

Lacaze, Yvon, 'Le Rôle des traditions dans la genèse d'un sentiment national au XVe siècle: La Bourgogne de Philippe le Bon', *Bibliothèque de l'Ecoles des Chartes*, 129 (1971), 303–85.

Laidlaw, J. C., *The Poetical Works of Alain Chartier* (Cambridge, Cambridge University Press, 1974).

———, 'Christine de Pizan, the Earl of Salisbury, and Henry IV' *French Studies* 36 (1982), pp. 129–43;

———, 'Christine de Pizan: an Author's Progress', *MLR* 78 (1983), pp. 532–50.

———, 'Christine de Pizan: a Publisher's Progress', *MLR* 82 (1987), pp. 37–75.

———, 'L'unité des "Cent Balades" ', in *The City of Scholars: New Approaches to Christine de Pizan*, ed. Margarete Zimmermann and Dina De Rentis (New York and Berlin, Walter de Gruyter, 1994), pp. 97–106.

Laing, D., *Facsimiles of Designs from Engraved Copperplates Illustrating Le Liure de la Ruyne des Nobles Hommes et Femmes par Jehan Bocace de Certald: Imprimé à Bruges par Colard Mansion, Annon M.cccc.lxxvi* (Edinburgh, privately, 1878).

Laistner, M. L. W., *Thought and Letters in Western Europe* (2nd edn London, Methuen, 1957).

Lamberton, Robert, *Homer the Theologian: Neoplatonist Allegorical Reading and the Growth of the Epic Tradition* (Berkeley, University of California Press, 1986).

Laurent de Premierfait, *Des Cas des Nobles Hommes et Femmes*, ed. P. M. Gathercole, *Studies in Romance Language and Literature*, 74 (Chapel Hill, University of North Carolina Press, 1968).

Lawall, Gilbert, 'Seneca's Medea: the elusive triumph of civilization', in *Arktouros: Hellenic Studies in Honour of Bernard Knox on the Occasion of his 65th Birthday*, ed. G. W. Bowersock, W. Burkert, and M. C. J. Putnam (Berlin and New York, Walter De Gruyter, 1979), pp. 419–26.

Le Fèvre de Ressons, Jean, *Les Lamentations de Matheolus et le Livre de Leesce (poèmes français du XIVe siècle)*, ed. A. G. Van Hamel (Paris, BEC, 1905).

Lefèvre, Raoul, *The History of Jason translated from the French of Raoul Le Fevre*, ed. J. Munro, EETS e.s. 111 (London, 1913).

——, *L'Histoire de Jason*, ed. Gert Pinkernell (Frankfurt, Athenäum Verlag, 1971).

——, *Le Recoeil des Histoires de Troyes: edition critique*, ed. Marc Aeschbach (Frankfurt and Berne, Peter Lang Verlag, European University Studies, section 13; Langue et Littérature françaises, 120, 1987).

——, *The Recuyell of the Historyes of Troye. Written in French by Raoul Lefèvre. Translated and Printed by William Caxton (About A.D. 1474)*, ed. H. O. Sommer (London, David Nutt, 1894).

——, trans. William Caxton, *Recuyell of the Historyes of Troye*, ed. F. Halliday Sparling (London, Kelmscott Press, 1892).

Lefkowitz, Mary, *Women in Greece and Rome* (Toronto, Samuel-Stevens, 1977).

——, *Heroines and Hysterics* (London, Duckworth, 1981).

——, *Women in Greek Myth* (Baltimore, Johns Hopkins University Press, 1986).

Le Goff, Jacques, *The Medieval Imagination*, trans. Arthur Goldhammer (Chicago and London, University of Chicago Press, 1988; orig. 1985).

——, 'Naissance du roman français' in *La Nouvelle Revue Française*, 238 (1972), pp. 163–73.

Lemaire, N. E., ed., *Poetae Latini Minores* IV (Paris, Teubner, 1825)

Levine, Joseph M., *Humanism and History: Origins of Modern English Historiography* (Ithaca, Cornell University Press, 1987).

Lewis, C. S., 'The Fifteenth-Century Heroic Line', *Essays and Studies* 24 (1938), pp. 28–41.

Lumiansky, R. M., 'Dares' Historia and Dictys' Ephemeris: A Critical comment', in *Studies in Language, Literature, and Culture in the Middle Ages and Later*, ed. E. Bagby Atwood and A. A. Hill (Austin, University of Texas Press, 1969), pp. 200–9.

——, 'The Story of Troilus and Briseida according to Benoît and Guido', *Speculum* 29 (1954).

————, 'Structural Unity in Benoît's *Roman de Troie*' *Romania* 79 (1958), pp. 410–24.

Lydgate, John, *Lydgate's Fall of Princes*, ed. Henry Bergen, EETS e.s. 121–4 (London, 1924–7).

————, *Lydgate's Troy Book*, ed. Henry Bergen, EETS e.s. 97, 103, 106, 126 (London, 1906–33).

McLeod, Glenda K., ed. *The Reception of Christine de Pizan from the Fifteenth through the Nineteenth Centuries: Visitors to the City* (Lewiston, Edwin Mellen, 1991).

Machaut, Guillaume de, *Oeuvres*, E. Hoepffner (Paris, Firmin-Didot et Cie., 1908).

Macrobius, *I Saturnali di Macrobio Teodosio*, ed. Nino Marinone (Turin, 1967).

————, *Saturnalia*, trans. P. Vaughan Davies (London, 1969).

Malkaraume, Jean, *La Bible de Jehan Malkaraume (Ms Paris, Bibl. Nat. F. Fr. 903) (XIIIe/XIVe Siècle)*, ed. J. R. Smeets (Amsterdam, Van Gorcum Assen, 1977–8).

Mallinger, Léon, *Médée: étude de littérature comparée* (Louvain, 1897).

Mann, Jill, *Chaucer and Medieval Estates Satire* (Cambridge, Cambridge University Press, 1973).

————, *Chaucer* (Feminist Readings, New York and London, Harvester Wheatsheaf, 1991).

Manuel, Frank, *Isaac Newton Historian* (Cambridge, Mass., Belknap Press of Harvard University, 1963)

Enée et Didon: Naissance, fonctionnement et survie d'un mythe, ed. René Martin (Paris, CNRS, 1990).

Matthew of Paris, *Chronica Majora*, ed. H. R. Luard (London, Rolls Series, 1872).

Meale, Carol, 'Legends of Good Women in the European Middle Ages' *Archiv für das Studium der neuren Sprache und Literaturen* 144 (1992), pp. 55–70.

Merkle, Stefan, *Die Ephemeris belli Troiani des Diktys von Kreta*, Studien zur Klassichen Philologie, 44 (Frankfurt am Main, P. Lang Verlag, 1989).

Meyer, Paul, 'Les premières compilations française d'histoire ancienne', *Romania* 14 (1885), pp. 1–81.

Mezzadri, Bernard 'Jason ou le retour du pécheur: esquisse de mythologie argonautique', *Revue de l'Histoire des Religions* 208 (1991), pp. 273–301.

Mimoso-Ruiz, Duarte, *Médée Antique et Moderne: Aspects rituels et socio-politiques d'un mythe* (Paris, Ophrys, 1982).

————, 'Medea', *Companion to Literary Myths, Heroes, and Archetypes*, ed. Pierre Brunel, trans. W. Allatson, J. Hayward, and T. Selous (London and N.Y., 1992; orig. Paris, Rocher, 1988), pp. 769–78.

Alastair Minnis, *Medieval Theory of Authorship* (2nd ed., Philadelphia, University of Pennsylania Press, 1988).

————, *Chaucer and Pagan Antiquity* (Cambridge, D. S. Brewer, 1982).

———, 'John Gower *Sapiens* in Ethics and Politics', in *John Gower's Confessio Amantis: a critical anthology*, ed. Peter Nicholson (Cambridge, D. S. Brewer, 1991), pp. 158–80.

———, A.B. Scott, eds., with the assistance of David Wallace, *Medieval Literary Theory and Criticism c.1100–c.1375: The Commentary Tradition* (Oxford, 2nd edn 1991).

Miola, Robert, *Shakespeare and Classical Tragedy: the Influence of Seneca* (Cambridge, Cambridge University Press, 1992).

Moers, Ellen, *Literary Women* (London, L. H. Allen and Co., 1977).

Momigliano, Arnaldo, 'The Place of Herodotus in the History of Historiography', in *Studies in Historiography* (New York, Harper and Row, 1966), pp. 127–42.

———, *The Classical Foundations of Modern Historiography* (Berkeley, University of California Press, 1990).

Morabito, A., 'La Diffusione della storia di Griselda dal XIV al XX secolo', *Studi sul Boccaccio* 17 (1988), pp. 237–85.

Morris, William, *The Life and Death of Jason* (London, Kelmscott Press, 1895).

Morse, Ruth, 'Historical Fiction in Fifteenth Century Burgundy', *MLR* 75 (1980) 48–64.

———, 'Problems of Early Fiction: Raoul Lefèvre's *Histoire de Jason*', *MLR* 78 (1983) 34–45.

'Medieval Biography: History as a Branch of Fiction' *MLR* 80 (1985) 257–68.

———, *Truth and Convention in the Middle Ages: Rhetoric, Reality, and Representation* (Cambridge, Cambridge University Press, 1991).

———, 'Absolute Tragedy: Allusions and Avoidances' *Poetica* 38 (1993), 1–17.

———, 'Telling the Truth with Authority: from Richard II to *Richard II*', *Common Knowledge* 4 (1995) xx–yy.

Moss, Ann, *Poetry and Fable* (Cambridge, Cambridge University Press, 1984).

Nolan, Barbara, *The Gothic Visionary Perspective* (Princeton, Princeton University Press, 1977).

———, *Chaucer and the Tradition of the* Roman Antique (Cambridge, Cambridge University Press, 1992).

Norman, Andrew P., 'Telling it Like it Was: Historical Narratives in their Own Terms', *History and Theory* 30 (1991), 119–35.

Nussbaum, Martha, *The Therapy of Desire: Theory and Practice in Hellenistic Ethics* (Princeton, Princeton University Press, 1994).

Olender, Maurice, *Les Langues du Paradis: Aryens et Sémites: un couple providentiel* (Paris, Gallimard-Le Seuil, 1989).

Orosius, Paulus, *The Seven Books of History Against the Pagans*, trans. Roy J. Deferrari (Washington, DC, Catholic University of America Press, The Church Fathers, 1964).

Brooks Otis, *Ovid as an Epic Poet* (Cambridge, 2nd edn, 1970).

Ovid, *Heroides and Amores*, ed. Grant Showerman, revised G. P. Goold (Cambridge, Mass., Loeb, 1977; orig. 1914).

Ovidius Naso, *Heroïdes*, ed. Arthur Palmer (Hildesheim, 1967; orig. Oxford, Clarendon Press, 1898).

Ovid, ed. F. J. Miller (Cambridge, Mass. and London, Loeb, 1916).

P. Ovidii Nasonis, *Metamorophoses*, ed. W. S. Anderson (Leipzig, Teubner, 1972).

Ovid, *Metamorphoses*, trans. Mary M. Innes (Harmondsworth, Penguin, 1955).

Ovide en France dans la Renaissance (Toulouse, Publications de l'Université de Toulouse, 1981).

Ovide Moralisé: poème du commencement du quatorzième siècle publié d'après tous les manuscrits connus, ed. C. de Boer, Martina G. de Boer, and Jeannette Th. M. Van 'T Sant, in *Verhandelingen der Koninklijke Akademie van Watenschappen* 15, 21, 30, 37, 43 (Amsterdam, 1915–38).

Ovid, *La Bible des Poetes*, compiled by Colard Mansion (Paris, 1484, BL IC. 49428), reprinted Antoine Vérard, etc.

Ovid, *Les Metamorphoses d'Ovide: traduites en prose françoise, et de nouueau soigneusement reueuës, corrigees en infinis endroits, et enrichies de figure à chacune fable. avec XV. discours contenans l'explication morale et historique*, ed. N. Renouard (Paris, Langelier, 1618).

The Metamorphoses of Ovid: translated by William Caxton 1480 (New York, George Braziller in connection with Magdalene College, Cambridge, 1968).

———, *Six Books of Metamorphoses*, trans. William Caxton, ed. George Hibbert (London, Roxburghe Club, 1819).

Ovyde: Hys Booke of Metamorphose, ed. Stephen Gaselee and H. W. W. Brett-Smith (Oxford, for Magdalene College, 1924).

M. Pacuvvi *Fragmenta*, ed. G. D'Anna (Rome, 1967).

Perret, Jacques, *Les Origines de la légende troyenne de Rome* (Paris, Presses de la Sorbonne, 1942).

Panofsky, Erwin, *Renaissance and Renascences in Western Art* (London, 1970; orig. 1965).

Partner, Nancy, *Serious Entertainments: The Writing of History in Twelfth-Century England* (Chicago, University of Chicago Press, 1977).

———, 'Making up lost time: writing on the writing of history', *Speculum* 61 (1986) 90–117.

Patterson, Lee, *Negotiating the Past: The Historical Understanding of Medieval Literature* (Madison, University of Wisconsin Press, 1987).

———, '*Thirled with the Poynt of Remembraunce*: Memory and Modernity in Chaucer's Poetry' in *Modernité au Moyen Age: le défi du passé*, ed. Brigitte Cazelles and Charles Méla (Geneva, Droz, 1990), pp. 113–51.

Paulys Real-Encyclopädia der Classischen Altertumswissenschaft, ed. G. Wilson, rev. W. Kroll (Stuttgart, 1914–).

Pausanius, ed. W. H. S. Jones, R. E. Wycherley, and H. A. Ormerod (London, Loeb Classical Library, 1918–35).

Paxson, James, *The Poetics of Personification* (Cambridge, Cambridge University Press, 1994).

Pearsall, Derek, *John Lydgate* (London, Routledge and Kegan Paul, 1970).

Perizonius, Jacques, *De Bello et Excidio Troiae* (Amsterdam, 1702)

Perry, Ben Edwin, *The Ancient Romances*, Sather Classical Lectures (Berkeley and Los Angeles, University of California Press, 1969).

Phillippy, Patricia A., 'Establishing Authority: Boccaccio's *De claris mulieribus* and Christine de Pizans's *Le Livre de la Cité des Dames*', *Romanic Review* 77 (1986), pp. 167–94.

Pindar, trans. R. Lattimore, *The Odes of Pindar* (Chicago, University of Chicago Press, 1947).

G. de Poerck, *Introduction à la fleur des histoires de Jean Mansel*, in *Annales du cercle archéologique de Mons* 54 (1935).

Pomeroy, Sarah, *Goddesses, Whores, Wives, and Slaves* (London, Robert Hale, 1975).

Poole, Adrian, *Tragedy: Shakespeare and the Greek Example* (Oxford, Blackwell, 1987).

Postan, M. M., and E. Power, *Studies in English Trade in the Fifteenth Century* (London, G. Routledge and Sons, 1933).

Pratt, Norman T., *Seneca's Drama* (Chapel Hill, University of North Carolina Press, 1983).

Presson, Robert K., *Shakespeare's 'Troilus and Cressida' and the Legends of Troy* (Menasha, Wisconsin, 1953).

Propp, V., *Morphology of the Folk-tale*, trans. Laurence Scott (Austin, Texas, University of Texas Press, 1968).

Quilligan, Maureen, *The Language of Allegory: Defining the Genre* (Ithaca and London, Cornell University Press, 1979).

——, *The Allegory of Female Authority: Christine de Pizan's Livre de la Cité des Dames* (Ithaca and London, Cornell University Press, 1991).

Rambeaux, C. 'Le Mythe de Médée d'Euripide à Anouilh ou l'originalité psychologique de la Medée de Seneque', *Latomus* 31 (1972), pp. 1010–36.

Rand, E. K., *Ovid and his Influence* (London, George Harrap and Co., 1925).

Ray, Roger, 'Bede's Vera Lex Historiae', *Speculum* 55 (1980), pp. 1–21.

——, 'The Triumph of Greco-Roman Rhetorical Assumptions in Pre-Carolingian Historiography' in *The Inheritance of Historiography*, ed. Christopher Holdsworth and T. P. Wiseman (Exeter, Exeter University Press, 1986).

Recueil de chants historiques français depuis le XIIe siècle jusqu'au XVIIIe siècle, ed. Le Roux de Lincy (Paris, C. Gosselin, 1841).

Reiffenberg, Baron de, 'Poëme sur la Toison d'Or (XVe siècle)', *Annuaire de la Bibliothèque Royale de Belgique* 8 (1847), pp. 95–101.

Reinhardt, Karl, *Eschyle. Euripide*, trans. Emmanuel Martineau (Paris, Editions de Minuit, 1972).

Renoir, Alain, *The Poetry of John Lydgate* (London, Routledge and Kegan Paul, 1967).

Ricks, Christopher, 'Metamorphosis in other words', in *Gower's Confessio Amantis: Responses and Reassessments*, ed. A. J. Minnis (Cambridge, D. S. Brewer, 1983), pp. 25–49.

Roques, Mario, *L'Estoire de Griseldis* (Geneva, Droz, 1957).

A. Rosa, ed., *Letteratura italiana: Le Opere*, I. *Dalle Origini al Cinquecento* (Turin, Einaudi, 1992), pp. 473–592.

Roscher, W. H., *Ausfürliches Lexikon der Griechischen und Romischen Mythologie* (Leipzig, 1890–7).

Rosenmeyer, Thomas G., *Senecan Drama and Stoic Cosmology* (Berkeley, University of California Press, 1989).

Sainte-Beuve, Charles-Augustin, 'Etudes sur l'Antiquité: de la Medée d'Apollonius', *Revue des Deux Mondes* (1845.11), pp. 873–99.

Sale, William, *Sickness, Tragedy, and Divinity in the Medea, the Hippolytus and the Bacchae* (Melbourne, Ramus Monographs, 1977).

Samaran, Charles, 'Pierre Bersuire', in *Histoire Littéraire de la France* 39 (1962), pp. 259–450.

Scheid, John, 'The Religious Roles of Roman Women', in *A History of Women in the West, I. From Ancient Goddesses to Christian Saints*, ed. Pauline Schmitt Pantel, trans. Arthur Goldhammer (Cambridge, Mass., Belknap Press of Harvard University Press, 1992), pp. 377–408.

Schmitz, Götz, *The Fall of Woman in Early English Narrative Verse* (Cambridge, Cambridge University Press, 1990).

Scott, Kathleen, *The Caxton Master and his Patron* (Cambridge, The Bibliographical Society, 1976).

Séchan, Louis, 'La Légende de Médée', *Revue des Etudes Greques* 40 (1927), pp. 234–310.

Segal, Charles, 'The Two Worlds of Euripides' Helen', *Transactions and Proceedings of the American Philosophical Association* 102 (1971), pp. 553–614.

———, 'Nomen Sacrum: Medea and other Names in Senecan Tragedy' *Maia* 34 (1982), pp. 241–46.

———, *Pindar's Mythmaking: the Fourth Pythian Ode* (Princeton, Princeton University Press, 1986).

———, *Interpreting Greek Tragedy: Myth, Poetry, Text* (Ithaca, Cornell University Press, 1986).

Seneca, *Medea*, ed. C. D. N. Costa (Oxford, Clarendon Press, 1973)

———, *Medea*, ed. Léon Hermann, Budé edition (Paris, Les Belles Lettres, 1924), I.132–74.

Seneca's Tragedies, ed. F. J. Miller (Cambridge, Mass., Loeb, 1917)

Servii Grammatici, ed. G. Thilo (Leipzig, Teubner, 3 vols, 1881–1902).

Severs, J. Burke, *The Literary Relationships of Chaucer's Clerk's Tale* (New Haven and New York, Yale University Press, 1942).

Seznec, Jean, *The Survival of the Pagan Gods: the Mythological Tradition and its*

Place in Renaissance Humanism and Art (New York, Bollingen Foundation, 1953; orig. 1940).

Sharman, Julian, *The Library of Mary Queen of Scots* (London, Elliot Stock, 1889).

Shaw, M., 'Female Intruder', *Classical Philology* 70 (1970), pp. 255–66.

Sidney, Sir Philip, *An Apology for Poetry*, ed. Geoffrey Shepherd (Manchester, Manchester University Press, 1973; orig. 1965)

Sklar, Elizabeth C., 'Guido, the Middle English Troy Books, and Chaucer: the English Connection', *Neophilologus* 76 (1992), pp. 616–28.

Smith, J. M., *The French Background of Middle Scots Literature* (Edinburgh, Oliver and Boyd, 1934).

Southern, Richard, 'Aspects of the European Tradition of Historical Writing', *Transactions of the Royal Historical Society* 20 (1970), pp. 173–96.

Spiegel, Gabrielle, 'History, Historicism, and the Social Logic of the Text in the Middle Ages', *Speculum* 65 (1990), pp. 59–86.

——, *Romancing the Past: The Rise of Vernacular Prose Historiography in Thirteenth-Century France* (Berkeley, University of California Press, 1993).

Stair Ercuil ocus a bas, ed. Gordon Quin (Dublin, Irish Text Society, 38, 1939).

Statius, P. Papinius, *Thebaid*, ed. J. H. Mozley (London and Cambridge, Mass., Loeb Classical Library, 1928).

Stein, E., 'Caxton's *Recuyell* and Shakespeare's *Troilus*', *Modern Language Notes* 45 (1930), pp. 144–6.

Steiner, George, *Antigones* (Oxford, Clarendon Press, 1984).

Streuver, Nancy, *The Language of History in the Renaissance* (Princeton, Princeton University Press, 1970).

Strubel, Armand, *La Rose, Renart, et le Graal: La littérature allégorique en France au XIIIe siècle* (Paris, Champion, 1989).

Suzuki, Mihoko, *Metamorphoses of Helen: Authority, Difference, and the Epic* (Ithaca and London, Cornell University Press, 1989).

Taillevent, Michel, *Un Poète bourguignon du XVe siècle: Michault Taillevent (édition et étude)*, ed. Robert Deschaux (Geneva, Droz, Publications romanes et françaises, 132, 1975).

Thielemans, Marie-Rose, *Bourgogne et Angleterre: relations politiques et économiques entre les pays-bas bourguignons et l'Angleterre, 1435–1467* (Brussels, Presses Universitaires de Bruxelles, 1966).

Thon, A., 'Analyse et extraits des documents relatifs à l'histoire des Pays-Bas au XVIe siècle', *Bulletin de la Commission Royale d'Histoire* 77 (1908), pp. 37–133.

Tidworth, Simon, 'The Roman and Medieval Theseus', in *The Quest for Theseus*, ed. Ann Ward (New York, Praeger, 1970).

Trambling, Jeremy, *Dante and Difference: Writing in the 'Commedia'* (Cambridge, Cambridge University Press, 1988).

Trevet, Nicholas, *Il Commento di Nicola Trevet al Testo di Seneca*, ed. Ezio Franceschini (Milan, Orbis Romanus, 1938).

Tuve, Rosamund, *Allegorical Imagery: Some Medieval Books and their Posterity* (Princeton, Princeton University Press, 1966).

Twycross, Margaret, *The Medieval Anadyomene: a study in Chaucer's Mythography* (Oxford, Medium Aevum Monographs, *n.s.* 1, 1972).

——, review of J. Engels, *Werkmateriaal, Medium Aevum* 37 (1968), pp. 320–3.

Tyrrell, William B., *Amazons: a study in Athenian Myth-making* (Baltimore, Johns Hopkins University Press, 1984).

Van Dyke, Carolynn, *The Fiction of Truth: Structures of Meaning in Narrative and Dramatic Allegory* (Ithaca and London, Cornell University Press, 1985).

Richard T. Vann, 'Louis Mink's Linguistic Turn' in *History and Theory* 26 (1987) 1–14.

Vaughan, Richard, *Philip the Bold: The Formation of the Burgundian State* (London, Longman, 1962).

——, *John the Fearless: The Growth of Burgundian Power* (London, Longman, 1966).

——, *Philip the Good: The Apogee of Burgundy* (London, Longman, 1970).

——, *Charles the Bold: The Last Valois Duke of Burgundy* (London, Longman, 1973).

——, *Valois Burgundy* (London, Longman, 1975).

Vernant, J.-P., 'Le Tyran boiteux: d'Oedipe à Périandre', Pierre Vidal-Naquet's *Oedipe et ses mythes* (Paris, Editions la Découverte, 1986), trans. as 'From Oedipus to Periander: Lameness, Tyranny, Incest in Legend and History', in *Arethusa* 15 (1982), 19–38.

——, *Le Chasseur Noir* (Paris, Maspero, 1981).

——, *La mort dans les yeux: figures de l'Autre en Grèce ancienne* (Paris, Hachette, 1985).

P. Vergili Maronis *Opera*, ed. F. A. Hirtzel (Oxford, Clarendon, 1900).

Publi Vergili Maronis Aeneidos Liber Quartus, ed. A. S. Pease (Cambridge, Mass., 1935; repr. Darmstadt, Wissenschaftliche Buchgesellschaft, 1967).

The Eclogues, Georgics, and Aeneid of Virgil, trans. C. Day Lewis (London, 1952).

Verducci, Florence, *Ovid's Toyshop of the Heart: Epistulae Heroidum* (Princeton, Princeton University Press, 1985).

Vessey, David, *Statius and the Thebaid* (Cambridge, Cambridge University Press, 1973).

Vincent of Beauvais, *Speculum Historiale* (Augsburg, 1474).

Warton, Thomas, *Observations on the Fairy Queen of Spenser* (London, 2nd edn, 1762).

Webster, T. B. L,. *The Tragedies of Euripides* (London, Methuen, 1967).

White, Hayden, 'Historiography as Narration', in *Telling Facts: History and Narration in Psychoanalysis*, ed. Joseph H. Smith and Humphrey Morris (Baltimore, Johns Hopkins, 1992)

————, *Tropics of Discourse: essays in cultural criticism* (Baltimore and London, Johns Hopkins University Press, 1978).

Will, E., *Korinthiaka: Recherches sur l'histoire et la civilisation de Corinthe des origines aux guerres médiques* (Paris, E. de Boecard, 1955).

Williams, Jr., Clem C., 'A Case of Mistaken Identity: Still Another Trojan Narrative in Old French', *Medium Aevum* 53 (1984), pp. 59–72.

Williamson, Margaret, 'A Woman's Place in Euripides' Medea', *Euripides, Women, and Sexuality*, ed. Anton Powell (London, Routledge, 1990), pp. 16–31.

M. Wilmotte, 'Observations sur le Roman de Troie', *Le Moyen Age* 27 (1914), pp. 93–119.

L. F. Winkler, *Studien zur Geschichte der Niederländischen Miniaturmalerei des XV. und XVI. Jahrhunderts* (Vienna and Leipzig, 1915).

Woledge, Brian, 'La légende de Troie et le début de la prose française', *Mélanges de linguistique et de littérature romanes offerts à Mario Roques* (Paris, Editions Arts et Sciences, 1950–1953), vol. 2, pp. 313–24.

————, *Bibliographie des romans et nouvelles en prose française antérieurs à 1500* (Geneva, Droz, 1954 et suppl. 1975).

Woodford, Susan, *The Trojan War in Ancient Art* (London, Duckworth, 1993).

Wright, H. G., *Boccaccio in England from Chaucer to Tennyson* (London, Athlone Press, 1957).

Wulfing, J. E., 'Das Laud-Troybook', *Englische Studien* 29 (1901), pp. 374–96.

————, 'Das Bild und die bildliche verneinung im Laud-Troy-Book', *Anglia* 27 (1904), pp. 555–80; 28 (1905), pp. 29–80.

R. F. Yeager, *John Gower's Poetic: the search for a new Arion* (Cambridge, D. S. Brewer, 1990).

Michel Zink, 'Une Mutacion de la conscience littéraire: Le langage romanesque à travers les exemples français du XIIe siècle', *Cahiers de Civilisation Médiévale* 24 (1981), pp. 3–27.

INDEX